Additional Praise for *The Missing Ring*

"When it comes to Alabama football, nobody does a better job of research and reporting than Keith Dunnavant, and this is another masterful job."

—Tony Bernhart, *The Atlanta Journal-Constitution*

"Keith Dunnavant has written yet another fabulous book about the fabled Alabama football program. You will be amazed at how one of the great injustices in the history of college football cost them their rightful place in history. And you just thought the system was screwed up now."

—Jim Dent, author of *The Junction Boys*

"Keith Dunnavant nails it: All the sacrifices the 1966 Alabama team made to win three national championships in a row and how we were robbed at the ballot box."   —Jerry Duncan, one of the boys of 1966

"Dunnavant infuses reportage and passion into a tale that every Alabamian of a certain age knows: for all the crying about Penn State in 1969, Penn State in 1994, or Auburn in 2004, no team ever got shafted the way the 1966 Crimson Tide did. It's all here: the churning legs, the churning stomachs, the dreaded gym classes where Bear Bryant's boys made the sacrifices he demanded in order to become champions. They conquered their opponents on the field, but proved to be no match for the politics of the day off the field. The '66 Tide is still waiting for the missing ring. Thanks to Dunnavant, we don't have to."

—Ivan Maisel, senior writer, ESPN.com, coauthor of *A War in Dixie*

"*The Missing Ring*, a stirring tale of Southern football set against a backdrop of the Vietnam War and the civil rights movement, tells the story of the greatest disappointment of the Bear Bryant era—and tells it unforgettably."

—John Pruett, *The Huntsville Times*

ALSO BY KEITH DUNNAVANT

Coach: The Life of Paul "Bear" Bryant

Time Out! A Sports Fan's Dream Year (with Edgar Welden)

The Fifty-Year Seduction

HOW BEAR BRYANT
AND THE 1966
ALABAMA CRIMSON
TIDE WERE DENIED
COLLEGE FOOTBALL'S
MOST ELUSIVE PRIZE

The MISSING RING

Keith Dunnavant

THOMAS DUNNE BOOKS
ST. MARTIN'S GRIFFIN ◆ NEW YORK

THOMAS DUNNE BOOKS.
An imprint of St. Martin's Press.

www.thomasdunnebooks.com
www.stmartins.com

Book design by Jonathan Bennett

Library of Congress Cataloging-in-Publication Data

Dunnavant, Keith.
    The missing ring: how Bear Bryant and the 1966 Alabama Crimson Tide were denied college football's most elusive prize / Keith Dunnavant.
        p. cm.
    Includes index.
    ISBN-13: 978-0-312-37432-7
    ISBN-10: 0-312-37432-1
    1. Alabama Crimson Tide (Football team)—History.   2. University of Alabama—Football—History.   3. Bryant, Paul W.   I. Title.

GV958.A4 D86 2006
796.322'630975184—dc22

2006045469

First St. Martin's Griffin Edition: September 2007

D 10 9 8 7 6 5 4 3 2

To my big brothers: Tom, Ron, and Jim.
Thanks for the classy and ambitious example you set for me,
for your support of this project in a variety of ways,
and for a lifetime of encouragement.

CONTENTS

The MISSING RING

INTRODUCTION

In the distance, a siren blared. It was barely audible at first, and then, as the procession moved up Graymont Avenue and toward Birmingham's massive Legion Field, the unmistakable sound of several different high-pitched police horns overlapped in a deafening chorus. The jarring wail cut through the huge throng like a royal fanfare as Bill Graham squeezed his son's shoulders and smiled broadly.

"Look!" Graham said to his boy, pointing to the buses and state police cars being waved around the stalled traffic prior to the 1966 Alabama-Auburn football game. "Here they come!"

It was like Christmas morning for eleven-year-old Bruce Graham, and he could barely contain his excitement.

Every day back in his hometown of Phil Campbell, a small community in northwest Alabama, Bruce devoured the sports pages of *The Birmingham News* for information about his beloved Crimson Tide. In fact, this was how the precocious son of Bill and Nell Graham had learned to read. On Saturdays, he listened to the Alabama games on the radio and tried to imagine what Denny Stadium and Legion Field and all those other mystical places really looked like. On Sundays, he planted himself in front of his family's black-and-white console television and soaked up every moment of *The Bear Bryant Show,* which provided him with a rare glimpse at the heroes who filled him with so much pride in calling Alabama home.

But it was his dream to see a game in person. Just once. Understanding this, his uncle Dwight had taken great delight in going to the expense and trouble of procuring two tickets to the state's biggest sporting event, no small feat in a year when the Crimson Tide was bidding for an unprecedented third consecutive national championship.

"Going to that game was the biggest thing that had ever happened to me at that point in my life," Graham recalled many years later. "I can't adequately describe what it meant. It just meant everything."

After bolting out of bed before dawn and putting on their best Sunday clothes—including coats and ties—Bruce and his father, a middle-aged educator at a local college, had spent more than two hours on the road, traversing the two-lane highways of northern Alabama in their 1964 Chevrolet station wagon, bound for the Magic City, the self-proclaimed football capital of the South. They stopped only to buy some take-out fried chicken for later.

By the time the buses finally pulled up next to the stadium and the sirens abruptly stopped, a crowd of several thousand fans surrounded the 'Bama players and coaches as they disembarked in the misty rain. Strategically positioned between the buses and the fence to the stadium, Bruce, small for his age, struggled to catch a glimpse of his favorite players, whose pictures he had studied closely in the paper.

Too short to see over the mob, too big for his daddy to hold up, he started maneuvering to peer through and around the legs of the men around him.

"I couldn't go high, so I decided to go low," he recalled.

Looking up from this vantage point, he spotted offensive lineman Cecil Dowdy, then quarterback Kenny Stabler, and receiver Dennis Homan.

Dressed in matching crimson blazers, wearing expressions of serious contemplation, the entire travel squad walked through the crowd and toward their nearby locker room with an air of unmistakable confidence, saying not a word.

"They all looked like giants to me," Graham said. "I remember thinking, I sure would like to get me one of those red jackets for Sunday. And so many of them seemed to have flat tops, which made a real impression on me."

Eventually, while staring up from around some taller person's ankles, he glimpsed for the first time in the flesh the towering figure of Paul "Bear" Bryant, the larger-than-life coach who had built the Crimson Tide into the most dominant football program in the land.

"I couldn't believe I was actually getting to see Coach Bryant up close," Graham said. "It was a pretty overwhelming experience."

Like the diminuitive Graham, the vast majority of Alabamians looked up to those young men and their legendary coach. Because in 1966, the Crimson Tide was more than a football team. It was also a mirror. And a shield. A source of inspiration. And validation.

After watching Alabama crush archrival Auburn 34–0 from their end zone seats—and gathering up as many discarded crimson and white shakers as he could carry—Graham and his father drove into the night, into a seemingly endless incandescent trail of headlights and brake lights. While negotiating the stop-and-go traffic, the pilgrims from Phil Campbell marveled at the toughness of the 'Bama defense, the masterful performance of Kenny Stabler, the speed and hands of Ray Perkins. Before long, they were home.

The next day at church and the day after that at school, all the kids wanted to know: *What was it really like?*

"It all seemed so big," he explained breathlessly, first once and then again and again. "I couldn't believe that the field was only a hundred yards, because it seemed so much longer than our field back home . . ."

"How close did you get to Coach Bryant?" demanded his good friend Eddie Glasgow. "You think he saw you?"

Even his fifth grade teacher, Mrs. Bragwell, was curious. She asked him to make a presentation to the class, in which he displayed one of those shakers and a game program—which he had already read, cover to cover, at least a dozen times—like artifacts from a distant land.

Later that week, Bruce begged his daddy to take him to the barber . . . so he could get a flat top.

1. BROKEN PLATES

The door flew open, and the room fell silent.

"Nobody had to tell us to shut up," recalled Louis Thompson, a Tennessee farmboy seated somewhere toward the back. "You just knew."

As Paul "Bear" Bryant walked to the front of the Foster Auditorium meeting room on the first day of September 1963, he looked out over the gathering without saying a word, carefully studying the faces of his fifty-one newest recruits to the University of Alabama football program. He glanced at the big clock on the wall, above the blackboard, and started winding his wristwatch. It was so quiet, even the guys in the back row could hear the metallic tumbling of the stem.

Seated in old wooden chair/desks—which some of the more robust specimens found confining to the point of discomfort—the players looked up at their new coach, who loomed over them like a giant. With his chiseled face and towering frame, the charismatic Bryant, just eleven days shy of his fiftieth birthday, exuded an unmistakable toughness, even to a bunch of eighteen-year-old tough guys. Tough, after all, was a language they all understood. His steely eyes said, "Don't mess with me. I may be getting older, but I can still whip your scrawny little ass."

"Well, we're a little bit early, but we'll get started anyway," he finally said in a gravelly voice deepened by too many unfiltered Chesterfield cigarettes, a voice dripping with the sound of whiskey-drenched nights, a voice reverberating with tons of ambition and precious little regret.

After welcoming the newest members of the Crimson Tide and telling them to go back to their dorm rooms that afternoon and write a letter home, Bryant started talking about the importance of working hard, getting an education, and setting high goals.

"Look at the men on either side of you," he said, and heads immediately turned back and forth. He told the players that many of them would not survive the grueling days to come—that many would not be willing to pay the price.

At this suggestion, the very same thought shot through the mind of every one of those cocky young athletes: Not me! He's not talking about me!

"But," Bryant continued, his piercing eyes moving around the room, "if you're willing to pay the price and do the things I ask of you . . ."

Then he challenged them to win the national championship, placing the ultimate achievement in college football within their reach but beyond their grasp.

Toward the middle of his little speech, Bryant noticed a player in the second row not looking him directly in the eyes. The coach walked up to the young man and slammed his large right hand on the player's desk with a loud crash.

"Boy, you look at me when I'm talking!" Bryant said.

"That was a message none of us would ever forget," recalled Decatur recruit Byrd Williams, seated nearby.

In the moments before Bryant walked through the door, the players had noticed that the old wooden desks creaked with the slightest fidget, so as they sat rapt, their eyes focused on him like lasers, the young men struggled against their own bodies to remain perfectly still. No one wanted to make a sound, even if it meant freezing in an uncomfortable position, even if it meant defying the laws of physics.

"I was scared to death I was going to move without thinking and that old desk would creak," Louis Thompson said. "I already had so much respect for Coach Bryant that I didn't want to do anything to displease him, so I sat there practically paralyzed, trying not to move a muscle."

Enormous power surged through all that motivated silence. All Bryant had to do was flip the right switch.

The obsession of an entire state began with one man and one football.

In the fall of 1892, after graduating from Phillips-Exeter Academy, the prestigious Massachusetts prep school, William G. Little returned to his home state and enrolled at the University of Alabama, then a sleepy military college. Twenty-three years after Rutgers defeated Princeton, 6–4, in the first intercollegiate football game on American soil, the sport was all the rage in the Northeast and Midwest, but it remained little more than a rumor in the Deep South. The athletic Little returned to the Heart of Dixie all fired up about the game, and, as far as anyone knows, the leather football he brought back from Massachusetts was the first ever possessed on the Alabama campus.

Soon after his arrival in Tuscaloosa, Little convinced a small group of students to form the University of Alabama's first football team. Naturally, he was elected captain, and a local man named Eugene Beaumont, who had learned about the game during his days at the University of Pennsylvania, was selected as coach. On November 11, 1892, the Alabama contingent crushed a unit consisting of Birmingham area high school students, 56–0.

Over the next three decades, the Alabama football program slowly grew in scope and accomplishment, consistently producing winning teams and becoming a source of pride for the student body. In the early years, the team was often known as the "Thin Red Line," a moniker most historians believe was borrowed from a Rudyard Kipling poem of the day. In 1907, after watching Alabama battle cross-state rival Auburn University to a 6–6 tie on an extremely muddy field, *Birmingham Age-Herald* sportswriter Hugh Roberts referred to the boys from Tuscaloosa as the "Crimson Tide," and the label stuck. In 1915, when most players chose not to wear headgear, flimsy as it was, a fearsome lineman/fullback named W. T. "Bully" VandeGraaff became Alabama's first All-American. According to news accounts at the time, VandeGraaff was so tough and so tenacious, he once tried to rip off his own badly mangled and bloodied ear so he could keep playing against Tennessee.

The first truly great moment in Alabama football history happened on November 4, 1922, when the unheralded Crimson Tide traveled to Philadelphia and stunned the powerful University of Pennsylvania Quakers, 9–7. Some giddy fan whitewashed the score on the brick exterior of a Tuscaloosa drugstore, a reminder that could still be read more than twenty years later.

Acclaimed novelist Winston Groom, author of *Forrest Gump,* may have summed up the unlikely victory better than anyone else in 2000 when he wrote, "It was as remarkable to some as if today a team, from, say, Norway, came to Tuscaloosa and beat Alabama." Indeed, for in 1922, the South seemed like a foreign country to many in the North, who looked down on the poverty-stricken, largely agrarian, racially divided South as a bastion of inferiority in every human endeavor. In this context, beating Pennsylvania was more than a football victory; it was a triumph of the Southern spirit—proof that the South, that Alabama, could compete and win against the best of the North in football and perhaps other things, a provocative, radical thought at the time. The thousands of ecstatic fans who showed up at the Tuscaloosa train station to greet the returning warriors stood at the vanguard of a movement destined to sweep across the state. The Crimson Tide was no longer just a team. It was a symbol of pride, a symbol of hope, and in the years ahead, the vast majority of the state's residents would come to identify with it in ways many were not fully equipped to understand, bathing in the reflected glow of Alabama's glorious triumphs, and, in the process, feeling better about themselves and their beleaguered place in the world, when pride, like other life-sustaining commodities, was precious and hard-won.

The 1922 victory by the Xen C. Scott-led Crimson Tide gave Alabama its first taste of national notoriety, but the next coach, Wallace Wade, who arrived in 1923, fundamentally altered the program's arc. After capturing its second consecutive Southern Conference championship and finishing unbeaten and untied for the first time in 1925, 'Bama was matched against mighty Washington in the Rose Bowl, the only postseason game at the time. No one gave the Tide a prayer, so when the first Southern team ever invited to Pasadena shocked the Huskies, 20–19, on January 1, 1926, the news shook the sports world like an earthquake.

The victory gave the Crimson Tide its first national championship and strengthened the bond with its growing legion of fans, who could not help hearing echoes of the long-ago Civil War, which still cast a menacing shadow over their downtrodden corner of the world. When the Alabama train reached the South, it was greeted with huge throngs of cheering fans at every stop.

"We were the South's baby," remarked 'Bama end Hoyt "Wu" Winslett.

In 1926, Alabama finished another perfect season and was invited back for the second of six trips to the Rose Bowl, where the underdogs from Tuscaloosa tied Stanford, 7–7, to share another national title, a game broadcast coast-to-coast on the brand-new NBC Radio Network, spreading the fame of the Crimson Tide to every corner of the continent.

In the minds of sports fans across America, the name Alabama has been synonymous with excellence in football since the Roaring Twenties.

One of the most enduring dynasties in all of American sports, the Crimson Tide has claimed 12 national championships, more than any school except Notre Dame; played in an NCAA-record 53 postseason bowl games and won an NCAA-record 30 of those contests; finished 34 times among the nation's top ten since 1936, third among all programs; amassed an all-time record of 774-301-43 for a winning percentage of .712, fifth among all schools; won 10 or more games an NCAA-best 28 times; and captured 25 league titles, including 21 Southeastern Conference championships.

In the autumn of 1966, with the world and the sport on the brink of dramatic change, college football's most elusive prize tantalized one of the greatest of all Alabama teams.

After winning consecutive national championships in 1964 and 1965, Paul Bryant's loaded Crimson Tide entered the 1966 season with the chance to become the first team in modern college history to accomplish a threepeat—three straight years as the No. 1 team in the land.

Naturally, the Alabama players believed they controlled their own destiny, that they could write their names forever in the history books by winning every game and successfully defending their crown. But they had no way of knowing that in 1966 at least, winning was not the only thing. They had no way of knowing about the invisible obstacle lurking ominously in the shadows.

The wagon always kicked up a cloud of dust. Even as he chased national championships at Alabama, that's how Paul Bryant would remember those formative days of his youth. In a cloud of dust.

Sometimes, during the frigid Arkansas winters, young Paul and his beloved mother Ida, all bundled up, heated bricks in the fireplace and sat on them to keep warm as the team pulled the wagon along the dirt roads of Dallas County. He hated this chore most of all, more than chopping cotton, more than milking the cows, more than plowing the fields in the heat of the Arkansas summer. The trip to their customers in Fordyce from their modest farm in the countryside took the better part of the morning, but it was not the boredom or the work or the exposure to the elements that bothered Ida's youngest son.

It was the hateful voices, because the children who invariably showed up to tease him about being poor had the power to make him feel inferior.

"Paul never forgot how that felt," said his sister, Louise.

Truly understanding the powerful 1966 football team is impossible without first examining and comprehending the life of the man who shaped it. Paul Bryant was not the greatest college football coach of all time just because he knew how to skillfully manipulate Xs and Os. His success was much more deeply connected to his mysterious ability to manipulate—and inspire—all kinds of players to reach.

Bryant spent his whole life running from those hateful voices, but the feelings of inferiority and hopelessness they spurred made him strong, not weak. As he grew into a powerful figure, all those feelings of emptiness and doubt inspired him to push himself, to reinvent himself, making Bryant one of the hungriest and most driven men ever to draw a breath.

The story of the 1966 Alabama football team is an extension of Bryant's untrammeled ambition. The story of the 1966 Crimson Tide is a reflection of the fire raging inside his soul.

When a huckster came to Fordyce and offered the princely sum of one dollar to anyone brave enough to wrestle a black bear, young Paul, big, strong, and reckless, jumped at the chance. Not just to make a buck, although the chance to earn a nice payday was a significant motivator for a poor boy who gladly worked all day chopping cotton to make fifty cents. The experience with the bear was not just some ill-advised adolescent stunt that earned him a nickname. It was a window into his soul. Then as later, the need to prove something—to others as well as to himself—was a powerful force in Bryant's life. In time, it would motivate him to push so hard against the boundaries of his own potential that no one could ever again have the ability to make him feel small.

Stardom as a hell-raising high school football player defined less by raw talent than steely will gave Bryant his first taste of self-esteem, and the scholarship he earned to the University of Alabama—where he played end for Frank Thomas's Crimson Tide powerhouse, including the 1934 national championship team that knocked off Stanford in the Rose Bowl—represented his ticket to a better life, fortifying him from the need to ever again step behind a plow.

But he never forgot how it felt to be hungry. He understood hunger of all kinds, and he knew how to exploit it.

The man who once played the game of his life against Tennessee with a broken leg—yet always toiled in the shadow of the more graceful Don Hutson, destined to become one of the greatest receivers in the history of the National Football League—saw football as a metaphor for the human experience. In Bryant's Darwinist world, only the fittest survived, and the fittest were not always the most gifted athletes. In fact, he probably ran off more great talents than any coach in the history of the game because they refused to bend to his powerful will. Conversely, he loved overachievers who were not very gifted but didn't know it. The survivors of his rigorous physical and mental training always knew how to fight for every last ounce of potential, and if they got knocked down, they always got up.

"Coach Bryant was determined to push you so hard—physically and mentally—that one of two things would happen," said Howard Schnellenberger, who played for the Bear at Kentucky and later coached offensive linemen for him at Alabama. "Either you quit, because you couldn't or wouldn't bend to his will, or you kept on pushing yourself to please him and, as a result, you kept getting stronger, more confident, and more determined."

After building championship programs at Kentucky and Texas A&M, Bryant returned to Tuscaloosa in 1958 with a reputation as the most demanding coach in college football. If nothing else, his infamous Junction preseason camp at A&M branded him as a man who set the bar in the clouds—and was willing to live with the consequences. When two-thirds of his team quit, unwilling or unable to sustain the punishment, the Aggies were left incredibly short-handed for the 1954 season. But two years later, the survivors of those ten days in hell led A&M to the Southwest Conference championship, a turnaround inexorably linked to the high standard Junction represented. In fact, Junction as an object lesson would loom large in the Bryant mystique for the rest of his career.

Emboldened by the A&M experience and resolved to reverse the fortunes of a once-dominant program that had won only four games in three years, Bryant pushed his early Alabama teams relentlessly. More than one-third of the athletes he inherited from J. B. "Ears" Whitworth quit in the first year. Even fewer survived from his initial class of recruits. But, like the marines, Bryant was looking for a few good men, and the determined souls who persevered would lead the Crimson Tide to the 1961 national championship, laying the foundation for the most remarkable quarter-century in college football history.

By the time the Alabama coaching staff started scouting the players who would become the freshmen of 1963 and the seniors of 1966, the Crimson Tide was headed to a near miss in the fall of 1962. Behind the arm of sophomore quarterback Joe Namath and a defense, led by ferocious linebacker Lee Roy Jordan, that surrendered just 39 points, Alabama finished 10-1 and ranked fifth in both wire service polls. The single blemish came in the ninth game of the season, when No. 1-ranked, defending national champion Alabama lost a 7–6 heartbreaker to Georgia Tech at Grant Field in Atlanta. After scoring a touchdown in the closing moments, 'Bama opted for a two-point run to win, because Paul Bryant and the Crimson Tide didn't play for ties. It failed. But Bryant didn't pout. Instead, he made sure his men understood that principles have consequences.

Even as Bryant skillfully cultivated a neatly ordered world guided not only by rules but also by values, his character came under assault. After most of the incoming freshmen had signed to play for the Crimson Tide in the winter of 1962–63, *The Saturday Evening Post* published a bombshell story alleging that Bryant and former Georgia head coach Wally Butts had conspired to fix the 1962 Alabama-Georgia game, a 32–6 Tide victory. In the article, Atlanta insurance man George Burnett told a captivating tale about how he had somehow overheard—due to a telephone company switching error—a conversation in which Butts supposedly provided information about the Bulldogs to Bryant. Even though no one in Alabama believed a word of the story, and the Crimson Tide nation immediately closed ranks around their leader, who bought time on statewide television to categorically deny the charges, the scandalous allegation threatened to ruin Bryant's career.

While waiting for his libel case to reach a Birmingham courtroom, Bryant went on the offensive as a witness for Butts at the federal courthouse in Atlanta on August 8, 1963. After Butts's lawyer methodically destroyed the credibility of the *Post* and its primary source, Bryant took the stand and, as Walter Cronkite reported that night to lead off the *CBS Evening News,* "laid it on the line." Defiantly, he refuted the charges, charming the jury, portraying himself and Butts as victims of an overzealous, irresponsible media organization. It had been little more than a year since the same magazine accused Bryant of promoting "brutal football" after an unfortunate incident involving Georgia Tech player Chick Granning. The fix allegation was far worse, because some things were sacred to Bryant. The *Post*, which bungled the fix story to the point of absurdity, never had a chance. Bryant owned that room, like all others. Several days later, the jury awarded Butts $3.06 million in damages, a record amount that would later be reduced by a higher court. Six months later, just before his case landed in a Birmingham courtroom, Curtis Publishing Company, owner of the *Post*, paid Bryant $300,000 to go away and issued a retraction. Instead of being permanently damaged by the whiff of scandal, the vindication actually enhanced the Bear's already large national reputation.

While Bryant was no saint—he struggled for years with excessive drinking and developed a reputation for skirt-chasing—he lived by a certain code of right and wrong, especially in the context of the game. The hurt of the *Post* ordeal would never quite heal, producing an emotional scar that would linger for the rest of his life. Football had made him—and, in a way, saved him—so the suggestion that he would participate in such a sinister, cynical betrayal of the game's most fundamental values—and, by extension, his own—hit him where it hurt. It wasn't enough that he was eventually vindicated on the facts; the mere suggestion that he would fix a game was an insult to his character, because he knew somebody, somewhere might actually believe it, despite the evidence.

"They gave Coach Bryant a bunch of money but they could never give him back what he thought he'd lost," remarked former player and assistant coach Charley Pell, who testified on his behalf at the Butts trial.

Although the Alabama players tried to put the business out of their minds, the article hit them all hard. The allegation was a challenge to the integrity of the whole program, and as the eldest members of the 1966 team arrived on campus as freshmen during the Butts trial, the fix story struck them as yet another assault on the state of Alabama by the national news media. The year 1963 was a turbulent time to live in the Heart of Dixie, especially if you happened to be black, and in the view of many white Alabamians, the national media was contributing to the unrest roiling the state, not just covering it.

With Dr. Martin Luther King, Jr. leading the epic battle to destroy segregation and other forms of institutional racism and Governor George Wallace—who had been elected in 1962 on a platform of "Segregation now, segregation tomorrow, segregation forever"—marshalling resistance that often led to shameless violence, the image of Alabama as one gigantic battleground in the civil rights movement permeated the national news.

Bear Bryant's dominant Crimson Tide was one of the few institutions Alabamians could legitimately feel proud of in 1963, so the timing of the fix allegation helped shape the mentality of the boys of 1966, who learned the meaning of Alabama football while being conditioned to be skeptical of the national media.

The building of the 1966 Alabama football team began long before any of the players arrived on campus. The same forceful, larger-than-life persona that helped Bryant emerge unscathed from the *Post* scandal hung over every aspect of the program—especially in the hiring of assistant coaches.

Like all successful leaders, Bryant understood the critical importance of surrounding himself with good people. "I never hire anyone unless he knows something about the game I don't," he was fond of saying. But Bryant looked for more than men who were skillful with *X*s and *O*s, because he could always find good tacticians and good teachers. He sought out men who had such characteristics but who also were hungry, men to whom winning meant something powerful.

"We all had different backgrounds, but the key was that we all wanted to win more than just about anything in the world," observed freshman coach Clem Gryska, a native of Steubenville, Ohio, who played for the Crimson Tide in the late 1940s. "In Coach Bryant's world, that was always the key. If you valued winning, you were likely to do whatever it took, and that's the kind of guy he wanted."

Determined to maintain his dominant aura and the same level of intensity in instruction, Bryant liked to hire coaches with previous connections to his programs, either as players or assistants. He liked to hire young coaches, men with lots of fire who wanted to show him something and move on to bigger and better opportunities. He liked to hire tireless strivers who could form a connective tissue between him and the team, men who could transfer their passion for winning to their athletes like a virus in the bloodstream.

"If you were a football coach and you had any kind of drive, you wanted to work for Coach Bryant in those days," said Dude Hennessey, a former Kentucky player who took a $1,500 pay cut to join the 'Bama staff in 1960.

Bryant tended to be a magnet for a certain kind of coach who wanted to prove he could measure up, and such men were more than likely to be intimidated by him and anxious to do whatever was required to please him.

Case in point: In 1963, Ken Meyer happened to be in the right place at the right time, which attracted Bryant's attention. But he won a job on the staff with initiative, by proving how much he wanted it.

The week before Alabama played Georgia Tech in 1962, lightly regarded Florida State earned a 14–14 tie with Bobby Dodd's Yellow Jackets, and Bryant and several of his offensive coaches were watching the film. The boss was impressed with some of the ways FSU was attacking with its passing-oriented offense, and he turned to assistant coach Pat James.

"You know anybody on the staff down there who could talk to us about what they did against Tech?" Bryant said.

James nodded and went off to make a call.

Some months later, when Bryant found himself with a vacancy on the staff, he collared James on the way out of a meeting. "What about that guy down at Florida State? They had some pretty good ideas. Why don't you give him a call . . ."

Ken Meyer, who had served as a bombardier with the Eighth Air Force in World War II, surviving twenty-five missions into the heart of occupied Europe, had learned much about football and even more about high standards while playing for irascible taskmaster Woody Hayes at tiny Denison College in Ohio.

"It was right after the war, and Woody mashed us every day," said Meyer, born in Erie, Pennsylvania, the son of a lighthouse keeper who spent his formative years moving up and down the Great Lakes. "He got rid of the ones who didn't want to work. I didn't mind working . . . didn't mind it a bit."

Meyer, who recruited future All-Pro receiver Fred Biletnikoff, Florida State's second All-American, recognized an opportunity when it coldcocked him upside the head.

A few days after a short telephone conversation with Bryant early in 1963, Meyer set out from his home in Tallahassee to meet the Bear for an interview in Pensacola. The Alabama folks had sent him a plane ticket, but he didn't like the look of the weather.

"There was no way I was going to miss my one opportunity to interview with Paul Bryant," Meyer said. "I really didn't think I would get the job. I just wanted to be able to say I interviewed with him."

Just in case the weather prevented him from reaching Pensacola by air, Meyer drove to Panama City and spent the night. A couple of hours before dawn the next morning, when he got up and started off for Pensacola, the entire Florida panhandle was covered in fog, and all the airports were closed.

The sun was still trying to punch a hole through all that fog three hours later when Meyer pulled up to the gate at the Pensacola Naval Air Station.

Bryant, who had risen to the rank of lieutenant commander during World War II, had attended a banquet honoring Lee Roy Jordan up the road in Excel, Alabama, the evening before, and driven to the base to bunk for the night.

"Coach Bryant got in really late last night, and he's gone back to bed," the duty officer said.

"But I've got an appointment with him," Meyer said, insisting that the young gatekeeper wake up his famous overnight guest.

A few minutes later, Bryant appeared at the door, wearing his bathrobe.

"Hell, I got up early, saw this fog, and figured you wouldn't be able to get here," Bryant said with a grin. "So I went back to bed."

The two middle-aged veterans visited for a while, conversing about football, the military, and life.

"He didn't say it in so many words, but I think the fact that I did what it took to get there on time made an impression on Coach Bryant," said Meyer, who accepted a $1,000 pay cut to become Alabama's backfield coach. "That fog probably helped me get the job."

Meyer's determination to make his appointment, to live up to his obligation, to be as good as his word regardless of the obstacles, told Bryant all he needed to know about his character. Bryant surrounded himself with coaches who were prepared not just to teach, but to get the job done, somehow, and the impact of such intangibles on the 1966 football team would be felt from day one, helping creating a climate of discipline and commitment.

In some ways, the college football world the boys of 1966 were entering in 1963 had changed little since Bryant rode assistant coach Hank Crisp's rumble seat out of Arkansas and strapped on the pads the year Knute Rockne died. The rules limiting substitution remained strict, meaning one-platoon was still the order of the day. Rugged, multitalented souls with stamina and heart still carried more weight than studs with special skills. Freshmen still could not play on varsity teams. All of the southern programs remained lily-white, and most of the northern teams who had broken the color barrier continued to practice varying degrees of tokenism. Because the NFL was still fighting its way out of the dark ages, salaries for all but the biggest stars remained modest, meaning most student-athletes still approached college football as an end in itself rather than as a launching pad to professional riches.

However, the scope of college football was bigger. The game cast a larger shadow, thanks primarily to television and radio coverage, which caused more people to follow the sport. In 1961, Alabama's Denny Stadium was enlarged to 43,000 seats, more than three times its size during the days of those great Rose Bowl teams.

All the additional money from tickets, TV, bowl games, and such allowed programs like Alabama's to award large numbers of scholarships. It would be a decade before the National Collegiate Athletic Association ventured into the realm of scholarship limitations, and before the Southeastern Conference dipped a toe into that water in the late 1960s, Alabama routinely signed sixty or more players per year. The ability to bring in so many athletes gave Bryant the luxury of taking chances and also afforded him the opportunity to lock up some players just to keep them from signing with a rival program, especially Auburn.

"You could gamble a bit more in those days," said Clem Gryska, who recruited northern Alabama. "You might take someone who was borderline, if you had a good feeling about him, because you didn't have to worry about having only a limited number of scholarships."

Having so many recruits on hand at any given time enhanced his ability to push them all to the breaking point, because no matter how many players quit, there was always someone else willing and able to do whatever he asked, in order to move up the depth chart.

In addition to their on-the-field responsibilities, each coach on the Crimson Tide staff worked a specific recruiting territory. While Alabama trolled for players in the neighboring states of Tennessee, Florida, Mississippi, and Georgia, Bryant's strategy was built around dominating the acquisition of talent in the Heart of Dixie, where he went head to head with Shug Jordan's Auburn program, which had captured the 1957 national championship.

With few rules governing how much time recruiters could spend on the road, Alabama coaches traveled constantly in pursuit of talent, often hopping in their cars after practice and driving into the night to visit with some talented stud or a high school coach who could lend a hand. Like every other aspect of Bryant's program, it was an incredibly organized, disciplined activity. Usually, coaches watched spools and spools of film on every prospect and saw him play in person at least once, often several times, before considering the offer of a scholarship. It was a generation before Internet recruiting sites and television and radio shows devoted to the pursuit of tomorrow's stars, and the 'Bama staff relied heavily on a complex net of friendly high school coaches and alumni to make sure they saw anyone worthy of a look.

Rather than filling specific needs, Alabama tended to sign an inordinate number of fullbacks and quarterbacks, solid athletes who could play anywhere on the field. Size didn't matter. In the age of the one-platoon, sixty-minute man, Bryant wanted players who could be molded into versatile, supremely conditioned cogs, driven, hungry animals who could be pushed beyond their own perceived physical and mental limits. The freshmen of 1963, '64 and '65 who would grow up to chase a third straight national championship in 1966 represented the end of an era. The transition to the two-platoon game was just over the horizon.

The seniors of 1966 started out as war babies. The eldest, a hard-hitting full-back from Petal, Mississippi, named Ray Perkins, was born in 1941, a month before Pearl Harbor, but most of the young men who would become his class-mates were born toward the end of World War II. The youngest members of the team tended to fall into the first year or two of the massive Baby Boom generation, in the immediate aftermath of the conflict, although it would be some years before the Commerce Department's arbitrary statistical classification took on bold-type importance, turning the children born between 1946 and '64 into the most analyzed, hyped, and clichéd group in American history.

The boys of 1966 grew up learning the meaning of fear during the era of "duck and cover," their lives forever shadowed by the constant specter of the cold war against the Soviet Union. As teenagers, they watched with a sense of dread as downed American U-2 pilot Frances Gary Powers was put on trial . . . as the Communists built the Berlin Wall . . . as the world teetered on the brink of nuclear war during the Cuban Missile Crisis.

The vast majority of the young men who were recruited to play for the Crimson Tide during those three years grew up in modest homes. Very few of their parents had attended college, so the chance to earn a degree, to trade foot-ball skills for an education on someone else's nickel, represented a significant mo-tivation, a ticket to a better life. Many could have played and studied elsewhere. Nearly all chose Alabama for one reason—to play for Paul "Bear" Bryant.

John McKay, who won four national championships at Southern California and was a close friend of Bryant's for years, once said, "All of us as coaches would like to think a player comes to our school to play for us. But I honestly don't believe too many kids came to Southern Cal to play for me. With Paul, there was no doubt. They might've majored in business or education or what-ever, but their mamas and papas sent them to Tuscaloosa to play for him."

Camden's Billy Johnson considered Auburn, because he wanted to study forestry. "But I wanted to play for Coach Bryant more than I wanted to study forestry," he said.

Given Bryant's reputation as a hard-driving, no-nonsense disciplinarian, the kind of player who was attracted to the Alabama program in those days saw it as a test. The Crimson Tide was a standard for excellence, and also, for tough-ness. "If you made the decision to go to Alabama and play for Coach Bryant, a big part of it was wanting to prove that you could play for him . . . that you were man enough to play for him," said Byrd Williams, who turned down an appointment to West Point to sign with the Crimson Tide, where he became one of the seniors of 1966.

"You knew if you could play for Coach Bryant, you could play for anybody," said Kenny "Snake" Stabler, a talented quarterback from Foley, Alabama, who became part of the 1964 freshmen class. "I was just in awe of Coach Bryant. Plus, you knew you would win at Alabama, and winning was everything."

Stabler, one of the most highly recruited players in the South during his senior year of high school, turned down a $20,000 offer to sign with the New York Yankees organization in order to play for the Bear, but not before being courted relentlessly by most of the teams in the SEC.

Often, the big schools brought their hottest prospects to campus through the air, which was a new experience for most.

On a fall morning in 1963, the little four-seat turbo prop was bouncing all over the place in the soupy clouds, and David Chatwood was digging his fingernails into the armrest, trying to keep his breakfast down.

"Snake, you scared?"

"Hell, no, Chatwood!" came the twangy, high-pitched reply from the front seat, loud enough to be heard over the noise of the prop.

Stabler always was a talented liar.

Chatwood and Stabler, who played for rival high schools in Baldwin County (Fairhope and Foley, respectively) but had been close friends since grade school, were heading for their official visit to the University of Mississippi. It was the first airplane ride for both, and when the pilot landed the Piper Cub on the little grass strip in Fairhope to pick them up and circled the area so they could see their houses from the wide blue yonder, they felt like big shots, perhaps for the first time in their seventeen-year-old lives.

Like Chatwood and Stabler, most of the players headed for glory in 1966 were impressionable, wide-eyed innocents who could be simultaneously thrilled and frightened by such an event. The team was a product of a simpler world still steeped in traditional values, especially the vast majority who grew up in small southern towns, where things like air travel still seemed special, where high school athletes were valued but not coddled. The fact that they were not a bunch of worldly sophisticates would play a central role in defining the 1966 football team, because on the harrowing journey Bryant was preparing, characteristics like cynicism and cool were worthless, while traits like faith and character were absolutely essential. Theirs was a world before the end-zone dance and all of the self-indulgent behavior the act symbolized.

When the air started getting choppy on the flight through Mississippi, Chatwood wondered who would get his favorite shotgun.

"I mean I was petrified," he recalled.

The flight took the better part of two hours, and when the plane finally taxied to a stop in Oxford, someone from the university escorted them over to Johnny Vaught's office. Vaught, one of the most successful coaches in the history of the SEC, was in the middle of a 90-13-4 decade, including five conference crowns and a share of the 1960 national championship.

"At first my daddy didn't like the idea of my taking that trip, 'cause he knew I'd already made up my mind about going to Alabama," Chatwood said. "He didn't think it was right for me to lead Ole Miss on. So I called Coach Vaught and told him my mind was made up, that I was going to play for Coach Bryant. He said that was fine, that he sure would like me to come to Ole Miss and look around anyway. Maybe they could change my mind."

Not a chance.

When Chatwood packed his bags for Tuscaloosa, his daddy, a wholesale grocery salesman who never attended college, stopped him at the door. "Son, I'm breaking your plate," he said with a serious expression.

"I didn't need a translation," Chatwood recalled. "He meant that I had made a commitment to Alabama and Coach Bryant, that I was a man now, and that I better honor my commitment and go out and make a life for myself. I didn't have a home to come back to if I decided to quit, and I knew that even before he said it."

The image of the broken plate resonated across the entire team. One way or another, every man who signed with the Crimson Tide was negotiating a passage from childhood to adulthood, from dependence to independence, understanding that he was entering a world of enormous expectations with no real safety net, a Technicolor jungle where everyone he knew—and many he did not—would be counting on him, and, in no small measure, living vicariously through his adventures. The elder Chatwood was not being mean to his son; he was not banishing David from his life. Rather, he was demonstrating, with a memorable and easy to understand symbol of tough love, that he was not about to make it easy on him to view his commitment to Alabama frivolously by offering him a refuge from the moments of doubt and weakness surely to come.

In the land beyond mama's kitchen table, all plates had to be earned.

The idea of the broken plate spoke to the kind of hunger that could be sated only by learning to stand on one's own feet and achieve—the deep, abiding need to prove something to the world, to stake a claim, to earn a better life. Among the players who were destined to survive at Alabama, hunger was not an optional characteristic. It was a life force that drove, fortified, defined them all.

The broken plate was their connection to Bryant, who knew how to motivate such individuals better than any coach who ever lived.

For some, the Alabama scholarship was like a life preserver tossed into the drink at precisely the right time.

Fate smiled on onetime dropout Ray Perkins on the night when 'Bama assistant Dude Hennessey arrived in Mississippi to scout another player. After Perkins ran for three touchdowns and intercepted two passes, Hennessey offered him a scholarship on the spot. "You didn't have to be a genius to see what he had," Hennessey later said.

What he could not see was that Perkins, who was holding down a full-time job at a gas station while keeping his grades up and playing football, had essentially been on his own for years. His carpenter father struggled with alcoholism, and his mother suffered from an illness that often left her bedridden. Football had already saved him, in a way that Hennessey could not yet understand, and the brash splinter of a man had a fire inside him that no one could extinguish.

Even though Perkins had no other offers—not even from nearby Southern Mississippi—he played hard to get. "I'd like to hear it from Coach Bryant," he said.

That was the first time Hennessey realized there was something different about Ray Perkins, but not the last.

Like Perkins, Jerry Duncan had somehow escaped the notice of the big-time college recruiters, despite rushing for more than 1,700 yards as a senior. His only real opportunity to play college sports came from tiny Georgetown College in Kentucky, which forced him to try out for a scholarship that required him to play football and basketball.

By the time Duncan's high school coach pulled Bryant aside at a coaching clinic in Raleigh and told him about the hard-driving guy who wasn't very fast, big, or strong but who had something deep inside that made him play his guts out on every snap, graduation had come and gone and the leading rusher in the state of North Carolina was reluctantly preparing to head to Georgetown. He wasn't too excited about the idea, but it sure beat milking cows for the rest of his life.

Clem Gryska could not believe it when Bryant told him to drive to Sparta,

North Carolina, a speck of a town high in the Blue Ridge Mountains, and sign a player none of the coaches had seen.

"You don't want me to watch some film first, talk to his coach?"

"No. Just sign him."

"That was very unusual," Gryska said many years later. "It was just one of those gut feeling things."

When Gryska treated Duncan and his father, a dairy farmer, to lunch at a local diner and gave his sales pitch about Alabama football as they munched on country ham sandwiches, he asked Jerry if the high school had any film of him running the ball.

"Shoot, we don't even have a camera," Duncan said with a devilish grin.

From the perception of a more complicated age, the way Duncan arrived on Alabama's doorstep seems difficult to believe. He wasn't an afterthought. He was a reject. No big-time school wanted Duncan, and the only reason he landed a scholarship to Alabama was because Bryant took a shine to his high school coach, admired his persistence, and gave him his word, which was like gold.

Years later, Bryant told a reporter, "In the meantime, we'd checked film on Jerry, and he didn't show us much. If I hadn't promised his coach a scholarship, I really don't think we'd have gambled on him."

In a very real sense, Duncan owed the chance much less to his demonstrated ability on the football field than to Bryant's sense of honor in living up to his word. But an opening was an opening, and with a foot in the door, the farmer's son was determined to make something good happen.

The recruiting classes destined to provide the athletes for the 1966 team were filled with Jerry Duncans, relatively untalented, overachieving players whose potential could not be fully measured on film.

Several of the boys of 1966 caught the attention of Alabama's recruiters by having older brothers who played for the Crimson Tide, including a talented kicker from Georgia named Steve Davis. In fact, Davis's father, Pig, had been the first athlete ever recruited by Bryant, when he worked as an assistant coach for Frank Thomas in the 1930s.

Davis, who played on Alabama's 1937 SEC championship team, later regaled his six children with colorful stories about his days wearing crimson. During the 1938 Tennessee game at Legion Field, while trying to field a punt, Davis was clobbered from behind, a vicious hit which he thought deserved a flag. Once he pulled himself off the grass, Davis limped up to a nearby official, who had watched the play unfold in front of him.

"Hey, Ref, did you see that?" Davis said with a look of frustration.

The official glared at him. "Son, there are men playing here today. If you're not one, get off the field!"

After completing his undergraduate studies, Pig became a highly successful high school football coach in south Georgia, winning more than two hundred games while building powerhouse programs in Tifton and Columbus. After eldest boy Tim, with an assist from his daddy, earned a football scholarship to Alabama, second son Steve followed in his footsteps, arriving as a freshman in 1964. Younger brother Bill would continue the family tradition, kicking for 'Bama from 1971 to 1973.

Tough like their coach father, the Davis boys grew up as hard-hitting position players—until the accident. When Tim hurt his knee as a high school sophomore and required surgery, which led to a freak infection, he lost fifty pounds and nearly died. Deeply affected by the situation, Pig encouraged his sons to take up kicking, where they would be less prone to injuries. While big on education, Pig earned only about $5,000 per year as a high school coach, and he sat his boys down and told them he could not afford to send them to college.

"He encouraged me to kick and see if I could earn a scholarship, and there was never any doubt about me going to Alabama, if they would have me," Steve said.

On the recruiting trail, Bryant's dominant presence could be Alabama's secret weapon. He could walk into a home and charm mamas and papas as effortlessly as diagramming a belly play.

In the world of broken plates, most fathers and mothers connected with Bryant because they saw him as an extension of their values. In buying into his sales pitch, they viewed him as a surrogate parent who was providing a whole new family for their son, helping him negotiate the difficult transition to adulthood and his own set of plates, literal and metaphorical.

When Bryant walked through the front door of Joe Kelley's house in Skipperville, a small community near Ozark in southeastern Alabama, Florida State's Bill Peterson was on his way out. The two coaches shook hands and exchanged pleasantries, and Kelley's mother escorted the Bear to their big round kitchen table. While she served everyone coffee and homemade cake, Bryant poured her a cup of coffee. Then he sat down right next to her.

As Bryant spent most of the next two hours speaking directly to the mother, telling her how he would take care of Joe and help him get his education, he devoured two pieces of cake, sipped on the coffee, and smoked several cigarettes, finally wadding up a pack of Chesterfields on the table next to his plate.

During the conversation, Kelley, a highly sought quarterback, passed a note to 'Bama assistant Richard Williamson, seated next to him. "I've made up my mind," it read. "I'm going to Alabama." Williamson didn't want to interrupt his boss in the middle of a sales pitch—even though the deal was apparently closed—so he discreetly passed the piece of paper to Bryant, who ignored it.

"The whole time they were talking, my mother sat there eating her cake and drinking the coffee Coach Bryant had poured for her," Kelley said. "That was the first and last cup of coffee my mother ever drank. She didn't like coffee. But when he left and I asked her about it, she said she thought it would have been rude not to drink that coffee, after he had been so hospitable to serve it."

She kept the empty pack of cigarettes as a souvenir.

When Bryant showed up in Muscle Shoals to sign running back Dennis Homan, the whole town buzzed with excitement. Homan felt powerless to his charismatic presence as the big man sat in his living room. "It was sorta like Uncle Sam coming to see you. You don't say no to Uncle Sam," said Homan, who signed up to help make the state's football team safe from mediocrity.

John David Reitz and Steve Spurrier, two hot prospects from east Tennessee, rode to Tuscaloosa for an official visit in the backseat of Reverend Spurrier's car. Every time they stopped along the way, they prayed. The morning after touring the campus and meeting with some of the players and coaches, the Presbyterian minister and the two recruits sat down for breakfast at the Stafford Hotel in downtown Tuscaloosa with Bryant and several members of his staff.

When Bryant picked up his fork and started to dig in, the preacher gave him a nasty look. "Bear, don't you think this food is worth praying for?"

"I never will forget the look on the face of those coaches," said Reitz, who subsequently signed with Alabama. "I thought every last one of them was going to crawl under that table."

Bryant put down his fork and the preacher blessed the food. But when signing day rolled around, he lost Spurrier to Florida.

Chris Vagotis grew up tough on the mean streets of Canton, Ohio, the middle child of Greek immigrants. His mother worked three different waitress jobs to support her three kids, who had been abandoned by their father, a gambler on a long losing streak.

Like most of the tough guys in their working-class neighborhood, Vagotis appeared headed to a life in the steel mills or the military.

But his size and strength helped him become an outstanding lineman at Canton-Lincoln High School, and he already had an offer on the table from Georgia when Alabama called and asked him to visit. When he started telling his friends that he had the chance to play for Bear Bryant, no one believed him. *Yeah, Chris. Sure. Let us know when Vince Lombardi calls!*

During the trip to campus, fullback Eddie Versprille pulled him aside. "Let me give you a piece of advice," he said. "If you only like football, you'd better not come here. Come here only if you *love* football. You gotta love football to make it here."

Vagotis lacked the maturity to know whether Versprille was letting him in on a little inside information or trying to work him with reverse psychology. But it wasn't important for him to know.

"I'm eighteen and all full of piss and vinegar, and I'm thinking to myself: I'm as tough as any of you sons of bitches!" Vagotis recalled. "I was going to show them how tough I was."

The next summer, when Vagotis stepped off the airplane in Birmingham, he walked past a sign for a "colored restroom." As he came up behind the bus that would take him to campus, he noticed the "Heart of Dixie" license tag, which, in his distorted view of the South, equated to a vanity plate for the Ku Klux Klan.

"All of the sudden, I started feeling like I was in a different country," he said. "I started thinking that I probably wasn't prepared for how different it was going to be, how hard it was going to be for someone like me to adjust."

It was only a matter of time before Vagotis discovered how much he had in common with all those good ole' boys.

After all, the hunger that brought them all together was universal, and he was just another guy with a broken plate.

2. THE CRUCIBLE

A look of horror covered Howard Schnellenberger's usually stoic face as the ambulance pulled up to the curb.

Schnellenberger, Alabama's offensive line coach through the 1965 season, watched helplessly as the paramedics wheeled the huge, unconscious lineman away from the physical education building on a winter afternoon in 1964. Moments before, the hero of some town far from Tuscaloosa had fallen to the floor in the Crimson Tide's off-season conditioning program, known simply as gym class, with a thunderous thud. He just dropped, like a rock. The players, who were walking up the sidewalk to their own date upstairs with Alabama's version of hell, saw the flashing lights, the limp body, and all the color drained out of Schnellenberger's face, and naturally, feared the worst.

Soon after coming to at a local hospital, the talented stud with the bulging frame packed his bags and headed home. But the athletes who saw him all stretched out would never be able to shake the searing image.

Gym class. Those two words filled even the toughest Crimson Tide players with a sense of dread, at least the ones with the burden of knowledge.

In the Alabama football program of the 1960s, everyone was destined for forty-five minutes of pain in the little gym far from the adoring crowds. Some could take it. Some could not.

"I used to get sick in the morning, just knowing I had to go through that later in the day," said fullback David Chatwood.

Every time he became queasy in anticipation, Chatwood and others like him were having their minds manipulated—and trained—by Bryant.

To understand the 1966 Alabama football team, you first must understand the philosophy and climate that produced it.

Because the vast majority of the athletes who arrived on the University of Alabama campus in 1963, 1964, and 1965 were among the first generation in their families to attend college, because nearly all grew up in Alabama or in neighboring states, because they were young men with broken plates who wanted and needed to stake a claim in the world, the internal pressure they felt to live up to the faith of Alabama the team and Alabama the state was an enormous force. Most had no other way to attend college, and going home in shame was not a viable option. This climate made most incredibly susceptible to whatever Bryant asked them to do.

With 150 or more players on scholarship at any given time, nearly all filled with a sense of awe for the boss, Bryant enjoyed the luxury of being able to push his entire team to the breaking point—physically and mentally—without worrying about how many would quit. He knew some could not or would not muster the physical and mental toughness to sustain the punishment, and he knew some, like Chatwood, would let the process pray on their minds but keep pushing anyway. He wanted to make Chatwood feel sick, to see how he would react. In Bryant's world, Chatwood's queasiness in anticipation was not a product of weakness; the fact that he ignored his nerves and kept reaching to become a better football player ultimately was a sign of mental toughness, which, in Bryant's world, was the whole ballgame.

As soon as the players arrived, the program took control of their lives with the kind of force usually reserved for the military. Every aspect of their existence was dominated by Bryant's imposing shadow, his overarching sense of mission, his omnipresent ambition, his belief in the power of an all-consuming focus on winning. In his mind, pushing his players to reach was never quite enough. He demanded that they surrender to his will on a multitude of fronts, and as much as any combination of athletic skill, the 1966 Alabama Crimson Tide worked because the players bought into the idea that they could achieve great things by allowing Bryant to appropriate their individual lives for the benefit of a unified purpose.

Long before the boys of 1966 were forced to deal with the invisible enemy lurking ominously in the shadows, threatening their assault on the history books, they were all compelled to confront mental and physical obstacles from within. They all arrived as disparate individuals, but when placed in the crucible of the Alabama football experience—which included gym class as well as the pressure-packed practices, regimented dorm life, and other aspects of an incredibly disciplined existence, along with the lessons they could learn only by laying it all on the line before tens of thousands of fans on a crisp autumn Saturday—the ones who had the right stuff gradually were transformed into a mighty new entity, a team, thinking, acting, and striving as one, forged like impenetrable steel by the fusion of their collective tenacity, talent, faith, and will.

More than any other aspect of the Alabama football experience, the off-season gym class program, conducted each year between the end of the bowl game and the start of spring practice, laid the foundation for the 1966 Crimson Tide. The eldest members of this remarkable team started fighting off those queasy feelings in January 1964, continuing each winter for the rest of their college careers, as the next freshmen class joined the process, and the next.

The fear and loathing began soon after a new recruit arrived, when he was still trying to learn the playbook; perform on the practice field and in freshmen games; adjust to the strict rules of the athletic dorm; make friends with his roommate; coexist with a bunch of players eager to take his spot; and study enough to stay eligible . . . while trying to fight off homesickness. The varsity players would start dropping subtle hints during that already difficult and confusing time, messing with their minds. "Just you wait, rookie!" one of them would say, passing a freshman in the chow line at Bryant Hall. "Just you wait till the off-season!"

The cryptic psychological warfare heightened the sense of pressure and tension building on the new players.

"You try not to let that get to you," said split end Billy Scroggins. "But when you're on the other side of it, the fear of the unknown is pretty powerful."

Bobby Johns, destined to become one of the greatest defensive backs in Alabama history, remembered the warning of a former high school teammate, Joel White, who preceded him in Tuscaloosa. "He said if I could make it through a week of that off-season program, I might have a chance [of surviving]," Johns said. "He was right. It was horrible. There was no way to be prepared."

Three times per week from late January to early March, the players were required to show up for the off-season conditioning program, which tested their strength, endurance, and commitment to the cause. The need to develop and enhance quickness pervaded every activity. Each man was assigned to a specific group, and all but the first classes walked up those three flights of stairs to the top of the old athletic building, above the coaches' offices, while the previous class retreated in exhaustion, faces flushed, bodies aching, dripping sweat, struggling to catch a breath. The anticipation of pain was palpable.

"One of the first times I walked up those steps, I had to step over Joe Namath," said Ray Perkins, an All-America receiver who would catch balls from Namath, Steve Sloan, and Kenny Stabler during his Alabama career. "He was lying there on the staircase, all sprawled out, unable to move . . . trying to get up the strength to walk down."

The dusty old gym felt like a sauna. The ancient basketball goals at the ends went unused, except between classes, when the assistant coaches sometimes played shirts and skins while awaiting the next batch of victims. One area of the gym contained a large wrestling mat. Two ropes dangled from the ceiling. Each of the four corners featured a fifty-five-gallon garbage can, and no one needed to be taught its purpose.

"I can remember seeing players over there throwing up into one of those cans even before we started, they were so scared," said fullback Ed Morgan.

Sometimes, a player would wander off from his group during the middle of the action and pretend to vomit in one of those drums, just to catch a breath. But such devious behavior was inherently risky. Being caught faking it by a coach was a fate worse than death for an athlete who desperately wanted to measure up and someday run out on the field wearing a red jersey. Plus, those cans smelled like an open sewer, and standing near one for any length of time could render the act of pretending to be sick a kind of self-fulfilling prophecy.

On the way in, the athletes were divided into three rotating groups. When one of the coaches locked the doors, the rattle of those old chain locks intensified the sense of isolation and desperation that hung in the air alongside the smell of stale sweat and fresh vomit. The rattle of those old locks animated the nightmares of many players.

"I just thought I was going to die every time I walked in there," said defensive back David Bedwell.

The forty-five-minute sessions—divided equally into three fifteen-minute periods, featuring wrestling, wave drills, and isometrics—pushed every man to his physical and emotional breaking point. It was a grueling, nonstop assault on the body and the senses.

"It was so bad," remarked linebacker Bob Childs, "that I've tried to block that part [of my Alabama career] out of my memory."

The gym echoed with the sound of the Alabama assistant coaches pushing the players, challenging them, belittling them, motivating them to reach for a little more. Always more. Whistles overlapped with yelling voices, and yelling voices overlapped with whistles.

"You sorry turd! Can't you climb that rope any faster!!?"

"Don't you let that little chickenshit pin you!!"

"Don't you ever want to wear that red jersey!!?"

The order of group selection was completely arbitrary, and the worst draw of all was to be forced to wrestle first. Wrestling was the most physically taxing of all the activities, and if a player lost, he had to go again. In fact, he had to keep grappling until he pinned somebody, or until the whistle blew signaling for him to rotate to another station. Wrestling to lead off the session could leave a player incredibly drained heading to the subsequent group, and he knew that the next coach was not going to cut him an inch of slack.

Every player's worst nightmare was to be sent to the mat first and to be paired with Jimmy Fuller, a 6', 206-pound mound of muscle who played on both sides of the line for the Crimson Tide. The two-time state high school heavyweight wrestling champion could pin anyone on the team in the blink of an eye.

Fortunately for all those guys who wound up being twisted like a pretzel by Fuller and other strong men like Mike Hall and Cecil Dowdy, the gym class was not about developing superior wrestling techniques. It was about learning to fight.

The players who had been recruited by Alabama were all good athletes. Sitting in a little cinder block stadium 10 miles from nowhere, coaches could easily determine whether a player had the ability to pass, catch, run, block, tackle, or kick in the competitive environment of major college football. Some players were much more gifted than others, of course, and all kinds of variables merited consideration in the decision to award a scholarship.

But there was no way for those recruiters to measure the intangibles that transformed a talented athlete into a championship player.

There was no way to determine whether a player who got knocked down time and again would pull himself up and ask for more, until he couldn't spell his own name. There was no way to tell how a player would react when his body was telling him to shut down, to collapse in a pile of his own sweat, even as his coaches were pushing him to reach for a little something extra. There was no way to measure desire or heart or pride. The Alabama staff knew that talent alone didn't win most games, and certainly not championships. It took something extra, and Bryant and his coaches were determined to identify and cultivate that mysterious but powerful characteristic in every one of their players.

The primary purpose of the gym class was to push the players to the edge and, in the process, to make them physically and mentally tougher. In an age before Alabama placed much stock in weight training, the hardships they faced in gym class were intended to stiffen their tolerance for pain and increase their ability to endure and continue to perform in the face of debilitating fatigue. That's where desire and heart and pride could be found, in the warm glow of physical and mental desperation.

Those gut-wrenching afternoons in the hellish sweatbox were not some sadistic experiment. They represented a methodical search for truth—for the true measure of every one of those players who wanted to grow up to run out of the tunnel wearing a red jersey. Who would quit in the fourth quarter? And who would fight until the last drop of blood?

In the showers back at Bryant Hall and over adult beverages at a local watering hole, the players could be heard cursing the names of all those malevolent whistleblowers, especially those going through their first harrowing off-season. In those formative days of pain and doubt, it was easy for the athletes to resent Bryant, to see him simply as the source of their torment. But by

1966, they would understand. By 1966, they would all look back on those difficult days as the making of one of the greatest teams in college football history.
At least the ones who survived.

The strategy exemplified by gym class worked, and yielded tremendous results,
for one reason above all others: All those broken plates. A certain number of
players were absolutely desperate to succeed, which left them vulnerable to pay
any price, which is exactly the way the boss wanted it.

When David Chatwood and Kenny Stabler were growing up in Baldwin
County, wide-eyed country boys with an appreciation for good hunting dogs
and ice-cold beers, they often stood on the sidelines while out of the lineup and
counted the light poles.

It was a way to pass the time, and Chatwood knew the count at Fairhope as
well as his phone number: twelve poles with four lights each.

In the summer of 1964, when the two buddies were taking a breather from
practice leading up to the high school all-star game at Alabama's Denny Stadium, Chatwood looked around the mammoth horseshoe and started performing some basic arithmetic.

"Look, Snake," he said, punching his buddy in the arm. "There's over a
hundred lights on that one pole!"

Stabler smiled. "Yeah, man," he said. "We've made it now, haven't we?"

A simple truth oozed from the moment of youthful wonder, stripped of pre-
tense, uncomplicated by the cynicism of a later generation. It was hard for those
players to grasp the enormous difference between the world they had left behind
and the one they were entering, but they could see the lights. They could count
the lights. But, of course, the scene also reflected a profound naivete.

"We hadn't played a game, and we thought we had arrived," a bemused
Chatwood remarked four decades later. "We didn't have a clue."

Most of the players showed up on campus with little more than their
clothes. A player was considered prosperous if he owned a car, and most of
those guys drove around in old junkers. Some athletes were dirt poor, and relied
heavily on the $15 per month laundry money and the four complimentary tick-
ets they received to each game, which they could scalp, earning as much as several hundred dollars per season.

"If it hadn't been for those tickets, I don't know how some of us would have
made it," said lineman Frank Whaley.

Two weeks after arriving on campus in 1963, Whaley returned to the dorm
after class to find a note in his mailbox. Mary Harmon Bryant, the boss's wife,
wanted to see him.

"Oh, Lord," he thought to himself. "What have I done?"

An alumni group was hosting a banquet for the incoming freshmen in Birmingham several days later, and word had reached Mary Harmon that Whaley, who came from a very poor family, did not own a sport coat, required for the occasion. When they arrived at the Bryant home, she took the 6'4", 208-pound Whaley to her bedroom and opened the coach's closet, revealing dozens of coats in various styles.

"Coach Bryant and I were the same size, and she started pulling out jackets and having me try them on," Whaley said. "I hadn't said a word to anybody [about not having a sport coat], but somehow, she knew, and that wonderful lady wanted to make sure I wasn't put in a situation where I would feel uncomfortable."

In addition to demonstrating the kindness and thoughtfulness of the coach's wife, a gentle soul who was the epitome of a Southern lady, the episode offers a glimpse into the world of many of the players, who, while adored by a whole state, often lived lives of financial hardship. Yet, at least in the context of the Alabama football experience, a modest background, even grinding poverty, was more of a strength than a weakness, because it tended to magnify drive and ambition in a place that was all about drive and ambition. In Bryant's world, a player too impoverished to own a sport coat but filled with enough fire to have used his athletic skills to reach Tuscaloosa in the first place was likely to be much more self-motivated than a rich kid with a bulging closet and a fat wallet. The Frank Whaleys of the world were willing to put up with the enormous physical and mental demands of playing football at Alabama, from gym class to spring practice to the structured dorm environment, in order to be part of something that they considered special and ultimately, as the launching pad to a better life.

Young men who had little but aspired to something more, young men whose default setting was to respect authority figures, were especially susceptible to Bryant's aggressive and demanding system.

The freshmen of 1963 became the first class to move into Bryant Hall, the ultramodern, three-story brick athletic dorm often referred to as the Bear Bryant Hilton. The place seemed like a palace, especially compared to Friedman Hall, the previous athletic dorm. State of the art in every way, including wall-to-wall carpeting in the living areas, intercoms in all of the bedrooms, and air-conditioning throughout, Bryant Hall bespoke the first-class image that epitomized the program's aspirations. Most of the players had grown up in homes without air-conditioning, and in fact, the dorm was one of the few buildings on campus with air, and this represented a widely envied touch of luxury in a town where the late-summer temperatures often hovered near 100 degrees. The big lounge adjacent to the lobby on the first floor contained one of the first color television sets in town—the first nearly all of those players had ever seen. On Saturdays throughout the year, players rushed out of bed to claim a chair or a place on the floor to watch cartoons.

While Bryant wanted his players to attack like wild animals on the football field, he expected and demanded that they act like gentlemen in all other situations. One cardinal rule around Bryant Hall was that any time an adult entered a room, a player was obliged to stand up. In those early days of Bryant Hall, when it was widely considered the Taj Mahal of athletic dormitories, university officials frequently led tours of the facility. When yet another admiring group started walking around one Sunday afternoon in 1964, the players were so engrossed in some television show, they failed to hear the door open.

Seconds later, the big man cleared his throat, loud enough to be heard in Montgomery.

Turning toward the door, the players saw Bryant with several dignitaries and immediately jumped to their feet.

He looked around at the faces and flashed an irritated look.

"What are you supposed to do when a lady or a gentlemen enters the room?"

"Stand up," they all said in a feverish chorus of terror, standing at attention like officer candidates who had just failed to salute a superior officer.

"Well, don't I qualify?"

"Yes, sir!"

In his mind, some things were right and some things were wrong, and not standing up for grown-ups was a symbol that could not be ignored, behavior that could not be indulged.

None of those players ever made such a mistake again.

Bryant Hall was run like a military barracks. Players, scattered across two floors in two-man rooms, were required to get up by an appointed time every morning and show up for breakfast in the cafeteria downstairs, wearing collared shirts and long pants. They were expected to keep their rooms neat, and to make their beds every morning. Freshmen were required to attend study hall three nights a week. The nightly curfew—10:30 P.M. during the season—was strictly enforced, and all the outside doors were locked at the appointed time, making the place feel like a fortress. Or a jail. Being caught out of your room after curfew—even in one of the community bathrooms down the hall—was a punishable offense. So was walking through a corridor without shoes. Talking after lights out was verboten, a rule the dorm director actually tried to enforce. Most nights, the dorm director went door to door doing bed check, which made sneaking out incredibly risky. Alcohol was never to be possessed or consumed on the premises. Women were not allowed upstairs at any time. Even the married guys were required to stay in the dorm from Thursday to Saturday during the season, just to make sure their minds were properly focused.

"That dorm felt like a prison sometimes," said receiver Dennis Homan. "You just about had to ask permission to go to the bathroom."

The enforcer of all those regulations, dorm director Gary White, was viewed by some as a nitpicking tyrant, but in reality, he was a good man who had a tough job. A former head manager for the Crimson Tide, White had spent a year as a scout for the Dallas Cowboys before returning to the university, and his sense of mission was severe. He ran a taut ship, walking around the place like a warden. Behind his back, the players sometimes called him "Deputy Dawg," after the slow-talking cartoon character. After spot inspections, he was known to leave little notes on the players' desks, indicating a small fine— twenty-five or fifty cents—for infractions like overflowing trash cans or wrinkled bedspreads.

"The whole program was built on discipline, and I was responsible to Coach Bryant," said White, who lived in a first-floor suite with his family. "If I let something slide, I knew it was my job. It was that simple. [Coach Bryant] made me understand that what we were doing was important in creating the climate to have a winning football team."

Players needed permission from the boss to get married. Permission. Bryant was not very happy when halfback Ed Morgan married his sweetheart after his freshman year. Morgan endured several specially designed gut checks after his nuptials. "Coach Bryant told me that more times than not, getting married was not good for a football player, and he was going to find out in short order whether it was good for me or not," he said.

Sometimes Bryant flatly refused to grant his approval for his players to walk down the aisle, not because he opposed the institution, but because he thought most athletes could not handle the responsibilities of football, school, and marriage at the same time.

Dennis Homan once gathered his courage, went to see Bryant in his office, asked the question, and watched his coach become irate, especially as he recalled how he got married prior to his senior year, which he hid from his coaches. "You've got all your life to be married, but you've only got one chance to become an All-American," he told Homan, who, naturally, went to see his girl and told her they would have to wait until after his senior season. "After that, there wasn't enough money in the state of Alabama—or anywhere else— to make me get married until I finished my Alabama career," Homan said.

Wayne Trimble wanted to put the ring on his girl's finger prior to his senior year, but he knew better. "I didn't want to go see him, didn't want to push the situation, so I told Barbara we would have to wait," Trimble said.

"At the time, we all just understood," Barbara Trimble said. "That's just the way it was, and while we were anxious to get married, Wayne didn't want to do anything to make Coach Bryant think he wasn't serious about football."

In an era when nearly all of the athletes who stayed for four years eventually graduated, some were better students than others, but cutting classes was not tolerated. The academic advisor, Grover Niles, checked to see if players were attending class and in good academic standing. Missing an academic class usually resulted in a special 5:00 A.M. gym class with one of the assistant coaches, or an early morning trip to the stadium to run steps. The punishment for such offenses was not pleasant, and the negative reinforcement usually worked. Most players attended class regularly, and generally toed the line on the other rules around the dorm, because they knew any behavior that progressed from isolated to serial was destined to be turned over to the boss. And no one wanted to make that lonely journey to Bryant's office before the crack of dawn. Such experiences were never positive, and often ended with a player being compelled to pack his bags for home.

By creating such a structured environment, Bryant was able to live up to his word to all those mamas and papas. He looked after all those players by placing them in a box that allowed them little opportunity to be lured astray. Some, of course, proved incredibly adept at finding trouble anyway, and it was not uncommon for assistant head coach Sam Bailey—the designated first-responder—to be awakened in the middle of the night to bail some player out of jail for fighting or causing some alcohol-related disturbance at some redneck bar far from campus. Such incidents never made the papers, but they usually marked the end of some promising player's Alabama career.

One time a visiting recruit was being treated to a few beers at a rough joint on the edge of town, and after a scuffle with a bunch of drunk locals, the players had to explain to the recruit's parents about the brick that shattered the windshield of his new sports car.

The transition to adulthood was full of flying bricks, even for the heroes of Bryant Hall.

A big part of the process of molding the team, preparing it for all those battles to come, was creating a sense of brotherhood, a oneness, among the players. More than anything else, this was a byproduct of all those moments of shared sacrifice, but it was also cultivated far from the football field. Like soldiers, the Alabama players grew closer not only by spending time around each other, but also, by learning to care about each other, to trust each other. The combination of all those sweaty days in gym class and the off-hours hunting in the woods, playing cards around the dorm, and just sharing the large and small moments of each other's lives would prove instrumental in shaping the 1966 Alabama football team. Feeling like brothers made the players fight for each other on the field; it made them fight with all their might until the bitter end, and this was an intangible that could not be overstated in the making of a championship team.

Many of the players enjoyed hunting, which explained why Bryant Hall typically was filled with enough shotguns and rifles to overthrow a small country. In small groups, the athletes headed off to hunt for birds and deer in the nearby countryside, often snatching no more than an hour or two between classes and practice.

Frank Canterbury, a city boy from Birmingham who learned to hunt after going off to college, came across an old junker 1955 Buick and bought it for a hunting car. Enlisting the help of Wayne Cook, Billy Johnson, John David Reitz, and Harold Moore, he borrowed some equipment from a local garage and chopped the top off the car, giving them the funkiest-looking convertible in town. Sometimes they even buzzed sorority row, and the jalopy always turned the girls' heads. The guys liked to trap beavers as well, and they often brought the carcasses back to the dorm and gave them to the custodian, a beloved black man known as Big Ed, who would take them home to make beaver stew.

On the way back to campus after one hunt out toward Moundville, Cook was behind the wheel of the sawed-off Buick when they came up behind a stopped school bus, unloading a bunch of black schoolchildren. He pumped the brakes, but nothing happened. The pedal went all the way to the floor. Suddenly, with Cook unable to stop the car, the players started yelling out to the schoolchildren: "Get out of the way! Get out of the way!"

Forced to chose, in the blink of an eye, between a potentially fatal collision with the bus or running the car off the road into a bunch of pine trees, Cook opted for the trees and told his buddies to hang on. After a skillful crash landing, Cook brought the car to a stop at about a 45-degree angle near the shoulder of the road as the stunned schoolchildren watched. No one was hurt.

"Ol' Cook saved us," Canterbury said.

Most members of the team liked to hang out at The Tide, a little dive bar in downtown Tuscaloosa owned by a beloved middle-aged lady who always looked out for the players. The Tide was like a clubhouse for the 'Bama teams of that era, a peaceful place where they could have a cold one or two and laugh and tell stories and escape all the pressures of their daily lives. Some impoverished players traded football tickets for beers. You could drink for weeks on a prized admission to a big game like LSU or Tennessee. The Tide, which had a jukebox and a shuffleboard table, was their turf, and the coaches, understanding their need for a zone of privacy and a temporary respite from the regimentation of Alabama football, knew to stay away.

Even the coaches needed their space, and the players learned to respect certain boundaries. After seeing several members of the team show up at the bar of a barbecue restaurant in Northport, the town just across the Black Warrior River from Tuscaloosa, line coach Howard Schnellenberger took his wife by the arm and walked out the door without ordering. The next day, he told the players, "You've got your places and I've got mine. I don't want to ever see you in there again."

Players knew better than to challenge the rule forbidding alcohol in the dorm, but some pushed the line further than others. It was a popular routine for some players to drive away from practice, stop at a little convenience store on the way to the dorm, and suck down a beer or two on the way to the evening training table, often guzzling that last bottle of suds while the car idled in the parking lot.

Trouble often came in a cloud of innocence, like when Creed Gilmer, who completed his playing eligibility in 1965, found himself admiring a teammate's new shotgun, aimed it out the window, drawing a bead on a passing car, and pulled the trigger. He didn't think the gun was loaded, until the buckshot exploded in a flash, splattering against the side of the car and scaring a bunch of frat boys half to death.

The process of forging a team capable of kicking ass on Saturday required placing a large number of competitive, and not always compatible, personalities under one roof. The brotherhood of gym class made everybody tough, and made most feel a strong connection to each other, but the price was a certain amount of unavoidable tension.

The card game rook was a popular pastime around Bryant Hall, and during one night of shuffling, a tightly wound athlete walked up to Johnny Mosley and pointed a .357 Magnum revolver inches from his head. "Mosely, I'm tired of your crap," he said, "and I'm going to kill you right now."

Mosley turned as white as a sheet, and his nemesis pulled the trigger.

The gunman started laughing when the pistol fired a blank, as planned, and retreated down the hallway, cackling with delight.

Many players tested the boundaries of their corseted existence with harmless mischief, like the group led by Frank Canterbury that kept a pair of hound dogs—which they used for hunting—in the attic. After a few too many close calls with the barracks sergeant, they built a chicken wire pen for the pooches in the woods out back. Many nights, they would sneak the dogs a bunch of steaks from the training table, understanding full well that if Gary White found out, somebody would be huffing and puffing in the wee hours.

The same crowd once built a flying saucer out of laundry bags and balsa wood. When it got dark, they launched the craft out of somebody's window and watched it climb into the night sky. The candles attached to the top gave it an eerie glow as it headed up over Foster Auditorium. The next day, local police and federal officials were dispatched to investigate sightings of a UFO over campus, as Canterbury, John David Reitz, and Harold Moore laughed knowingly.

Bryant didn't want his players to cower in the face of their restrictions. He wanted them to be men, a little fearless, a little cocky, but ultimately, responsible. He understood that they would push the line, that they would need to let off steam from time to time. He understood the inevitability of a certain amount of reckless behavior in developing a powerful football team capable of performing on Saturdays.

He knew they were going to drink a little beer, chase a little skirt, and drive fast, but it was his job to keep their eyes on the road, safely headed toward the national championship. All those rules were like speed bumps. If nothing else, they motivated a certain level of good sense among a crowd still young enough to feel bulletproof.

Because so many people across Alabama looked upon Bryant as the ultimate expression of American manhood and viewed his rigorous program as the supreme test of that macho standard, the opportunity to play for him—after surviving his various demands—was seen as proof of a profound manliness. The perception that it took someone incredibly tough to play for Bryant tended to reinforce the cycle, helping turn perception into reality.

But in his world, being a man was about much more than strength. It was also about character.

Like mainstream America, the Crimson Tide football program was anchored by a strong sense of right and wrong. It was not some pristine colony of choirboys, but it was a neatly ordered world of mostly decent young guys who were always guided by the shadowy presence of obligations and consequences. Most of them were raised with a powerful understanding of these societal bookends, which provided the context for everything in Tuscaloosa.

Toward the end of his freshman year in 1963, defensive end Frank Whaley found out that his high school sweetheart was pregnant with his child. Growing up in the small town of Lineville, his mother and father could not give him much in the way of material things, but they instilled him with something much more valuable, which the Alabama program reinforced.

"Back then, if you made a mistake, you didn't run and hide from it," he said. "You owned up to it and dealt with it. You did the right thing."

Although he was quickly moving up the depth chart and figured to play the next season, Whaley reluctantly gave up his scholarship and his place on the team, moved back to Lineville, married the mother of his child, landed a part-time job pumping gas to support them, and borrowed $310 from a local bank to cover the medical expenses, knowing he could not pay it back for a while.

"Coach Bryant was not happy about the mistake I made . . . but he understood I had to take care of my responsibilities," Whaley said. "I learned a lot of things from Coach Bryant, but probably the number-one thing was . . . if you've got a problem, you should face it like a man and try to do the honorable thing."

Unable to blend into the wallpaper like other students, the players always felt that they were being watched. The overriding feeling of needing to live within certain parameters that would reflect well on the Alabama program often transcended the specific rules that governed their daily lives.

After practice one day, a bunch of the players decided to see how many of them could squeeze into David Chatwood's dilapidated Ford station wagon, an old postal vehicle, which had been driven more than 350,000 miles, even before he had bought it at a government auction for $200. The guys were young and full of vigor, and it seemed like a fun thing to do. By the time they started off for the dorm, the wagon was crammed with bodies. Arms and legs dangled from open windows. One brave soul straddled the hood, precariously teetering in the wind.

Halfway to the dorm, they passed the boss on the street, and his eyes followed the wagon barrelling down the road with a look of disgust.

"Oh, God!" one of them yelled. "Do you think he saw us?"

"Yes," Chatwood said with a groan. "He looked right at me."

When they arrived at the dorm, the student who manned the front desk handed Chatwood the telephone.

"Was that your car?" Bryant said firmly.

"Yes, sir."

"You wanna keep it?"

"Yes, sir."

"Well, don't ever let me see you doing anything like that again."

The desire to maintain at least the appearance of a total focus on football extended even to their social lives. Some players would make their dates scrunch down in the seats of their cars to avoid eye contact with Bryant when they saw him coming out of the dorm or the athletic offices. Nobody said they couldn't have a girlfriend, of course, and most did, but they didn't want to shove it in his face. God forbid, he might get the idea that football was not the most important thing in their lives.

"You knew if you screwed up in practice some time after that, it would all come back to the fact that you weren't concentrating 'cause you were out with some girl," Jerry Duncan said.

No one gave a serious thought to challenging the system, or to Bryant's right to invade every corner of their lives.

"In those days, you listened to authority figures, and wanted to please them, even if you disagreed," said defensive back Mike Sasser.

Beyond the desire to protect the players from their own slowly evaporating immaturity, the structure existed and was enforced rigorously because Bryant believed that discipline was the foundation of any kind of success. Winning is a habit, and he wanted his players to maintain a winning attitude at all times. If you took pride in your living space and made your bed like a champion, it would positively affect your self-image, and that would spill over into all aspects of your life, including how you performed on the football field. Players who could muster the discipline to master the little things off the field were likely to be equally diligent between the white lines, translating into fewer missed assignments and fewer penalties. In a sport where one bad play could mean the difference between winning and losing, it all connected. Bryant believed you could draw a line between missing curfew and fumbling a ball in a critical situation. It was all part of the same universe of responsibilities and consequences.

Whether it was going full speed in gym class or studying hard enough to turn a B into an A, he wanted a commitment to excellence to permeate the lives of every one of his players, until it was second nature for them to demand the best in everything.

"We don't want ordinary people here," Bryant was fond of saying in his team meetings. "We want special people who are willing to do the things that are required to become champions."

It was all about paying the price. If a player demonstrated a willingness to live within Bryant's structured world, he was displaying a commitment to the cause of building the most powerful football team in the country.

One bed at a time.

The importance of living within Bryant's rules, large and small, landed like a mighty thud even before the seniors of 1966 had completed their first semester on campus.

The week of the Kennedy assassination in November 1963, junior quarterback Joe Namath and several of his teammates were caught up in a minor disturbance at a little hamburger joint off the Strip, the main drag adjoining the west end of campus. Some of the guys got a little loud, and it was obvious that Namath had been drinking, which was a violation of team rules. The owner of the place called one of the coaches, and while most of the other members of the team were able to maintain their anonymity as they all retreated into the night, Namath could not escape his already glowing notoriety. After two years as the Crimson Tide's starter, the Bomber from Beaver Falls, Pennsylvania, was being hailed as one of the top quarterbacks in the country—some were already calling him one of the greatest of all time—and virtually every living soul in the state of Alabama knew his face.

When word reached the boss that his best athlete had been seen drinking, he immediately went over to the dorm and pulled Namath into a room.

"Is is true?" Bryant asked.

"Yes, sir," Namath said flatly.

Honesty was one of the hallmarks of the program, and Namath knew better than to lie.

Bryant suddenly felt sick. Because he knew. He knew what he had to do.

During a meeting with his assistant coaches the next morning, Bryant explained the Namath situation and asked for their input. Virtually every assistant in the room wanted to punish him in some painless way. After all, in that less media-conscious age, when stories about troubled athletes were more likely to be swept under the rug than splattered in bold type, it would have been very easy to ignore the incident, or at least to consider it a meaningless aberration that required little more than a slap on the wrist.

While most of his staff members were thinking about how they were going to beat Miami on the road and Ole Miss in the Sugar Bowl, and the significant bowl bonus that rode in the balance, Gene Stallings struck a contrarian view.

"If it'd been me," said Stallings, one of the survivors of the famed Junction preseason camp at Texas A&M, "you'd have kicked me off."

Nearly a decade after Junction, the epic event still reverberated across Bryant's career.

Bryant's mind was already made up, and the dutiful Stallings, destined to win a national championship as the head coach of the Crimson Tide a generation later, was the only coach who passed the test.

When Bryant suspended Namath and head manager Jack "Hoot Owl" Hicks—one of Joe's closest friends, who was nailed because the coaches knew he always drove his old jalopy wherever Namath went—and forced them to move out of the dorm immediately, the news spread like a wildfire. The other players—including freshman defensive back Johnny Mosley, destined to become one of the senior leaders on the 1966 team—waited nervously for the other shoe to drop, unaware that only Namath and Hicks had been fingered.

"I just sat there waiting for the knock on the door," said fullback Steve Bowman, headed for All-SEC acclaim in 1964 and 1965. "I knew if they were kicking Joe and Jack off, I didn't have a prayer. That's the only time in my life I've ever been scared of losing something, and I was scared of losing everything."

One of the most remarkable attributes of Bryant as a leader was his willingness to place the team in short-term peril while concentrating on the big picture. Understanding that the right thing and the tougher thing are usually the same choice, he built his career on creating a system held together by discipline that worked because it was always applied consistently and fairly. And he was always prepared to live with the consequences.

When Bryant suspended Namath for the final two games of the year and told him he could try to win his job back during spring practice in 1964 if he kept his nose clean, he was sending a clear message to the star quarterback, but also to the rest of the team. In addition to teaching Namath a lesson about the importance of following the rules and living up to his obligations—and reinforcing the notion that no one player was bigger than the team—Bryant's highly publicized act spoke loudly to the rest of the Crimson Tide.

"You can draw a line between that one event and the discipline that helped make that 1966 team so great," said center Jimmy Carroll, then a redshirt freshman. "We knew if he would kick his best athlete off the team . . . one of the best quarterbacks of all time . . . there's no telling what he would do to some of us, if we got out of line. The memory of that was always in the back of our minds. It made us respect Coach Bryant even more . . . and probably fear him even more, too."

While the freshmen played their own schedule and remained somewhat isolated from the upperclassmen, the young men who would one day be the seniors of 1966 watched the varsity stumble to a disappointing season in 1963, at least by Alabama's lofty standards. Even with Namath at the controls and a punishing defense that surrendered an average of just 8.8 points, the Crimson Tide lost two games it should have won: 10–8 to Auburn and 10–6 to Florida, the latter one of only two defeats Bryant would suffer in Tuscaloosa during his entire tenure as head coach. It was the first time Alabama had dropped two regular-season games since Bryant's first year in 1958.

With senior Jack Hurlbut and sophomore Steve Sloan taking turns trying to fill Namath's enormous shoes, the Crimson Tide looked unimpressive in scoring a 17–12 nationally televised victory on the road against Miami, a game postponed until December 14 because of the Kennedy assassination, making it the latest regular-season contest in modern 'Bama history. Without Namath, Alabama headed toward the Sugar Bowl as a big underdog to undefeated SEC champion Ole Miss.

What happened in New Orleans on New Year's Day 1964 became the stuff of Crimson Tide legend. To nearly everyone's surprise, Bryant appointed the still green Sloan as the starting quarterback, and the quiet, studious young man from Cleveland, Tennessee, displayed a tremendous amount of poise in leading Alabama to a 12–7 upset, which seemed about as improbable as the freak snowstorm that descended on the Big Easy on the eve of the game. While not spectacular, Sloan was steady and made few mistakes, guiding 'Bama close enough for Tim Davis to set a Sugar Bowl record with four field goals, and the opportunistic defense forced six turnovers and twice stopped the Rebels inside the Tide's 10-yard line.

Clearly, Bryant had been prepared to risk losing those two games in order to reinforce his sense of strict discipline, but in winning two big victories despite Namath's absence, the Alabama players made a bold statement about the power of working as a team and overcoming adversity—to the nation and to themselves. The boys of 1966 watched and learned.

While forever acutely aware of the importance of the team concept, especially in light of the Namath suspension, each player competed on a daily basis as an individual not only against his teammates, but against the constantly moving target of his personal athletic potential.

Forged in the crucible of intense physical and mental strain and rigid discipline, the athletes who became productive players slowly felt themselves getting stronger. It wasn't just a matter of bulging biceps. They could stand to run for longer periods, push the blocking sleds on the practice field with greater force, survive afternoons of tremendous heat without running out of steam. They could also sense a growing ability to more easily harness the power of their will while simultaneously ignoring the pangs of doubt rattling around in their heads. Hardened by the cumulative effects of Bryant's demanding regimen, those destined to play important roles on the 1966 Crimson Tide gradually felt emboldened by a gathering resolve.

"Surviving all that stuff made you realize you could do just about anything," said lineman Billy Johnson.

The players who survived and prospered in the crucible to come out the other side as winning athletes lived in constant fear—four distinct kinds of fear.

In the pressurized world of 'Bama football, the fear of retribution from the man at the top hung in the air at all times. If a player fouled up, or if the team performed badly in a practice or lost a game, everyone realized that the ultimate result of such a failure was that Bryant and his coaches would start pushing even harder. This could take the form of longer, more grueling workouts, or a player might be kicked off the team and lose his scholarship. The desire to avoid such additional grief was primal, like a child learning to dread a paddle.

As they began to see Bryant as more than an authority figure who wielded power over them, a different kind of fear came bubbling up from someplace deep. After experiencing a certain amount of training and being exposed to him for a period of time, the kind of player who grew to respect him and under-stand what he was trying to help them accomplish was driven by a fear of let-ting him down. The possibility of doing something to disappoint him was a powerful motivator to work even harder, to concentrate even more intently.

Even before the players arrived in Tuscaloosa, most were conditioned to un-derstand that their role on the Crimson Tide football team was a source of tremendous pride for their family and friends back home. The rare and special honor of playing for Alabama was a thought reinforced in many different ways. Once on campus, this feeling tended to intensify, and they started to see how they were representing not only their families and friends, but an entire state living in the shadow of their glory. The desire to be worthy of this widely en-vied privilege loomed large, and the fear of being unworthy drove them to push still harder, and to hold on for dear life.

"I knew there was no way I could quit at Alabama, because I couldn't go back and face those people in Enterprise," said center Jimmy Carroll, one of the seniors of 1966. "Let me tell you, that was a tremendous incentive. How could I go home with my tail between my legs?"

Eventually, after spending enough time sweating and reaching with a bunch of guys, a certain kind of player looked inside himself and found something even more powerful. The bond he had developed with all those young men took on a life of its own, and he could not imagine doing anything to let them down. This was where all those moments of shared sacrifice assumed a whole new power, not to mention all the carefree times at The Tide, playing rook around the dorm, and building flying saucers and such. The level of determi-nation a player felt to live up to his responsibilities on the field was a reflection of his personal investment in the larger cause, because he knew if he didn't do his job, it affected all those guys who felt like they were his brothers.

All of the players who made the conscious decision to suffer through all the physical pain and mental anguish, and to cede a significant amount of control over their daily lives, saw the Alabama football experience through the lens of at least one of those fears.

"You were willing to pay any price, because winning and being on that team meant so much," said defensive lineman Randy Barron.

A master psychologist, Bryant deftly cultivated his larger-than-life persona, making certain that raw intimidation remained the dominant fixture of the motivational package. However, he also knew how to subtly push all of the buttons, reminding his players how many people were counting on them, and why.

"Some people thought all that stuff he used to say about mamas and papas was corny, and in a way, I guess it was," said longtime 'Bama assistant Jack Rutledge, who coached the centers in 1966. "But Coach Bryant knew exactly what he was doing. He understood all kinds of ways to make a kid push himself."

During one steamy scrimmage, he noticed fullback Ed Morgan dragging back to the huddle, wheezing. Running to his side, he grabbed the player, lifted him off the ground, and shook him like a rag doll.

"Goddamn it, Ed Morgan, you run around here like you've got shit in your blood!" he thundered. "I know your mama and daddy, and you're not that way. You need to be a man!"

Morgan worked harder to catch his breath faster—and so did every athlete who witnessed his moment of truth.

Every player struggled with the thought of quitting. Every single one. To some, it seemed like the only sane option, compared with the insanity of putting up with gym class, spring practice, the regimented dorm, the mandatory for-credit football classes that were really just an extension of practice, and all the other aspects of life under Bear Bryant that more closely resembled Marine boot camp.

"The training was inhumane," said Chris Vagotis, the Ohio lineman who had arrived determined to show his toughness. "Inhumane! They talk about Junction, but that was what, ten days? Hell, we put up with that kind of crap for four years."

During the hottest periods of the spring and summer, the coaches frequently outfitted some of the young players in a padded contraption known as the Zoot Suit, which intensified the heat and limited mobility while allowing other players to attack at will. Wearing the Zoot Suit was like having a target on your chest. You were going to be hit hard and often, and the trick was to learn to suck it up and take it for as long as the drill lasted, a metaphor that could be applied to the entire Alabama football experience.

Quitting was easy, since no one was holding a gun to their heads, and there were less demanding places to play football.

Dozens of players quit, including many great talents, like Terry Owens, a gigantic lineman who transferred to Jacksonville State and later played for the San Diego Chargers. The first year was always a mass exodus. The trail of defectors would start during the unrelenting pressure of two-a-days, when they practiced for hours and hours in the heat of the Alabama summer without water breaks, and accelerate in the middle of the gym class hell. His freshman year alone, Louis Thompson roomed with three different players who eventually quit, some no doubt pushed to the door by his own bitching and moaning.

After a harrowing set of two-a-days in 1964, Tom Somerville and Stan Moss took lightning-quick halfback Herbie Phelps, the previous year's Kentucky high school player-of-the-year, to the Greyhound bus station.

"We're right behind you, Herbie," Somerville said with a sense of brotherhood.

"Yeah, we're gone in a couple of days," Moss yelled after him.

But they were both made of something different, so they stayed.

The sound of footlockers and suitcases banging against the dorm stairs filled many nights, even as some of the athletes who tried to distract themselves by playing cards or studying wondered what it would be like to disappear into the night.

Sometimes during their freshmen year, long after the fascination of the light poles had faded, roommates David Chatwood and Kenny Stabler would lie in their beds, physically spent and frustrated, and talk about heading home for good.

"We could be there before breakfast."

"Yeah, I wonder what mama would fix us?"

But it was just talk. They couldn't go home, broken plates and all.

On the field and in team meetings, Bryant often looked out at his men and said, "It takes two things to win football games: Preparation and dedication. I'm responsible for the preparation and you're responsible for the dedication."

Dedication often came disguised as desperation.

Receivers coach Richard Williamson, a split end on the Crimson Tide's 1961 national championship team who led 'Bama in receptions two straight years, understood the psychological battle brewing in every player's head. One day after an especially tough practice early in his playing career, Williamson packed his bags, got in his car, and started out for his home in Fort Deposit, Alabama. He could not take it anymore.

"Daddy, I'm coming home, be there in time for supper," he said from a phone booth along the way.

"What do you mean, son?"

"Well, I've quit the team and—"

"Son, if you quit down there, you don't have a home to come back to."

Discouraged, and having nowhere to turn, Williamson got back in his car and drove back to the dorm. He did not yet understand that his father had saved him from making the biggest mistake of his life.

"When you're a player, you get to a point where you think, I just don't want to put up with this any longer," said Williamson, bound for a long and distinguished career as a college and NFL coach. "It wasn't always easy to understand the brilliance of what Coach Bryant was doing."

The unrelenting nature of the pressure, punctuated by the obscenity-laced rants of the coaches, forced every player to confront some very basic questions.

"You eventually start thinking to yourself, What kind of man am I to let these people treat me this way?" said All-America defensive lineman Richard Cole. "I must be some sort of coward. Believe me, that stuff played with our minds."

It was not just the dilemma of whether to stay or go that tormented so many players. They also wrestled with the thought of what the choice would say about them as men.

Was it the cowardly thing to quit? To disappoint all those people who were counting on you? To throw away your education? To say you were not tough enough to take what they were dishing out? Or was it more cowardly to stay? To allow yourself to be humiliated day after day? To let them appropriate your manhood, your sense of dignity, your body, for some future glory that might never come?

Determined to create a team of supremely conditioned, mentally tough players, Bryant was never concerned about the quitters. He understood that a significant amount of his recruits would always choose to leave rather than pay the price. He understood that every one of his players thought about bolting at one time or another, and that's the way he wanted it—to push players to that edge, to see how they would perform under the most difficult conditions. In fact, he wanted to force the quitters to show their true colors on the practice field or in the gym, before they could do real harm by costing him a game.

More than naked aggression, his practices also included various instances of methodical scheming designed to test the way his players thought and reacted.

While taping Byrd Williams's slightly injured knee in the training room before a practice in 1964, head trainer Jim Goostree looked up at his face and smiled. "Today's your day!"

"What do you mean?" Williams asked with a puzzled expression.

"Today's your day. Better be ready."

Sooner or later, Bryant put every player on the team through what he liked to call a gut check. The gut check could take various forms, but the central theme was always the same. He wanted to see how you would react to the most severe conditions under absolute pressure.

"That day, I couldn't do anything right," Williams said. "It was horrible. Somebody was always pushing me or telling me what a screwup I was . . . making me do something extra. But I survived, kept fighting. They weren't going to run me off, and that's what Coach Bryant wanted to find out."

The gut check usually consisted of equal parts physical and psychological, but sometimes it wasn't physical at all.

During one especially rough practice, Bryant was jerking players around, pulling them in and out of a one-on-one blocking drill.

"Alright, who hasn't been in here?" he said, looking around at a group of about thirty exhausted athletes.

Not a single player raised his hand. In fact, volunteering to jump into that fray would have been nuts. But that's not the way Alabama players were trained to think. They were taught to be honest—and always eager for battle, no matter what.

"You, you haven't been in here!" Bryant said, pointing to one player whose performance had already caused him doubts.

The Bear was right. He knew exactly who had been hitting and who hadn't.

"Dude," he yelled out to assistant coach Dude Hennessey, "I want you to take this one over there and run him till he quits. Don't want to ever see him again."

In the blink of an eye, one player made a choice out of weakness that cost him his Alabama playing career.

The 1966 team was built on such moments, because they reinforced fundamental values that measured more than athletic talent.

Sometimes, he checked the whole team's guts at the same time.

Like many others, offensive guard Johnny Calvert's belief in his teammates and himself was fortified by a harrowing afternoon during the spring heading into his sophomore year. Every year, the alumni were invited to practice on a certain day, and in 1964, it just happened to coincide with one of the biggest gut checks of all. After seeing something that bothered him, Bryant climbed off his tower, sprinted to the center of the action, and started chewing on his team. He asked the boosters to leave, and then he kept one group of offensive players and two defenses on the field. For the next hour or so, he forced the offense to drive from one end of the field to the opposite goal line and back again, without substituting, without being able to call time-out, while running two different defenses in and out of the action, fresh and motivated.

After a certain amount of time, every player on the offense was straddling the precipice of physical and mental exhaustion. Les Kelley, one of Calvert's high school teammates, fumbled near the goal line, and Bryant pitched a huge fit. He forced Kelley to run 26 give, the team's basic off-tackle play, more than a dozen times in a row, without a huddle. The defense knew it was coming, and they pulverized him every time. But no one quit. Not that day. They all sucked it up, and kept fighting through the pain. Bryant learned a little something about those players, and they learned a little something about themselves.

"You felt like if you could survive a day like that, you could survive anything," Calvert said.

When assistant coaches Charley Pell and Jimmy Sharpe forced him to run wind sprints after practice several days in a row, Chris Vagotis, one of the few Yankees on the roster, made a big mistake. He asked why. In those days, nobody asked why.

When they refused to tell him, he went to see the big man, who scared the hell out of him, but said he would check into it. After supper, Pell and Sharpe appeared at the door to his dorm room.

"What are you doing going to see Coach Bryant?" Pell said.

"I wanted to know why I'm being punished."

The exchange started getting salty, the hotheaded Vagotis suggested they take it outside, and the coaches eventually backed off. The pride of Canton didn't see any more playing time for a while.

"That first year or so, I felt like a foreigner on that team," Vagotis said. "It was like some of [the coaches and players] thought I was taking up a spot that should have gone to some Southern boy."

One way or another, they all felt like aliens in a strange land, desperately trying to learn the language. Some reached a breaking point, and broke, choosing to leave rather than continuing to take the punishment while trying to decipher the meaning of it all.

Most of the players who left voluntarily shared one common thread. It wasn't necessarily a matter of toughness, and certainly not of ability, but generally speaking, the game didn't mean as much to them.

"It reached a point for me where it just wasn't worth it," said Norton Bond, a 6'4", 205-pound defensive end, who quit the team in 1965 and eventually became an attorney. "My identity wasn't wrapped up in football. It was never that important to me, so [quitting] was not a difficult choice."

Injuries forced many others to leave, including Bill Cherry, described by his teammates as one of the most talented running backs of the time. When Louis Thompson picked him up during a scrimmage in 1964 and slammed him to the ground with a thud, Cherry felt like a boy among men.

"I was a competitive guy and loved the game . . . loved hitting and being hit, but I had never been hit like that," said Cherry, who later became an attorney. "I mean, Louis just laid one on me, and it tore up my shoulder."

Cherry attempted a comeback, but his tattered body eventually led him to a difficult choice. "I just felt if I stayed out there, I was going to get killed," he said.

The potential of sustaining a career-ending injury was a subject all of the players tried to avoid, but the reminders of how quickly potential could be rendered to past tense were never difficult to find. The eldest members of the 1966 team arrived on campus in time to see Mike Fracchia complete his journey from stud to cautionary tale. One of the greatest runners ever to wear an Alabama jersey, a player with tremendous moves, speed, and strength, Fracchia led the Crimson Tide in rushing during the championship season of 1961. But a serious knee injury prematurely ended his career, and though he attempted a comeback, Fracchia was never the same. His former teammates could see him struggling to understand who he was without being able to define himself as a warrior for the Crimson Tide.

For many, quitting the Alabama football team was a shame they would carry for years. In a state where football was more than a game, it marked them, like a scarlet letter. One of the defectors from the 1966 team later became a high school coach and frequently attended Bryant's coaching clinic on the Crimson Tide's practice field. Colleagues noticed that whenever Bryant showed up, he always vanished. It became a running joke, and some of his friends liked to tease him.

"Here comes Coach Bryant! Better hide."

Invariably, he would turn to look. Just in case.

Even after the passage of more than a decade, the quitter could not face his old coach. He could not bear to see the disappointment in his eyes.

When he talked to his squad about life after football, Bryant often contrasted the adversity they faced on the field with hardships beyond the huddle.

"You think this is hard?" he would say. "This isn't hard. This is nothing. What are you going to do when you lose your job . . . and you've got three or four kids and one of 'em is sick . . . and your wife has run off with some drummer? Are you going to quit then? Or are you going to fight?"

Many of the remaining athletes tended to be incredibly self-motivated individuals who viewed football as an extension of themselves. To them, the game was the equivalent of a vital organ, manufacturing self-esteem like adrenaline. It was difficult for such competitive athletes whose identity was so intertwined with the game to walk away without feeling that they had somehow devalued and even debilitated themselves. Beyond the four fears, this feeling motivated players to reach because succeeding on the football field was an essential part of their lives—because football somehow made them whole. If a player viewed the game in such a way, he could not possibly tolerate anything less than a full-frontal assault on every last ounce of his potential.

Bryant loved players who saw the game in such dramatic terms, because he knew they would find a way to win championships.

This sort of drive permeated the 1966 Alabama Crimson Tide. You could almost see it tattooed on their foreheads.

Bryant's ability to dominate the state's news media also played a vital role in shaping the team.

Newspapers remained the primary source of sports reporting in those days, and the various papers across Alabama devoted significant space to covering the Crimson Tide. The most important sportswriters of the day—including Benny Marshall, Alf Van Hoose, and Clyde Bolton of *The Birmingham News,* Bill Easterling and John Pruett of *The Huntsville Times,* Bill Lumpkin of the *Birmingham Post-Herald,* Jimmy Smothers of *The Gadsden Times,* and Charles Land of *The Tuscaloosa News*—provided a critical link between Alabama football and its large fan base. Still in the grips of a romantic era when sports figures were placed on pedestals and bad news was often ignored, Alabama's newspapers played a central role in the veneration of Bryant and the enormous shadow cast by Crimson Tide football. The daily ritual of turning to the sports pages was more than a search for information; it was a quest for a narrative connection with the Crimson Tide. The major writers of the era helped make 'Bama football a living and breathing entity for many devoted fans who had never attended the university or, in many cases, even seen a game in person.

On most days, Tuscaloosa's Land was the only reporter to cover practice. Once or twice a week, he was joined by a scribe from Birmingham, Huntsville, Montgomery, or Mobile. Bryant usually was very tight-lipped in his impromptu postgame press conference, which often consisted of a hasty conversation while walking toward the dressing room with one or two writers.

Players were forbidden from speaking with a member of the press without special permission, which was rarely sought, even more rarely granted. When Birmingham's Van Hoose once approached offensive tackle Jerry Duncan about an interview, Duncan refused to talk with him until the columnist proved he had received permission from the boss. "I've cleared it with Coach Bryant," Van Hoose insisted.

"No offense, but I need to hear that from somebody else," Duncan said, demanding to receive confirmation from sports publicity director Charley Thornton before he would answer the first question.

By maintaining a tight 'grip on the information flow, Bryant was able to carefully craft the program's message—to the outside world and among the players themselves. Even as he manipulated the players' minds and developed their bodies in the crucible, he skillfully used the media to help create the carefully controlled environment that fostered the formation of a powerful team. Prohibiting his players from speaking to the press reinforced the team concept, limited dissent, and formed a protective boundary between the program and the outside world, which prevented the players from becoming distracted.

At the same time, he skillfully used the media in a variety of ways, to communicate not only to the Alabama nation but also to the players themselves. Several months before the 1966 season, defensive end Frank Whaley was surprised to see his name in the sports section of *The Tuscaloosa News.* "If he comes down to Tuscaloosa as the old Frank Whaley and not the new one I knew last year, then I'll fire him," Bryant said for all the world to see. "We don't have any use for folks who aren't thinking 100 percent all the time." Instead of calling Whaley into his office, Bryant clearly believed the message was more effective delivered in the afternoon paper. Whaley needed no interpretation.

One of Bryant's most effective tools in shaping the way his team thought was his incredibly popular Sunday afternoon television program. *The Bear Bryant Show,* broadcast statewide, featured the coach and cohost Charley Thornton narrating the highlight film from the previous day's game. In 1966, it became one of the first locally produced programs in the state of Alabama to be shown in color. Sponsored by Coca-Cola and Golden Flake potato chips—the unifying slogan, "Great Pair, Says the Bear," became as ubiquitous as his chiseled face—the show was required viewing for Alabama fans, especially because so few games of the era were televised live.

While the show made Tide supporters feel closer to their team and their coach, the players watched for an entirely different reason.

"You wanted to see if he would mention your name," said defensive tackle Richard Cole, who usually joined many of his teammates crowded around the television in the first-floor lounge at Bryant Hall. "Of course, there were times when you didn't want him to mention your name, if you'd make a mistake."

The fans across the state who often heard him stumble over someone's name probably thought he took the show lightly. He did not. Bryant approached everything having to do with the shaping of his football team very seriously, including his television show. Because he knew his players watched, Bryant often sent messages during the show.

After letting his grades slip into a dangerous zone, Birmingham's Eddie Propst received a letter from the boss over the summer informing him that he was losing his scholarship. He stayed on the team, but would have to pay his own way until he pulled up his grades. After making several tackles on special teams against Mississippi State in 1966, Propst took a special thrill in watching the show with the guys in the Bryant Hall lounge. When the image of him slamming a State player to the ground filled the screen, his heart raced.

About that time, Bryant said, "Well, there's ole Eddie . . ." Launching into a few complimentary words, he finally said, "I guess I'll put him back on scholarship."

Not all messages landed with such glee, but in ways both positive and negative, Bryant used the program to great effect to reinforce the all-consuming focus of producing a championship football team.

No bell rang. No buzzer sounded. No whistle blew. But it was the end of something, just the same.

The eldest members of the 1966 Alabama Crimson Tide were the last athletes recruited to play the one-platoon game in Tuscaloosa, and in this respect, they became the personification of a dying breed, soon to be as anachronistic as singing cowboys, soon to join blacksmiths, soda jerks, and service station attendants in the graveyard of American cultural extinction.

The game was changing, and the days of a certain rugged ideal were coming to a close. All aboard. Next stop, the future. Please have your gigantic body, your breakneck speed, and your specialized skill out for the attendant.

After several years of rigorous debate, the college football rules committee completely liberalized the substitution guidelines prior to the 1964 season, allowing coaches to bring players on and off the field as they pleased. The change ushered in the era of two-platoon football for good, a shift destined to fundamentally alter the sport, and Bryant was not the least bit happy about it.

Although Alabama was better equipped than most programs to handle the change, considering the massive number of solid athletes it attracted and the unsurpassed level of training they received, the Bear resisted the two-platoon game because he understood that it de-emphasized stamina and versatility in favor of skill and fresh legs. It promoted the development of a whole different sort of player, and his philosophy of small, quick athletes who won by outlasting the other guy was living on borrowed time. The future belonged to big, strong men pumped up in the weight room, specialists who would not need to worry about enduring for sixty minutes.

The present still belonged to the mostly diminutive, superbly conditioned Crimson Tide.

Alabama would continue to recruit the same sort of athletes for several more years, despite the change and, in fact, Bryant started the 1964 season by using several of his best athletes both ways. But that didn't last long, because it didn't take a genius to understand that even a talented and determined player going both ways was no match for a guy who could spend half the time on the sidelines catching his breath and swigging on a cup of water.

While the shift to the two-platoon game represented a significant turning point, the 1964 season would be best remembered as the year of Joe Namath's dramatic comeback.

In the weeks and months after his suspension at the end of the 1963 season, when he was totally isolated from his teammates and his story was being tossed about all over the country like a cautionary tale, several major colleges tried to lure Namath out of Bryant's doghouse. But he took his punishment like a man, further reinforcing the legitimacy and primacy of Alabama's strict code of discipline. As promised, the boss allowed him to go out for the team again in the spring. After working his way up from the bottom of the depth chart, Namath won his job back. In the fall of 1964, his arm and his command of the offense stronger than ever, the man who would one day be known as Broadway Joe led the Crimson Tide to an undefeated regular season, capped by the school's second national championship in four years, awarded by both the AP and UPI polls.

In the fourth game of the season, a 21–0 victory over North Carolina State, Namath sustained a knee injury, which would hamper him for the rest of the year. Even in such moments of crisis, Bryant was always acutely aware of the messages he communicated to his team, so as head trainer Jim Goostree and others attended to the grimacing Namath, he immediately turned his back on the injured quarterback, put his arm around backup Steve Sloan, and walked him several yards onto the playing surface.

Sophomore lineman Byrd Williams, standing nearby, never forgot the image—or the point Bryant no doubt was determined to convey. "He was sending a signal to the rest of the team: This is my guy and I've got confidence in him. He wanted us to know that he believed that having Namath go down was not the end of the world . . . that it was a team game and we would adjust and win as a team. What a great management lesson. So many little things like that shaped the confidence of the '66 team, things that most people away from the team never saw or noticed."

Despite being significantly hobbled by the injury, which caused him to share playing time for the rest of the year with the increasingly effective Sloan, Namath could still stun opponents in the blink of an eye. With less than two minutes remaining in the first half of a scoreless game against Georgia Tech, Namath came off the bench and threw two long touchdown strikes, giving the Tide an eye-popping 14–0 lead, en route to a decisive 24–7 victory.

Backfield coach Ken Meyer had already started his journey from the press box to the dressing room when Namath entered the game, so, unaware of the dramatic turn of events, he was at the blackboard diagramming a strategy to get the Tide on the board early in the second half when his grinning quarterback interrupted him. "But coach," he said. "We're ahead now."

"I couldn't believe it," Meyer recalled. "It had all happened so quick, I was standing there completely unaware. That's how good Joe was. That's how quick he could make something happen and completely change the complexion of a game."

About two hours before Namath's heroics, thousands of fans were treated to one of the most memorable sights in the storied annals of Alabama football.

Relations between Alabama and Georgia Tech had been strained since 1961, when Alabama's Darwin Holt blocked Tech's Chick Granning while running downfield on a punt return at Legion Field, resulting in severe injuries to Granning's face. The Atlanta media blew the incident way out of proportion, suggesting Holt had struck Granning with the intention of hurting him and insinuating that Bryant taught such behavior. The injury was unfortunate, but Holt and Alabama were unfairly victimized by a smear campaign that obscured the most basic facts about an incredibly rough sport. For reasons beyond the dispute, Tech had announced its decision to leave the SEC and become an independent after the 1964 season, which gave the school the excuse to cancel the series with Alabama, making the 1964 game the final game of a long and hotly contested rivalry.

Two years after nearly being hit by liquor bottles thrown by rowdy Tech students in Atlanta, Bryant arrived at Grant Field in November 1964 determined to protect himself. Even the Bear bled, after all, and he wanted to avoid ruining his new sports jacket—and have a little fun in the process. Before the ritual pregame walk around the field, Bryant started moving from locker to locker trying on helmets, but most were too small. Finally, he pulled on the large No. 78 helmet worn by sophomore lineman Louis Thompson, which fit snugly.

"Hell, this'll work," he said, and walked out onto the field to a combination of jeers and cheers, creating an image that no one in the stadium would ever forget.

In truth, the stunt probably was motivated as much by Bryant's desire to break the tension of a big game as a desire to keep from getting hit. After all, he walked the sidelines for the entire game without a helmet, and no one touched him. Seeing the boss walk out in the headgear gave everyone on the team a lift and a chuckle, while subtly mocking the bad blood between the two schools. He was sticking it to all those high and mighty Georgia Tech folks who didn't want to play in his conference anymore, the same folks who tried to brand him as some sort of ogre after the Chick Granning affair. The helmet said, "Take your best shot. You can't touch me!"

As the eldest members of the 1966 team played increasingly important roles on the 1964 squad, their development was influenced in various ways. The 1964 Tide won several close games, and the players learned early not to panic, which would pay enormous dividends later. Several loomed large, including receiver Ray Perkins, who caught sixteen passes; tight end Wayne Cook, who started nearly every game and blocked a punt in the victory over Tennessee; and lineman Jimmy Fuller, who made many big plays on defense.

The most enduring image of all from the championship season of 1964 happened on New Year's Night 1965, in the electric atmosphere of the first prime time Orange Bowl in Miami, televised from coast to coast by NBC.

With the Crimson Tide trailing once-beaten Southwest Conference champion Texas 21–7 in the third quarter, Namath came off the bench to replace the struggling Sloan and led a furious Alabama rally. With his gimpy leg heavily bandaged, Namath gave one of the gutsiest performances ever seen in a big college game, completing 18 of 37 attempts for an Orange Bowl–record 255 yards. One of his two touchdown passes was a seven-yarder to multitalented sophomore Wayne Trimble. Namath's knee was hurting so badly at times, he could hardly run, but he drilled the ball time and again in the face of a menacing Texas rush, keeping millions of anxious television viewers on the edge of their seats as the time dwindled.

After the game, which occurred at the height of the war between the established National Football League and the upstart American Football League, Namath would sign a $427,000 deal with the New York Jets, the richest contract in the history of sports at the time. Bad knee and all, he was showing football fans all across the country why many experts were calling him the next Johnny Unitas. Within a short time, the man whose career had dangled by a flimsy thread in the uncertain weeks after the Kennedy assassination would be the toast of New York, a cultural icon for a new age, headed for the immortality of Super Bowl III, when he promised and delivered an unlikely victory over the mighty Baltimore Colts and helped give the AFL the clout to merge with the NFL, setting the stage for a whole new era of professional football.

With 'Bama down 27–17 in the fourth quarter, Jimmy Fuller intercepted a Longhorns pass, and once again, Namath trotted onto the field, ignoring the pain, reaching deep. Methodically, he marched the Tide downfield, toward the go-ahead touchdown. On a first-and-goal call from the Texas 6 yard line, full-back Steve Bowman bulled his way to the two. On second down, Bowman churned forward to the one. On third down, Bowman hit the line hard, with all he had, but he was stopped by a crowd of white shirts just short of the goal.

What happened next remains one of the most controversial and frustrating plays in Alabama football history.

Calling his own number, Namath lunged forward behind center Gaylon McCullough and disappeared into a sea of red and white jerseys around the goal line, colliding with a defensive wall led by All-America linebacker Tommy Nobis, a dominating player who would win both the Maxwell and Outland trophies the next season. Namath and his nearby teammates believed he had scored when they all climbed off the grass, a view momentarily vindicated by one official who raised his arms to signal a touchdown. However, he was quickly overruled by another official, the ball went over on downs, and Texas ran out the clock to secure a 21–17 victory.

Like McCollough and Bowman, Namath later publicly insisted that he had crossed the goal line, but Bryant refused to second-guess the officiating. In fact, the way he handled the situation taught every man on the team yet another lesson, especially those athletes still being forged in the crucible of the Alabama football experience for future assaults on glory.

"We didn't deserve to win after failing in four cracks from the six," Bryant told reporters afterward. "When something means that much to you, you should push people out of there far enough to remove all doubt."

Instead of pouting or causing a stink, Bryant was telling his players that in football as in life, they should be prepared to do whatever is required to win convincingly enough to prevent one debatable call from determining the outcome.

Still, the "did he or didn't he?" argument may live forever in the lore of Alabama football.

More than three decades after the play, an Alabama alumnus attending a cocktail party at New York's Waldorf-Astoria Hotel prior to the College Football Hall of Fame induction ceremony was introduced to Nobis, who had gone on to a stellar career with the Atlanta Falcons.

"One thing I just have to ask you," the Alabama man said with a sheepish grin.

"No," Nobis said, interrupting in midsentence, his smile suddenly fading into an icy stare, "I know what you're going to ask, and the answer is no. He didn't score!"

Even after all those years, Nobis was still defending his end zone.

Because the wire services still held their final votes at the conclusion of the regular season, the Tide's loss to Texas did not have any effect on the 1964 championship, which was safely in the bag. However, in 1965, a pivotal change was coming. After several years of rigorous debate, the AP's poll of sportswriters decided to count the votes after the bowls. Through the years, several national champions had been knocked off in bowl games, including Oklahoma in 1950, Maryland in 1953 and Minnesota in 1960. Alabama was the latest, and the alteration, billed as an "experiment," was intended to prevent a repeat of 1964. No one could know the decision would play right into Paul Bryant's hands in 1965.

With a talented cast returning, including All-America center Paul Crane, All-SEC fullback Steve Bowman, and quarterback Steve Sloan, who had helped Namath pilot the way toward the 1964 title, Alabama was loaded once again.

Regardless of how the national championship was decided, Bryant kept his players focused on following his demonstrated ability to lead them to the promised land.

When they first arrived in Tuscaloosa, the men of the broken plates found the adjustment to life under Bryant an incredibly harrowing, unnerving experience, which is exactly what the boss wanted them to feel. In time, however, the ones who stuck it out found a comfort zone in the box he created for them, which ultimately made it all much more effective.

By itself, gym class never would have yielded the intended results. The same could be said of every other demanding aspect of the Alabama football experience. The crucible worked, methodically forming a powerful new entity, because it existed as a zone of absolute control and commitment. In isolation, gym class might have seemed too extreme, but in the context of all the rest, it made complete sense. Players might have rebelled against one or more aspects of the system, if they lived in a much looser overall environment, but the ones who chose to stay understood that they were buying into not just certain rules and regimens, but a whole philosophy.

The system was geared around the belief that Bryant knew how to mold championship teams, and the various parts fit neatly together like pieces in a puzzle: The rules around the dorm cultivated a sense of pride and personal responsibility. Gym class taught the players to challenge their own physical and mental boundaries. Gut checks like the infamous Alumni Day motivated a sense of gathering oneness. Punishment for rules violations fostered a climate of accountability and reinforced the importance of living up to one's obligations to his teammates.

The success of the 1966 football team was firmly rooted in how all of these seemingly disparate areas of emphasis joined to create a mighty unit capable of thinking and acting as one.

The ultimate payoff was winning the big one, and enjoying the satisfaction of pulling that national championship ring on your finger for the first time, watching the light glint off the stone and remembering the high price you paid for it.

The whole system worked, ultimately, because it worked. Success bred success. The players put up with the enormous strain required to live up to Bryant's expectations because they repeatedly were rewarded for their efforts. They could see how their sweat eventually led to something.

Even as he kept his players pointed toward the big prize, Bryant understood the critical importance of what motivational experts call intermediate levels of motivation. Because the whole process was invested with such a potent combination of pride and pressure, playing enough minutes to win a precious varsity letter loomed large in the minds of every player. Earning a letter also represented another torturous test—yet another opportunity for the athletes to prove how much they wanted to be part of the Alabama family.

Before being formally admitted into the A Club, the Alabama letterman's association, new members were forced to withstand the kind of demanding and degrading initiation process usually reserved for Tuscaloosa's politically connected and tradition-rich Greeks. After all, Crimson Tide football was the most exclusive fraternity of all on the Alabama campus, and many of the brothers of Bryant Hall took a special thrill in the hazing process.

Most of it fell into the nuisance category, like being forced by an upperclassman to fetch a pack of cigarettes in the middle of the night, or the realm of physical pain, like being compelled to allow an upperclassman to whack you repeatedly with the wooden paddle you made especially for him. Some have frightful memories of being dropped off out in the middle of nowhere on a cold night wearing nothing but their underwear. The lettermen always tossed them a dime as the car pealed off into the night. The problem was finding a place to use it.

"Some of that stuff would get you thrown in jail today," Dennis Homan said with a forgiving chuckle.

On one especially cold day, the initiates were sent out wearing only T-shirts, jeans, and sneakers and told to kneel in front of a first-floor window outside one of the girls' dorms and beg for water. The coeds, of course, were hip to the gag. They proceeded to pour one bucket of water after another onto the shivering Crimson Tide warriors.

During Kenny Stabler's initiation, he was sent out with a string tied to a pencil on one end and, unseen, to his genitals on the other. His mission was to go out across campus and convince a certain number of girls to autograph his notepad with the pencil. Because the string was strung so tight, every Jane Hancock scribbled in lead was a new experience in pain.

The initiation process always culminated on a cold winter day, when the new lettermen were awakened before dawn and forced to march down University Boulevard in their underwear, shivering as a large crowd of students looked on, gawking at the mighty Crimson Tide heroes being publicly humiliated. Once they reached the Sigma Nu house, the upperclassmen made the rookies jump into the ice-cold fountain out front and fish for a bunch of specially placed trout—with their bare hands.

Sometimes, a little improvisation was required.

On the cold and rainy day of completion for Homan and Stabler, the upperclassmen stopped the procession to compel them to lie down in a puddle in the middle of the street and pretend to make out with each other.

"You should have seen that," Homan said. "We were a sight . . . laughing like crazy, just trying to get through it . . . all those people looking at us like we were nuts."

Among the many pressures designed to harden the Alabama football team, hugging and pretending to kiss and fondle a teammate of the same sex on a public street may have been the oddest, but for the new initiates into the brotherhood of the Crimson Tide, the frigid walk down University Boulevard in front of all those prying eyes was an important passage. All of those men had paid a high price for the privilege. It was like a victory parade, and they all walked tall and proud.

Even those players who managed to survive the various stages of the crucible to make the team and earn a letter felt constant pressure to do the things necessary to win significant playing time. Even the starters—especially the starters—felt forever under the gun to do the things required to protect their jobs.

The trip to the equipment cage adjacent to the locker room before practice was fraught with a tension all its own. Far from the frigid initiation process, it could be chilly in a very different way.

The commandant of the cage, equipment manager Willie Meadows, was a gruff former Korean War tank driver who didn't so much talk as bark.

"What the hell do you want, boy?" was a typical greeting when he stuck his head up to the edge of the chain-link fencing, especially for some young punk freshman with an eye on making the varsity.

God help the player who ever tried to pilfer a jersey or a pair of sweats.

Under Meadows's direction, head manager Sang Lyda and his staff of students were responsible for a variety of equipment and logistical operations, including the all-important practice schedule. Every morning around seven, Lyda made the trip to Bryant's office to see if the boss had any special needs for the day and to go over that afternoon's schedule, which was timed down to the minute. So many minutes for this group, so many for that group, so many for a scrimmage, and so on.

The schedule was guarded like a state secret. None of the players was supposed to see it, but Byrd Williams became known to his teammates as "Scoop Man" because he often succeeded in his daily quest to sneak a peak at the daily lineup, so he could mentally prepare for the parameters of the physical strain. "Byrd didn't want to go to practice until he saw the schedule," Lyda said. "It just drove him nuts if he couldn't get a look."

The most important duty of all for Lyda and his managers, or at least the one that loomed largest in the minds of the players, was the daily preparation of the baskets. Laundry was handled off site in those days, so after the cleaning was delivered, the managers rushed back from scarfing down lunch at Bryant Hall and carefully loaded each basket with a fresh jock strap, socks, practice pants, and jersey.

The color of the jersey corresponded to the player's place on the depth chart: red for first team, blue for second team, green for third team, and so on. At any given time during the start of two-a-days—before the great escape began—the team might consist of five or six different units, but any jersey below green might as well have been invisible.

The depth chart fluctuated on a daily basis, and when a player walked up to the cage and retrieved his basket, he always approached with a sense of trepidation.

"If a player got a basket with a blue jersey and he had been on the first team the day before, that was devastating," Lyda remarked.

Many aspects of the program were carefully calculated to create a sense of status, which produced an incentive to achieve in order to earn certain privileges. Making training table was important, not only because the player was able to eat steak every night while some players munched on spaghetti or chicken, but also because it meant he probably had a chance to play.

The first milestone that truly felt like an accomplishment in every Alabama player's career was walking up to a list posted outside the locker room door and seeing his name listed on the travel squad. Sometimes, Bryant, having seen something disturbing, would call Lyda over during a practice and tell him to scratch one name off the list. Of all the torturous moments of life as an Alabama football player, perhaps the only thing worse than sprinting off the practice field and not finding your name typed in bold letters was sprinting off the practice field and seeing your name typed in bold letters, but scratched out.

The team traveled in style on two chartered airplanes—usually a Martin 404 and a Douglas DC-3—and two chartered Greyhound-style buses, and being assigned to the first plane and the first bus—where Bryant always sat in the first row—was another reflection of accomplishment, which could be earned only through performance, on the field and off.

While motivating his players to keep reaching in order to be rewarded—as well as to please him, which was a reward in itself—Bryant skillfully cultivated a climate in which he could make them feel both vulnerable and invincible. It was quite a trick, abounding with various management lessons, not only in accomplishing both so deftly, but in knowing when to pull the lever and switch from one to the other.

"Coach Bryant always knew how to keep you guessing," said linebacker Eddie Bo Rogers. "Somehow he knew when you needed a pat on the back and when you needed a kick in the butt. It was eerie sometimes."

One dividend of the rigorous training regimen was that Bryant was able to convince his players that because they had worked so hard, the games were destined to be easy by comparison, and the only way they could lose was if they somehow slacked up in their preparation. At once, this posture, while sold in the larger context of the Alabama football experience, filled their heads with both incredible confidence and significant diligence.

Beyond the vital connection between preparation and performance, Bryant's psychological hold on his players was so firm that he was able to transfer a sense of unbending belief to many of them with a precious few words. It wasn't magical, but it was mysterious and it was powerful, and the men who played for him in those days inevitably struggle to describe how one man could inspire them all so expertly.

But even inspiration has limits. Sometimes it takes a little guile to finish the job.

Alabama players wanted to avoid two places if at all possible. The first was Bryant's office, because no good ever came out of walking through that door. The second was the training room. Of course, visiting the training room on occasion was inevitable, since some players required tape every day, and the taping process was unavoidable. But no one wanted to stay long, because frequent trips to the training room for anything other than some routine like tape could knock a player off the depth chart. Starting positions were lost forever by athletes who lingered a little too long in Jim Goostree's lair, and many players were willing to play with significant pain to avoid such a risk.

Goostree, who studied as a student trainer under Tennessee's legendary General Robert Neyland before arriving in Tuscaloosa toward the end of the Whitworth regime, worked at Bryant's side for his entire quarter-century at Alabama. A wily and colorful character who spoke with a deep Tennessee twang, Goostree was widely admired as one of the most skilled athletic trainers in the business. Like his boss, he didn't believe in coddling players. He understood how much of the trainer's job was psychological, how critical it was for him to communicate to the players the difference between hurts and injuries, and to prevent them from falling into a cycle of allowing themselves to be dragged down mentally by a physical ailment.

He was also the players' connection.

He had the good stuff.

Several times a month, usually in the dark of night, Goostree carefully mixed the powder in the proper doses, mashed it into a bunch of pills and left them to harden overnight. He always waited until he was alone, because he did not want any witnesses.

Forever cryptic with the players, he refused to tell them exactly what the jumper, his little magic pill, contained. And they didn't need to know. All they needed to know was that it would give them a little lift of extra energy, a little burst to help sustain them during a rough practice. He told them it was potent, and that's why he didn't dole it out like candy. On especially demanding days, some players made a special trip to the training room because they needed a little extra steam in their stride.

But it was all in their heads.

The jumper was an elaborate con, conceived by Goostree, approved by

Bryant, and swallowed time and time again by athletes who needed to believe in something stronger than their own will. It was a placebo, a sugar pill, absolutely worthless and harmless, and most of the players never knew until years later—yet another psychological ploy used to help forge a steely championship team.

The chartered airplane thundered through the clouds between Birmingham and Athens, Georgia, on the seventeenth day of September in 1965, encountering one patch of turbulence after another. All around the cabin, the Alabama players, headed for a nationally televised season opener against Vince Dooley's Georgia Bulldogs, struggled to keep their breakfast down on the extremely bumpy ride. Seated somewhere toward the back, sophomore halfback Dicky Thompson, a native Georgian returning to his home state for his first varsity game, was also taking the first flight of his life.

"I remember being scared to death," Thompson said. "Because I had never flown before, I wasn't real sure we were going to make it."

The 1965 season was destined to be full of turbulence as well, and it would take all the skill and determination that Bryant and his staff could muster to keep the players from panicking and losing faith while they plotted a course for a second consecutive national championship.

Leading Georgia 17–10 as the clock approached two minutes remaining in the game, fifth-ranked Alabama was stunned by one of the most controversial and debated calls in the history of the SEC. On a second-and-eight from his own 27 yard line, Georgia quarterback Kirby Moore passed to the outstretched arms of a tumbling Pat Hodgson, who lateraled to Bob Taylor, who eluded the Alabama defense and streaked downfield for a 73-yard touchdown. Moments later, Moore hit Hodgson for a two-point conversion, giving the Bulldogs an unlikely 18–17 victory over the Crimson Tide.

The problem, as many Alabama players, coaches, and fans pointed out at the time, and stop-action film would demonstrate the next day: Hodgson's knees appeared to be on the ground before he lateraled the ball, meaning the play should have been called dead. The official ruling contended that Hodgson had actually "batted" the ball, despite significant evidence to the contrary.

Although the game was televised, instant replay was still in its infancy, and it would be another four decades before the colleges indemnified themselves from bad calls by allowing the use of taped replays to challenge the officials' rulings.

The Alabama players felt robbed, but despite being beaten for a second straight game on a questionable call, despite believing the lateral should have been whistled dead, Bryant was not the sort of man to whine about an event he could do nothing to reverse. "You don't win games in the movies on Monday," he said.

In Bryant's mind, Alabama should have beaten Georgia decisively, rendering one contested touchdown relatively irrelevant. That's the way he thought, and that's the way he trained his players to think. In the aftermath of the loss, he was much less concerned about Pat Hodgson's knees than the heads of every one of his players. He was steaming mad that his defending national champions had wallowed around and allowed Georgia to stay close enough to be in a position to win at the end, and he was determined to get their attention.

Freshman linebacker Mike Hall, who had received permission to go home to Tarrant for the weekend, watched the game on his mother and daddy's television with a sense of impending doom. "I had to have a real serious talk with myself about whether I wanted to go back," Hall said. "I knew there was going to be a steep price for that loss, and we would be the ones paying it. I knew it was going to be pure hell down there."

Convinced that his team had wilted toward the end of the game in the extremely humid mid-September conditions, Bryant pushed the Tide through a series of grueling practices the next week.

The Monday after a 27–0 victory over Tulane, as they started preparations to face heavily favored Ole Miss, the coach walked into the locker room before practice and all activity immediately stopped. Silence fell across the sweaty room as he slowly looked around at his young men, finally placing his hand on one player's shoulder.

"I know your mother," he said.

Then he walked up to another player. "I know your father."

Finally, he turned to face the entire team. "I didn't recruit any losers here," he said. "We can win this game. Nobody thinks we can, but we can."

Four decades later, offensive guard Bruce Stephens still chokes up when thinking about the powerful simplicity of the moment. "I get goosebumps just thinking about it," he said. "He knew just what to say, just how to get to all of us."

Practice that day was rough. Bryant spent much of the afternoon out of his tower, running around the field snatching and grabbing. In those days, Alabama kept at least one official on the practice field at most times during scrimmages, because Bryant wanted an impartial individual to call his players on the kinds of mistakes that would result in penalties during games. The man in the striped shirt kept throwing flags over and over again, and every time he dropped a yellow cloth onto the green grass, Bryant could be seen fuming on the sideline.

Finally, the boss, clearly disgusted, blew his whistle and told his players to head for the showers, which was very unusual. He never ended practice until he was happy, and they all could see he was not happy, which was quite disconcerting.

Several minutes later, the door to the dressing room flew open and Bryant filled the shadow of the doorway with his seething anger. Every player in the room froze in place, many of them naked, some dripping wet.

"I don't give a damn if you don't get to class, don't get to eat, don't get to sleep, I want every one of you ready to go at 5:30 in the morning, 'cause we're gonna learn how to play football in the morning."

Then he walked out the door.

Starting tight end Wayne Cook listened with a sense of dread like everyone else, but he believed something much more devious was in play. Walking off the field, he had approached referee Eddie Conyers and asked about all those penalties.

"He said Coach Bryant had told him to throw all those flags," Cook said. "I was convinced he had it all planned. It was a setup, so he could have a reason to get upset."

Sleep came fitfully for most that night, and when players started bolting out of bed around 4:00 A.M. Tuesday, driven as always by the terror of being late, one of the cardinal sins in Bryant's world, defensive lineman Richard Cole nudged his roommate.

"Wayne! Time to get up," he said with a yawn.

"I don't want to!" Cook said, burying his head under his pillow.

"You got to, Wayne! You know what Coach Bryant will do if you're late!"

"I'm not going! I don't care if I never play again! I'm not going . . ."

Cook, a 6'1", 197-pound junior from Montgomery, was quiet and something of a loner, but he was also one of the toughest characters on the team. Players knew not to mess with Cook.

After several more attempts to coax him out of bed, Cole looked at his watch and started worrying about being late himself. He could have just gone to practice and left Cook to deal with the consequences of his sleepy-eyed choice. But Alabama football was a brotherhood, and oneness was not just some buzzword; it was a way of life. If a teammate slipped, you helped him up, partially out of a sense of obligation, but also out of the strong bond, reinforced during all those moments of shared sacrifice.

"I kept thinking to myself, if I were Wayne, what would I want him to do for me?" Cole recalled.

Feeling the need to pull his roommate off the turf, he ran down the hall to enlist the help of lineman Billy Johnson, Cook's closest friend on the team. Johnson called the dorm director, who turned the matter over to Pat Dye, the newest coach on the staff.

Dye learned to chop cotton before he learned to read and write very well, which was just one of the many things he had in common with Paul Bryant. Growing up hard on his family's farm in rural south Georgia, in a fertile patch of land near the Ogeechee River, Dye was toughened by a demanding father and strengthened by both parents' powerful sense of right and wrong. He was tough and he was country and he was full of ambition. Football gave him a purpose and the chance at a life beyond the farm. After an All-America career with Wally Butts's Georgia Bulldogs, followed by a hitch in the U.S. Army, he wanted to see if he could coach. He didn't know what it took to be a coach. Not yet. But it sounded like the right thing to do, so after talking with Butts, who gave him a great recommendation, he pulled out a pen and paper and . . .

28 April 1965

Dear Coach Bryant,

I heard recently that you were looking for some assistant coaches. I wrote Bill Rice to find out if this were true. He call [sic] me last night and said I should contact you.

I have a Canadian football contract but I would give up playing if I had a chance to work for you at Alabama. I don't have any coaching credentials other than playing experience. I am happily married and have two children, a boy three years of age and a girl one year old. My degree from Georgia is in Recreation. I get out of the Army June 2nd of this year.

I have always had the highest respect for you, your assistant coaches, and your football players. To me, the opportunity to coach under you at the University of Alabama would be the finest thing that could happen to a young man who plans to coach football. Thank you for your consideration.

Sincerely,

Pat Dye

Several weeks after posting his letter, Dye made an appointment for an interview, and, wanting to show some initiative by beating the big man to the office, drove off from his home in Atlanta at 2:00 A.M. He had even bought a new suit for the occasion, and looked pretty good for a country boy applying for his first real job.

When he arrived at the athletic offices in Tuscaloosa before dawn, 'Bama assistant Richard Williamson met him at the door and poured him a cup of coffee.

"Pat, how long have you had that suit?" Williamson asked.

"Just got it," Dye said with a glint in his eye.

"I thought so," Williamson said with a laugh, pulling at the tags still attached to the back.

After finding a pair of scissors, Dye met with Bryant and landed a job coaching Alabama's linebackers for $6,000 per year. "Actually, he said I could watch the linebackers," Dye said with a grunt some four decades later. "Watch 'em. I didn't know quite what that meant, but I guess he was sending a little message, even with that."

It would be a while before Dye could afford to spring for another new suit, even as he became active in the Alabama National Guard to make ends meet, but he was about to learn a thing or two about coaching.

Officially, Dye's primary responsibility was to turn folks like Jackie Sherrill, Mike Hall, and Stan Moss into winning football players, and he did one fine job of it through the years. But Alabama was not a place where protocol ever got in the way of a job that needed to be done, so when the fiery young coach fresh out of the army was presented with the problem of Wayne Cook on a tense Tuesday morning no Alabama player of the time would ever forget, he attacked the situation like a linebacker pursuing a ballcarrier.

Barging into the room Cook shared with Cole, he literally pulled the sleeping player out of bed. "You're going to practice," Dye said, yanking him up from out of the covers. "You can quit later if you want, but you're not gonna lay up here in bed like some sorry dog. If you want to quit, you can go to Coach Bryant's office, look him in the eye, and quit like a man."

Cook knew Dye was right, but he walked to practice with his blood boiling.

"That business with the flags had really gotten under my skin," Cook said. "I didn't want to take any more of that stuff."

Assistant coach Dude Hennessey beat everyone to the field. Afraid he might oversleep, Dude had spent the night on an office couch.

When the players walked out onto the practice field, the sky was still dark, and in the glow of the stadium lights, Bryant was pacing back and forth along the adjoining cinder track, holding a football. He was dressed in street clothes and hunting boots. He looked mad.

Practice under Bryant was usually so organized, so scripted, but none of the coaches knew quite what to do that morning, because they had all shown up on the field without the smallest semblance of a plan. Instead of their usual routine, they spent most of the next half hour watching the boss push every member of his team to the edge—testing not only their performance, but their willingness to absorb the intimidation he was doling out. No one knew what the Bear was going to do, and the uncertainty fueled a tremendous level of anxiety as he jerked players in and out of huddles, kicked some in the rear end, challenged the offense to score and score again, and demanded that the defense suck it up and hold the line.

"There wasn't anybody on that field who wasn't scared to death," said junior lineman Byrd Williams.

Four decades later, no one can say for certain whether Bryant the master manipulator of minds helped orchestrate the lousy Monday practice in order to provoke the Tuesday morning from hell. But even if it was at least partially a stunt, he accomplished the mission of placing his players in an extremely tense situation so he could see how they would react.

When junior Cecil Dowdy, who would be remembered as one of the greatest offensive linemen in Alabama history, missed a block, Bryant grabbed him by the cage and spent several tense moments in his face. The coach was determined to impress upon Dowdy the need to avoid such mistakes, and he also wanted to see whether he would seize the opportunity to push harder or start feeling sorry for himself, the prelude to mental surrender.

Several players quit that day, unable to withstand the pressure, but not Wayne Cook. He was not a sorry dog. He was a champion.

Pushed to the brink by his demanding coach, Cook had been rescued from the ledge not only by his teammates, not only by a wily young coach who earned every nickel of his $6,000 salary, but, ultimately, by his own pride. In time, it would be clear that his decision to persevere on that most demanding of all days was one of the turning points in the making of the 1966 Crimson Tide.

Although it has largely been obscured in the history of Alabama football, the game against Ole Miss at Legion Field on October 2, 1965 ranks among the most important the Crimson Tide has ever played. Two weeks after the devastating loss to Georgia, defending national champion 'Bama entered the game as an underdog against Johnny Vaught's powerful Rebels.

After a frustrating first half, Alabama trailed, 9–0, and Bryant tore into his team in the locker room. With the unthinkable possibility of losing a second game looming like a pointed gun, the Tide rallied in the second half.

Even with Dicky Thompson's three interceptions and two fumble recoveries stoking the Alabama defense, the Crimson Tide still trailed, 16–10, heading into the final minutes. But the fourth quarter belonged to Alabama. That's when all those puke-ridden gym classes truly became a source of strength . . . when Tuesday morning before dawn and all those other days of mental and physical strain coalesced to create a powerful sense of confidence and determination.

With the moments dwindling, quarterback Steve Sloan marched the Crimson Tide 88 yards in 14 plays for the winning touchdown, capturing a 17–16 victory, one of the most dramatic and pivotal in school history. Three times on the drive, 'Bama converted on fourth and short, including a 22-yard gain on a gutsy tackle eligible pass to junior Jerry Duncan.

Not only did the victory keep the Crimson Tide in the hunt for the 1965 national championship, it taught every player on the team what they were all capable of when backed into a corner, when the situation appeared desperate. The memory of such a feeling and such a performance in the face of adversity would come in handy down the line.

When Bryant walked into the jubilant locker room, the players were singing a familiar tune, and their voices echoed across the tight quarters with a triumphant resonance:

"I don't give a damn about the state of Mississippi . . . the state of Mississippi . . . the state of Mississippi . . . I don't give a damn about the state of Mississippi, 'cause I'm from Ala-bam."

The proud coach stood in front of a bench for a moment without saying a word, looking out over his men before finally pulling a drag on his cigarette as silence fell across the room.

"I tell you what," he said with a big grin, "When you wear that red jersey, you're too good to piss on the ground!"

Bryant was so gratified by the way his team had fought, the way it had won despite many lingering doubts outside the program, the way it had persevered time and again during the desperation of the winning drive, he clearly was struggling for some original way to express his delight. "Too good to piss on the ground" was a phrase straight out of his roots in rural Arkansas, where indoor plumbing was a high-class luxury, and in his own colloquial way, he was trying to tell his young men that they were a special bunch, still capable of great things despite their rocky start.

Two weeks later, backup quarterback Kenny Stabler made a mistake in the waning moments against Tennessee at Legion Field that would live in the annals of Alabama football forever. With the score tied and the ball on the Tennessee 4-yard line, Stabler glanced at the scoreboard clock, which still said third down, and threw the ball out of bounds to stop the clock, to set up for a David Ray field goal. But he hadn't looked at the yardage marker. It was actually fourth down, and the ball went over on downs, allowing the Volunteers to escape with a 7–7 tie.

When the Alabama team ran off the field, head manager Sang Lyda was temporarily occupied with trying to retrieve the game ball from Tennessee, and he had delegated responsibility for opening the locker room door to another manager. But while Lyda was fighting over a ball, one of his boys dropped the ball. By the time a very steamed Bryant approached the dressing room, the Alabama players were lined up outside, unable to penetrate the locked door.

Never more than three feet from Bryant's side on game day was his bodyguard, Alabama State Patrol Captain Smelley, a rotund middle-aged man with a taste for whiskey and a gift for telling good jokes. He carried a pistol, but no one on the team had ever seen him use it.

"Smelley, shoot that damn lock off!" Bryant ordered.

"Well, I . . . I can't do that, coach," he said. "I might—"

"Alright, then, get the hell out of the way!"

The door was made of steel, but Bryant was mad, and he was in no mood to wait around. The fifty-two-year-old man took a few steps back and rammed the door two or three times with his shoulder, finally knocking it off the hinges in front of his stunned team.

After the players and coaches filed in and found seats, Bryant stood before them and took full responsibility for the loss, which he attributed to confusion on the sideline at the end. His fault. He took all the pressure off.

"But you can still win the national championship, if you think you can," he said. "Unless I've misjudged you . . ."

No one in the whole country would have bet on an Alabama team already burdened by a loss and a tie. No one except those young men in red who dared to believe in something bigger than themselves.

Six weeks later, after the Crimson Tide streaked the rest of the way untouched, Bryant, who maintained tremendous clout in the bowl selection process, wrangled an invitation for his SEC champion Crimson Tide against Big Eight champion Nebraska in the Orange Bowl. With the final vote being delayed until after the bowls, the guys from Tuscaloosa suddenly had a chance to prove the old man right.

In a meeting with his team, Bryant predicted an incredible scenario: UCLA would upset undefeated, No. 1-ranked Michigan State in the Rose Bowl and LSU would knock off undefeated, No. 2-ranked Arkansas in the Cotton Bowl. He told his 8-1-1, No. 4-ranked Crimson Tide that if they could beat Bob Devaney's undefeated, No. 3-ranked Cornhuskers, the big prize would be theirs.

Nebraska, favored by seventeen points, was both talented and huge, especially compared to Alabama. Hardly anyone gave the Crimson Tide a prayer. All those demanding conditioning programs tended to weed out most large

players, leaving Bryant with a bunch of relative runts, whom the boss profoundly referred to as his "quick little boys." The Cornhuskers outweighed the
Crimson Tide on the line by an average of more than 35 pounds per man, including the apparent mismatch between 185-pound 'Bama tackle Jerry Duncan
and 245-pound consensus All-America Nebraska defensive tackle Walt Barnes.

Two days before the game, when the players and coaches lined up to have
their pictures taken in groups, Bryant refused to pose with his linemen.

"I don't want to be seen with those scrawny little guys," he said, loud
enough for all to hear. "They're gonna get their asses whipped."

They all felt about two feet tall as the boss walked away.

Prior to the game, the coach stood before his players in the Orange Bowl
locker room and noted that most of them were about to play against blacks for
the first time. While Nebraska was integrated, Alabama remained all white, like
every other team in the SEC, and because of a long list of acts of racist defiance
and violence in the state of Alabama in the wake of the civil rights movement,
many Americans struggled to distinguish between the bigotry epitomized by
segregationist Governor George Wallace and the segregated Crimson Tide.
"Now, we've got a chance here tonight to show the whole country how much
class we have in Alabama," Bryant said, looking around the room.

"I want you to treat 'em like anybody else. Knock 'em on their ass and then
help 'em up."

All night long, millions of fans from coast to coast watched the members of
the all-white Crimson Tide knocking the Nebraska players, black and white, on
their rear ends, en route to a stunning upset victory. And they watched, time
and again, as those mighty warriors for a state struggling for its very soul
reached down and pulled their opponents off the grass.

Some images are more powerful than others, and in an age when men like
Birmingham Public Safety Commissioner Bull Connor pushed Alabama further into the darkness, ordering his police officers to attack black protesters
with dogs and fire hoses as the whole country watched in horror in the spring of
1963, it was difficult for the Crimson Tide to compete in the court of public
opinion. Some images dance right past the eyes and pierce the heart.

The sight of those white Alabama hands reaching out in sportsmanship on
the first night of 1966 was much subtler. It did not lead the evening news. It
did not cause the Ku Klux Klan to disrobe. But it was a start.

Most eyes were too busy watching Alabama crush Nebraska into submission
to pay much attention to the racial angle.

Understanding that Alabama would need to outscore Nebraska to win,
Bryant junked his usually conservative offensive philosophy and gave senior

quarterback Steve Sloan the freedom to pass at will. He also called several trick plays, and it was a rout from the opening kickoff. Alabama led 24–7 at the half, and the 39–28 final margin did not adequately reflect the true nature of the blowout.

The quickness of the Alabama offensive line proved absolutely devastating, allowing Sloan to methodically plunder the Nebraska defense in one of the greatest offensive displays in Orange Bowl history, completing 20 passes for 296 yards, both Orange Bowl records. Cecil Dowdy, Jerry Duncan, and the rest stunned the gigantic Cornhuskers, who could not believe they were being bested by a bunch that attacked like tiny does of lightning at precise angles, mitigating all that size.

"You don't block right! Why don't you block right?" was a familiar refrain of frustration heard across the neutral zone.

Junior split end Ray Perkins, a one-time fullback from south Mississippi, spent much of the night lunging for balls and taking off toward the end zone, amazing the national television audience with one great catch and run after another. His Orange Bowl record nine catches—including two for touchdowns—accounted for 159 yards, a phenomenal stat for the era.

In the first quarter, Alabama safety Johnny Mosley made a devastating open field tackle on All-America Nebraska tight end Tony Jeter. As the 5'10", 176-pound Mosley tried to help him up, the 6'3", 223-pound Jeter pushed him away with an angry look.

"You little son of a bitch!" he said. "I'll get you!"

When Nebraska broke the huddle and approached the line, Mosley kept one eye on quarterback Bob Churchich and the other on Jeter, because he could see the guy meant business. After the ball was snapped, Jeter headed downfield and collided with another 'Bama player, administering a devastating lick, which forced him out of the game.

Great hit. Wrong little SOB.

Like many opposing players, Jeter had a hard time distinguishing one little twerp from another.

Writing in the next day's edition of *The Birmingham News*, Alf Van Hoose told his readers, "If the No. 4-ranked Tide isn't voted a second straight U.S. crown after this spectacular show, a proud, bubbling Paul Bryant ought to appeal to a higher court: national opinion."

After one of the most improbable upsets in college football history, at the banquet attended by both official parties and various dignitaries and fans, a beaming Bryant stepped to the microphone as they started presenting the commemorative bowl watches. "I've got six guys I want to introduce to you . . . want to have 'em stand up," he said with a sly grin.

Then he started calling their names:

"Paul Crane . . . Jerry Duncan . . . Cecil Dowdy . . . Bruce Stephens . . . Johnny Calvert . . . Wayne Cook . . ."

He paused to give them all time to reach the front of the room, then singled out his diminutive offensive linemen—the ones who were supposed to get their asses whipped—for special recognition in helping win the football game.

Still upset about the photo snub, Calvert, a junior who was destined to be one of the leaders of the 1966 team, walked back to his table dumbstruck, but grinning from ear to ear.

"That old man had gotten us again," Calvert said. "That photo deal was just another psyche out, and we were so focused on what we were trying to do, we didn't even realize it."

In the process of forging a powerful team, Bryant had skillfully fortified his players with an unmistakable faith in themselves, a belief that allowed them to overcome tremendous obstacles and achieve something virtually no one thought possible. Their steely resolve was a mighty force.

Just as Bryant had predicted, all three undefeated teams lost, in the wackiest New Year's ever, so two days later, the Alabama players walked down to breakfast at Bryant Hall to find a typed note taped to the cafeteria door:

Congratulations on being named national champions for the second year in a row! Let's start today to make it three in a row.

> *Sincerely,*
> *Paul Bryant*

Even in the glow of incredible and improbable accomplishment, Bryant was sending an unmistakable signal: Champions never lose the hunger.

The little note was the final ingredient in the shaping of the 1966 Crimson Tide, the last deftly applied touch in the formative crucible of the Alabama football experience.

The players returning in 1966 had a chance to make history—if they wanted it bad enough.

3. BLOWIN' IN THE WIND

On a hot summer night in 1964, when Joe Namath was still working his way back into his coach's good graces and the first of the Crimson Tide's successive national championships was still only a dream, Alabama players Jerry Duncan and Dan Kearley jumped in one of their cars and headed off to eat supper.

Until preseason practice started in August, Duncan and Kearley were sharing a house trailer in the Alberta City community outside Tuscaloosa, which made up in freedom what it lacked in comfort, since it would be time to move back in to regimented Bryant Hall soon enough. The two good buddies had just returned from a trip to Jerry's home in North Carolina, in time for the start of summer school.

Armed with a card that allowed them to receive deeply discounted meals at the local Morrison's cafeteria on University Boulevard, the two college students pulled up to the restaurant and wound up in the middle of a civil rights war zone. Because the cafeteria had been successfully integrated after the passage of the landmark Civil Rights Act of 1964—the climactic event of the long and often violent political struggle against segregation—members of the Ku Klux Klan were walking a picket line, urging whites to boycott the establishment. The small number of nervous African-American people inside were breaking down an important barrier by eating at a once-segregated restaurant, but no whites were crossing the picket line.

With little money to blow on food, Duncan and Kearley viewed their discount cards like gold. Determined not to be intimidated by a bunch of thugs, they crossed the picket line amid racist taunts, walked through the cafeteria line, and sat down to eat their meals. At one point, they looked around to see that they were the only two white people in the restaurant.

"When we came out of that place, the first thing [the Klan members] did was take our pictures," recalled Duncan, then heading toward his sophomore season. "They wanted to make sure they knew who had defied them, I guess. But they didn't realize we weren't trying to make some statement. We were just a couple of hungry college kids who didn't have much money and wanted to get something to eat."

Around the same time, the Klan protested the integration of a movie theater in downtown Tuscaloosa on the night Hollywood actor Jack Palance happened to be in town visiting relatives. When Palance crossed the picket line with his family, an angry mob filled the streets, forcing local police to evacuate them from the theater for their own safety. In the area for some reason, Duncan and Kearley approached the theater to see what was going on and watched in horror as white supremacists threw rocks and bottles at the car that carried the Palance family out of town and to the Birmingham airport. The ugly incident made national news and gave the state yet another black eye, the same month when three college-age civil rights workers were murdered near Philadelphia, Mississippi.

Ginger Turner and her boyfriend considered themselves typical students who loved to get all dressed up and go to the football games, where they cheered for the Crimson Tide with all their might. But that evening, they became unlikely revolutionaries. The only two whites besides Palance and his family to cross the picket line, they were chased away from the theater by the angry mob, finally seeking refuge at a nearby church, which Turner remembers as her "moment of consciousness-raising."

"I couldn't believe that those ignorant people thought they could tell us where we could and couldn't go . . . and finally it dawned on me: that was the way black people felt all the time," she said.

Remembering the scene, Duncan said, "Where I grew up we never had any racial trouble, at least not that I knew anything about, so watching Jack Palance get chased out of town was a pretty unnerving experience. Watching those folks get violent like that, I just couldn't understand it. It seemed so wrong."

While Bryant tried to insulate his players from the dangers and distractions of the outside world, the segregated Alabama football program was on a collision course with the civil rights movement.

In Alabama during the 1960s, the epic battle for racial justice seemed near and far at the same time.

In the years after the Supreme Court's landmark 1954 *Brown v. Board of Education* ruling, which overturned the doctrine of separate but equal in education, and the refusal of Montgomery seamstress Rosa Parks to step to the back of a city bus, the historic events that launched the movement, African Americans methodically attacked the indignities and inequities of institutional racism. Most of the political leadership of Alabama, like other Southern states, opposed the challenge vigorously, pandering shamelessly to a large percentage of citizens motivated by a toxic mix of fear, hate, indifference, and resistance to

federal intervention in local affairs. Because the violence was isolated, far removed from most cities and towns across the state, the fight for equal rights existed to most whites and blacks alike as a distant abstraction seen largely on the
evening news, if at all.

In a world of separate schools, water fountains, hotels, restaurants, and restrooms, where only a tiny fraction of African Americans—or Negroes, as they
preferred to be called at the time—could exercise their constitutionally guaranteed right to vote, the state of Alabama became identified most often in the
national consciousness with racism. After Parks's courageous stand, which introduced the world to an eloquent young preacher named Dr. Martin Luther
King, Jr., the American public watched in horror as one bunch of bigots after
another gave the whole state a bad name. In 1956, white supremacists, including agents of the Ku Klux Klan, rioted in protest of the first attempted integration of the University of Alabama, transforming Autherine Lucy into a tragic
footnote in the history of a proud institution. The infamy of Bull Connor's fire
hoses and dogs turned Birmingham into a symbol of racial intolerance. When
four little girls were murdered during the bombing of Birmingham's Sixteenth
Street Baptist Church in September 1963, it was impossible for any decent
white person to continue to see the civil rights movement as just a political
struggle. The horrible act of violence broke the whole nation's heart, especially
the vast majority of Alabamians who wept and prayed and hoped it would all
just stop, once and for all.

The 1966 Alabama football team was the product of a world on the
precipice of historic change, and just as Bryant could not protect his players
from the unexpected dangers of eating supper and going to the movies, he
could not keep the civil rights movement from encroaching on his neatly ordered world. Understanding how the fight to overturn a century of racial op-
pression affected the state of Alabama is essential in seeing how the 1966
Crimson Tide football team was formed, as well as how it connected to the rest
of the country.

During the tense scene on June 11, 1963, when Governor George Wallace
stood in the door of Foster Auditorium in a symbolic and futile attempt to prevent the permanent integration of the University of Alabama—scripted like the
TV show it was—various state and federal officials watched the proceedings
from the windows of the nearby athletic department. The delegation from
Washington camped at the sparkling new athletic dormitory, even as workers
applied the finishing touches. Tanks guarded the entrance to the quadrangle
and members of the Alabama National Guard, federalized by President John F.
Kennedy to keep order, walked the campus carrying automatic rifles.

"We were all scared to death something terrible was going to happen," said student Jo Ann Boozer, who watched the events on television while locked away in the administration building with other student leaders.

With the campus sealed off like a war zone, and the university administration supporting the integration of African-American students Vivian Malone and James Hood, the violent yahoo fringe stayed away, leaving the stage clear for Wallace's rhetorical nonsense to further sully the state's image.

According to his autobiography, Bryant was in Chicago on the day of Wallace's stand, heading for a coaching clinic in Montana. Forced to leave his name in order to get a table at a restaurant, while awaiting a flight at nearby O'Hare Airport, he was recognized, and even in such a seemingly benign environment, the state of Alabama's image problem across the rest of the country confronted him. When he left a big tip after finishing his meal, the waiter, a white man, glared at him, said, "I don't want your money!" and walked away.

To much of the outside world, which considered Alabama a pariah state, George Wallace and Bear Bryant were synonymous. Most did not understand that Bryant and his team were victims of the poisonous climate exploited by Wallace and others.

Inside the state, most parents on both sides of the struggle endeavored to prevent their children from getting involved. However, many young people found themselves drawn into the social revolution by the pangs of an awakening social conscience, or simply by circumstance, which is how Alabama receiver Ray Perkins wound up watching the aborted first Selma-to-Montgomery march in support of voting rights in the spring of 1965. Perkins served in the Alabama National Guard, and his unit was mobilized to search bridges for bombs.

"At the time, I just looked at it as doing my job, trying to make sure nobody got hurt," Perkins recalled. "You didn't think of it in terms of a historical moment, but, of course, it was."

After the violent first march, forever known as Bloody Sunday, a small number of white University of Alabama students believed they were risking their lives by marching in a rally led by African-American church leaders in downtown Tuscaloosa.

"There was a real divide at the university in those days," recalled Ginger Turner, who was ostracized by some members of her sorority for participating in the march, "between those who wanted [the civil rights movement] to just go away and those of us who saw [segregation] as a matter of a clear injustice . . . that needed to be dealt with."

Alabamians approached the controversial issue of integration from various viewpoints, but the vast majority abhorred the violence, resented the pejorative image a small number of troublemakers were giving their state, and felt increasingly defensive about their place in the world. With little to brag about, the relatively poor state was already predisposed to see the powerful Alabama football team as a source of unity and pride. In the 1960s, however, the connection between Alabama fans and Bear Bryant's program was further hardened by all the negativity swirling in the ether, presenting a distorted view of their state, which was overwhelmingly peaceful and home to mostly decent, hardworking, law-abiding people, white and black. At a time when the whole country appeared to be looking down at them all through a prism of racial intolerance, the success of the championship Crimson Tide transcended pride. It was about validation. It proved that they were more than the sum of George Wallace, Bull Connor, and the forces of bigotry.

In 1966, as much as any institution of the time, Bryant's football program reflected establishment America—what the old order held dear, what it refused to tolerate.

Forever guided by a powerful sense of right and wrong, by adherence to a strict set of rules, by obligations and consequences, the program was propelled by the power of aspiration. Playing football for the Bear and being motivated by all those incentives and disincentives was just another part of the American free enterprise system. Success was something that could only be earned. Achievement meant something important to every member of the organization, and especially for the players who came from impoverished backgrounds and needed the scholarship to gain an education and a chance at a better life, the Alabama football experience was an extension of the American Dream. When Bryant spoke to his players about always "showing your class," he was promoting a code of duty and honor drawn from the noblest American traditions.

The discipline pervading the Crimson Tide program connected it to the culture in a critical way, exemplified by the suspension of Joe Namath, an easily accessible object lesson about the Bear Bryant school of life, which was really nothing more than a reflection of the old-school values embraced by the vast majority of mainstream America. Alabama football stood for certain things, and the punishment made clear that anyone who aspired to someday wear the red jersey had better be prepared to live within a code of conduct.

In the years ahead, the Namath suspension became a large part of the Bryant persona. The next generation of Alabama children—including many unborn at the time of the incident—grew up hearing the story as a kind of morality tale. Parents all across the Heart of Dixie used it to demonstrate the importance of following the rules and the need to stand for a set of principles.

The banishment—and eventual triumphant return—of the prodigal son strengthened the already sturdy bond between Alabamians and their favorite football team, giving them yet another reason to see Bryant's program as an extension of their own values.

To people all across the state who felt beleaguered on the race issue, the Alabama football team was like a shield deflecting all those slings and arrows of contempt and disgrace. It was their defense not only against the national news media, but ultimately, against their own shortcomings, their own gathering sense of shame at allowing an otherwise wonderful place to be defined by one glaring weakness.

The Bear and his boys made them feel special.

Watching the Crimson Tide on television or in their mind's eye, Alabama fans of various backgrounds believed they were looking at themselves. They saw a program defined by strength, class, and a pursuit of excellence not just as a representative of their state, but as a reflection of who they were and what they believed.

Embracing the idea of the Crimson Tide as a mirror image of their civilization was encumbered by one small problem, however. It reflected everything—including the ugly scar of segregation.

When it came to the most important moral and political issue of the age, the Alabama Crimson Tide was trapped on the wrong side of history.

By 1966, the tension between the segregated Crimson Tide and the civil rights movement was reaching a boiling point.

Five years earlier, the Rose Bowl seriously considered breaking its tie to the Big Ten and the forerunner of the Pac-8 and inviting the undefeated Crimson Tide. Several members of the Los Angeles news media wrote stories suggesting the folks in Pasadena were planning to welcome the Ku Klux Klan to town, robes and all.

When the bad publicity changed the Rose Bowl's mind, the Alabama athletic department convened a news conference in a Birmingham hotel to announce it was accepting a bid to play Arkansas in the Sugar Bowl. While Bryant stood at the podium answering questions, some drunk redneck wandered in and stopped him in midsentence.

"Hey, Bear," he said, loud enough to be heard down the adjoining hallway, "tell those nigger-loving sons of bitches to kiss your ass!"

Bryant looked at the man like he had lost his mind. He just glared at him and said nothing as the man, who introduced himself as an Alabama fan, continued his racist rant.

From the standards of a later era, the Bear should have taken the opportunity to distance himself from such bigoted remarks. He should have made it clear that the University of Alabama football team in no way condoned such behavior, but white men in positions of power did not stand up and put their arms around Martin Luther King and embrace his cause in those days, regardless of what they thought. Like most whites of the day, accustomed to seeing African Americans in menial roles, conditioned to their second-class social status, Bryant viewed blacks through a prism of paternalism, which was a long way from hate. Bryant was no racist, but he was no fool, either. He was just another pragmatic businessman who knew a large segment of his fan base felt about the same way as the drunk.

The scene perfectly captured the peculiar dilemma facing the Crimson Tide as the civil rights movement gathered momentum.

Even as Bryant and his coaches and players worked long hours to build a powerful football program that their state could be proud of, they were engaged in a contentious struggle for the meaning of Alabama in the nation's eyes. Was Alabama about excellence in football? Or bigotry?

The collision between sports and race was hardly new. Few events in American history threatened the nation's social order—and challenged the way Americans thought about race—like Jackie Robinson's shattering of baseball's color barrier in 1947. Creating a colorblind society in college football would take much longer. In the years after *Brown v. Board of Education,* most of the southern states adopted laws prohibiting blacks and whites from competing on the same field. In an era rife with tokenism, even many northern colleges continued to field teams with only a small number of blacks. As pioneers like Robinson could attest, bigotry was not limited to the South, but the institutionalized nature of segregation forced the region's major teams to remain all white and, in most cases, to avoid "race-mixing." Frequently, they became pawns of politicians who espoused white supremacy.

When Bobby Dodd's Georgia Tech powerhouse accepted a bid to play a University of Pittsburgh team with a black player—running back Bobby Grier—in New Orleans' Sugar Bowl in 1956, Georgia Governor Marvin Griffin called for the Yellow Jackets to forfeit the game. "The South stands at Armageddon," Griffin railed in a speech, saying it would be better to lose the game on principle than to engage in such dangerous race-mixing.

For the next seven years, the Sugar Bowl, one of the most iconic events in college football, bowed to pressure from local segregationists to avoid the repeat of such a calamity and matched only segregated teams.

During the same period, the University of Mississippi refused to play integrated teams in bowl games and Mississippi State University's basketball team was forced by state officials to turn down three invitations to the NCAA tournament for the same reason. After winning his fourth SEC title in 1963, which included an automatic bid to the big dance, State head coach Babe McCarthy literally sneaked his team out of Starkville in the middle of the night, defying the orders of the segregationist governor, in order to play in the national tournament against an integrated team.

For many years, various northern teams agreed to bench their limited number of black players on trips to the South, acquiescing to the caustic political climate that invaded the sports world.

In the late 1940s, Bryant had wanted to integrate his University of Kentucky team, but could not win the support of the university president, who feared that such a move would jeopardize the Wildcats' status in the SEC, which maintained a gentleman's agreement forbidding the signing of black athletes.

Soon after he returned to Alabama, the Bear publicly defied the forces of hate. In 1959, he engendered the wrath of the KKK—which made its Alabama headquarters in Tuscaloosa—and the prosegregation citizens councils by accepting an invitation to play Penn State, which featured one black player, in Philadelphia's Liberty Bowl. Some nuts threatened violence, but 'Bama played the game anyway, without incident, losing 7–0 in the first of Bryant's twenty-four straight post-season bowl appearances. Over the next several years, Bryant continued to accept bowl invitations against integrated teams, including Oklahoma, Nebraska, Missouri, and Colorado, believing, correctly, that such encounters would slowly melt much of the resistance to black faces in crimson jerseys.

However, for reasons of practicality in a state with an enormously popular segregationist governor who controlled the funding for his institution and a large number of fans who needed to have their hearts and minds changed on issues of race before they would be willing to accept black faces in red jerseys, Bryant refused to spend some of his own political capital by integrating his team. He told friends it was too soon, too dangerous to place an African-American player in such a volatile and potentially hostile environment, and he may have been right, but his caution played into the hands of the forces who wanted to equate him with George Wallace.

The world was full of people like the Chicago waiter, and as long as Bryant's football team remained all white, it was easy for members of the national media and others across the country to blur the lines, to reduce Alabama in all forms to a synonym for racism, to paint the Crimson Tide as yet another symbol of Southern defiance, yet another instrument of George Wallace, yet another kindred spirit of Bull Connor. This represented an enormous burden for the 1966 Alabama football team.

Even as the stain of segregation complicated the lives of Bryant and his team, one unknown act belied the stereotype of the coach and his Crimson Tide.

On a memorable night in 1963, Charlie Thornhill stood before a banquet room filled with people, dressed in his best Sunday go-to-meeting clothes, and proudly accepted the Player of the Year award from the Roanoke Touchdown Club. The powerful tailback, who had scored more than two hundred points in his senior season of high school, made history by becoming the first African-American player to win the prestigious trophy as well as the first black person ever feted in such a way by Roanoke's white establishment.

The guest speaker for the evening, duly impressed by the way Thornhill handled himself, not to mention his incredible statistics, pulled him aside at the end of the evening, draping his large right arm around the player's shoulders.

"Son, where you planning on going to school?" Paul Bryant asked.

Trying to fight off a case of nerves, Thornhill looked up at Bryant, unable to believe he was meeting the famed coach in the flesh.

"Well, I have an offer on the table from Notre Dame," he said.

"Don't sign anything yet," Bryant said. "I want to tell somebody about you."

Somebody was Michigan State head coach Duffy Daugherty.

As the region exploded on the issue of race, Bryant reluctantly continued to watch talented African-American athletes in his state and across the South flock to historically black small colleges, like Florida A&M and Grambling, and to major universities in the Midwest, East, and West. Several native Alabamians who were unwelcome by their state university wound up playing in the National Football League during the period, including San Diego Chargers cornerback Leslie "Speedy" Duncan (Jackson State) and Cleveland Browns cornerback Ben Davis (Grambling).

The folks who wanted to equate Bryant with Wallace failed to recognize how the continued segregation of the Crimson Tide hurt the Alabama football team most of all, costing it many fine African-American athletes who could have made the Tide even stronger. Some bigots across the state and elsewhere certainly pointed to the dominance of the all-white Crimson Tide as an example of white supremacy, and while this ridiculous idea held no currency in the Alabama athletic department, the philosophy underpinning it caused some very misguided people who nevertheless loved Bryant's program to see him as a kindred spirit, simply because the door remained closed to African Americans.

This could not have been further from the truth. Unable to recruit blacks himself, he often steered talented players elsewhere, as demonstrated by the case of Charlie Thornhill.

No program pursued a more progressive policy toward minority athletes than the Michigan State Spartans, who became a Big Ten power by exploiting the political situation that kept southern teams segregated. Although MSU's percentage of minority students was not much higher than Alabama's in the mid-1960s, the football program recruited southern blacks aggressively—including Texas native Bubba Smith, one of the greatest defensive players of all time—making the colorful Daugherty a kind of Harriet Tubman figure, running a football equivalent of the Underground Railroad during the traumatic days of the civil rights movement.

Daugherty, one of Bryant's closest friends in the coaching profession, acted quickly on his buddy's tip and signed Thornhill out from under Notre Dame's nose.

"Coach Bryant said he would like to have me play for him, but the time wasn't right," said Thornhill, who turned down the chance to break the color barrier at the University of Maryland. "We talked about things opening up at Alabama in the future, and he seemed very anxious for that to happen, but he understood how tough it would be for someone like me to play at Alabama in those days. He told me about how Duffy was playing a lot of blacks . . . making a statement that was pretty hard to ignore . . . and that it would be a good place for me."

From the vantage point of four decades of history, the moment is awash in irony. At the very least, it accurately depicts the nuance of the time, as many people of goodwill tried to make sense of a social order that was impossible to justify and yet deeply entrenched in the southern mindset.

"If it hadn't been for me meeting him that night, I would have gone to Notre Dame, which did not have many black players at the time . . . and who knows how that would have turned out," Thornhill said. "Coach Bryant did something very nice for me at an important time. I'll always be grateful to him."

Toward the end of his freshman year, Thornhill was walking through a corridor at Jemerson Fieldhouse when running backs coach Danny Boyster passed him and punched him in the chest.

"How you doing, big boy?" Boyster said with a smile.

A look of rage crossed Thornhill's face, and he immediately hit Boyster in the chest. "Don't call me boy!"

Growing up in the segregated South, Thornhill had been conditioned to hear the word "boy" as a demeaning, racist term. In some ways, it was worse than the n-word, because it was used openly and without remorse among many whites as a subtle way of denying grown black men a little piece of their dignity.

"I misinterpreted [what Boyster was saying], and I was ready to retaliate," Thornhill said. "He was just being friendly . . . and I read it wrong. Something in my brain clicked. I was the one with the chip on my shoulder. It didn't take me long to realize what a big mistake I had made, but I couldn't take it back."

Branded as a troublemaker, Thornhill soon found himself demoted off the roster. Relegated to the scout team and moved to defense, he was humiliated when many of his family and friends made the trip to see the Spartans open the 1964 season at the University of North Carolina, only to find out that he had not made the travel squad.

"I was really devastated, but I knew nobody could help me except God and myself," Thornhill said. "So I got down on my knees one night and prayed that I could somehow find a way to make the football team."

During a scrimmage toward the middle of the season, one of the starting linebackers was forced to the sidelines with an injury. An assistant coach yelled out, "Get in there, Thornhill. You need some of this!"

Sensing his one chance to prove something while the whole team and staff were watching, Thornhill walked onto the field and buckled his chin strap with a sense of mission. The Spartans' offense ran five plays and the man who had been tagged with the dubious nickname "Mad Dog" after that hallway incident made five straight tackles. Diving. Chasing. Pounding. He owned the field. They ran another five plays, and he made five more tackles.

Finally, a shocked Daugherty approached the line of scrimmage. "Can't anybody out here stop Thornhill?"

"Not today!" he shouted defiantly, loud enough for Duffy and everyone else to hear.

As the offense huddled up, an assistant coach approached Mad Dog. "You've made the offense look really bad . . . and the whole offensive line is coming after you on this next play," he said.

Thornhill looked up to the heavens and said a little prayer. "Just one more play," he thought to himself, trying to catch his breath. "Just one more."

An instant after the ball was snapped, Thornhill crashed through the line and slammed the quarterback in the numbers. His helmet popped off and the ball squirted onto the ground as Duffy shook his head in amazement.

"Alright, Thornhill," Daugherty yelled out, "get over there with the first team, where you belong. I'm taking you to Wisconsin!"

In a world understandably focused on the overt bigotry of Bull Connor and George Wallace, hardly anyone knew how the subtleties of the racially charged climate had nearly prevented one of the best players on the pioneering Michigan State team from realizing his potential. Beyond fear and mistrust, the incident demonstrated the difficulties of trying to communicate when you speak different languages.

The Thornhill story was like a metaphor for all those whites and blacks being thrown together in the early days of integration. Often, outright racism was much less of a problem than the significant obstacle of trying to understand each other, to overcome disparate backgrounds amid all the pressure to make it work. Fortunately for Thornhill and many other African Americans like him all across the country, performance on the field was a universal language. His ability to fight off blockers and slam a quarterback to the ground needed no interpretation. The space between those bold white lines was truly a color-blind society, which was a lesson the Alabama program and its fans would learn soon enough.

At the time, Bryant did not know how the young man he steered to East Lansing would grow up to become a key figure on a team destined to frustrate his ambitions for a third straight national championship.

Like so many other aspects of the old order, Michigan State's southern pipeline was living on borrowed time, because the segregationists could not tie the hands of Bryant and the other southern coaches forever.

State-sponsored racism was dying a slow and painful death by the middle of the decade. The insidious "whites only" signs were disappearing all across the South, blacks were registering to vote in large numbers, and the first public secondary schools in Alabama were integrated. The dual system of schools for blacks and whites would linger into the early 1970s in many parts of the state, but the first tentative steps toward integration were accomplished mostly without incident, although tension permeated the process.

Social integration was another matter, but in Alabama as elsewhere, young white people were starting to listen to African-American music stars openly, which had once been strictly taboo. Motown groups like the Supremes, the Miracles, and the Temptations represented a new era because they were designed to appeal to both white and black audiences. The success of Berry Gordy's sound, which could be heard blaring from car radios across the South, was a powerful weapon against the forces of division.

On March 10, 1966, several months after the desegregation of the public schools in Huntsville began with the admission of a small number of African-American students to traditionally white schools, Butler High's Danny Treadwell integrated the state high school basketball tournament at the University of

Alabama's Foster Auditorium—the site of Wallace's stand. The landmark event produced a huge crowd, and many spectators taunted Treadwell with racial slurs, especially in the opening round game against Tuscaloosa. Describing the tense scene forty years later, John Pruett, the longtime sports editor of *The Huntsville Times,* wrote: "Danny Treadwell's heart was pounding and his hands were shaking. His legs felt like he was in quicksand. He had a hard time catching his breath. He thought he might throw up."

Dealing with enormous pressure, Treadwell helped lead Butler to the 4A state championship, breaking down an important barrier in the shadow of Wallace's infamy.

The movement gradually spread into college sports.

In a world filled with shades of gray, the 1966 NCAA basketball tournament championship game produced a moment of undeniable contrast and significance. When an underdog Texas Western team with five black starters knocked off Adolph Rupp's all-white Kentucky powerhouse, 72–65, the sports world changed forever. In the years to come, it would be looked back on as a tipping point in the slow, uneven process of integrating college athletics—a body blow to the forces of bigotry who wanted to believe in the superiority of the white race.

Although Rupp had resisted recruiting African-Americans, like the rest of his peers in the SEC, the climate was slowly changing. When a liberal Yankee, Dr. John Oswald, became the University of Kentucky's president in 1963, he began pressing to integrate the athletic program—as Bryant had wanted, some fifteen years earlier. Late in 1965, head football coach Charley Bradshaw, a former Alabama assistant, broke the color barrier in the SEC by signing two black players—Nat Northington, who would go down in the history books as the first athlete of his race inked by an SEC school and the first to play in an SEC game, against Ole Miss in 1967, and Greg Page, the second. At the start of the 1966 season, both players loomed as historic figures throughout the conference, but Page died after suffering a devastating neck injury during practice.

Two months after the historic Texas Western victory—on the heels of leading his Pearl High School team to victory in the first integrated state tournament in Tennessee history—Perry Wallace signed with Vanderbilt to break the color barrier in SEC basketball.

With the specter of George Wallace looming large, it was much easier for Kentucky and Vanderbilt to lead the way than the state university in the more racially charged climate of Alabama, and Bryant was perfectly content to wait a while longer. During this period, according to a deposition provided for a subsequent court case, Bryant said he advised one coach of a promising

African-American athlete who expressed an interest in breaking the color barrier in Tuscaloosa: "If he was my kid, right now I believe it is a little too soon. I
would direct him someplace else . . . I said, we want to win, color doesn't mean
anything to us, but . . . we are going to have to play in Starkville, Mississippi,
and Oxford, Mississippi, and Tuscaloosa, Alabama, and . . . I wouldn't want
the kid to be embarrassed or anything."

"Anything" was an oblique reference to violence.

In an era when a small group of vigilantes was willing to kill to prevent
James Meredith, a black man, from integrating the University of Mississippi,
Bryant and others worried what might happen if they fanned the flames of
football and race too quickly, before the state was ready.

Even if Alabama had been ready to open the door to black players in the
mid-1960s, the state's image—and, by extension, the university's—probably
would have scared many players off. Although 298 African-Americans were enrolled on the Tuscaloosa campus by 1966, the memory of Wallace's stand and
all the other moments of infamy still resonated. The thought of becoming Alabama's answer to Jackie Robinson in those days would have given any sane
player pause, even if he had grown up cheering for the segregated Crimson
Tide. Selling out-of-state blacks on the idea of taking a pioneering step into the
unknown would have proven even tougher.

"It was kind of ridiculous for us to think we could go to California . . . and
try to get a black athlete, with the image that we have here in Alabama . . .
[considering] what a black athlete sees on TV or reads and might think about
Alabama," Bryant later said of the dilemma.

From the vantage point of four decades of history, the continued segregation of the Alabama football program three years after Wallace stood in the
schoolhouse door is impossible to justify. Knowing what we know now, Bryant
should have invested some of his hard-earned political capital to knock down
the barrier for good, regardless of whether many of his fans were unprepared
for the change. Some, after all, would never be ready.

Imagine the powerful symbolism if Bryant had defied Wallace and all the
forces of hate by signing a black athlete shortly after the stand.

However, Bryant did not live in a theoretical world, and judging him in
such a manner is inherently unfair. For all his calculating boldness on many issues, he was just another leader of the white establishment, and like so many
others, he was trying to understand and react to the rapidly evolving culture
without throwing gas onto the flame of racial politics. He might have lost his
audience, and his team, by getting so far ahead of public opinion.

"Coach Bryant knew it was coming," said longtime assistant coach Clem

Gryska. "He was ready for integration, but he knew a lot of the people around the state weren't ready, and he didn't want to move too soon."

Contrary to what some people in other parts of the country no doubt believed, the Crimson Tide was not filled with a bunch of closeted Klansmen. Like the general population in the South, the members of the 1966 Crimson Tide, neatly tucked away in the cocoon Bryant built for them, spent little time thinking about the civil rights movement. Because most of the players were raised in the belly of segregation, their views tended to reflect their captivity in a poisonous time. No one went around speaking in favor of Martin Luther King Jr. or Malcolm X, but like many decent, hardworking white people who were accustomed to a separation of the races but didn't spend their time terrorizing black folks—and were generally repelled at the thought—they were starting to struggle with a sense of right and wrong on the issue of race.

"I think we would have accepted black players just fine," said defensive back Johnny Mosley. "First of all, Coach Bryant would not have tolerated anything less than treating them just the same as the rest of us, because he was not that way. Plus, if they were in there taking everything the rest of us took, we wouldn't have cared a lick. We just wanted to win."

By the time the 1966 Alabama Crimson Tide chased a third straight national title, even winning and competing for championships could no longer be isolated from the civil rights movement. A mighty crash was coming, a collision that would change the Alabama football program forever, setting off a chain reaction destined to reverberate throughout the culture.

The state's public relations problem even carried over into the Crimson Tide's scheduling. After Tulane University announced its intention to withdraw from the SEC, effective at the end of the 1965–66 athletic year, 'Bama officials started shopping for a season-opening opponent for 1966. The Tide approached several different major schools from outside the South about filling the vacancy.

"None of the teams we called wanted to play us because of the racial climate," said longtime assistant athletic director Charley Thornton. "The image of the state was so bad, they didn't want to play in Alabama."

Although the state laws prohibiting whites and blacks from playing on the same field had been swept away by the civil rights legislation, the pressure among prominent forces to continue to avoid such "race mixing" remained strong. Whether Bryant actually felt free to bring an integrated opponent to Denny Stadium in this climate remains unclear, but according to Thornton, more than one of the teams Alabama tried to schedule in 1966 was integrated, so apparently, Bryant was willing to test the climate.

Left with few palatable options, the Crimson Tide scheduled lightly re-garded, all-white Louisiana Tech to replace Tulane, a decision that would figure prominently in the national championship race.

Even as the 1966 Crimson Tide suffered for remaining segregated, eighteen-year-old Dock Rone struggled with the biggest decision of his young life. As he prepared for his first semester at the University of Alabama, the civil engineering major from Montgomery, who had turned down a scholarship to play football at a historically black college, started thinking about walking on to the 'Bama football team the next spring.

"When I first mentioned the idea to some of my family and friends, I heard a lot of concern and fear," said Rone, who played as a 5'8", 175-pound lineman at Montgomery's all-black Carver High School. "The thought made me a little nervous, too, because I didn't know what might happen."

For the moment, Rone mostly kept his little dream to himself, tucked away from the view of all who no doubt would have appreciated the irony of a black man yearning to be part of an institution whose only apparent weakness—indeed, its tragic flaw—was how it reflected the stain of segregation. The time was not quite right, so like many other Alabama fans, Rone watched the Crim-son Tide chase history with a sense of frustration. Closely watching every game, he anxiously waited for his opportunity to step onto the field and prove something that transcended skin color. His private ambition was about one man and one fragile dream. It was all about being young and full of life at a time when the world suddenly looked ripe for change, when the old rules no longer seemed so absolute.

In the case of Dock Rone, fear and hate were no match for a more powerful instinct. He was a big Alabama fan and a football player who believed in the might of his toughness, and he desperately wanted to see if he had the right stuff to play for the Bear.

The 1966 season was the beginning of the end of the segregated Crimson Tide, but as Alabama pursued a third straight national championship, none of the fans who kept one eye on the polls and another on their beloved team had a clue.

4. THREEPEAT

Cecil Dowdy pulled the hose out of his gas tank with a thunk and yelled to his roommate, sitting in the front passenger seat of the 1956 Ford, a rust bucket with balding tires and ripped cushions.

"You got any money?" he said with a worried expression.

"No. I don't have a dime," replied Frank Whaley. "I thought you had money."

Several weeks after the end of spring practice in 1966, the two buddies had driven off from Tuscaloosa with no real agenda. Far from the pressures of their responsibilities with the Crimson Tide football team, they relished the rare chance to feel like ordinary college students during the sweet spot in the schedule when the curfew rules were relaxed and they could drink a beer or two without risking the wrath of Gary White. With the AM radio cranked up, they cruised the two-lane roads of central Alabama, laughing and telling stories and living in the moment. They were about one hundred miles from campus when Dowdy yanked the hose out . . . and the realization landed like a thunderbolt.

"What are we gonna do?" Whaley whispered, aware that his friend had already pumped $5 worth of fuel, which filled the tank.

Something. They would think of something.

A good-natured country boy who had earned All-State honors as a high school lineman in the small northwest Alabama town of Cherokee, Dowdy was one of the fiercest competitors on the team. In the upset victory over Nebraska in the Orange Bowl, when just about everyone thought the Crimson Tide would be crushed by all those giants in the trenches, Dowdy repeatedly dominated one of the Cornhuskers' huge defensive linemen, who outweighed him by more than thirty pounds. Five or six times during the memorable night, the pride of Colbert County exploded off the ball with such force that he lifted his opponent up on his back, clearing yet another gaping hole for all those 'Bama jerseys. Overlooked like so many other members of the Crimson Tide's deceptively powerful offensive line, Dowdy was denied even All-SEC acclaim as a junior. But his time was coming.

After returning to the team in 1965, Whaley matured into a solid defensive player. He started several games at defensive end, but a broken ankle against Mississippi State marred his season and left him hobbling in spring practice. Although not as dominating a player as Dowdy, Whaley was an aggressive tackler who had impressed the coaches with a new fire before the injury, and he was determined to return to the lineup at full strength in 1966.

On that carefree afternoon of joyriding, of course, Whaley was quite focused on avoiding doing time alongside his teammate in the Talladega County jail.

Understandably embarrassed by their honest mistake, Whaley and Dowdy pleaded their case with the gas station attendant and tried to work out some sort of deal so they could get back on the road. Finally, Whaley pulled his commemorative Orange Bowl watch—worth much more than $5—off his wrist and agreed to leave it as security until he could return the next day with the money. The clerk's eyes grew as big as saucers while running his fingers over the little band of gold.

"You can bet I'll be back to get that," Whaley said as they walked away.

After all, it was more than just a valuable timepiece. The watch was a tangible reminder of the power of faith.

The unlikely 1965 season represented an enormous triumph for the Crimson Tide on several different levels, but more than anything else, it proved that great achievements were possible despite overwhelming odds—if they dared to believe. It was easy for Bryant to stand before his battered team at mid-season and encourage them to reach beyond their adversity, but the players who bought into his message and then somehow rebounded from a loss and a tie to capture the big prize were profoundly affected by the experience. Even to the men who trusted him without hesitation, his uncanny calling of those other bowl games, which placed the Tide in position to vault to the top of the rankings, fell somewhere between brilliant and spooky. 'Bama's 1965 season was more than the sport's most electrifying rally from oblivion to the throne room. To the players, trained to think of football as something more than a game, something transcendent, it was one long exercise in overcoming hardship with perseverance and faith. Even as several key players graduated, the sweet residue of 1965 lingered in the air, infusing the 1966 Crimson Tide with a potent combination of inspiration and confidence.

"We were riding such a wave heading into [the 1966] season," said offensive tackle Jerry Duncan. "Coach Bryant had us believing in each other, in him so firmly . . . none of us would have questioned him if he'd said we were about to fly to the moon from his front porch."

"There was a feeling of supreme confidence that permeated that group, funneled down from the senior class," said sophomore Conrad Fowler.

In the months leading up to the season, most of the players landed jobs or registered for summer school. Cash and credit hours were usually coveted with equal dilligence, and regardless of which path a player chose, he was expected to spend a significant amount of time working out so he could return for preseason practice in superior shape.

When California junior college transfer Kenny Martin started looking around for a way home for the summer, teammates Jerry Duncan, Byrd Williams, Frank Canterbury, and Harold Moore offered to drive him. None of them had ever traveled outside the South, and they thundered off in Canterbury's car with a sense of youthful adventure, taking turns driving, munching on baloney sandwiches along the roadside, stopping to spend the night in cheap motels. In Los Angeles, former 'Bama line coach Howard Schnellenberger, who had joined George Allen's staff with the Rams, invited the whole bunch over for grilled steaks and cold beer. They all felt like big men, sipping suds with a coach who had once pushed them so relentlessly. The side trip to Mexico turned a little hairy when somebody broke the seal on a fifth of tequila at a liquor store, and the wide-eyed Alabama boys had to talk fast to stop the clerk from calling the *federales*.

On the way home, the expedition hiked to the bottom of the Grand Canyon. They planned to stay the night at the base, but after a while, they all got bored and started heading back up the narrow eight-mile trail. It didn't take long for them all to have a change of heart. Huffing and puffing, struggling to keep moving, gasping for air, their spirited run turned into a brisk walk, bordering on a trail of tears. Along the way, they started ditching their sleeping bags and other camping equipment—anything to lighten the load. With no way out of the massive hole in the ground except straight ahead, they kept moving up and around, up and around, and just like gym class, just like practice, just like all those other hellish aspects of the Alabama football experience, they pushed each other to keep pressing toward the goal line.

"I thought we were never going to get out of there," Duncan said. "But we sure weren't going to quit. We wouldn't let each other quit."

By the time they reached the top, it was well past midnight and the sky was a blanket of stars. They all collapsed on some nearby picnic tables and slept till dawn.

Around the same time, Bryant was busy fulfilling the ever-growing demand for speaking engagements and public appearances befitting one of the sport's premiere coaches. Everyone wanted a piece of him, wanted him to talk about winning in football and winning in life, and he had a hard time saying no. While delivering a speech at California's Pepperdine University in June, the Bear suddenly stopped talking and clutched his chest. "I don't know what it is," he said with a troubled look. "Is there a doctor in the house?" Then the crowd gasped as he fell onto a nearby brass rail, bruising his head and lying unconscious until the paramedics arrived several minutes later.

The news that Bryant had collapsed of some mysterious ailment, presumed to be a heart attack, landed in bold type in newspapers across the country, and on front pages in Alabama. Charles Land, sports editor of *The Tuscaloosa News,* flew to Los Angeles to report on his condition and scooped the competition the next day. "I thought I was dying," Bryant told Land. "When I woke up on the floor, I was glad . . . because I remember having thought I was dying."

Doctors, who diagnosed the problem as some sort of stomach ailment, advised him to cut down on some of his off-the-field demands. Relieved that he had not suffered a heart attack, which might have tempted him to quit coaching, the old warrior, who would turn fifty-three on September 11, had a twinkle in his eyes when he told Land, "I always heard that you thought of all the bad things you had ever done at a time like that. But I didn't have that much time."

The Bear was out of the hospital in a couple of days, and after he and Mary Harmon spent a few relaxing nights at their cabin on Lake Martin in southeastern Alabama, he returned to Tuscaloosa with a spring in his step and started back on his routine of sixteen-hour days. Because he was still hungry, even after all those years, and he could smell another championship.

Regardless of how or where the Alabama players and coaches spent their summer vacations, the object of their obsession was never far from their thoughts. The threepeat was not just a goal. It was a quest.

The concept of the mythical national championship in big-time college football dates to the early years of the twentieth century, but a largely forgotten journalist named Alan J. Gould was primarily responsible for launching the modern obsession with poll-watching. In 1936, Gould, the sports editor of the Associated Press, the nation's leading wire service, combined his love of college football with his appreciation for the sort of hype that sold newspapers to create a weekly top 10. "Just another exercise in hoopla," Gould once said, somewhat dismissively, of his creation.

By establishing a panel of sportswriters from coast to coast, Gould succeeded in selling the survey as a fair, if unscientific, pulse of expert opinion. Charges of bias filled the air from the start, of course—especially after Minnesota captured the first AP national title, despite a loss to once-beaten Northwestern, which finished seventh—but Gould figured the controversy proved he was onto something. He was right. In 1950, rival United Press, which later merged with International News Service, joined the fray by starting its own weekly survey, utilizing the trained eyes of college head coaches. The two polls agreed more often than not, and when they occasionally named different champions, the resulting debate stirred the pot still further, giving football fans something else to argue about, even as the lack of consensus slowly undermined the idea of choosing the nation's best team with a glorified popularity contest.

Across the sixty-plus years when the colleges and the sporting public generally conceded the primacy and legitimacy of the wire service polls—which filled a vacuum left by the National Collegiate Athletic Association's inability to determine a champion on the field—programs captured one or both crowns in consecutive years a total of ten times. Traditional powers Alabama (1964–65 and 1978–79), Oklahoma (1955–56 and 1974–75) and Nebraska (1970–71 and 1994–95) accomplished the feat twice.

The possibility of winning three straight national championships tantalized all of those dominant teams. Several came relatively close, including Red Blaik's 9-0-1 Army Cadets in 1946, who finished second to Notre Dame after being tied by the Fighting Irish. In 1956, Bud Wilkinson's famed Oklahoma Sooners entered November riding an NCAA record forty-seven game winning streak, within reach of a third consecutive title. But a mediocre Notre Dame team pulled a 7–0 upset, stopping the streak and leaving the Sooners to finish 9-1 and ranked fourth in both polls.

Around Bear Bryant's Alabama program, the national championship was the target each and every year. The big man placed little emphasis on winning the Southeastern Conference, arguably the sport's toughest league, because he wanted his players to aim higher. Well aware of their chance to achieve one of the most elusive feats in all of American sports, the two-time defending national champion Crimson Tide approached the 1966 season with a sense of mission.

"Bryant, himself, scoffs at the mention of three titles in a row," suggested the season preview in the Alabama media guide, penned by longtime publicity man Charley Thornton. "He won't even discuss it publicly. Neither will the players or the coaches. But deep down, the thought inspires them all."

In a less-guarded moment, Bryant confessed to Benny Marshall, the sports editor of *The Birmingham News:* "We have an opportunity to do something no other team in history has done. . . . I get fired up just thinking about it."

Usually Bryant, an accomplished practitioner in the art of poor-mouthing, played down the strengths of his team, which was primarily intended for the consumption of the players, to prevent them from becoming "fat-headed." "It's awful easy for people to read about themselves and just say it's going to happen," he said during the summer.

But it was difficult for him to convince anyone he wasn't holding a very strong hand heading into the 1966 season. On one occasion, he struck a cautious tone with a reporter: "I'm stall-walking," he said, pulling out a horseman's metaphor. "I'm worried to death about a lot of different things . . . [like] whether we are quick enough to overcome our smallness." This, of course, reflected a valid concern. But he could also flip the switch and turn positively optimistic. "Biggest thing we've got I think is confidence," he told another reporter. "These little ole kids think they can win. It's pride, poise, and confidence and right there are ingredients you have to have to be a winner."

Even before 'Bama hit the trail in search of its fourth national title in six years, the word dynasty was being thrown around with increasing regularity. The spotlight focused on the program grew even brighter in August, when *Sports Illustrated,* in an unprecedented move, published a five-part cover package on Bryant entitled, "I'll Tell You About Football." In the series, Bryant and veteran football writer John Underwood—who later collaborated on his best-selling 1974 autobiography, *Bear*—explored everything from his poverty-stricken childhood in Arkansas to *The Saturday Evening Post's* scandalous "fix" allegations. Like one gigantic billboard for the Bear and his Crimson Tide, the coverage further enhanced the national stature of Alabama football.

Underwood, who traveled around the country with Bryant for several months to squeeze bits and pieces of interview time into the coach's jam-packed schedule, had been with him the day he collapsed. He even rode in the ambulance alongside his famous subject—and held his wallet. Several days later, after reluctantly canceling a few speaking engagements to rest a bit, Bryant called the writer. "Meet me in New York," he said. "We have to finish what we started."

Television, still rare and special, played an unquestionable role in validating and strengthening 'Bama's reputation as a football powerhouse. Since returning to Tuscaloosa in 1958, Bryant's teams had already appeared on the tube fourteen times, more than any other program. NCAA rules limited teams to no more than one national and one regional appearance during the regular season, and each year, the network scrambled to cover Alabama and a small number of other prominent teams as often as the rules allowed. In June, ABC Sports, which had regained the rights to NCAA football for the first time since 1961, convinced Alabama and Auburn to move their regular season finale at Legion Field from November 26 to December 3, so it could be seen by a national audience. ABC also planned to televise the Alabama-LSU game at Legion Field regionally.

When the Associated Press announced its preseason poll, Alabama was ranked No. 1, receiving 15 first-place votes, followed by Michigan State (12 first-place votes), UCLA (6), Nebraska (2), Arkansas, Notre Dame, Syracuse, Purdue, Southern Cal, and Tennessee. After experimenting with holding its final poll after the regular season for the first time in 1965—which allowed 'Bama to leap from fourth to first after stunning Nebraska—the AP announced that it was reverting to the old way for 1966. The culminating poll would be held at the end of the regular season—a week after the UPI coaches' survey—rendering the bowl games once more little more than meaningless exhibitions in the process of selecting the national champion.

It was easy to see why the writers picked the Crimson Tide to win a third straight national title. Despite several significant losses—including a pair of All-Americans in quarterback Steve Sloan and center Paul Crane, plus three other All-SEC performers in fullback Steve Bowman, defensive end Creed Gilmer, and split end Tommy Tolleson—'Bama was loaded on both sides of the ball. The fifteen returning starters included virtually the entire offensive line; two of the nation's best receivers, Ray Perkins and Dennis Homan; halfback Les Kelley, who emerged from the shadows to score two touchdowns against Nebraska and was moved to fullback to replace Bowman; and the guts of a defense that surrendered fewer than 10 points per game, including All-SEC cornerback Bobby Johns.

Like all Alabama teams, the 1966 bunch would rely heavily on senior leadership. Three years after the memorable first squad meeting in that old classroom, three years after fifty-one talented athletes who dreamed of wearing the red jersey struggled not to make a sound, the ranks were thinned considerably. The silence of the departed ones was the loudest sound of all. Only thirteen of the fifty-one remained to play as seniors, although four others had joined the class after being redshirted. The specter of high attrition rates was a constant in the demanding world of Alabama football. A large number of juniors and sophomores would play important roles for the Crimson Tide, a trend exacerbated by the transition to the two-platoon game, which prevented the coaching staff from relying so much on a small group of rugged and proven athletes.

The biggest question mark heading into the season surrounded the quarterback position. The battle to fill the shoes of Sloan, the *Nashville Banner*'s SEC Player of the Year in 1965, was expected to be won by junior lefthander Kenny "Snake" Stabler, who had played only sparingly. Stabler's athleticism could have made him a star most anywhere on the field; in fact, he briefly started in the secondary in 1965. Privately, many around the program were saying the fleet-footed Stabler could be even better than Sloan. His running ability gave 'Bama's option-oriented attack many more dimensions, but he was still unproven through the air, having completed only 3 of 11 passes as a sophomore backup to Sloan.

After spending two years grooming the free-spirited but incredibly talented Stabler, the polar opposite of the devout, focused, disciplined Sloan, Bryant understood that Snake was the key. A mature Stabler could be the last piece of a powerful puzzle. "Quarterbacks are more important than coaches," Bryant told reporters during the preseason. "You can find head coaches anywhere. Quarterbacks are hard to come by."

While most of the attention gravitated to Stabler, Wayne Trimble was not yet prepared to concede the race. The most versatile athlete on the entire squad, Trimble had been signed off Cullman High School's 1962 state championship team and was considered a major recruiting prize. But he entered his senior season in a haze of disappointment, a victim of poor injury luck and his vaunted adaptability. After finding a home on defense in 1965—highlighted by an interception against Auburn—Trimble, possessed with a stronger arm than Stabler's, at least at that point in their respective development, gave up his starting position and asked to be given the chance to compete for the quarterback job during the spring heading into his senior year.

The coaches were more concerned about replacing Paul Crane, one of the greatest centers in school history. Crane, a devastating blocker and nearly flawless snapper who had been drafted by the New York Jets, cast a large shadow over a bunch of pretenders. "Why, yes, we've got a weakness," Bryant told reporters, trying to build up his team. "We've got a weakness at center." Auditions for the position stretched from spring to the preseason, and the man who finally won the job owed his place on the 1966 team to a moment of heartbreak and frustration in 1963.

After working his way up the depth chart and earning a spot on the travel squad as a sophomore, Jimmy Carroll injured his ankle and sat out the first several ballgames. In the fifth game of the year, the Crimson Tide was crushing Tennessee at Legion Field, en route to a 35–0 victory, and the boss started clearing the bench. His time was coming, and he couldn't wait to go out and hit somebody.

"Carroll! Jimmy Carroll!" Bryant yelled.

A shiver of electricity ran up Carroll's spine, and he sprinted to his coach, who draped his right arm around the young man's shoulders while looking at the clock. "I don't know how much you'll get to play the rest of the year," Bryant said, launching into what amounted to a one-way discussion with himself on whether to send the kid from Enterprise into the game. Finally, he said, "I think I'll save you," indicating that he had decided to redshirt Carroll, giving him another year of eligibility.

"I was crushed," Carroll said. "I mean, crushed, because I wanted to play. That was my first reaction. Then, it began to dawn on me: That means another off-season conditioning program, another spring training. I've got to go through all that stuff for another year!"

Had it not been for Bryant's split-second decision, Carroll would have completed his playing eligibility in 1965, and probably never would have had the chance to start for the Crimson Tide.

In addition to Frank Whaley, two other key defensive players were coming off devastating health problems. Jimmy Fuller, a strong athlete and a great competitor who had played on both sides of the line, separated a shoulder against Florida State. He was expected back to fill a slot up front on defense, and having him at full speed would make the unit much tougher. Dicky Thompson, who started at halfback before being moved to fill a need in the secondary, was still trying to overcome the lingering effects of a rare kind of pneumonia that nearly cost him his life.

On his Sunday television show, the Bear always called him "little Dicky Thompson from Thomasville, Georgia." He said it with such conviction that Thompson, who stood 5'9½" and weighed 167 pounds soaking wet, started seeing his relatively small size as a point of pride, which was the whole idea. A few words, sprinkled like pixie dust . . .

Growing up in a middle-class south Georgia family, Thompson gravitated to sports early, like his two brothers, and their participation in football, basketball, and baseball was a unifying force. Their father, a skilled and meticulous carpenter, was a strict disciplinarian.

Whenever Dicky played sports around Thomasville, he knew where to find his father: On the top row of the bleachers, watching intently. His presence was an anchor in young Dicky's life, and their close but demanding relationship always included the father's carefully scribbled notes on how his son could improve his performance.

After becoming an all-state running back and signing with Alabama, to the surprise of many skeptics around town, Dicky rode off to Atlanta in the summer of 1964 to start practice for the upcoming state high school all-star game. It should have been one of the highlights of his life, and it was until the phone rang, until something in him shattered as he heard his mother crying. His father was dead. The massive heart attack had taken him quickly.

Immediately, he hopped in a car and headed South, and when he arrived, the devastated son hugged his mother, hugged her tight. After the funeral, he got in his car and drove back to Atlanta, because he felt an obligation to his team. He dedicated his Most Valuable Player trophy to his old man, and he had to stop himself from instinctively looking toward the top row.

"My father taught me that there are times when you just have to be a man and live up to your responsibilities," he said.

He also taught his son to fight.

During practice the week of the 1965 Auburn game, Thompson started feeling incredibly weak, struggling to catch his breath. Reluctantly, he went to see trainer Jim Goostree. Next thing he knew, he was lying in a hospital bed surrounded by doctors, and they were talking about surgery to remove one of his lungs. Within a few days, he lost more than twenty pounds, and doctors told the coaches he would never play football again.

After several weeks in and out of three different hospitals, and experimenting with a variety of drugs, Thompson started to recover, slowly. The decision not to remove his lung was a point of contention among all the doctors and his worried mother, and if they had opened him up and ripped out one half of his breathing capacity, his football career most certainly would have been over.

The coaches refused to let him dress in the spring. But he wanted it. Bad. Because football was everything to him, he kept begging, and after passing a physical, little Dicky Thompson could be seen running all over the practice field during the preseason in 1966, intercepting, tackling, making his daddy proud.

"There was never a thought in my mind that I wouldn't come back," Thompson said. "I wouldn't even entertain the thought of quitting. I had this feeling that I was representing all those people who believed in me . . . including my dad. And I didn't want to let them down."

Like many of his teammates, Dicky Thompson was defined less by his rather ordinary physicality than by his oversized heart. He thought big, he acted big, and he dreamed big. He just happened to be trapped in a little man's body.

As Alabama prepared to chase history in 1966, the world was hurtling with great momentum toward the turbulent late 1960s, which still loomed beyond the view of all the guys who sweated in Bryant's disciplined world. The Crimson Tide pursued the threepeat while the country negotiated a pivotal bridge year between two distinct eras, between order and rebellion, which makes the culture a big part of the story of the 1966 team.

The eldest members of the Crimson Tide arrived in Tuscaloosa before that horrible moment on November 22, 1963, when the assassination of President John F. Kennedy forever shattered the nation's innocence, and matriculated against the backdrop of the gradually escalating war in Vietnam and the climactic battles of the civil rights movement. Many of the most sacred aspects of establishment culture were soon to be challenged, and the players on the 1966 team represented the end of an era. Among the last athletes to arrive on campus who reached maturity unaffected by the coming age, they grew up in a world before illicit drugs became commonplace, before authority became a dirty word, before Vietnam exploded into the defining issue of a generation, before the guiding words of obligations and consequences became obscured by a blur of cynicism and relativism.

Beyond the issue of race, the state of Alabama and the university remained a place of order and conformity. Born to parents who had survived the deprivations and hardships of the Great Depression and World War II, the students who attended the University of Alabama in the mid-1960s were conditioned to be more concerned with responsibilities than rights, which instilled them all with a powerful sense of boundaries.

Female students were required to meet strict curfews, prohibited from visiting a man's off-campus apartment, and forbidden from wearing shorts or slacks in public. Proper young ladies wore girdles at all times. Drinking was officially forbidden, but the rule was broken with a wink and a nod, especially at the weekend frat parties, where rock 'n' roll bands like Dr. Feelgood and the Interns performed as they all walked around sipping from unmarked Dixie cups.

However, those who were caught overindulging on alcohol often paid a high price. Sorority sisters and dorm mates were encouraged to squeal on girls who came in drunk or committed other offenses, and being written up usually resulted in a trip to the women's judicial board—the girls called it "Judish"—where punishments ranged from temporary house arrest to suspension.

"In those days, you might bend some rules a little, but you didn't even think about questioning authority," said sorority sister Jo Ann Boozer. "There was this overriding feeling that this is the way things are and this is the way things are supposed to be."

In those days, the vast majority of students were firmly hinged to some sort of marriage track by the end of their undergraduate experience. Premarital sex remained a forbidden fruit. Abortion was illegal, and the stigma of unwanted pregnancy was severe. Nothing presaged the coming age of women's liberation—and the sexual revolution—quite like the still-new birth control pill, but most doctors refused to prescribe it unless a young woman had a ring.

"As soon as someone got engaged, the first thing they would do was go to the doctor to get a physical . . . [so they could] get the pill," said Boozer, who graduated in 1965.

The women's movement was just over the horizon, but even at the staid University of Alabama, subtle signs of the future could be seen.

Women's intercollegiate athletics were nonexistent in the Southeastern Conference in those days, and when Alabama signed Alexander City tennis phenom Roberta Allison to play on the men's team in 1962, no one fully appreciated the significance of the event.

"I didn't go into it wanting to be a pioneer," said Allison, the first female to earn an athletic scholarship to Alabama. "I just wanted to play tennis."

At the urging of the tennis coach, Bryant, Alabama's athletic director, helped push a rule change through the conference to allow women to compete on men's teams in noncontact sports. Several coaches and players at rival schools resisted, some to the point of forfeiting matches to avoid facing a woman on the court.

"Some people just weren't ready for women athletes in those days," said Allison, who played for the Crimson Tide a decade before Title IX led to the creation of broad-based women's sports programs across the country.

Most women who planned to pursue careers chose traditional female professions like teaching or nursing. When Jo Ann Boozer and a few other women decided to major in business, a bastion of male dominance, they frequently walked into Bidgood Hall amid a barrage of catcalls.

"What are you doing over here, honey?" some guy would shout. "This is a man's school!"

"I know why you're here!" another would yell. "Just looking for a husband!"

No. They were looking for the door to the future.

The desire to live within the rules in order to avoid dire consequences could be seen in the traffic jams that clogged sorority row on Friday and Saturday nights. In the moments before the midnight curfew, the guys rushed their dates home, often double-parking while sneaking a final kiss—or more—and the sisters on duty started flashing the porch lights, the Tuscaloosa equivalent of a two-minute warning. At the stroke of midnight, the lights went out and the sorority houses and dorms were locked, leaving anyone outside with an automatic appointment before the stern enforcers of Judish.

Like the overall society, the Alabama football team's reliance on a strict set of boundaries went unchallenged at least partially because resisting authority remained anathema to the whole culture. "Why?" was a question being asked with increasing frequency in places like California, where hippies and those pursuing alternative lifestyles were fast becoming a force, but not in Alabama, not in the vast majority of the heartland. One of the reasons Bryant's all-consuming philosophy worked was because the world sent him sons who were already conditioned to respect his jurisdiction over their lives, because the term generation gap had precious little currency, at least in Alabama.

On a memorable night in February 1964, the still-approaching conflict between young and old could be seen when Young Boozer, Jo Ann's father, stared at the television set as his daughter swayed to the music. The middle-aged Tuscaloosa insurance executive was walking through his living room when four lads from Liverpool appeared for the first time on *The Ed Sullivan Show.* Something disturbing caught his eye.

"Looks like they need a good barber," he said with a dismissive grunt.

Bear Bryant's college roommate never trusted a man who was not well groomed.

Jo Ann wanted to roll her eyes when her father criticized the Beatles. In addition to being captivated by their sound, she thought they all looked so neat in those three-button suits. But even rolling her eyes was a form of rebellion in 1964, and polite, well-raised young Southern ladies didn't sass their daddies—even with their pupils.

"Oh, daddy," she said playfully, instead.

The elder Boozer, a gregarious gentleman who played halfback and defensive back for Frank Thomas's Alabama football powerhouse in the 1930s before becoming a very successful businessman, never understood the allure of rock 'n' roll. It was all noise to him.

While the music struck Boozer and many other adults of the time as an uncrackable code—nearly a decade after Elvis Presley's raw sexuality threatened the conventions of American society—the long hair that John, Paul, George, and Ringo sported on national television was easy to see and impossible to overlook. More than a fashion statement, it was a form of rebellion. In an age when the ubiquitous crew cut reflected a world of order and obedience, appearing in such a way was a provocative act, a tangible symbol of the revolution looming on the horizon, when all once sacrosanct aspects of American culture would be open to challenge and defiance.

The Beatles made it cool to have long hair, but in Alabama, as in many other parts of the country, it was not yet cool to be cool.

Not just yet.

Not in Bear Bryant's America.

Even after the British Invasion, the fans in the Heart of Dixie who grooved to the music of groups like the Beatles, the Rolling Stones, and the Byrds clung almost universally to short hair—and all it symbolized.

Two years after the height of Beatlemania, the mop tops still cast a large shadow as Alabama plotted a course for the 1966 national championship. Their latest album, *Revolver,* released in August, featured the timeless portraiture of "Eleanor Rigby" as well as the youthful exuberance of "Good Day Sunshine," and audiences all across the world continued to see their work as both meaningful and easy to dance to. However, the Beatles were drenched in controversy when John Lennon made some remark about the Beatles being "bigger than Jesus," which they all insisted was misinterpreted. The outcry from religious leaders was enormous. In Birmingham, deejays at WAQY-AM drew national attention with their decision to "ban the Beatles," but it did nothing to help the struggling station's ratings. As the group prepared for what would turn out to be their last official concert at San Francisco's Candlestick Park in late August, the continued dominance of the old order could be seen in the fact that Lennon felt compelled to hold a news conference to explain himself. Some mothers and fathers already thought rock 'n' roll was the devil's music, especially in Alabama, the heart of the Bible belt, and his original comment played into their fears. "I'm sorry I opened my mouth," Lennon said. "I'm not anti-God, anti-Christ or antireligion. I was not knocking it. I was not saying we are greater or better."

The year 1966 saw several important albums released, perhaps none better or more groundbreaking than the Beach Boys' landmark *Pet Sounds.* In many ways, one of the record's hits, "Wouldn't It Be Nice," which was working its way up the charts when the players returned to campus in August, seemed emblematic of the time, offering not just a wonderful harmonic statement about the transition between adolesence and adulthood, but also a respectful nod to innocence and traditional values.

The soundtrack of the year also included classics like "Monday, Monday" by the Mamas and the Papas, "You Can't Hurry Love" by the Supremes, "When a Man Loves a Woman" by Percy Sledge, "(You're My) Soul and Inspiration" by the Righteous Brothers, "Ain't Too Proud to Beg" by the Temptations, and "Cherish" by the Association. Patriotism remained a source of national unity, which explained the success of SSgt. Barry Sadler's rousing anthem, "The Ballad of the Green Berets," which became the year's top-selling song.

The cynicism of fast-approaching motion pictures personified by 1967's *The Graduate* and 1969's *Easy Rider* still remained mostly unimaginable to movie audiences in 1966, who flocked to see sex kitten Rachel Welch filling up the screen—and her skintight outfit—in *Fantastic Voyage*; Walter Matthau and Jack Lemmon trying to perpetrate a scam before eventually experiencing a change of heart in *The Fortune Cookie*; and Michael Caine's *Alfie* epitomizing the carefree life of the swinging bachelor.

As the major record labels took the first tentative steps toward issuing recorded music on eight-track and cassette, two mediums destined to become big hits with consumers, the transistor radio still seemed like a marvel. The sight of an Alabama coed walking across campus holding a tiny radio tethered to an earphone bespoke the era of the quick little boys like few other images.

Two technological innovations were nearing critical mass.

In 1966, fewer than 10 percent of the nation's homes contained a color television set, but as the three networks shifted the last of their shows to color with the fall season and the cost of the once enormously expensive appliance slowly dropped, the transition from black-and-white rapidly gained momentum. All across the country, children and wives were starting to bug fathers and husbands about plunking down the bucks for a new set, so they could watch shows like *Bonanza*, which finished number one in the Nielsen ratings, as well as *The Andy Griffith Show, Bewitched*, and *Gomer Pyle, U.S.M.C.*, starring Alabama native Jim Nabors.

Television still reflected and reinforced traditional values. Nudity, graphic language, and strong sexual content remained taboos in all aspects of public American life, especially TV. The sardonic wit of *The Smothers Brothers Comedy Hour* remained several months from its debut on CBS, and the raw realism personified by *All in the Family*, which would hit the airwaves in 1971, still seemed inconceivable to audiences who found comfort and reassurance in Andy Griffith's neatly ordered world.

At the same time, folks were starting to buy FM radios in increasing numbers. Most cars still came equipped only with the long-established AM band, but many audiophiles bought expensive FM converters to increase their listening choices. AM, where top 40 was king, would still dominate the radio business into the 1970s, but the signs of crystal-clear FM's slow ascendance were starting to be felt, including in Alabama, where many fans listened to the Crimson Tide games on FM stations such as WJOF in Athens, which covered the Tennessee Valley and points north.

In 1966, when the median household income was $7,254 and only 34 percent of women worked outside the home, you could buy a three-bedroom house in Alabama for $10,000, a gallon of regular gas for 32 cents, a bottle of Coca-Cola for a nickel, and a pack of cigarettes for 30 cents. Cigarette advertising still could be seen all over network television.

After the U.S. Supreme Court's June 13 decision in *Miranda v. Arizona*, law enforcement officers were suddenly required to advise accused criminals of their Constitutional rights.

At a time when the gross national product was $787 billion, the outstanding federal debt was $328.5 billion, and the federal budget was $134.5 billion, President Lyndon Johnson directed a costly war on poverty, which included the July 1 launch of the Medicare program. But the news increasingly was dominated by the war in Vietnam.

When the seniors of 1966 arrived on campus as freshmen in 1963, very few Americans could identify Vietnam on a map. The escalation began gradually, even as young men like Johnny Mosley, Wayne Trimble, and Jerry Duncan struggled to survive gym class and spring practice. By the fall of 1966, the war cast an ominous shadow across many aspects of American life. With more than 200,000 American troops on the ground in southeast Asia, casualties mounting, and no end in sight to U.S. involvement, the once insignificant antiwar movement was slowly gaining momentum on campuses far from Tuscaloosa.

Flag-waving patriotism was still a powerful, unifying force at Bryant Hall, where many members of the team belonged to either the Army or Air Force ROTC. The draft loomed like a dark cloud for all young men, even the heroes of Bryant Hall, giving them yet another reason to attend to their studies and hold on to their all-important college deferment.

The distant war often arrived in the form of a letter, delivered to Bryant Hall, shaking the athletes out of what remained of their complacence. A marine colonel who had participated in 'Bama's gym class program in order to get in better shape before being shipped off to Vietnam periodically dropped a line to the friends he had made on the team. "I remember he said [gym class] was tougher than boot camp, which didn't surprise any of us," Jerry Duncan said. Gathering around the small post office, a tiny alcove near the front door, the players always read the missives from the jungle war with a combination of thrill and dread. Eventually, the letters just stopped coming.

Jacqueline Susann's *Valley of the Dolls*, one of the biggest-selling novels of the year, gave Middle America a glimpse into the New York fast lane of clawing ambition, unrepentant sex, and rampant drug use, a shocking portrayal, which readers devoured to the surprise of the publishing community. Truman Capote's *In Cold Blood* read like a novel, but the grisly tale of murder was a landmark in nonfiction. Even as journalist Tom Wolfe hopped on Ken Kesey's multicolored bus to chronicle the rise of the counterculture in 1966, a journey that would spawn the seminal book *The Electric Kool-Aid Acid Test*, very few Alabama students had ever experienced marijuana, much less harder drugs like LSD. The news was full of a former Harvard professor named Timothy Leary championing the mind-expanding properties of such psychadelics. His advice to "turn on, tune in, and drop out" was the clarion call of a new generation, but most folks in Alabama remained blissfully unaware of him or the movement he embodied.

Defensive lineman Louis Thompson was listening to a band at a fraternity party in 1966 when someone came up to him and offered him a toke on a funny looking cigarette, the first hit of grass he had ever seen. "I didn't even know what it was, until the guy told me," Thompson said. "I knew I didn't want any part of marijuana."

More than a personal danger, drug use symbolized all of the challenges to the established order lurking just over the horizon. It was only a matter of time before the younger generation started questioning everything. Soon, the whole country would be divided into longhairs and buzz cuts—even the Bear's hometown.

Inside the cocoon of Bryant Hall, the distractions of the outside world remained mostly filtered out by the players, who were concerned only with winning another national championship, a drive that began with two stressful events on the first day of preseason practice in mid-August: the weigh-in and the mile run.

The determination to produce a lean, quick, superbly conditioned team led, inevitably, to two concrete measurements, and the scales and the stopwatch never lied. Every summer, the players were provided with personally calculated weights and times, which they were expected to meet. Or else. If a player failed to make his numbers, the coaches interpreted it not only as a sign that he had allowed himself to fall out of tip-top shape over the summer, but also as a reflection of a lack of commitment to live up to his responsibilities to the team.

Defensive lineman Louis Thompson, the heaviest man on the roster, frequently struggled with his weight, and consequently, experienced trouble making his time. As a sophomore, he reported weighing 226 pounds, and Bryant ran him until he dropped. Two years later, heading into his senior season of

1966, he received a handwritten note from the boss instructing him to report weighing no more than 218. Home for summer in Tennessee, he took the missive seriously and went straight to the bathroom scales, which showed him at 215. Too close to the limit for his own comfort, he went on a starvation diet for several days, just in case.

Three weeks later, when he reported to Tuscaloosa, Louis waited his turn in the long procession of players wearing nothing but their underwear, and when he finally stepped on the scale, he felt a hand tapping on his shoulder. Turning, he saw Bryant looking over his shoulder to see the face of the scale, which read somewhere slightly below 218. Bryant didn't say a word. He just patted Louis on the back and walked away.

The mile run was yet another way for the coaches to promote the importance of endurance and conditioning. Times were tailored to individual players to make them reach, and while some sprinters on the team like Ray Perkins, Dennis Homan, and Donnie Johnston found the process manageable if they pushed themselves during the summer, others saw it as a kind of torture. Running didn't come easily for everyone, and yet it was a universal activity all were expected to master in order to make them better football players. Some athletes dreaded it every bit as much as gym class. A player who failed to meet his time was forced to keep running . . . and running . . . and running. It was often ugly—and painful. Some players could not take the constant punishment near the height of the Alabama summer, which was one central point of the whole exercise.

When the team reported in August of 1966, the athletic department was in the process of resurfacing the cinder track adjacent to the practice field, so Ray Perkins, one of the Crimson Tide's senior leaders, was assigned the task of plotting a one-mile course. Either out of a lack of precision in his measuring or something more conspiratorial, Perkins laid out a track somewhat short of a mile—perhaps as much as fifty yards. Nobody missed their appointed number.

"We had some guys running close to world-record times," said Perkins, the fastest man on the team, who needed no help in that department.

Fortunately for all concerned, none of the coaches noticed Perkins's little stunt, or some of those guys might still be running.

Every successful team is built on a delicate balance of competition and camaraderie. Like the military, the Alabama system promoted a strong bond among the players and, at the same time, was driven by the individual ambition that inevitably forced them to push and chase each other.

The tension bubbling up between defensive linemen Richard Cole and

Louis Thompson in the summer of 1966 was a microcosm of the competitive climate that ultimately made the team stronger.

Louis grew up on a farm outside Lebanon, Tennessee, and when a coach noticed the strapping ninth grader in the hall and asked him to come out for football, he jumped at the chance, thinking it would allow him to get out of his hated afternoon chores. Wrong. His daddy let him play, even encouraged him to play, but was waiting for him when he arrived home that first night after practice.

"Time to milk the cows, son," he said, pointing to the barn.

Although his plan didn't work out as he had envisioned, Thompson enjoyed the game enough to live with all the extra work. All those years on the farm hauling hay and performing other physically taxing activities had made him big and strong, which helped him become an outstanding defensive end and fullback. During his junior year, Alabama assistant coach Dude Hennessey drove north to see another player, and it just happened to be the night when Thompson turned into a demon on defense. Hennessey pulled him aside after the game, telling him Alabama would keep an eye on him the next year.

"That really fired me up, because up till that point, I had never thought about being able to go to college," he said.

Highly recruited the next year, he chose Alabama over Tennessee, even though he had grown up a big Volunteers fan, and hoped to play fullback in Tuscaloosa. In those days, 'Bama recruited a dozen or more fullbacks every year and most wound up playing somewhere else on the field. On the first day of practice, when the coaches divided the large freshman class into position groups, Louis started jogging toward the area designated for fullbacks.

Assistant head coach Sam Bailey, who oversaw the freshmen team, grabbed him by the jersey. "Thompson, where are you going?"

"Over with the fullbacks, coach."

Bailey sneered at the rookie.

"Get over there with the linemen."

His career as an Alabama skill player lasted about three seconds.

Over the next three years, Thompson struggled to please the coaches and earn much playing time. Someone always seemed to be in his face, usually line coach Ken Donahue. He could do very little right in their eyes, and at times, it was the big man himself who climbed down from his tower and challenged him to lay it on the line.

From his perch high above the practice field, Bryant looked out over the activity below with a keen eye. Unless the team was scrimmaging, the position coaches worked their squads in separate drills, planned to the minute in advance, separated by periods that commenced when head manager Sang Lyda blew the whistle. The linemen practiced on the far edge of the field, behind a bunch of pine trees, and yet Bryant could see everything from his tower, which offered a panoramic view. Every so often, the players and coaches below would hear his bullhorn click on and he would make some pronouncement that turned heads across the field: "Hey, Louis, too high on that! Bring it down!"

While trying to concentrate on their drills, every player and assistant coach also listened out for the clank of the chain that kept the Bear from falling out of the tower. When he unfastened the chain, it rattled against the metallic tower, which meant the Bear was on his way down. The sound of the chain was practically Pavlovian; it scared the hell out of everybody, because they were all conditioned to hear it as a prelude to something unpleasant. The noise was usually a warning that Bryant had noticed something disturbing and someone was about to be chewed out. On many such occasions, Louis Thompson found himself on the wrong end of Bryant's wrath, being corrected by the Bear in front of the whole team.

During two-a-days in 1966, the coaches were giving Thompson an especially hard time. Finally, during a scrimmage, something inside him snapped and he walked off the field, across the adjoining track, and toward the gate. Sam Bailey saw him and followed him.

"Get your butt back across that track," Bailey said. "You ain't quitting now. Not after coming this far."

Thompson looked at his coach with an agonized expression and slowly started walking back across the track. Because he knew Bailey was right.

Players often talk about Bryant's ability to know how to push a player to his limit and his brilliance at knowing where the line was. Many players, of course, were shoved past the boundary, and their decision to stay and suck it up or leave in a fit of rage was deeply entangled in all sorts of personal issues.

"I was just so mad," Thompson said of that fateful day. "I'd gotten to the point where they had pushed me so hard, I'd had enough. They were probably pushing me so hard because they could see I wasn't laying it all on the line . . . that I was feeling sorry for myself. I almost gave it all up. If it hadn't been for Coach Bailey . . ."

If Louis had not been so focused on the pain and frustration, he might not have missed the road sign. He was now entering the land of the committed Alabama football player.

Thompson never considered quitting again, and a few days later, his determination to become a significant contributor to the team could be seen in a hallway conversation with Richard Cole, the starter at right defensive tackle in the Crimson Tide's three-man front.

"Cole," he said, "Get ready, 'cause I'm gonna take your position away from you!"

The two were friends, and Cole, a mild-mannered Baptist preacher's son, was not the sort to get too excited. "Well," he said, "you do your best and I'll do my best, and we'll let the coaches decide."

Growing up in the small northeastern Alabama towns of Altoona and Crossville, Cole learned to be gritty to survive playing tackle backyard football with his two older brothers. Talented enough as an eighth grader to start on the high school varsity at tiny Crossville—where he was forced to practice against the upperclassmen he was supplanting, mostly bigger guys who relished the chance to exact their revenge—he nevertheless didn't warrant much attention from Alabama or Auburn. Someone from Shug Jordan's staff watched him play a time or two, but wasn't very impressed. Lowly Memphis State offered him a scholarship but after he turned it down, his high school coach took the initiative of calling Bryant personally and telling him they were making a big mistake. He must have been a good salesman, because several days later—more than a week after signing day—assistant coach Clem Gryska came calling, saving Cole from joining the marines.

While not the most gifted player on the team, Cole's toughness and steady play had propelled him into the starting lineup, where he became one of the most pleasant surprises of 1965. Although he put on a tough front when Louis Thompson announced his ambition, the banjo-picking country boy was concerned. "It worried me because I knew, sizewise, strengthwise, speedwise, he very well could take my position," Cole said.

For the next couple of weeks, the competition between the two players raged as just another one of numerous battles that gave preseason practices a certain dramatic texture. At any given time, some fire-breathing second-teamer was always challenging to leap to the top of the pyramid. As the coaches watched intently, Louis Thompson and Richard Cole pursued ballcarriers with a vengeance and, in the process, made each other better.

Impressed by the way Thompson had elevated his game, gratified by the way Cole had defended his turf, Bryant eventually shuffled the lineup to make room for both players at the tackles, with Johnny Sullivan between them at noseguard. It would turn out to be a brilliant strategic move, getting those three players on the field at the same time, providing a textbook example of how a rivalry between two athletes ultimately lifted the whole team to another level.

Still, the Bear prowled the sidelines in the weeks before the season opener worried, as usual. After the first scrimmage of the preseason, he bitched about how the first-team offense, led by Kenny Stabler, had been "embarrassed" by the second-team defense.

"I didn't recognize anyone out there today who played in the Orange Bowl," he growled after the first scrimmage of the preseason.

The poor-mouthing followed a familiar script, but who was he kidding?

The Bear was loaded and everyone in college football knew it.

The Alabama schedule appeared favorable for another run to glory. Benefiting from the vagaries of the SEC's opponent rotation, the Crimson Tide would not face Georgia or Florida, two of the league's best teams. The road trip to tenth-ranked Tennessee on the third Saturday in October represented a major test, as well as a journey into hostile territory to face Johnny Vaught's Ole Miss Rebels. 'Bama faced Charley McClendon's always tough LSU Tigers at Birmingham's Legion Field, the program's second home, also the site of the season-ending showdown with archrival Auburn, when the tickets were split down the middle. But the season-opening date with Louisiana Tech spelled trouble, making it look, to the uninformed, that the two-time defending national champion had gone out of its way to schedule a creampuff.

On the Monday before Alabama opened the season, the new wire service rankings landed like a thud in Tuscaloosa. Inexplicably, without playing a game, the Crimson Tide had fallen from first in the preseason AP poll to third, behind Michigan State and UCLA, who had notched their first wins. The initial UPI poll ranked Alabama fourth, behind Michigan State, UCLA and Southern Cal.

The demotion was historic.

Alabama fans wondered how in the devil their two-time defending national champions could be ranked number one in the preseason poll and then tumble to third without playing a game. No good answer was readily available, but the speculation centered on the Louisiana Tech game. Perhaps a few voters had been convinced to knock the Crimson Tide down a notch after noticing the lightweight opener? Or was something more sinister at work? No matter, most Alabama folks thought. It was early. The Tide had plenty of time to convince the voters. Winning would take care of everything.

Like Alabama, Michigan State returned a talented and experienced team, including a punishing defense led by lineman Bubba Smith and a potent offense led by quarterback Jimmy Raye. Duffy Daugherty's Spartans, who had captured the UPI national championship in 1965 before being upset in the Rose Bowl, which allowed Alabama the opening to win the AP title, were being called one of the strongest Big Ten teams of all time. With Michigan and Ohio State rebuilding, the Spartans' biggest test appeared to be a late-October home game against Purdue, led by quarterback Bob Griese, one of the early favorites in the Heisman Trophy race. The Boilermakers had taken Michigan State to the wire in '65, losing a 14–10 squeaker.

The dark horse in the national championship race looked like eighth-ranked Notre Dame, led by third-year coach Ara Parseghian. After a decade of mediocrity under three different head coaches—Terry Brennan, Joe Kuharich, and Hugh Devore, who combined for an uninspiring 51-48 mark and three losing seasons—Notre Dame hired Parseghian away from Big Ten lightweight Northwestern in 1964. Parseghian, an intense man and a terrific Xs and Os coach who ran a taut ship, won immediately. In 1964, the Fighting Irish arrived at the season finale undefeated and ranked atop both polls, then lost a 20–17 heartbreaker to Southern Cal, which allowed undefeated Alabama to ascend to the No. 1 ranking. With several major holes, including at quarterback, the Irish had slipped to a 7-2-1 finish in 1965. The presence of a veteran cast and a promising sophomore quarterback named Terry Hanratty gave Notre Dame fans renewed hope in 1966.

Alabama, however, controlled its own destiny. All the Crimson Tide had to do was win. The rest would take care of itself.

Unconcerned by the polls so early in the season, Bryant was understandably worried about how his team would react to playing such a clearly overmatched team. The Crimson Tide's 34–0 victory over Louisiana Tech before 65,000 fans at Legion Field was never close, and featured some bright spots, including the overall play of the defense, which limited the Bulldogs to minus 32 yards rushing. Linebacker Eddie Bo Rogers, a junior college transfer, made a terrific play to intercept a Phil Robertson pass, setting up the Tide's second touchdown. But the offense frequently sputtered. It was early yet, and the defense was clearly ahead of the offense, although Kenny "Snake" Stabler showed flashes of brilliance, including the 79-yard touchdown strike to his roommate, Dennis Homan.

"Anybody could look at the statistics and see that the Red [first-team offense] couldn't move the ball, and they won't be the Red team Monday," Bryant told reporters after the game. "I don't think I developed any oneness in them. That's my job, my responsibility, and we didn't have it."

When the players reported for practice Monday afternoon, as the third-ranked Tide prepared for a big game against Ole Miss, and checked the personnel roster, several members of the first team offense had been demoted to the second team (known internally as the Jetts), including tackle Jerry Duncan and guard Johnny Calvert. Both had graded well below passing in the Tide's strict performance evaluation system.

The coaches rode their butts all day long. They couldn't do anything right. Duncan and Calvert absorbed all the abuse and kept battling, crashing the line with tremendous force on every snap. At the end of practice, the two linemen took it upon themselves to retreat to the far side of the field and start running wind sprints as dusk fell across Tuscaloosa.

"That was us saying to Coach Bryant, who could see us from the tower, that we weren't going to surrender just 'cause we had a bad game," Duncan said. "We were willing to do whatever it took to get our positions back."

Especially after the dramatic comeback against Mississippi in 1965, which set the stage for all that was to come, the Alabama players took the date with Johnny Vaught's Rebels seriously. Ole Miss was Alabama's most ardent rival for SEC supremacy during the period. Long before Bryant returned to Tuscaloosa, forever altering the arc of Southern football, Vaught established Ole Miss as a college power. An offensive innovator who introduced the Split T to the South in the years after World War II, he also produced some of the greatest defenses in league history. His players hit hard and kept coming, and the two programs shared a grudging respect for each other.

The rivalry usually was contested from afar, because the two schools met only sporadically. The six-game rotation in the SEC, coordinated by the conference commissioner's office, required various compromises, which explained how two of the best teams in Ole Miss history—the undefeated national champions of 1960 and the undefeated, third-ranked Rebels of 1962—benefitted by not having to face 'Bama squads that finished fifth and ninth, respectively. It worked both ways. In 1961, the No. 1-ranked Tide caught a break by avoiding the No. 5 Rebels.

With many of the players returning from a team that finished 7-4 and knocked off Auburn in the Liberty Bowl, Ole Miss represented a closely watched test for the third-ranked Crimson Tide.

In the dressing room at Memorial Stadium in Jackson, Bryant stood before the players, announcing the lineup for the second game after a tough week of practice.

"Dowdy . . . Carroll . . ."

Then, while calling out the offensive linemen, he paused and looked up from his notes.

"Alright, Calvert and Duncan, I guess I'll give you one more chance," he said, manipulating the linemen with as much ease as during the photo stunt prior to the 1966 Orange Bowl.

Even with one of the greatest teams in Alabama history, Bryant knew how to make his players keep reaching toward an infinite horizon. Some things were beyond their grasp and some things were beyond their reach. In time, they would all learn the frustrating difference.

5. THE SNAKE

The game usually commenced after supper, behind closed doors in a meeting room upstairs at Bryant Hall.

"OK, here's a situation," Alabama backfield coach Ken Meyer would say in his nasally Pennsylvania accent, launching into a description of down, distance, field position, and conditions as he looked across the small round table at his quarterback. "What's your call?"

Kenny "Snake" Stabler sometimes stared into his coach's eyes without saying a word for a few precious seconds, milking the moment for all it was worth. Even as the situation congealed in his mind and he prepared to give his answer, his angular face usually contained the trace of a smile, because nothing ever bothered Slim Stabler's boy. Nothing.

After a solid rookie season backing up Steve Sloan in 1965, when he showed some electrifying moments running the option, great things were expected of the junior quarterback with the slithery moves. Despite tossing two touchdown passes and running for another score in the victory over Louisiana Tech, Stabler entered the second game of the 1966 season against Ole Miss still unproven as an SEC passer.

Apparently, the two-time defending national champions still had plenty to prove, too. Stuck in third place in the AP poll and fourth in the UPI poll, Alabama suddenly could feel Notre Dame's breath. After knocking off seventh-ranked Purdue, 26–14, on national television, the Fighting Irish jumped to fourth in the AP and third in the UPI. With young phenom Terry Hanratty outdueling Bob Griese, Notre Dame was beginning to look like a prime contender for the big prize. The possibility was greeted with a groan by Alabama fans everywhere, because competing against Notre Dame in the national championship wars was like running for Homecoming Queen against the prettiest girl in school.

While bugged by the poll situation, the Alabama players kept their minds focused on the trip to Jackson to face Johnny Vaught's Rebels. Stabler was making his first start against a conference opponent, and Alabama fans were anxious to see how Snake would perform under pressure.

Through the years, Bryant often explained how he liked to win with one or two great players and a bunch of others who were not so talented but thought they were great. This was an important part of the whole dynamic, and in 1966, the one great player, the single athlete for the ages, was Kenny Stabler. No one else was even in his league. Stabler was the real deal, and all it took to realize this was to watch him take a football in his hands, when his quick feet and deft passing touch became potent weapons in the cause of Alabama's championship thrust. He could absolutely take your breath away.

Forty years later, given the enormous changes in the game, how many of the athletes from 1966 could play on Alabama teams in the twenty-first century is debatable—not many—but along with Ray Perkins and Dennis Homan, Kenny Stabler was blessed with the right stuff to make him a star anytime, anywhere. Snake's ability was timeless, like Sinatra's voice or Shakespeare's way with words.

Meyer, who tutored Joe Namath and Steve Sloan to greatness, could see the fun-loving good ole boy from lower Alabama was something special even before he ascended to the starting job. Heading into the Ole Miss game, his left arm remained something of a question mark, but it didn't take a Phi Beta Kappa to see how Stabler could turn the corner on the option.

One reason for Meyer's faith was the methodical and calculating way Stabler approached those twice-weekly tactical exercises, which allowed the coach to see how his star pupil's mind worked.

To test his decision-making skills, his mastery of the offense, and his understanding of the defensive personnel he was scheduled to face, Meyer required Stabler to provide him with a play, a formation, and a snap count, and then the coach concocted a defensive reaction out of his own mind. Often, Meyer asked Snake to justify his call, which provided a revealing expedition into his reasoning process. Sometimes, playing God in their make-believe world, he threw his quarterback for a big loss or called a penalty, just to complicate the situation and force him to react on the spot.

"Kenny was a quick learner and a very logical thinker," said Meyer, who spent five years on the 'Bama staff. "He knew how to apply what he had learned to make good decisions, and you could see that in the game we played."

But some things could not be simulated, measured, or learned.

Some intangibles could only be stimulated in the heat of heart-pounding, adrenaline-pumping, sweat-dripping competition.

Nobody taught Stabler to be fearless. He acquired this mysterious characteristic the hard way, in a dark, sad, painful place, and it was more than a weapon or a plate of armor or a muscle he flexed in the face of an oncoming rush. It was his essence.

Like many of his friends in Baldwin County, Lee Roy "Slim" Stabler answered Uncle Sam's call and went off to fight in World War II, becoming an army machine-gunner in the drive to defeat Hitler. But he never came back. Not all of him. Not quite all. Slim left something over there, and after he returned to Alabama and carved out a career as an auto mechanic, married one of the prettiest girls in Foley, and started a family, he struggled to deal with the lingering pain.

"My father always had these demons inside, and I think it had a lot to do with the war," said Kenny Stabler, born on Christmas Day in 1945, in the glow of the post-war euphoria. "It probably also had to do with the guilt of not making more money, not being able to support my mother the way he wanted. He was a big, tough, mean alcoholic, and he took his frustrations out on my family."

Most of the time, Slim was fun-loving and affable, especially when he was hunting with his boy and his friends, strumming his guitar, or playing the occasional practical joke, but he was prone to dark moods, which arrived without warning, no doubt exacerbated by the drinking.

Despite Slim's abuse, his wife Sally, a beloved figure in the community who worked as a nurse for a local doctor, endured for years without leaving or fighting back. The alcoholism that controlled Slim became a burden for his oldest son, forcing him to deal with all sorts of grown-up responsibilities and consequences way before his time. "It really worked on Snake that he couldn't do more to protect his mama," said Alabama fullback David Chatwood, his childhood friend.

One night, sixteen-year-old Kenny walked into his house some time after dark to find his father pointing a shotgun at the rest of the family. Slim, who smelled of alcohol, said he intended to blow them all away. He offered no reason. But it was the whiskey. Kenny knew it was the whiskey talking. Slim's finger twitched on the trigger as tears rolled down Sally's face.

After trying to talk his father down from his madness, Kenny, a splinter of a man at 6'1" and 165 pounds, struggled to wrestle the shotgun away from his daddy, a towering figure who stood 6'5" and weighed 240 pounds, with especially large and powerful forearms. At one point, Slim turned the gun on his boy. Kenny stared into the barrel, which filled up his world, and in that instant, not knowing whether he would live or die, he instinctively kept fighting, because he knew it was time for him to be strong.

After he finally won control of the gun and Slim stumbled away to sleep it off, Kenny tucked the weapon away where his father couldn't find it the next time he went on one of his rampages.

"I had to be the one to stop that . . . I had to keep my father from killing my family," Stabler said.

The experience of growing up with an abusive father marked Stabler deeply. It wounded him immeasurably, but on another level, it toughened him, infusing him with the belief that he could handle anything, which also inured him to a certain amount of pain.

Rebelling against the pathos and belligerence that dominated his father's life, Stabler grew into a gregarious, happy-go-lucky young man. Although tormented by the past, it was as if he thought he could will himself to be carefree, and so he did, with all the apparent ease of a quarterback draw. In the process, he rejected some of the things his old man represented, even as Slim remained an ambivalent constant in his life, even as Kenny loved and idolized his daddy, continuing to share a mutual appreciation for fast cars, hunting, and music. Slim often showed up at practice in Tuscaloosa, walking the sideline like some rich alumnus, and was destined, despite all that had come before, to one day save his boy's career and very likely his life, in one fell swoop. Even the fine line between love and hate can be blurred by two competing moments dripping with such irony.

Forever living in the moment, Snake's effortless charm and country-boy authenticity made him the life of every party. On any given night during his college days, his twangy, high-pitched voice could be heard entertaining a crowd of players in somebody's dorm room, because Kenny always had a good joke at the ready. He enjoyed making people around him feel good.

"It was impossible not to like Kenny," said fellow quarterback Joe Kelley. "He was just such a loveable guy."

All fun all the time, Stabler was not the type of young man to spend much energy considering that his appreciation for a stiff drink might be another dangerous aspect of his father's legacy. Years later, while Stabler was leading the Oakland Raiders to the Super Bowl, head coach John Madden related a conversation when he complimented Snake on his ability to throw a certain low-trajectory pass. "That's right," he replied with a big grin, "I'm a low-ball thrower and a highball drinker."

Stabler enjoyed living on the edge. On many nights during his Alabama days, he and roommate Dennis Homan sneaked out of the dorm to have a few beers and chase girls.

For a while, they dated a pair of lovelies at the Mississippi University for

Women, frequently making the long drive home when they were in no shape to sit behind the wheel. Numerous times, Stabler hopped in his souped-up 1963 Chevrolet Impala and negotiated the four-hour trip to his hometown of Foley after practice just to see some girl, and then drove back in the wee hours of the morning. Homan often covered for his buddy, placing the pillows in his bed just so, to make dorm director Gary White think Stabler was snoozing when he opened the door for bed check.

"Snake was such a free spirit," Homan said. "I had a tough time keeping up with him. He had tremendous stamina. He could get by on two or three hours of sleep and still be sharp the next day."

In 1966, Stabler and Homan developed an eye for the same girl during one of their post-practice drives through sorority row, which could have spelled trouble with some competitive athletes. Not those two. Snake tried to get a date with her but for some reason threw an incomplete pass. He laughed it off, even as his buddy made another thrilling catch. Slightly more than a year later, the beautiful coed became Homan's wife.

One night during the off-season leading up to the 1966 season, Stabler and Homan sneaked back into the dorm after curfew. Neither one was feeling any pain. For some reason, as they crept up the stairs to their bedroom, Snake pulled one of the fire extinguishers off the wall and prepared to squirt his buddy. When they rounded the corner, Gary White loomed in the hallway like a stop sign, a lit cigarette dangling from his lips. Stabler, startled to see the dorm director, pointed the fire extinguisher at him playfully and pulled the trigger, spraying foam across the hall and soaking White, causing sparks to fly off his cigarette.

"Get to your room!" a furious White scolded the giggling players, wiping the sudsy liquid from his face.

Several hours later, well before dawn, White awakened the quarterback and his intended receiver and told them to report to the practice field, where defensive line coach Ken Donahue was waiting to administer their punishment. Donahue forced them to run until they threw up. Then he ran them some more . . . until they couldn't stand up.

Snake often pushed the boundaries of Alabama's regimented system, but, like every other member of the team, he always paid the price. No one cut him an inch of slack.

"I probably spent as much time on the practice field at five o'clock in the morning as five in the afternoon," Stabler conceded.

Even as he struggled to escape his difficult childhood, Stabler was ruled by it in ways he was still too young to understand. The same invisible hand that often tempted him down a reckless path also led him toward greatness on the football field. Like so many other people, he drew the strength that made him whole from a moment of heartbreaking anguish.

"When you've stared down the barrel of a shotgun in your own home at sixteen," he said, "third-and-twenty's not so bad."

In a more conventional sense, Kenny could trace the roots of his athletic career to a combination of his father's support, meddling, and genes.

An outstanding high school athlete who was forced to drop out to help feed the family when his own father died, Slim cultivated a love of sports in his son from an early age. Slim, Sally, and Kenny became a constant presence at the Foley High football and basketball games when Kenny was growing up, and when he started playing himself, he had no bigger fan than the old machine gunner. Sometimes, many times, he pushed his son too hard, such as the time when, after an afternoon of drinking, he forced Kenny to apologize to his baseball teammates for making an error that cost them the game, charging way past the fine line between correcting his boy and humiliating him.

Like many frustrated former athletes, Slim lived vicariously through his son's accomplishments, and it was the father who started thinking about college scholarships and pro contracts way before the son. By the time Kenny reached Foley High, his skills on the football field and the baseball diamond caught everyone's attention. Playing mostly defense for an undefeated team as a tenth grader, he also returned kicks, and after the stadium full of people roared while watching him juke and cut and zig and zag back and forth across the field on an electrifying punt return for a long touchdown, one of his coaches said, "Damn, that boy runs like a snake."

When Stabler eventually won the starting quarterback job, his quickness and moves running the ball became the catalyst to an undefeated season and a conference championship. The chance to play pro baseball briefly enticed him—as a pitcher, he once outdueled future major leaguer Don Sutton, from nearby Pensacola—but the chance to play for Bryant was too much to turn down, and besides, his daddy convinced him he could make more money in the long run playing pro football.

In Tuscaloosa, Pat Trammell set the standard. A good athlete but a great leader, the fierce competitor who quarterbacked Alabama's 1961 national championship team cast a mighty shadow over all those who followed in his footsteps, despite his comparatively modest skills. "He can't run. He can't pass. All he can do is beat you," Bryant often said in praise of Trammell, exaggerating to make a point that connected with all who labored in the hopes of someday wearing a red jersey. With the intense future doctor in the huddle, the Bear didn't have to worry about kicking ass, because Trammell's footprints could often be seen on the other players' pants. At once feared and beloved, Trammell transcended his rather ordinary skills, setting an example others were expected to follow.

After watching the enormously talented Joe Namath and the precise Steve Sloan successfully follow in Trammell's footsteps, earning All-America honors while leading the Crimson Tide to the national championship, Stabler realized he was stepping into one of college football's most pressurized situations. To be considered a success, he would have to do more than score touchdowns and dazzle fawning crowds. He would be judged on whether he could lead 'Bama to the promised land, like Trammell, Namath, and Sloan.

More than a dozen high school quarterbacks annually signed with the Crimson Tide in 1963, '64, and '65, and in the beginning, Stabler was just another promising talent who needed to be tested.

Wayne Trimble, one of the best all-around athletes ever to suit up in Tuscaloosa, seized the early lead until he suffered an injury in relief of Joe Namath as a sophomore in 1964.

Several other players competed for the position at one time or another, including Columbiana's Conrad Fowler, Haleyville's Jimmy Israel, and Birmingham's Bobby Johns. After a tremendous high school career, Gadsden's David Beddingfield made a run at the job in the spring of 1966 before being sidelined with a severe back injury.

"Coming in, I thought for sure I was going to be the next Joe Namath," said Johns, who starred at quarterback for the famed Shorty White at Birmingham's Banks High School. "It didn't take me long to figure out there were a bunch of guys who thought the same thing."

After a dispute with his high school coach, which caused several programs, including Alabama, to stop recruiting him, Birmingham's Eddie Propst turned down scholarship offers from Clemson, Arkansas State, and Utah State to walk on in Tuscaloosa in the spring of 1964. His daddy, an Alabama law school grad, sold a piece of property to pay Eddie's way through school and allow him to reach for his dream. A huge 'Bama fan who had always yearned to play for the Bear, Propst competed for the quarterback job as a freshman, and like so many others, was eventually moved elsewhere. But he earned a scholarship.

"Playing quarterback at Alabama was special, and a lot of guys wanted to follow in that line," said Joe Kelley, who entered the season third on the depth chart, behind Stabler and Trimble. "But Kenny was just better than the rest of us."

Instead of coddling Stabler, Bryant leaned on him. Hard. Constantly chal-

lenging him to reach beyond his natural ability, the coach also spent a significant amount of time playing with Snake's mind, reinforcing the team concept,
making sure he didn't get too big for his britches.

In practice, whenever Stabler rolled down the line on the option and tossed
some wild pitch at precisely the right time, the Bear often clicked on his bullhorn and yelled down from the tower: "Stabler, you're luckier than a shit-house
rat!"

The big man also liked to remind him, in front of the team, "I've never
trusted left-handed crap shooters or left-handed quarterbacks."

But Stabler was tough. He could take it all.

It was easy to see how his talent lifted the 1966 Crimson Tide to another
level, but his mental toughness was an equally formidable force.

The psychological games could be internal, as well. Many quarterbacks
would have been permanently scarred by the experience of throwing the ball
out of bounds on fourth down in the waning moments against Tennessee. Not
Stabler. It certainly bothered him, because he was an incredibly competitive
athlete, but it didn't linger in his mind. It didn't dent his confidence. That
space belonged to him, and it was untouchable, shielded by the mental toughness, which pervaded every aspect of his life.

Instead of wilting from the pressure, Stabler embraced the challenge of trying to measure up, determined to satisfy Bryant, who became the most important influence in his life.

After Stabler threw a jump pass in a game—a maneuver former Alabama
quarterback Harry Gilmer made famous at the end of World War II, but not
embraced by the boss, because it was inherently risky—Bryant collared him on
the sideline and blessed him out like crazy, no doubt utilizing some of his favorite obscenities for emphasis. Homan approached Snake after Bryant walked
away and asked what coach had told him. "He said he didn't recommend it,"
Stabler said with a grin.

Bryant believed in winning with defense and special teams. Because his defenses usually dominated so completely, the Alabama offenses rarely needed to
score very often to close the deal, which allowed him to attack with a ball control philosophy, placing an emphasis on establishing the run. In the mid-1960s,
as the sport transitioned to the two-platoon era, the vast majority of major
teams clung to a similar philosophy. The wide-open passing attack remained
rare, mostly limited to marginal names like Tulsa, Florida State, and Brigham
Young. In 1966, Florida, which relied on the cannon of Steve Spurrier, was the
only member of one of the big conferences to rank among the NCAA's top ten
in passing.

Alabama's aerial game was potent, but sparingly applied. Namath, one of the greatest passers of all time, threw the ball a total of 146 times in 1962, his most prolific season—fewer than 15 times per game. When the situation required him to win through the air, Bryant proved incredibly flexible and pragmatic, as evidenced by the Orange Bowl victory over Nebraska, when Steve Sloan put on a clinic. Depending too much on the pass was an unnecessary risk, however, and he could often be heard reminding reporters that "three things can happen when you pass, and two of them are bad" [an incompletion and an interception].

Operating mostly out of the I-formation and sometimes out of the pro set, Alabama's option-oriented offense was a relatively simple union of power and finesse. No one held the title of offensive coordinator in those days, but Meyer, who was directly responsible for developing schemes and managing the playbook, handled most of the duties usually associated with the position. He added various wrinkles to the 'Bama offense to take advantage of Namath's talents, and then tweaked the system to exploit the unique gifts of Sloan and Stabler. Stabler's mobility allowed more rollouts, where he forced the opposition to defend against the run and pass.

Alabama rotated a series of solid fullbacks and halfbacks, including Les Kelley, Gene Raburn, Frank Canterbury, Ed Morgan, and David Chatwood. But without a game breaker in the backfield, Stabler, who had already demonstrated his ability to beat people with his feet—rushing for 328 yards as a sophomore—was the key. The 'Bama offense was geared around his ability to run, pitch, fake, pass—and improvise.

"Kenny was the most creative of all the quarterbacks we had in those days," Meyer said. "There were times [during their tactical games at the dorm] when he would come up with something that was a little off the wall, and I learned to try not to kill that, because Kenny's improvisational skill was one of the things that made him so good."

With both Dennis Homan and Ray Perkins returning at receiver, defenses were expected to double-team one or the other, creating plenty of opportunities for a quarterback with Stabler's gifts.

Looking for a way to empower Stabler's creativity, Bryant and Meyer devised a new wrinkle. It was called the automatic, and in an era before college quarterbacks routinely checked off at the line of scrimmage, the ploy featured some of the characteristics of an audible. On certain pass plays, if Stabler could look out and see that Perkins or Homan was double covered, he would change the play at the line and give it to the fullback, usually Les Kelley. If the defense walked the strong safety up to the line of scrimmage after he called the Tide's bread-and-butter off-tackle play, the flanker and wideout knew to run eight-yard quick outs, because Snake was going to fake to the fullback and dump it off short.

Like all of the Alabama quarterbacks of the day, Stabler called most of the plays within a tight framework. Generally speaking, the Alabama game plans tended to prevent passing in certain situations, and the wristband he wore served as a cheat sheet for plays and formations, just in case. Stabler was charged with complete authority to call whatever he wanted in nearly all situations, but he was also accountable to the big guy, and if he decided to stray from the game plan, he knew he'd better have a damn good reason, especially if it failed to work.

"Kenny was the kind of quarterback who knew how to make something happen, one way or another, and Coach Bryant loved that about him," said longtime assistant coach Clem Gryska.

Like Namath before him, Stabler gave Alabama not only a potent threat to run and throw, but also an innate knack for being able to see the whole field and read defenses in a flash. His ability to perceive and plunder vulnerabilities often amazed his teammates as well as his coaches, who learned to trust his vision and his judgment.

Despite the fact that Stabler was, in the words of his good buddy Dennis Homan, "no mental giant," something happened to him when he stepped onto a football field. Long after his college playing days, sports psychologists began talking about "the Zone," the mental state, which allows an athlete to achieve a level of supreme focus, creating the climate for optimum performance. The world is full of talented athletes, but reaching such a mysterious and powerful state can be the difference between greatness and wasted potential. The way Stabler was able to block out all distractions, tap into a sometimes spooky calm, and perform consistently, even in the face of the most adverse conditions, suggested he was able to flip a switch and lead Alabama's offense from the Zone.

"I think he might have been the first one there," joked Homan.

Like most of the other starters on offense, Homan broke into the lineup under the direction of Sloan, an incredibly disciplined player who set school records for passing efficiency but was much less of a threat to run than Stabler.

After starring as a back at Muscle Shoals High School in the northwestern corner of the state, Homan appeared headed for a career as an Alabama runner. In those days, the Alabama varsity tossed very few passes to the backs, but the freshman team often was used to experiment offensively, and so the coaches were impressed when Homan caught several passes out of the backfield during his freshman season. With a bunch of solid backs battling for playing time, the coaches moved Homan to wide out heading into his sophomore year, but with veterans David Ray, Tommy Tolleson, and Ray Perkins ahead of him on the depth chart, he didn't play a snap for the first six games.

On a fateful day in the middle of the 1965 campaign, with 'Bama locked in a tight battle against Mississippi State in Jackson, Homan was standing on the sidelines watching the offense struggle. He had a tendency to talk to himself in those days, and as he noticed a weakness in the Bulldogs' defense, he blurted something out, without thinking.

"That cornerback can be beaten inside!" Homan yelled above the din of the crowd. "He's playing too far outside!"

Bryant, standing nearby, heard Homan and grabbed him by the jersey, pulling him out of his trance.

"Go in there and do it!" he said.

Momentarily stunned, his heart racing, he trotted onto the field, substituted himself for Tolleson, and told Sloan about the exchange with the boss. Moments later, Sloan stood in the pocket and zipped the ball with authority as Homan ran a route toward the center of the field.

"I was so wide open it looked like I was out to practice early," Homan recalled. "I remember watching the ball coming toward me like it was in slow-motion, thinking to myself: There's no way you can drop this ball!"

The 65-yard touchdown strike proved to be the difference in 'Bama's 10–7 victory, and Homan's bold-type introduction to the Alabama nation.

Teaming with Stabler, Homan would quickly become a household name all across the state of Alabama.

Timing was everything for Homan, Stabler, and many others who owed their positions to opportunities presented and seized. In Stabler's case, the flashes of brilliance he displayed in backing up Sloan—including his two-point conversion scamper on a fake kick against Florida State—counted even more than his methodical dominance of the quarterback derby during practice heading into the '66 season.

Like the three men who preceded him, he brought something more to the huddle—something invisible but powerful. On the field as off, the Snake could not be rattled. A cool customer who thrived under pressure, the man who once saved his entire family from tragedy was propelled by an unshakable confidence, insulated by a feeling of supreme invincibility.

The players could smell such certitude, and they were prepared to follow the scent all the way to the history books.

The sun was starting to fade by the time Ray Perkins stepped off the bus, into the procession of red blazers cutting through the crowd at Jackson's Mississippi Memorial Stadium.

"Raymond?"

The boss, standing off to the side in a coat and tie, was the only person in the world who called Walter Ray Perkins by the full extension of his middle name.

"Yes, sir," the senior receiver said as he approached his coach.

"Raymond, how would you feel if you had to ride a bus all the way from Oxford to Jackson and then play a game?" Bryant asked.

Perkins let the question tumble in his head for a moment.

"Well, coach," he said, "I think I'd be a little tired."

Bryant, whose team had flown to Jackson the day before and had spent most of Saturday relaxing around the Holiday Inn, nodded his head and walked away without saying a word.

Never known to whip his players into a frenzy before kickoff, like the clichéd version of some fire-breathing coach, Bryant nevertheless was always attuned to the psychology of the game. He never stopped looking for an edge, even on game day, and he knew how to use one seemingly innocuous exchange to infuse his players with another jolt of confidence. In this case, he wanted to plant the seed in Perkins's mind—and probably several others—that while Alabama was rested and primed for battle, Ole Miss must be a little weary from the journey.

Little things. So many little things coalesced in the making of another championship team.

As a packed house of 42,345 converged on a cool early October evening, the Crimson Tide and the Rebels fought to a 0–0 first quarter dominated by defense. On Ole Miss' third play, Dicky Thompson stepped in front of a pass and returned it 20 yards, putting 'Bama in business at the Rebels' 35 yard line. Stabler methodically led the Tide downfield, mostly with his arm . . . five yards to Perkins . . . nine yards to Wayne Cook . . . three yards to Homan. The pressure on Snake was stout, and the Ole Miss defenders minimized 'Bama's yards after the catch. When Les Kelley was stopped on third and short, Steve Davis came on to attempt a 36-yard field goal, but missed, wide left.

After the 'Bama defense forced a punt from deep in Ole Miss territory with just 1:57 remaining in the first half, the game still scoreless, Stabler hit Jerry Duncan, the one-time North Carolina reject, on first down for 15 yards on a tackle eligible pass, one of the gadget plays that had proven crucial in beating the Rebels in 1965. Five snaps later, Les Kelley bulled his way in from the one and Davis booted the extra point to give 'Bama a 7–0 lead with forty seconds left in the half.

After trading punts in the third quarter, Stabler marched the Tide downfield. The drive started with a 19-yard pass to Perkins on first down and ended with a 28-yard touchdown to the pride of Petal, Mississippi, who was on his way to a memorable night in his home state.

Early in the fourth quarter, with Alabama holding a convincing 14–0 lead, Dicky Thompson stepped in front of an Ole Miss pass near midfield, pulled it to his chest, and headed upfield. Out of the corner of one eye, he saw one of the Rebels' biggest and baddest offensive linemen lumbering toward him.

"I'm full of steam, all wound up, and I'm thinking to myself: I'll really punish that guy when he tries to tackle me," Thompson recalled. "Well, we collided and I bounced off that big ole' boy like a basketball. He about killed me."

Thompson tumbled to the ground, but he held on to the ball, and then pulled himself off the turf. Not even a mad giant could ruin little Dicky's career night.

What would have been Thompson's SEC record fourth interception of the evening was called back when safety Johnny Mosley was flagged for interfering with another receiver, a hit that did not affect the play. Instead, the tenacious young man whose football career had nearly been destroyed by a severe lung problem was forced to stay in the game, and for a few moments, he was not quite sure where he was. But after a while, his head stopped spinning, and he kept chasing the ball, eventually stopping yet another Ole Miss drive dead in its tracks with his school-record third interception of the night. One breath at a time, he kept proving all those doctors wrong.

While the defense rose to the occasion time after time, holding the Rebels scoreless on four trips inside the 'Bama 35 yard line, the night belonged to Kenny Stabler.

Facing one of the SEC's toughest defenses, Stabler ran the option like a pro, dipping and dodging and making people miss, while silencing all lingering doubts about his passing skills. Completing a school record 16 of 19 attempts for 144 yards, many of them against a menacing rush, he led Alabama to a decisive 17–7 victory. Displaying a deft mastery of the short pass, recognizing and exploiting vulnerabilities in the Ole Miss defense, he methodically attacked the Rebels, connecting 9 times with the rested and relaxed Perkins, another Alabama record, for 94 yards.

"[Stabler] surprised us," Vaught said after the game. "He's a lot better player than we thought he was. He's quicker, he throws a much better short pass, and he just keeps you off balance."

Across the state of Alabama, fans of all ages crowded around radios, listening to every syllable out of play-by-play man John Forney's mouth with sweet anticipation. With every clutch completion, every moment of poise in the face of a clawing rush, Alabama supporters slowly started to take Stabler into their hearts. It was early yet, and he still had a long way to go to be considered in the same league with Trammell, Namath, and Sloan, but on that memorable night when everything went right, when he could hardly miss, Snake began to earn his place in the sacred pantheon of Crimson Tide football heroes. More than an important victory, it was also a night of reassurance—that the torch had been successfully passed.

In the next day's edition of *The Birmingham News*, veteran columnist Alf Van Hoose gave voice to the thought ringing in many heads: "Kenny Stabler answered once and for all the persistent questions about his left arm. The Snake can throw."

During his postgame press conference, Vaught became the first notable figure to say aloud what many knowledgeable observers around the Alabama program had been privately thinking for months. "They're a better football team than they were last year," he said. "They are more dangerous . . . and they punch it at you."

This was a staggering thought, to suggest that the 1966 Alabama football team was already better than the 1965 Crimson Tide, which had fought back from the brink to capture the big prize. But Vaught was no blowhard. He was not packing the Bear's head. He was the first to say it, but he would not be the last.

6. QUICK LITTLE BOYS

After guiding his Crimson Tide through a typical Friday walk-through in sweats prior to the campus opener against Clemson, Bryant bolted through the locker room door wearing a big grin. A mischievous grin. The rotund man at his side looked around at the Alabama players, scattered about the room in various states of undress, unaware that he was walking into a trap.

Bryant wanted to show Frank Howard some of the quick little boys who were bidding for a third consecutive national championship.

"Hell, Bear," the Clemson head coach said. "You ain't foolin' nobody."

Like many others, Howard, a native Alabamian who had played on the line for the Crimson Tide in the days of Wallace Wade, believed Bryant had to be exaggerating the weights of some of his players. No way some of those guys could be as small as they were listed in the program.

In the days leading up to his highly anticipated first meeting with his alma mater at Denny Stadium, Howard seized several opportunities to raise a skeptical eye at Alabama's program weights. "I notice that Bear's got some mighty small boys," he said. "My doctor told me I had to lose some weight, so while I'm down there I'm going to weigh on his scales."

At some point after seeing that quote or one similar to it, a lightblub clicked on in Bryant's head.

Raised on a farm outside the tiny community of Barlow Bend, Alabama, near Mobile, the once 185-pound Howard was one of the smallest players on the unusually large 1930 Crimson Tide, a unit so big that an Atlanta sportswriter compared it to a herd of stampeding elephants, launching the school's long association with one of the sport's most iconic mascots. Despite his relatively slight stature, he became a ferocious competitor on Wallace Wade's final Alabama team, which capped an undefeated season by clobbering Washington State in the Rose Bowl, 24–0.

One of the most colorful characters ever to walk a sideline, Howard led the underdog South Carolina school to most of its greatest moments on the gridiron up to 1966. Playing for many years in the old Southern Conference before becoming a founding member of the Atlantic Coast Conference, then considered a second-tier football league, Howard produced two undefeated teams, including the 1948 Tigers, who upset Missouri in the Gator Bowl to finish eleventh in the final AP rankings.

He also knew a thing or two about drama and self-promotion. Following his lead, Clemson started referring to Memorial Stadium as "Death Valley," which eventually led to an unusual demonstration of fandom. In the early 1960s, Clemson alumnus S. C. Jones made a trip to the remote outpost of Death Valley, California, and returned to South Carolina with a piece of white flint, which, for some unknown reason, he had picked up out in the desert. Jones presented the rock to Howard as a gift—from one Death Valley to another. The stone lingered in Howard's office for several years, but after a moment of inspiration, Jones and the piece of white flint gained a measure of immortality on September 26, 1966—just two weeks before the Tigers ventured to Tuscaloosa—when Howard's rock was mounted on a pedestal at the stadium and dedicated prior to a big victory over Virginia. Why it is supposed to be significant was long ago lost to history, but forty years later, Clemson players still run down the hill and touch Howard's Rock for good luck.

The most venerated figure in the history of Clemson athletics was once asked by successor Charley Pell—also a former 'Bama lineman—why he had turned down Bryant's application for an assistant coach's position prior to World War II. "There was no way I was going to hire Bear," Howard told Pell with a familiar laugh. "In no time, he'd have slit my throat, drank my blood, and had my job."

Well known for his quick wit, which made him a hit on the rubber chicken circuit, the man who doubled as Clemson's athletic director once was petitioned by a group of students to launch an intercollegiate sculling program. "I'm not wasting any of our money on a sport where the object is to sit down and go backwards," he quipped.

Frank Howard loved a good joke.

After introducing the Clemson coach to some of his players, who greeted him warmly, Bryant escorted him to a nearby scale, an industrial-sized contraption with a large face that could be read halfway across the room. Howard said he wanted to take a measure of 'Bama's scales, and here was his chance.

Suddenly wondering if he was being set up, especially since a photographer was standing by to take his picture, the potbellied Howard, who normally weighed more than 260 pounds, stepped onto the scale and watched as the needle jostled back and forth before settling at 237 pounds.

"By God, Bear, they're accurate after all!" he said with a grin.

Surreptitiously, Bryant had instructed equipment manager Willie Meadows to make sure that the scale subtracted about 30 pounds off anyone who stepped on it, just to poke a little fun at the intense interest in Alabama's weights.

Paul Bryant loved a good joke, too.

Despite the skepticism and the good-natured ribbing, there was absolutely nothing phony about Alabama's numbers. The weights that appeared in the program were measured during the grueling heat of two-a-days, which tended to represent a low point for most of the athletes, but the reality that the Crimson Tide was dominated by a bunch of skinny runts was impossible to deny.

Size mattered. It most certainly mattered, empowering Alabama in unusual ways as the Crimson Tide plotted a course for the history books.

Heading into the 1966 season, a feature in the *Birmingham Post-Herald* captured the perception hanging over many of Alabama's athletes: "There must be times when Tom Somerville feels like writing across his chest, 'I'm a football player.' He looks more like a manager than a starting football player on a championship team."

Somerville, a native of Memphis, visited Vanderbilt and hoped to win a scholarship to play for the lowly Commodores, who routinely battled Kentucky and Tulane to break out of the SEC cellar. Although he wanted to play somewhere more prestigious, he was realistic. Even those hopes were dashed, however, when a Vandy assistant coach called him several days later. "I'm sorry," he said, "but we're just not recruiting linemen as small as you are." He was devastated.

Fortunately, Howard Schnellenberger, who recruited the area for the Crimson Tide, saw him play and liked his tenacity and quickness. As a sophomore in 1965, the 5'9", 179-pound Somerville started at noseguard and routinely whipped offensive linemen who outweighed him by thirty pounds or more.

A tough customer who was determined to leave it all on the field, Somerville, like many of his teammates, played way above his head. Once, after making a tackle on a sweep, the man known affectionately as Stumpy pulled himself off the grass and walked back to the huddle. "Think I'm hurt," he said with a grimace, as he held up what turned out to be a compound dislocation of his finger. His whole hand throbbed with pain. The digit looked so bad, two of his teammates started throwing up, just looking at the way the bone was contorted, and the official was forced to move the ball to the opposite hash mark to avoid all the vomit.

Naturally, Somerville sucked it up and kept playing.

It seemed inconceivable that Alabama, the most dominant football program in the South, could sign a lineman like Somerville who was deemed too puny to play for Vanderbilt, a program then in the midst of eight straight losing seasons. Inconceivable, but true. Somerville was just one example. The team was filled with similar tales. In addition to the highly recruited studs like Kenny Stabler and Wayne Trimble, the Crimson Tide included many athletes who were passed over by other programs because they were considered too small or not talented enough.

The tension between brute force and finesse is as old as the game itself, and for as long as coaches have salivated over gigantic specimens who could administer punishment in family-size doses, the lure of a quick little squirt who could zoom to the ball or with the ball has been equally irresistible. The choice always represented a trade-off. Putting a bunch on the field that was too small tended to leave a team vulnerable to being pummeled. Playing a group that was too big tended to leave a team handicapped in the face of an opponent's mobility, especially with the passing game. Even as athletes, like the general population, started growing larger during the twentieth century, the one-platoon game acted as a kind of buffer against too much size, because running up and down the field for sixty minutes and playing both offense and defense required a tremendous amount of stamina and versatility. With the advent of two-platoon, those days were numbered.

Because they had learned from experience what great equalizers quickness, stamina, and steely resolve could be, the Alabama coaches did not automatically rule someone out just because he failed to meet some preconceived standards for size and strength. Alabama recruited plenty of impressive-looking athletes, but the emphasis the program placed on speed, quickness, and conditioning tended to eliminate many of the large players who signed with the Crimson Tide, such as the giant lineman who collapsed during gym class and was carried out on a stretcher, never to be seen again. How much talent a player possessed was irrelevant, if he was unable to stay vertical in February.

Driven by the desire to produce versatile, scrappy players who could be trained to persevere, Bryant hated "fat bellies," and even as the sport transitioned to the age of the specialist, which lessened the need for endurance, he refused to tolerate large athletes unable to withstand the punishment. A big player caught absolutely no slack at Alabama. If anything, a giant who towered over the midgets was pushed harder. In fact, Bryant and his coaches tended to assume that a player with a large body should naturally be able to muster a similarly oversized level of desire and work ethic. According to the Bear's Theory of Proportionality, he didn't see a thing in the world wrong with expecting more from a player who obviously came to practice with an abundance of natural ability. If a big player could not play big, he really was not so big after all.

Case in point: Steven Wright, a highly recruited lineman from Louisville, Kentucky, arrived in Tuscaloosa in 1960 as a 6'6", 280-pound mountain of muscle and athleticism. He could have gone anywhere, and indeed, he turned down more than seventy other scholarship offers because he wanted to play for the best in the business. He didn't realize he was a square peg trying to fit into a round hole. Because the smaller, quicker players could run circles around him, the Alabama coaching staff struggled with how to deal with him. Instead of being gratified by his size and strength, Bryant told him he was too big and demanded that he lose sixty pounds with all deliberate speed.

Desperate to measure up, Wright went on a crash diet and eventually dropped fifty pounds, but in the process, lost most of his strength. "I was damned if I do and damned if I don't," said Wright, who later played for the Green Bay Packers. "They were winning with all those small players, and I just didn't fit the mold. I was just in the wrong place at the wrong time. They didn't know what to do with me."

When Alabama coaches spoke about quickness, they generally referred to a player's relative ability to react and reach the point of attack. The player who could get out of his stance first and beat his opponent to the punch invariably was able to seize the advantage, and when empowered with good technique, he was often able to turn an opponent's superior size into a disadvantage.

Deeply intertwined in the mysterious process of how the brain processed information and telegraphed instructions to various parts of the body, Alabama's determination to promote quick reactions among its athletes permeated everything from the wave drills in gym class to the three-on-three Oklahoma drills during the heat of two-a-days. The staff knew that they could not produce quickness in a player, but certainly believed that they could coach an already quick athlete to lean on his internal accelerator.

More than a winning strategy, Bryant's reliance on so many small players became a central part of the team's identity, tapping into the mythology of Alabama football. To Alabamians who felt like underdogs and clung to the Crimson Tide as a validation of their little corner of the world, the stunning achievements of the undersized teams of the mid-1960s assumed a kind of David vs. Goliath higher truth, making the players seem even more heroic.

Especially after the stunning victory over Nebraska in the 1966 Orange Bowl, the Alabama offensive line attracted significant attention. The starting unit, which returned intact from 1965 except at center, included senior tight end Wayne Cook (6'1", 197), senior tackle Cecil Dowdy (6'0", 206), junior guard Bruce Stephens (5'11", 181), senior center Jimmy Carroll (6'0", 193), senior guard Johnny Calvert (5'11", 197) and senior tackle Jerry Duncan (5'11", 185). In many ways, the rugged bunch, which averaged a skinny 192 pounds per man, smaller than every opponent on its schedule, smaller than many high school lines of the day, was emblematic of the entire team. A group including Byrd Williams, Chris Vagotis, Terry Kilgore, and Billy Johnson also saw significant action. Loaded with overachievers who somehow found a way to win, the unit's success represented a triumph not only of quickness but also of steely will, clever tactics, malleability, and an abiding need to hang on to Alabama football for dear life.

No one personified all of these qualities quite like Jerry Duncan, the one-time high school fullback from North Carolina who owed his scholarship to Bryant's gut feeling. Considered too untalented to win a job in the backfield, he first broke into the lineup as the sprint man on the kickoff team in 1964. His assignment was to race downfield and take out the leading edge of the kick coverage team by attacking at the feet and trying to wipe out three men with one good lick. Think bowling ball. It was like rolling to convert a tricky split into a spare.

Against Mississippi State, Duncan sprinted downfield, lowered his head, went in for the kill . . . and was creamed. The first thing to hit the ground was the back of his head, and the resulting concussion required a spinal tap, as well as several stitches. He recovered quickly, but kept bouncing around the lineup, looking for a home.

The coaches kept trying to run Duncan off, but he would not go.

Eventually moved to offensive tackle, where many careers went to die, Duncan languished near the bottom of the depth chart at the end of spring practice heading into his junior year. After a tense meeting in Bryant's office, when the boss made it perfectly clear that his career was dangling by a thread, he went home for the summer, anxious for a little time off from all the pressure of school and football.

Two or three days later, at his parents' North Carolina home, the telephone rang.

"I've decided to try to save you," Bryant said. "And I've decided that you need to be in Birmingham this summer."

Duncan's heart raced.

Birmingham? What's this about Birmingham?

"Coach," Duncan said, trying not to offend, "I really appreciate your thinking about me, but I've already got all my stuff up here. Got my plans made . . ."

Firmly, Bryant interrupted him in midsentence. "Here's what you're gonna do," he said. "I want you to be at Baggett Transportation in Birmingham in three days."

Schools like Alabama often arranged jobs for their players during the summer, and the owner of the trucking company was a friend of the program who always needed help on the loading dock, where a strong back came in handy. It was a good way for players to stay in shape over the break.

If the coaches wanted you to stay around Tuscaloosa or Birmingham during the summer, it was usually a good sign; it suggested they thought you were worth something, that you might have a chance to play. In this case, Duncan realized it was either a signal or a test, or both, and yet, he was torn. He knew if he refused what sounded like a direct order from the boss, he could probably kiss his football career good-bye. It was already late May, and he was looking forward to a break, but ultimately, he decided he wanted to keep playing football enough to abandon his plans for the summer, so he reluctantly negotiated the twelve-hour trip back to Birmingham. At least he would have the chance to make a little money, although the whole thing happened so fast that he arrived in the Magic City without a place to stay and wound up rooming with Frank Canterbury and Jimmy Fuller for a few days, until he could look for an apartment.

Thanks in part to all the heavy lifting at his summer job, Duncan reported in the best condition of his career. When the first-string tackle came in overweight and failed the mile run, Bryant refused to issue him a uniform. He quit. Several days later, the second-string tackle was sidelined with a season-ending knee injury, and because he was in good shape and in the right place at the right time, Duncan suddenly wound up with a starting position.

"It was gonna take a helluva player to get that red jersey away from me," Duncan said. "Not because I was all that good, but because it meant everything in the world to me."

Like Duncan, guard Bruce Stephens was ignored by other colleges. Considered too small, with little discernable athletic talent, the native of Thomasville, Alabama, warranted a look from Alabama only because his two older brothers, Gerald and Charlie, had played their guts out for the Bear. No other school offered him a scholarship, probably because he looked like he belonged in the tuba section. A converted back, like so many other 'Bama linemen of the era, Bruce played most of his high school career weighing 158 pounds and reported to Tuscaloosa after working hard to bulk up to a tubby 175.

Following a frustrating freshman season in which he was used mostly as a tackling dummy, Stephens moved to Demopolis during the summer and landed a job at a paper mill. The stench was unbearable, but the pay was pretty good, and it gave him time to think about how much he hated getting knocked around without any chance of playing. The week before he was supposed to report for the beginning of preseason practice, he quit his job at the mill, and, in a fit of youthful stupidity, moved to New Orleans and landed a job as a carpenter.

After several weeks of backbreaking work, including time on a crew build-ing a grocery store, homesickness started to set in, as well as the revelation that he probably could not make a very good living as a carpenter. The topper was watching the 1965 Orange Bowl on television, and seeing his big brother Charles catch a pass from Joe Namath. Suddenly, he missed it. He missed it all, even the days when he felt like a punching bag, the days when he could not fig-ure out that his gathering toughness was leading to something. Nervously, he placed a call to Tuscaloosa and managed to make an appointment to see his old coach several days later.

The boss left him sitting in the lobby for more than forty-five minutes, which, as it turned out, was just another test. When Bryant finally ushered him into the office, and he took a seat on the couch with no springs, which swal-lowed him like quicksand, Stephens looked up at the coach, seated behind his big, slightly elevated desk. He apologized for leaving the team in the lurch, and then asked if he could have his scholarship back.

"No. I won't give you your scholarship back," Bryant said, pulling a drag on his cigarette.

Bryant stared at him through a fog of smoke.

Crushed, not knowing what to say, not wanting to beg, not wanting to leave without exhausting every possibility, Stephens was willing to do whatever it took. Just as he struggled to come up with some response to having his hopes dashed, Bryant broke the icy silence.

"Tell you what I will do," he said. "I'll give you a uniform."

Although he would have to figure out a way to pay for the next semester of school—and a place to live—Stephens jumped at the chance to regain his scholarship during spring practice.

The color of his jersey on the first day of practice was yellow, which was a message. Yellow was the color typically reserved for injured players, and the only thing hurt about Stephens was his pride. Determined to prove something to the coaches, Stephens went on the offensive from the start, and his renewed sense of dedication could be seen in the way he exploded off the line. He grinded opposing linemen into the dirt, took every little punch of abuse from the coaches, and kept fighting for more.

Several days into the spring, after working his way up the depth chart, he walked up to the cage and retrieved his basket. When he looked down and saw the neatly folded red jersey, signifying his elevation to the first team offense, he literally felt a chill run up his spine.

On the way out to practice, Stephens passed his coach, and he kept on walking for a few more steps. Then he stopped. He stopped because he needed to know. Retracing his steps, he tentatively approached Bryant.

"Coach, what do I have to do to get my scholarship back?" he said.

Bryant looked at him with a steely expression. "What color's your shirt?"

"It's red, coach."

"Well, you can move back into the dorm today."

Bryant walked into the distance as Stephens struggled not to scream. He was good, but also lucky. He didn't quite understand how lucky.

Often asked whether he treated all of his athletes the same, Bryant replied with an answer that caught some by surprise: No. "You can't treat 'em all the same, 'cause they're all different," he said. "But I try to treat them all fairly." The Bear's structured world allowed some room for nuance. The even application of discipline was one of the foundations of the program, and yet, when it came down to the decision of giving players a second chance after failing the team in some important way, Bryant often lived off his gut. Some players were banished forever. Some were saved.

"After that spring practice, they could have done anything they wanted to me," Stephens said. "They could have set me on fire. I wasn't going anywhere." That's why.

Somehow, Bryant could look him in the eyes and tell, and that's why the boss gave him a second chance.

The common denominator connecting Duncan, Stephens, and many others on the 1966 Alabama Crimson Tide was a zeal to retain the red jersey at all costs, which left them desperate enough to bear any burden. Their individual vulnerability actually made the whole team stronger. Their fear of losing everything became one of the foundations of the whole team, because the fear could be exploited in a variety of ways to make them reach, which made them stronger and more committed players, which lifted the Crimson Tide to another level of performance.

Late in the second quarter on a steamy Saturday in early October, virtually every one of the 48,000 sets of eyeballs in Denny Stadium focused on Kenny Stabler as he rolled down the line and headed for the corner.

After leading Alabama to a touchdown and a field goal on its first two possessions, Stabler nursed a 9–0 lead over Clemson as he pitched to Les Kelley, who broke into the open field and rambled for an electrifying 30-yard gain. Three plays later, Stabler sneaked in from the 1-yard line, staking 'Bama to a 16–0 halftime lead.

With Stabler and Kelley attracting the spectators, hardly anyone watched the offensive line, but a drama was unfolding among all those clinched bodies just the same. More than the springboard to a successful play, the unit's dominance was one of the keys to the entire season to come.

Most teams of the era, when linemen could not use their hands, attacked by attempting to drive the defensive linemen straight back play after play, using brute force. The drive block, or any of its various strongarm cousins, required a tremendous amount of upper body strength to push defenders off the ball and maintain contact while the play developed. For Alabama, hitting the line play after play in such a way would have been suicidal, the equivalent of a fast-break basketball team trying to play a half-court game against a mammoth front court. The Alabama coaches were way too smart to play somebody else's game just to prove a point.

"There was no way we could have beaten a bunch of those teams playing straight up, just trying to knock their heads off," said offensive line coach Jimmy Sharpe, who inherited most of the unit from the previous coach, Howard Schnellenberger. "We would have gotten killed."

Instead, they exploited an innovative strategy to emphasize the strength of their players and their system.

Largely a carryover from the one-platoon days, Alabama's blocking schemes tended to avoid straight-ahead collisions. Instead, the players attacked at precise angles, relying heavily on their superior quickness to reach the point of attack first. The Tide linemen usually attacked the thigh, just above the knee. Executed correctly, a skinny little boy who had the jump on a big strapping guy still trying to get out of his stance could seize the advantage, and turn his opponent's size and strength into a disadvantage, if only for a precious few seconds.

Especially after the Orange Bowl, coaches flocked to Tuscaloosa from all over the country to watch demonstrations—especially of the unit's signature move, the 'Bama block.

When Stabler rolled down the line on the option, tackle Jerry Duncan's mission was to explode off the ball with one gigantic stride, slam his head gear and shoulder into the defensive end's outside thigh, and use the momentum of his thrust to try to force the player to turn inside. The object was to either isolate the player from the action or, better yet, knock him off his feet. The defender usually knew what was coming, after watching film, and so the moment Dun-

The boys of 1966 included, left to right, first row: Wayne Trimble (10), Dudley Kerr (11), Kenny Stabler (12), Joe Kelley (14), Melvin Brunson (15), Mike Sasser (16) and Steve Davis (17); second row: Donnie Johnston (20), Donnie Sutton (23), Johnny Mosley (24), Dennis Homan (25), Dicky Bean (26), Frank Canterbury (28), Junior Davis (30), and David Chatwood (31); third row: Les Kelley (32), Gene Raburn (35), Wayne Owen (36), Bobby Johns (37), Kenny Martin (40), John David Reitz (41), Harold Moore (42), and Eddie Propst (43); fourth row: Ed Morgan (45), David Bedwell (46), Stan Moss (50), Ed Wright (51), Terry Kilgore (52), Jimmy Carroll (53), Mike Hall (54), Bob Childs (56), and Ken Busbee (34); fifth row: Tom Somerville (60), John Calvert (62), Norris Hamer (63), Mike Reilly (65), Johnny Sullivan (66), Billy Johnson (67), Bruce Stephens (68), Allen Harpole (69), and Dicky Thompson (44); sixth row: Byrd Williams (61), Cecil Dowdy (70), John Sides (71), Jimmy Fuller (73), Nathan Rustin (74), Taze Fulford (75), Chris Vagotis (76), and Jerry Duncan (77); seventh row: Robert Higginbotham (57), Randy Barron (72), Louis Thompson (78), Richard Cole (79), Mike Ford (81), Charles Harris (82) and Wayne Cook (83); eighth row: Eddie Bo Rogers (84), Don Shankles (85), Billy Scroggins (86), Wayne Stevens (87), Richard Brewer (21), Ray Perkins (88), and Conrad Fowler (89).

Paul "Bear" Bryant, pictured at his home with Wayne Trimble (left) and Ray Perkins,
two of his senior leaders, dominated the Alabama program with his imposing presence.
(Courtesy of the Bryant Museum)

In the years after his infamous stand in the schoolhouse door, in a futile attempt to prevent the integration of the University of Alabama, Governor George Wallace's popularity was not universal, especially in Tuscaloosa.

(Courtesy of the Bryant Museum)

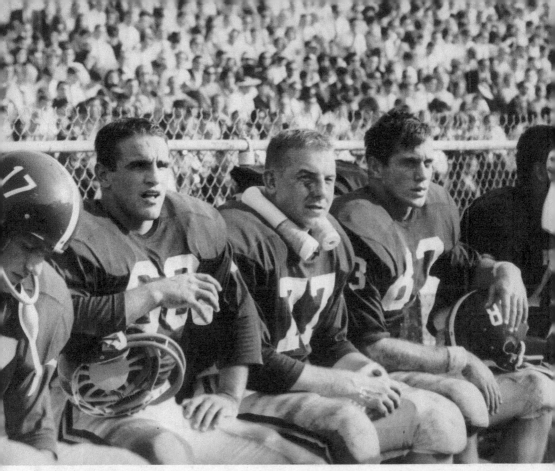

Each in their own way, kicker Steve Davis and offensive linemen Bruce Stephens, Jerry Duncan, and Wayne Cook learned about paying the price before becoming key figures on the 1966 Alabama Crimson Tide. *(Courtesy of the Bryant Museum)*

After suffering a devastating head injury, one-time fullback Ray Perkins willed himself to become one of the nation's finest receivers.

(Courtesy of the University of Alabama Sports Information Office)

RIGHT: While most eyes watched quarterback Kenny Stabler handing off to halfback Gene Raburn, the Alabama offensive line methodically dominated yet another defense.

BOTTOM LEFT: After recovering from a severe lung problem, Georgia native Dicky Thompson made one big play after another for the Crimson Tide.

BOTTOM RIGHT: Assistant coaches Ken Donahue (left) and Sam Bailey played a vital role in molding the Crimson Tide.

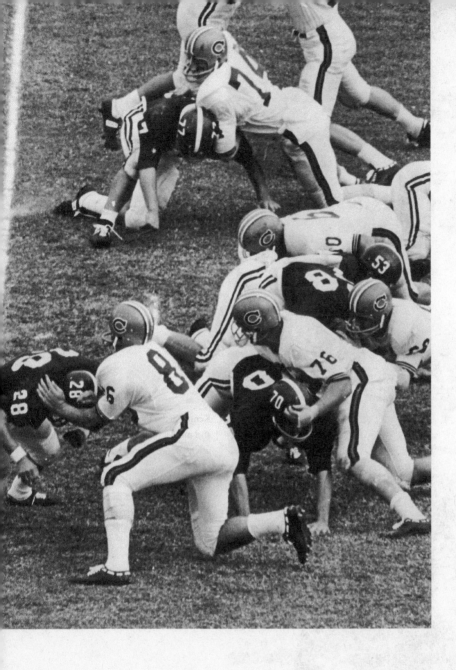

Kenny Stabler's cool-headed leadership and mental toughness lifted the Alabama offense to an entirely different level.

Muscle Shoals native Dennis Homan started his Alabama career as a running back, until fate intervened, leading him to become one of the Crimson Tide's greatest receivers.

In a dramatic road game in Knoxville, Kenny Stabler led the Crimson Tide out of a mighty hole.

(All photos on this spread courtesy of the University of Alabama Sports Information Office)

Jerry Duncan earned a measure of fame with the tackle eligible, one of his coach's favorite gadget plays. *(Courtesy of the Bryant Museum)*

One of several sophomores to play important roles on Alabama's dominating defense, linebacker Mike Hall was a fearsome presence. *(Courtesy of the Bryant Museum)*

After a frustrating career, Wayne Trimble experienced a memorable day against Mississippi State, with the help of Jerry Duncan (left) and Ray Perkins. *(Courtesy of the University of Alabama Sports Information Office)*

RIGHT: After a minor disciplinary problem, fullback Les Kelley returned to help the Crimson Tide chase history.

BELOW: A sign held up during the nationally televised Alabama-Auburn game captured the sentiment of many who believed the Crimson Tide was being treated unfairly by the wire service polls.

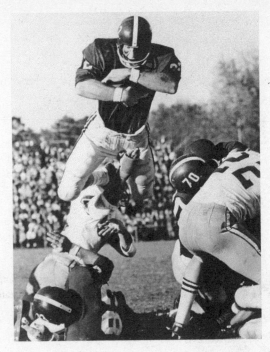

BAMA PLAYS FOOTBALL
N.DAME PLAYS POLITICS
IN YOUR ♥ YOU KNOW WE'RE #1

On the day Alabama arrived in New Orleans to prepare for the Sugar Bowl, Kenny Stabler celebrated his twenty-first birthday with the boss.

NUMBER 3 — HELL!

After the AP awarded the national championship to Notre Dame and ranked undefeated, two-time defending titleholder Alabama third, a memorable cartoon reflected the frustration of Crimson Tide fans everywhere.

Kenny Stabler plundered Nebraska's defense all day long in the Sugar Bowl.

Very few defenders managed to stop Ray Perkins from hauling in the pass, especially during his big day against Nebraska. *(Courtesy of the of University of Alabama Sports Information Office)*

In the glow of a Sugar Bowl victory that completed a season for the ages, Kenny Stabler and Ray Perkins share a light-hearted moment in the locker room. *(Courtesy of the Bryant Museum)*

can took that first step and reached toward him, he would be fighting to move to the outside. Quickness was the key. If Duncan was quick enough to reach the point of attack first, and own the defender's knee before he could move, as he usually was, then he could influence the defender's center of gravity enough to turn him toward the middle of the field. If the block succeeded, the quarterback was liberated to move on down the line and pitch or keep. If Duncan lost the battle, the end was able to move to the outside and take the pitch man, which usually killed the play.

"We were asking our guys to do something with the 'Bama block that was virtually impossible for most players, especially players who had a good bit of size," Sharpe said.

The 'Bama block also required precise footwork, which is why the linemen worked most every day pushing a sled around the practice field, using their ability to keep it straight and even as a barometer of their technique. The first step was precarious, and executed poorly, an offensive lineman could get his feet tangled up, which left him incredibly vulnerable to being knocked down.

"Ordinarily, when I'm teaching somebody to block, I'll tell you to never cross over with your feet, because it's real easy to lose your leverage," Sharpe said. "One of the things that made the 'Bama block so difficult was that need to cross [your feet] over during that first step. If they're as quick as you are, they're going to be able to knock you off your feet."

A 260-pound giant could never make such a move. Then again, a 260-pound giant would be much more useful just knocking his opponent's rear end across the line of scrimmage.

The undisputed leader of the group, All-America tackle Cecil Dowdy, was the only player to tip the scales past 200 pounds. His teammates sometimes called him "Chief." With a relatively long body and short legs, Dowdy excelled at keep his back straight and stiff, and extending his blocking surface, as the coaches referred to the process of slamming one body into another with a certain violent force. "A blocking machine," Duncan said. The short legs allowed him to produce short steps, and to a greater degree than most of his teammates, he had the ability to sustain a block despite his unimposing frame, which gave the coaches options regarding how to use him.

The way Alabama controlled the line of scrimmage with a combination of quickness and technique was a sight to see, especially when Dowdy and tight end Wayne Cook—the only three-year starter on the unit—frequently doubled-teamed the defensive tackle. Using their combined quickness to reach the lineman before he could get out of his stance, their mission was to knock him into or near the approaching linebacker, who would have to pull off some mighty fancy footwork to avoid being thrown to the ground or isolated from the oncoming ballcarrier. This was especially effective in creating a seam for the halfback on 66 drive, a basic running play with a lead-blocking fullback, which was tough to defend.

In the face of all those physical mismatches, the Alabama offensive line personified the notion of the overachiever. Demonstrating game after game that size need not be an insurmountable impediment, the unit symbolized the spirit of somehow finding a way to overcome a liability with a combination of tenacity and innovative thinking. Week after week, they proved, if the game means enough to you, somehow you can find a way to get the job done, to beat someone with greater physical gifts by emphasizing your strengths and minimizing your weaknesses. This thought permeated the 1966 Crimson Tide, but nowhere was it more essential to the success of the entire football team.

The way the Alabama line dominated kept Kenny Stabler from running for his life on every play, allowed the Tide to establish the run, enabled Ray Perkins and Dennis Homan to reach their potential, and took enormous pressure off the defense by keeping it off the field for long stretches.

An offensive line is like a car battery, attracting attention only when something goes wrong. So it was a sign of strength that most eyes turned elsewhere as the Crimson Tide clobbered eventual Atlantic Coast Conference champion Clemson, 26–0, to go 3–0 on the season.

Sometimes, the line's contribution was clear to see, like when Wayne Cook leveled his man to spring Stabler for a nine-yard keeper on the third play of the second quarter. At most times, however, the linemen who exploded off the ball, reached the ball quick as a hiccup, and hammered those thighs, turning the Clemson defenders inside or outside, toiled in the shadows of the skill position players, which is the way it has always been and the way it will forever be. Not many folks in the stands were drawn to the blocking when Dennis Homan rambled thirty-eight yards on a reverse in the third quarter, but the seam the guys created was pivotal all the same.

While Stabler led the Tide to scores on four of his five possessions at the helm, linebacker Stan Moss recorded an interception and caused a fumble to pace a dominating defensive performance. Even though Bryant started emptying his bench in the third quarter, Clemson never seriously threatened. Sobered by the weight of evidence as Alabama methodically controlled every phase of the game, Frank Howard said, "Alabama has one of the finest football teams I've ever seen."

Even for the forever confident overachievers from Tuscaloosa, who were accustomed to finding a way to win despite enormous odds, the poll obstacle seemed increasingly large and formidable. Some problems could not be solved by lowering your head and out-quicking the guy in front of you. Some problems could not be tackled with innovative technique.

The combination of Alabama's stunning drop in the polls and the program's inability to get a shot at any of the other contenders meant 'Bama needed either to sway the voters or hope all of the other title chasers were knocked off.

The sport remained captive to a rigid system of regionality and an antiquated approach to the bowls, and no one was stuck further in the past than Notre Dame.

During a trip to Tuscaloosa to speak at Bryant's annual coaching clinic in early August—where he joined, among others, Michigan's Bump Elliott and Oklahoma's Jim Mackenzie—Fighting Irish head coach Ara Parseghian was reminded that Notre Dame and Alabama, two of the most successful programs in the history of the sport, had never met on the field. He said he would welcome a future game. "The only trouble is that our schedule is completed through something like 1974," he said. "Who knows what the situation will be ten years from now. Coach Bryant and myself might not even be coaching then."

This illustrated the problem looming in Alabama's championship quest. While the Crimson Tide embraced the bowl system, which allowed it to claim the national title in 1965, Notre Dame refused to play postseason games, for reasons of internal university policy. All the Fighting Irish needed to do in order to play Alabama was to take a step out of the dark ages and challenge the Crimson Tide in the Sugar Bowl or Orange Bowl. Imagine the bidding war. At the same time, the Rose Bowl controlled the champions of the Big Ten and the forerunner of the Pac-8, which further hampered the process of equitably awarding the national title.

Suddenly, the sport's structural flaws with regard to the postseason were starting to occupy the minds of Alabama players and fans. Ranked fourth in both wire service polls—it had tumbled from third in the AP survey—the Crimson Tide could not hope to get a shot at No. 1 Michigan State of the Big Ten, No. 2 UCLA of the Athletic Association of Western Universities, or No. 3 Notre Dame, which played as an independent. Southern Cal of the AAWU, ranked fifth in the UPI and sixth in the AP, also was inaccessible.

The linkage between the polls and the national championship process was still evolving, and the big prize was not the Crimson Tide's birthright, but no one appeared capable of explaining how a team that had won consecutive titles and returned the guts of the previous year's squad could be ranked so low—especially after starting the year as the AP's preseason No. 1, especially after winning its first three games without a serious challenge.

The Crimson Tide intended to earn its way into the history books, but without the ability to challenge any of the higher ranked teams, Alabama was facing an unusual position for a defending champion, especially a loaded, two-time defending champion.

However, with a big road trip to Knoxville on the horizon, Bryant was determined to keep his players' minds focused. Tennessee. The word alone made him scowl.

7. ROCKY TOP

The rain started on Thursday, so by the time Alabama's two chartered airplanes touched down at the Knoxville airport on Friday morning, the tarmac was littered with puddles. The sky loomed dark and gloomy. As the players and coaches began loading onto the assembled buses, which would take them to their hotel, a delegation from the local chamber of commerce approached Bryant, welcomed him to their fair city, and handed him a manila envelope filled with a map and some tourist information.

Digging through the envelope with an irritated look, he pulled out a commemorative key chain and flipped it from one side to the other in his gigantic hand, revealing a tiny artist's rendering of the University of Tennessee's Shields-Watkins Field. Scowling, he crumpled up the envelope, handed it back to one of the stunned civic leaders, and tossed the key chain into the distance. Heads bobbing above crimson blazers turned to watch the trinket skip across the rain-soaked tarmac.

"We didn't come here for a damn tour," he said gruffly, and stepped onto his bus.

The game was still more than twenty-four hours away, but Bryant already had his game face strapped on, good and tight.

He didn't want to do any sightseeing.

He didn't want to meet a bunch of dignitaries.

He sure didn't want a keepsake of the stadium "the General" built.

He just wanted to whip Tennessee. And go home.

Bryant's rudeness was out of character, but perhaps he instinctively knew he needed to show his game face to his players so they would understand that it was time to be serious and focused on the task at hand. Tennessee was not just another game, and the 1966 renewal of the South's most intense rivalry would test not only the athletic skill of the participants, but also Bryant's ability to exploit his team's mental toughness.

"Tennessee was like a dirty word to us," said defensive lineman Richard Cole. "Coach Bryant really got fired up to play those guys in orange, and he made sure we got fired up, too."

Like the other Alabama coaches before him, Bryant considered the annual showdown on the third Saturday in October a pivotal test on the road to greatness. "You find out what kind of person you are when you play Tennessee," he often said.

Bryant treated every game like it was a referendum on his manhood, but Tennessee had been a source of motivation and torment for much of his adult life, and playing the Volunteers truly stirred his blood. Consequently, around the Alabama football program, Tennessee week was substantially different. You could feel it in the air. The preparation was more intense, and fraught with greater potential peril.

Chased inside Foster Auditorium, the university's ancient basketball gymnasium, by the rain earlier in the week, Alabama was running through drills when Bryant suddenly jumped up from his seat in the first floor bleachers. With an angry look on his face, he approached one of his defensive players. "Get your sorry ass out of here!" he thundered. "Go to the dorm, get your stuff, and don't ever come back!"

The team was stunned. No one knew what the coach was reacting to, but he obviously had perceived something disturbing in the player's performance, perhaps some lack of concentration. Boom. A career was over.

Didn't the player know it was Tennessee week?

Didn't he realize beating the Volunteers would require every ounce of his soul?

"Talk about a spark," recalled offensive tackle Jerry Duncan. "That said something to every member of the team. We knew we'd better lay it all on the line, or we'd be gone, too."

Some of the athletes who watched in disbelief could not help wondering whether Bryant orchestrated the event with the sole purpose of manipulating their minds, motivating them to reach with even greater intensity, in order to avoid being banished. Perhaps the dismissed player was just a prop, exploited for their benefit. Regardless of whether it was a moment of genuine outrage or a scripted monologue ripped from the pages of his own personal psychological handbook, Bryant succeeded in creating a sense of heightened insecurity heading into one of the biggest games of the year, which he knew how to utilize better than any coach alive.

The next day, Bryant called the team together and told the players he had overreacted. The prodigal son was allowed to return to the squad.

Instead of lessening the effectiveness of the mental exercise, his decision to take the player back actually enhanced his psychological clout. Fear was a powerful motivator, but fear mixed with a perception of mercy and fairness gave his kind of player, the kind of athlete who had already proven susceptible to his methods, even more of a reason to believe in him. Where they were headed, it was critically important that they all believed.

The Alabama-Tennessee series began in 1901, but the genesis of the rivalry can be traced to a crisp October afternoon in 1928.

Before kickoff at old Denny Field in Tuscaloosa—a collection of wooden bleachers overflowing with an estimated 15,000 fans for the occasion, many of whom were forced to sit on the grass—Robert Neyland, then in his third season as the Tennessee head coach, humbly approached 'Bama head coach Wallace Wade and asked for a favor. Would Wade mind shortening the second half, in case the score got out of hand? Neyland didn't want his boys needlessly embarrassed.

After leading the Crimson Tide to two Rose Bowl appearances and national championships in 1925 and '26, Wade was already a giant figure in Southern football. His team was heavily favored. Still largely unknown, Neyland had been hired with the primary mandate of finding a way to beat powerhouse Vanderbilt, led by famed coach Dan McGugin, a disciple of Michigan's legendary Fielding Yost, who fashioned a dominating 197-55-19 record at the Nashville school from 1904 to 1934. When Tennessee tied the Commodores, 7–7, in 1927, ending Vanderbilt's run of six straight victories in the series, the event was cause for celebration in Knoxville.

No one gave Tennessee a chance against Alabama in 1928, and Neyland's plea for mercy made perfectly good sense. According to Al Browning's history of the series, *Third Saturday in October,* Wade played down the possibility of such a rout, but agreed to suspend the game early "in the unlikely event we have a halftime lead that justifies such action."

But Neyland was messing with Wade's mind.

He knew his team was good, and his attempt at a little pregame gamesmanship was nothing but a clever con.

On the opening kickoff, Gene McEver, one of the greatest runners in Tennessee history, rambled 89 yards for a touchdown. McEver was fast, but he was also tough, so when two Alabama defenders braced near the 50 yard line to bring him down, he barreled straight toward them, bowed his neck, and leveled them both on the way to the end zone. Tennessee never relinquished the lead, but it was a terrific battle all the way.

In the fourth quarter, as Tennessee held on for a 15–13 upset victory over the Crimson Tide, darkness started to fall across Tuscaloosa, and fans were encouraged to pull their cars up to the field and turn on their headlights, so the competitors could see well enough to finish the game.

Never again would a Tennessee coach be able to plead for mercy—against Alabama or anyone else. The win established Tennessee as a major Southern power and launched the annual border clash into an entirely new realm, as one of the most heated and meaningful rivalries in college football.

Educated at the United States Military Academy at West Point, where he played football and baseball, Neyland was a career army officer who left his post in Knoxville twice to serve his country, including a distinguished tour during World War II, when he attained the rank of brigadier general. He lost precious few battles on the sidelines. A hard-nosed disciplinarian who won with dominating defenses and a bland but effective single wing offense, the General led Tennessee to a 173-31-12 mark, capturing five SEC titles and the 1951 national championship. His 1939 Volunteers, perhaps the best of all, finished unbeaten, untied, and unscored upon during the regular season—the last team ever to accomplish one of the most remarkable feats in college football.

The fierce battles for Southern supremacy between Neyland's Vols and Frank Thomas's Crimson Tide during the 1930s and '40s cast an ominous shadow on both sides of the border. The rivalry became a yardstick for both programs, especially in the days when a bitter feud prevented cross-state brothers Alabama and Auburn from competing on the field of play.

"You never know about a football player until he has played against Alabama," said Neyland, who was known to take his desire to beat the Crimson Tide to unusual lengths.

For years, Tennessee scheduled the lightly regarded University of Chattanooga the week prior to Alabama, because Moccasins head coach Scrappy Moore, a pupil of Frank Thomas, ran the Notre Dame box offense—just like the Crimson Tide. When Thomas retired due to ill health after the 1946 season and new 'Bama coach Harold "Red" Drew installed the T-formation, Neyland supposedly called Moore and threatened to cancel the series—which represented a big payday for Chattanooga—unless the Moccasins switched to the T-formation.

In the years after he played against Tennessee with a broken leg, Bryant closely studied the General's incredibly disciplined program, which informed his development as a coach. Despite incorporating many of Neyland's strengths as his own, Bryant was unable to beat the General during his days as the head coach at Kentucky, which tormented him to no end.

By the time Bryant returned to Tuscaloosa—where he was destined to go

16-7-2 against the Vols, including a string of eleven straight victories—the General was long gone from the sidelines. But he was still chasing him, all the same, as evidenced by his decision to hire former Tennessee player Ken Donahue as his defensive line coach in 1964, at least partially to learn more about the General's philosophy.

After Neyland's retirement in 1953, Tennessee slipped a notch, just as Alabama was entering the dark ages that would eventually lead to Bryant's triumphant return. Except for Bowden Wyatt's 1956 SEC championship team—featuring Heisman Trophy runnerup Johnny Majors in the backfield—the Volunteers spent most of the late '50s and early '60s wallowing in mediocrity. Alabama reeled off three straight blowout victories over the Volunteers, including a 35–0 blistering at Legion Field in 1963, which sealed first-year coach Jim McDonald's fate.

The decision to hire Doug Dickey in 1964 marked a turning point in Tennessee history. Dickey, a former Florida quarterback who would lead the Volunteers to SEC championships in 1967 and 1969 and to three straight victories over Alabama, rebounded from a 4-5-1 mark in his first year to 8-1-2 in his second, including the shocking tie against the Crimson Tide, which felt like a victory for the Volunteers, who had lost the three previous games by a combined score of 96–10. Two days after the game, the springboard to Tennessee's first bowl bid since 1957, Dickey's team was devastated when three of his assistant coaches—Bill Majors, Bobby Jones, and Charlie Rash—were killed on the way to work when their automobile was struck by a train. The tragedy hung over the program just as it was rising out of the doldrums.

After shutting out Clemson, Alabama jumped from fourth in both polls to third, but still trailed No. 1 Michigan State, which knocked off Michigan, 20–7, and No. 2 Notre Dame, which blanked Army 35–0. The Tide benefited from UCLA's close call with lowly Rice. The Bruins held on for a 27–24 victory, but tumbled to fourth. The rest of the AP top ten included Southern Cal, Nebraska, Georgia Tech, Florida, Purdue, and Baylor.

Even as the Crimson Tide chased history, a small group of players facing the military draft were hauled to Montgomery for army physicals. The bus was one gigantic bundle of exposed nerves during the two-hour drive. Passing an army physical was the first step toward having your ticket punched for Vietnam, and college deferments could last only so long.

Most of the players flunked their physicals, which many wanted to believe Bryant had something to do with, though it seems unlikely that even the Bear exerted such power. After a stunned army doctor examined reserve defensive back David Bedwell's X-ray, he told the player he had a broken vertebra and advised him to take the film back to his team doctor before donning another set of pads.

"He said I was a fool to be playing any more football, that I could be paralyzed if I got hit wrong," said Bedwell, a native of Cedar Bluff. "Just about scared me to death. The doctor said I didn't have to worry about Vietnam . . . said they'd take women and children before they sent me, I was in such bad shape."

He kept practicing, but the coaches, spooked by the X-ray, held him out of contact for several weeks.

Another doctor later took one look at linebacker Bob Childs's banged-up knee and told him, with a straight face, that he could eventually pass a physical and get in the army and go to Vietnam if he was willing to have surgery to repair the damage to the knee. Childs, whose father had been a tank commander in World War II for the army led by General George S. Patton, resisted the urge to laugh in the doctor's face.

Tom Somerville made a special trip to his hometown of Memphis to take his physical. With all his various ailments—a history of asthma, as well as problems with his back and his finger—Somerville took the advice of his future father-in-law doctor and rolled the dice, believing he would flunk the physical. When he was rejected, "it was like the greatest burden in the world being lifted off my shoulders."

The team was full of players with a variety of physical problems considered debilitating enough to prevent them from being sent off to war, but not severe enough to keep them from chasing a third straight national championship.

Although Alabama was favored heading into the Tennessee game, the improbable ending of the previous season gave Volunteer fans reason for optimism. Tennessee returned a talented and experienced team, and the 2-1 Vols—who had blown out Auburn and Rice and lost 6–3 to ninth-ranked Georgia Tech—were not intimidated by the mighty Crimson Tide. A victory over Alabama could catapult Tennessee into the thick of the race for its first conference championship in a decade.

On the night before the big game, the two teams showed up in the lobby of a Knoxville movie theater at the same time.

Alabama center Jimmy Carroll turned to his teammate Louis Thompson, who grew up in middle Tennessee. "Which one's Baby?"

Trying not to be obvious, Thompson pointed out 5'9", 212-pound noseguard Bobby "Baby" Morel. Carroll took a good look across the room at the man he would be facing in the trenches the next day, and Morel took a good look back.

For a few tense moments, the two teams stared at each other and tried to look tough, as the aroma of freshly popped popcorn wafted through the air.

About the time the Tide was relaxing in a darkened movie theater, something was happening in Huntsville, about 150 miles southwest of Knoxville, that represented the first tentative step toward the integration of the Alabama program.

Actually, the story began more than two months earlier, with a historic game of eight ball.

On a summer day in 1966, John Meadows, the new head football coach at Huntsville's Butler High School, walked through the door of a boys' club in a black section of town and challenged teenager Leonard Thomas to a game of pool. Meadows, a middle-aged white man, was not a hustler, at least not in the traditional meaning of the word, when applied to the game, but he was hustling just the same, and in approaching the African-American youngster, he was laying down a gutsy bet—gambling that, even in George Wallace's Alabama, especially in George Wallace's Alabama, football could transcend hate.

The journey to the pool room started several months earlier, when the Huntsville Board of Education, in a controversial move, voted to close Councill High, the local black school, making the district in Alabama's fourth-largest city a leader in the movement toward desegregation. Twelve years after the Supreme Court ordered the desegregation of schools "with all deliberate speed," political leaders across the country, especially in the South, continued to drag their heels. The culture of dual school systems remained a fact of life in cities and towns across Alabama, although many traditionally white schools had begun the process of limited, token integration, the first step toward the eventual merger of the systems in the years ahead.

Like many other school districts, Huntsville was hampered by forces who opposed integration and wanted to delay it for as long as possible, but at a time when the city was critically dependent on the jobs provided by the U.S. Army's Redstone Arsenal and Marshall Space Flight Center, a key installation of the National Aeronautics and Space Administration (NASA), the motivation to avoid the possibility of federal retribution was even more powerful. Starting with the fall semester in 1966, black students in Huntsville could choose to attend any of the Rocket City's three traditionally white public high schools— Huntsville, Butler, or Lee—a change that marked the beginning of a closely watched cultural revolution. In a volatile climate tinged with fear, burdened with a legacy of bigotry, division, and mistrust, and poisoned by the shameful demagoguery of George Wallace and many other politicians, no one could say what might happen.

Even though the once pervasive separate restrooms and water fountains were largely gone, and restaurants and other public places were forbidden from discriminating, mixing of the races remained extremely limited. Although Huntsville was much more diverse and cosmopolitan than other parts of Alabama, due to the influx of NASA and military personnel, the two cultures remained largely separate and many mothers and fathers, black and white, approached the integration of the schools with significant trepidation.

The full-scale integration of the system coincided with the beginning of football season, and in Huntsville as well as the rest of Alabama, high school football—white and black—towered over the landscape. Many of the same fans who hung so much of their lives on the fortunes of Alabama and Auburn simultaneously invested tremendous passion in their favorite high school teams. In towns like Decatur, Enterprise, and Leighton, high school football was the foremost expression of hometown pride, where sons, neighbors, and friends became gladiators in the intense competition with nearby communities. Entire towns shut down to attend big games. The culture encouraged young men to play the sport, valuing its various lessons as key ingredients in the making of a man. The cumulative glow of stadium lights on a Friday night in Alabama was a source of enormous energy, capable of being harnessed for a much higher purpose.

With so few black students attending traditionally white high schools across the state, nearly all of the schools continued to field all-white athletic teams.

Hired to revive the moribund Butler program after winning a state championship at nearby Scottsboro, the driven, incredibly competitive Meadows—who won nearly three hundred games at Cullman, Scottsboro, Butler, and Tennessee's Lincoln County—saw an opportunity to strengthen his football team by tapping into the suddenly available black athletes.

"I didn't think it should be a big deal," said Meadows, who had played service ball with African Americans before embarking on his coaching career. "I was just looking to field the best possible team, without regard to color. I didn't care about color. I cared about winning."

When Meadows asked one of the old Councill coaches about talented and available athletes who might be interested in playing football for him at Butler—where the Rebels waved the Confederate flag and at one point, featured the symbol on their helmets—he mentioned several names, including two players who turned out to be too old to qualify under Alabama High School Athletic Association rules. Leonard Thomas was only 16—and he was good.

Thomas grew up of modest means in northwest Huntsville, without a father in the picture. "It was tough not having a dad," he said. "The only role models

I had were the older guys around the neighborhood, and they did their best to keep me out of trouble." Deeply religious—he became a deacon in his church as a teenager—Thomas was drawn to sports from an early age. In the backyard football games, the other kids always wanted him to run with the ball, because he was fast and he could cut sharper than anyone had ever seen.

Named all-city after leading undefeated Councill in rushing in 1965, Thomas was still trying to decide where he wanted to go to school when he showed up at the boys' club, where he spent much of his time hanging out with his friends, staying out of trouble. With his old classmates scattering among the three schools, he was not looking forward to starting over, and remained apprehensive about playing football at a white school.

"There's a man here who wants to talk to you," one of the counselors said, as he walked through the door.

After Meadows introduced himself and suggested they play a game of pool, the hustle began. He picked up a cue, broke, and started sinking one shot after another. The crisp whack of stick on ball filled the dingy, poorly lit little room. They talked casually, the white man and the black teenager, about pool, about music, about family, about nothing at all, and Meadows kept filling the pockets.

"I liked him from the start," Thomas said. "I hadn't had that many dealings with white people, and he seemed like a real good guy. He made me comfortable. We didn't even talk about football while we were playing pool."

After whipping him in two straight games, Meadows told Thomas, "I've heard you're a pretty good football player," and started talking to him about playing for the Butler Rebels.

Finally, he said, "How would you like to visit the campus and meet some of my players?"

The white boys over at Butler gave Leonard Thomas a warm reception, making him and two other black players feel right at home, even as the school system was peacefully integrated. Within a short time, some of his best friends in the world were his white teammates, a revolutionary turn of events in Alabama or anywhere in 1966. "When the football players accepted me and took me in, I think it sent a signal to the rest of the kids at school, and they accepted me very quickly," Thomas said.

In the season opener against Cullman, Thomas started at running back. Early in the game, he took a pitch on what was designed as an off-tackle play, ran into a crowd, stutter stepped, and darted to the outside in a flash, turning what would have been a loss into a big gain. Several times during the night, while rushing for more than one hundred yards, the 5'11", 170-pound Thomas performed similar moves way beyond the other backs on the team. "At Councill, our traps were wider and our sweeps were wider," he said, "and when I got to Butler, they didn't have any white players who were fast enough to get outside like I could." The Butler players—and their opponents—were treated to a glimpse of the future of offensive football, that would be fundamentally changed by the introduction of the black athlete.

In the locker room after the victory, a beaming assistant coach approached Thomas with a big grin. "Man, you ran like a rabbit out there!"

His teammates quickly picked up on the idea. Rabbit Thomas had a nice ring to it. Within a few weeks, it was a name well known by football fans throughout northern Alabama, especially around the Tennessee Valley Conference, a fourteen-team league stretching across nine counties, from Huntsville to Russellville.

"Rabbit was tough to get a hand on, and tough to bring down if you did manage to get a hand on him," Meadows said.

The season progressed with surprisingly few racial taunts from other teams and fans, although during one road game, he ran out of bounds and was shocked to hear the opposing head coach yelling toward the defender pursuing him: "Get the nigger! Get the nigger!" On subsequent carries, he tried to avoid running out of bounds.

Every so often that autumn, as Rabbit Thomas was breaking down an important barrier, a bone-rattling rumble could be heard in the distance.

With slightly more than three years remaining to meet President John F. Kennedy's pledge to place a man safely on the moon by the end of the decade, the activity at Huntsville's Marshall Space Flight Center was never far from anyone's thoughts in the once-sleepy little town, which had exploded into a high-tech center of more than 120,000 residents. The race to beat the Russians to the moon was Huntsville's mission, every bit as much as Houston's or Cape Kennedy's, and it hung heavy in the air at all times, especially when the engineers tested the massive Saturn rockets, the firepower destined to take Neil Armstrong, Edwin "Buzz" Aldrin, and Mike Collins to the moon on that magnificent week in July 1969, when the world held its breath and everyone in the Tennessee Valley beamed with a special kind of pride.

At the end of World War II, Huntsville, with a population of just 16,000, was best known for producing cotton and watercress. The trajectory of the whole area was forever altered in 1950, when the U.S. Army moved Wernher von Braun and his team of German rocket scientists to Redstone Arsenal, where they built the country's first ballistic missiles. Even as the team of naturalized American citizens concentrated on cold war weapons and distanced themselves from their Nazi past, the publicity savvy von Braun became the country's foremost advocate of peaceful space exploration, promoting the idea of missions to the moon and Mars long before the Russians launched Sputnik in 1957, which changed everything.

On a memorable day in September 1962, the visionary von Braun, the first director of Marshall, who exerted tremendous influence on the entire space program, escorted President Kennedy around the Marshall complex, finally showing him one of the massive Saturn first stages. "This is the vehicle designed to fulfill your promise," von Braun said. "And by God, we'll do it!"

As the Crimson Tide chased history, engineers and technicians in Huntsville and elsewhere were preoccupied with expanding the reach of mankind. In the wake of the historic first successful docking maneuver in September, the tenth and final flight of the Gemini program, a critical test of several of the procedures required to eventually reach the moon, was set for November. Next up was Apollo, scheduled to start in early 1967. For all the turbulence of the civil rights movement, for all the gathering fear surrounding Vietnam, 1966 was a year of big dreams, and Huntsville was focused on the biggest of all.

Contrary to what some people in other parts of the country wanted to believe, Alabama was not defined simply by George Wallace's stand in the schoolhouse door, Bull Connor's dogs and fire hoses, or any other of the various isolated but deplorable acts of bold-type bigotry that combined to give the state a bad name. Alabama was many things, good and bad, but it was much more than could be seen through the lens of the national news media. Even as Huntsville, like the rest of the state, struggled to overcome the lingering effects of a century of segregation, the increasingly educated, progressive, white-color city plotted a course for Tranquility Base and thereby reinvented itself. The tension between yesterday and tomorrow could be seen all over town, but in many ways, the Rocket City was the face of Alabama's future.

"Most of us were rejecting all that hate," said Rod Steakley, a senior defensive back for the Huntsville High Crimson Panthers.

About the time the projector started to roll in Knoxville, undefeated archrivals Huntsville and Butler collided in one of the most highly anticipated high school games ever played in northern Alabama. Tickets to the showdown were in such demand, the city installed temporary bleachers to augment Huntsville Stadium's 10,500 seats. The traffic jam started more than two hours before kickoff. An estimated 15,000 fans crowded into the facility, many of them standing, all of them expecting a game for the ages.

When Thomas and his teammates walked onto the field to warm up, he happened to look up at the overflowing stands and noticed several crudely scribbled signs, all with the same message:

"Run, Rabbit, Run!"

He could hardly believe his eyes.

"I didn't think anybody knew who I was," he said.

He felt a lump in his throat as he stared up at the signs, perhaps realizing the full measure of his pioneering step for the first time.

After Huntsville jumped out to a 14–0 lead, Butler, led by Thomas and quarterback Carl "Junebug" Walker, stormed back to win a thrilling 20–17 victory that lived up to the enormous hype.

In the second quarter, with the Panthers up by two touchdowns, Thomas lined up at split end for a play specially designed for the occasion, which Meadows dubbed "Rabbit, Get Lost." When the ball was snapped, Walker faked a bootleg and then hit Thomas with a pass across the middle. Huntsville safety Rod Steakley lunged for him but missed as Rabbit made a move worthy of a highlight film, spinning once, then again before streaking into the end zone for a thirty-three-yard Butler touchdown as the Rebels' crowd erupted.

"Rabbit really had a way of making you miss," Steakley said.

Run, Rabbit, Run.

In the glow of a magical October night, in a city where blacks and whites had recently been forbidden from playing together on the same field, Rabbit Thomas achieved something stunning and once unthinkable. As whites and blacks together celebrated him, elevated him, invested their hopes and dreams in him—many wearing Crimson Tide caps and jackets—Thomas emerged as a symbol of unity in a culture struggling to cleanse itself of division.

"I was so young, I didn't really appreciate what a big thing I was part of," said Thomas, who later integrated the program at Florence State, a nearby small college, and became a high school coach in Huntsville. "I just wanted an opportunity to play, to show what I could do."

While the Alabama Crimson Tide continued to take heat for having no black players, the success of Thomas represented the first grassroots step, the first of many, on the way to the successful integration of the state's favorite team. The Alabama football team did not exist in a vacuum. Every time a high school player shattered a color barrier in the cities and towns across the state, forcing the fans conditioned to see the world through the prism of black and white to choose instead between love and hate, the integration of the Crimson Tide took on a sense of mounting inevitability.

Waking up to rainy skies the next morning, thousands of the fans who crowded Huntsville Stadium spent Saturday afternoon hunched over radios listening to

John Forney, the voice of the Crimson Tide, describe a classic battle on a sloppy field.

AstroTurf was a new invention in 1966, and it would be another two years before Tennessee led the SEC into the misguided artificial revolution, bastardizing an entire era with the whiff of sterility. Within a few years, a large percentage of the nation's major football schools, including Alabama, would plow up their grass to make room for artificial turf. Like so many other changes destined to roil the sport in the years ahead, fake grass was promoted as an instrument of progress.

Fortunately for all concerned, the progress of nylon and concrete was still approaching from the distant horizon. The 1966 Alabama-Tennessee game was not just a competition between two outstanding, hard-hitting football teams. It was also a battle against extreme elements, the way the big referee in the sky intended. The rain started long before kickoff and lasted much of the day, turning the natural grass field into a sludgy, soupy mess, forcing the competitors on both sides to contend with slipping and sliding feet, wet footballs, muddy uniforms and hands, and a pervasive sense of futility. It was so miserable, it was damn near perfect.

The punishment started even before the opening kickoff.

During pregame warmups, the Alabama coaches led some of the players through a drill known as "bull in the ring," which basically consisted of players taking turns knocking heads. Someone landed a ferocious lick on noseguard Tom Somerville, which left him stunned. Stumpy walked around in a daze while the rain poured from the sky, not knowing quite where he was, but with enough presence of mind not to say a word to the coaches, lest he lose his hard-earned spot in the starting lineup.

Given the harsh conditions, Bryant instructed his game captains, offensive tackle Jerry Duncan and defensive tackle Johnny Sullivan—one of seven native Tennesseans on the roster—to defer the option if they won the coin toss. Duncan, one of his coach's favorites, was a cocky little devil, and he subsequently went up to the boss and said the offense wanted the ball. Bryant admired confidence and thought it should be rewarded, so he approved the change. 'Bama won the toss and elected to receive in a driving rainstorm.

On the sixth play of the game, a second-and-15 call from the Alabama 20 yard line, Kenny Stabler approached the line of scrimmage and watched the Tennessee safety take several steps forward, out of his zone coverage. Interpreting the safety's movement as double coverage on receiver Ray Perkins, Stabler called the signals, pulled away from center, and stepped back with the ball, toward fullback Les Kelley.

On that particular pass play, which included a fake to Kelley, Stabler was empowered with the ability to employ the automatic and actually give the ball to Kelley, if he thought Perkins was facing double coverage.

But Kelley read the situation differently.

"The guy moved up about halfway, between a zone and man coverage, and I read it as single coverage," Kelley said.

When Stabler stuffed the ball into Kelley's arms, he refused to take it, because he thought it was a fake, and the ball tumbled onto the wet ground. Tennessee's Jim Weatherford recovered at the Alabama 23 yard line.

Knocked into a big hole less than two minutes into the game, the Alabama defense hunkered down, including Stumpy Somerville, still groggy from his pregame bell-ringing. On the first snap, Bob Johnson, Tennessee's 6'4", 231-pound All-America center, bound for a long career with the Cincinnati Bengals, plowed through the 5'9", 187-pound Somerville to spring wingback Charles Fulton for a nine-yard gain. Somerville could tell it was going to be a long day.

Three plays later, Tennessee quarterback Dewey Warren hit tight end Austin Denney on a screen for a six-yard touchdown pass. With Gary Wright's extra point and a subsequent 40-yard field goal—set up when the 'Bama offense was forced to punt out of its own end zone—the Volunteers led 10–0 before the end of the first quarter, even as the rain intensified.

A defensive struggle in which neither team accounted for 100 yards of offense, the first half was highlighted by the performance of Tennessee punter Ron Widby—the nation's leader in 1966—who kept booming balls over Johnny Mosley's head, forcing him to retreat and try to hang on in the slippery mud.

During the course of a game, Bryant always wanted his backup quarterbacks nearby, just in case, and so as the first half progressed, third-string signal caller Joe Kelley, standing no more than two feet from the boss, heard something whiz by his head at a tremendous velocity. Looking down, he saw a half-filled liquor bottle sticking up out of the mud, directly between the coach and himself. He knew whoever threw the bottle was not aiming for him.

"For the rest of the game, while I'm trying to concentrate on the action, I can't help wondering: How in the world I am going to get away from Coach Bryant? How am I going to get out of the target zone? This could be really dangerous!" Kelley said.

Toward the middle of the second quarter, Alabama caught a break by recovering a Tennessee fumble at the Vols' 31 yard line. Stabler, struggling to overcome one of the worst halves of his life, kept the ball on six of the next eight plays, including a gutsy fourth-and-three call when he darted for a six-yard gain behind the block of right guard Bruce Stephens. But on the next play,

the wet ball slipped out of his hands at the Tennessee six, and Paul Naumoff recovered for the Volunteers, who carried a 10–0 lead into halftime.

When the Alabama players started filing into the locker room, the click-
click-click of their cleats filling up the crowded space, Bryant approached head
manager Sang Lyda outside the door and told him to pull out the fresh uniforms. Forever planning for every possible contingency, Lyda and his crew carried a spare set of practically everything, for just such an occasion. Never
before had the boss told him to completely re-dress the team for the second
half, but being down 10–0 under such awful conditions represented a new experience for everybody, and Bryant understood the value of having his players
strip off all those wet, muddy uniforms so they could take the field feeling
clean and dry. If they felt clean and dry, if only for a few minutes, perhaps
they could also wipe away the lingering mental mud of their disastrous first
half.

Ten to zip.

Under the circumstances, the thought loomed before them all like a mountain.

As the players listened to their position coaches go over adjustments for the
second half, some of them scribbling on portable chalk boards, the smell of
sweat quickly filling the place, the thought of the mountain laying before them
competed with the pulsating fear of the unknown. Nobody knew what Bryant
would do, what he would say, but they all feared the worst.

Senior lineman Jimmy Fuller, who knew enough to be afraid, whispered to
rookie defensive end Eddie Bo Rogers: "Just find you a corner and hide."

Center Jimmy Carroll took a seat in the back and kept his helmet on—just
in case. "I thought for sure he was going to kill us," he said.

Suddenly, the door opened and closed abruptly, and the room grew deadly
silent. And then . . .

"What a friend we have in Je—sus . . ."

Holy crap. The very same thought shot through every player in the place.

Whenever Bryant walked into a room signing a hymn, his players knew to
duck. It was usually the prelude to a serious butt chewing.

But this time he had a big smile on his face, and he started clapping his
hands as he walked to the front of the room, a lit Chesterfield cigarette dangling from his lips.

"This is perfect! We got 'em right where we want 'em," he said, looking
around at the faces of his players, who were, to a man, stunned.

What game had he been watching? Didn't the Bear know Alabama was
down ten points to a good team in the middle of a monsoon?

He just kept smiling and putting a positive spin on the situation, and the players lapped it up like mother's milk.

"That was their half, and now this is our half coming up."

"What a chance we've got! What a chance we've got to show what we're made of."

He was not out of his mind.

Somehow, he knew.

The same relentless driver who spent so much of his life mashing his players into submission, making them feel vulnerable to his wrath, also understood how to make them feel invincible, and so now, just when they needed a jolt of bulletproof, he flipped the switch.

At the most precarious moment of a magical season, Bryant instinctively understood that his players needed something stronger than fear. They hungered for inspiration.

With a few simple words, he demonstrated his faith in them, and to the players in that room, his faith was a powerful thing, a force of nature capable of rivaling the mighty rain itself. None of the supremely confident 'Bama players would ever have admitted losing faith. They never considered the possibility of losing—at least consciously—and this was one of their most potent weapons. The confidence instilled as a matter of course by the system lifted 'Bama to another level routinely. "We played a lot of teams that had more talent than we did," noted kickoff specialist Dudley Kerr, "but once we pulled that red jersey on, we all had the attitude that we were tougher and better prepared than anybody we could possibly play."

Yet, the Crimson Tide was unaccustomed to falling so far behind under such miserable conditions, and Bryant no doubt understood they needed to be inoculated from the natural tendency to be poisoned by pangs of doubt.

"Coach Bryant could say two or three words and it would be like a book, and that was one of those times," said receiver Dennis Homan.

A lesser coach might have leaned too heavy on the gas, perhaps offering up some sentimental gusher about their responsibility to live up to the legacy of all those great Alabama teams of the past. But melodrama was not Bryant's style.

A brilliant stroke of reverse psychology, Bryant's short, simple message also tapped into the memories of all those moments of shared sacrifice, all those harrowing days of physical and mental torture, which prepared them to be able to deal with being ten points down on the road in the rain, when the situation appeared dire.

When he said, "What a chance we've got to show what we're made of," the players heard:

> This is it.
> This is the situation I trained you for.
> You've been knocked down.
> How are you going to respond?
> You want to be a champion?
> Prove it.

Bryant, who often spoke about the similarities between football and life, was known to remind his players how every football game is decided by three or four plays. However, he pointed out, no one can predict when those three or four plays will happen.

Throughout the third quarter, Alabama hung tough. On the second series, Tennessee mounted a solid drive from its own 28 to the Alabama 35, before the Crimson Tide's defense stiffened and forced a punt. The 'Bama offense drove from the shadow of its goal to near midfield before sputtering, and at least it managed to flip the field position and avoid giving Tennessee the ball once more within sight of the red zone.

Toward the end of the third quarter, with Tennessee still leading 10–0 and the rain still pouring, Alabama linebacker Mike Hall landed a thunderous hit on wingback Charles Fulton, who fumbled onto the muddy ground. Defensive end Mike Ford recovered the ball, putting the Crimson Tide in business at the Volunteers' 46 yard line.

The one-two punch by Hall and Ford smelled like one of those plays.

Stabler, unable to complete a single pass in the first half, went back to the air on first down, hitting Dennis Homan for a 14-yard gain. Four plays later, Snake sneaked in from the one, closing the gap to 10–6 with 14:29 remaining in the game.

In the press box, backfield coach Ken Meyer was thinking one.

His boss, still standing dangerously close to Joe Kelley, was thinking two.

"In my mind, I was thinking about playing the percentages and going for the one so we could potentially tie it with a field goal," Meyer said. "Coach Bryant was way ahead of me. He was thinking about winning it with a field goal, and as risky as it was, that was just the way he thought."

Playing for ties was not in Bryant's nature, even though a failed two-point play would require the Crimson Tide to score another touchdown to win.

After consulting with Meyer on the phone, Bryant told Stabler to call the pass play known internally as P-50, a tight end delay, specially designed for the situation.

When Stabler took the snap and rolled left, Wayne Cook broke free from

his man on the line and lumbered straight ahead into the end zone. Snake released the ball with a delicate touch just as the rush converged on him, and
Cook caught the spinner face-mask high, then pulled it to his chest as the
nearby official raised his arms toward the sky.

"I was surprised they called that pass to me," Cook said.

Indeed, Cook, known as a devastating blocker, caught only 14 passes the
whole year, for a grand total of 115 yards. The defense no doubt expected Stabler to run the ball or throw it to either Perkins or Homan. Cook was far down
on the list of offensive weapons, but his 3-yard reception against Tennessee
would be remembered by many of his teammates as the play of the year.

The story behind the catch, the story hardly anyone knew, made it even
more unlikely, even more dramatic.

Without the intervention of his teammates, especially roommate Richard
Cole and close friend Billy Johnson, without the strong-arm tactics of assistant
coach Pat Dye, without his own sense of unquenchable pride, Cook might very
well have quit the team on that Tuesday morning from hell in September 1965,
in which case he never would have been around to make the catch that helped
preserve Alabama's undefeated season.

He was not a sorry dog. He was a champion.

Because he kept the faith, because he continued to fight through his pain
and frustration, because he ignored the little voice that eventually wrestled for
control of every 'Bama player's innermost thoughts, Cook survived to play a
pivotal role on a special team.

Sometimes, a catch is more than a catch. In this case, Cook's tight end delay
was more than the play which kept the Crimson Tide alive heading into the
guts of the fourth quarter. It was a metaphor for the entire Alabama football experience.

Sometimes, one of those pivotal plays happens long before the opening
kickoff.

When the Crimson Tide bussed over to the stadium for a light workout on Friday afternoon, Stabler looked out the window and was surprised to see a
dummy dangling from a construction crane, hanging in effigy—a dummy
wearing a No. 12 red Alabama jersey, which just happened to be his number.

Snake laughed out loud.

He was amused, flattered even, but not the least bit bothered.

Nothing spooked Slim Stabler's boy, not even the infamous fourth down incompletion against Tennessee the previous season, which folks in the Volunteer
state were still jabbering about.

After the Alabama defense held Tennessee on three-and-out and Johnny Mosley negotiated another fair catch, the Crimson Tide, trailing 10–8, took over at its own 25 yard line with about nine minutes remaining. In his twangy, high-pitched voice, Stabler looked around the huddle and said, almost matter-of-factly, "Alright, shut your mouths. We're putting the ball in the end zone."

Four games into his tenure as Alabama's starting quarterback, Stabler had already endeared himself to his teammates and fans alike with his masterful command of the offense. He had silenced all of the skeptics who once wondered if he could pass as well as he could run.

But as the Tide broke the huddle, needing to drive the length of the field to win the football game, it wasn't Stabler's arm or his feet or even his knowledge of the playbook which impressed the rest of the offense. It was his cool-headedness. With the game on the line, as in all other situations, he was absolutely fearless, incapable of being rattled, and positively sure of the inevitability of their ultimate victory. Every player in the huddle fed off his contagious confidence.

"Kenny had this amazing presence in the huddle, which was just so calming, and you could see it in the way he handled things on that drive," said receiver Ray Perkins, who caught a pivotal pass to push 'Bama into Tennessee territory.

Looking around at the capacity crowd of 56,368, most of them cheering for the men in orange, Stabler, forever living in the moment, walked back to the huddle after one play with a big grin and said, to no one in particular, "Man, isn't this fun?"

Pressure?

What pressure?

"Kenny acted like we were already ahead," said offensive guard Bruce Stephens.

As the heir to Trammell, Namath, and Sloan, Stabler was more than just a guy with fleet feet and a strong arm. He was, in a very real sense, an extension of Bryant, and on the field in the second half, he was implementing a vision straight from the "got 'em right where we want 'em" school of thought. While his record-setting game against Ole Miss convinced everyone in the world he could pass with deadly accuracy, his performance in the second half against Tennessee transcended his mediocre statistics. Snake proved he could lead his team out of a mighty hole, in the clutch, despite horrible conditions, and in the process, he assumed the full mantle of the Alabama quarterback.

"I didn't have any doubt in my mind on that drive," Stabler said. " 'Course, I never had any doubt at any other time, either."

Fighting off fatigue and the cumulative effects of an extremely hard-hitting game against a stingy Tennessee defense which would finish the season surrendering just 8.7 points per game, the entire offensive unit was running on adrenaline by the fourth quarter. But the fourth quarter belonged to Alabama. This was an idea which permeated the program. From gym class to two-a-days, the coaches pushed the players to their physical and mental limits in order to make them tough enough to close the deal in the final stanza, when many other teams were prone to surrender to their fatigue. The Alabama players believed in the power of their superior conditioning. They also believed in the power of their collective will to win, which glowed inside every athlete who had proven his commitment by withstanding Alabama's demanding system.

Stabler methodically marched the Crimson Tide downfield, mostly on the ground. In addition to running the option left and right, planting his feet carefully in the treacherous mud, and handing off twice to halfback Gene Raburn, he kept calling Kelley's number, and the 6'3", 210-pound fullback from Cullman—bigger than every one of the offensive linemen blocking for him—kept lowering his shoulder and churning up short yardage. Exhausted, on the way to a twenty-six-carry day, the most prolific of his career, he once tried to wave Stabler off in the huddle. But Snake looked him in the eye and repeated the play, and Kelley dutifully hit the line once more, punishing the men who tackled him, pushing further toward the Tennessee end zone.

"I remember being dog tired on that last drive, but determined to keep going," said Kelley.

When the swarming Tennessee defense stopped Kelley just short of the goal line on third-and-two, Stabler called time-out, unbuttoned his chin-strap, and walked to the sideline to see what the boss wanted to do.

Like General Neyland and many other old-school coaches, Bryant placed tremendous emphasis on the kicking game. Less concerned with how far a punter could boom the ball than how quickly he could get it in the air, Bryant reduced the process to a mathematical equation. In order to punt for him, an athlete was required to kick the ball in 2.2 seconds or less. In the competition for the job heading into the 1965 season, Birmingham's Stan Moss punted for a higher average, but Davis won the position because the stopwatch showed he got the ball off in about 1.8 seconds. Davis's punting average of 38.9 yards per kick was nothing to brag about, but he never came close to getting one blocked.

Field-goal kicking was still considered an act of desperation by most coaches, especially hard-nosed guys like Bryant, who were conditioned to believe they should be able to stick it in for seven when they pushed down close.

This way of thinking played a role in the frustrating loss to Georgia Tech in 1962. But the Bear was learning to be more pragmatic. After All-America end-kicker David Ray graduated following the 1965 season, junior Steve Davis, a National Merit Scholar, took over the field goal and PAT duties. Entering the Tennessee game, he had attempted five field goals, nailing three.

By the time Bryant decided to put the game on Davis's shoulders, the latest of the kicking brothers from Georgia was ready for the most important boot of his life.

The big question surrounded the holder.

Ordinarily, defensive back Bobby Johns held for Davis, but during the time-out, Johns hesitated on the sideline while Bryant and assistant head coach Sam Bailey, who oversaw the kicking game, discussed their options.

"I think we should go with Johns—he's got dry hands," Bailey said.

But Bryant overruled him. He decided to let Stabler hold, because he had been handling the wet ball all day. He wanted to avoid the chance of a bobble on the tee.

Just before the teams lined up, guard Bruce Stephens approached Davis, whose uniform was conspicuous because it was still nearly spotless. "If you don't make this, I'm gonna kill you," Stephens said. He was not smiling.

"Look Bruce," Davis said, trying not to lose his concentration, "I want to make this as bad as you do."

Few positions in football toil in as much anonymity as the snapper and holder on field goals and extra points, and yet the two jobs are absolutely essential for the placekicker to have a chance to score. Precise timing drives the whole process. As soon as the placekicker sees the ball snapped, he starts his motion, knowing it will arrive in a certain period of time—usually less than 1.4 seconds. The holder must pull the ball down and have the laces turned to the proper spot before the kicker's leg reaches the tee, or his rhythm is disturbed, which significantly increases the likelihood of a blocked kick.

Center Jimmy Carroll was known as a fun-loving guy. He especially liked to joke around with head manager Sang Lyda, a splinter who weighed no more than 108 pounds after a good meal. Always prepared for a multitude of contingencies, Lyda kept a piece a chalk in his pants pockets during practice—just in case the coaches wanted to use a blackboard—and during scrimmages at the practice field, he often scribbled little notes on the ball, usually profane phrases, knowing no one would see them except Carroll. It was a running joke between the two south Alabama boys, a harmless way of passing the time between head-knockings. One day, after Lyda scribbled "Eat Shit" in chalk on the side of the ball and placed it on the line of scrimmage, Bryant called a break in the action and told Lyda to bring him the ball so he could demonstrate something. Sang nearly peed in his pants. He furiously wiped his message clean and delivered the ball, without letting the big man see what he was up to.

When the action started, Carroll was a competitive animal who played his guts out. Burdened with the chore of filling the shoes of departed All-American Paul Crane, who was revered for his snapping skills as well as his leadership ability, Carroll had already proven himself as a very competent snapper as well as a good offensive center. Against Tennessee's Morel, he gave as well as he took.

Determined to perfect a deep-snapping technique in which the ball landed with the laces in the correct position, preventing the holder from needing to turn it, Carroll often spent time after practice snapping the ball to Johns, who held for most extra points and field goals.

"OK," Carroll would yell out to his rear after snapping the ball, still in his stance. "Where are the laces?"

"Most of the time with Jimmy, it was so perfect all you had to do was put it on the tee," Johns said.

During the time-out, Carroll asked for a dry ball, but the official would not allow it. "That kinda hurt my feelings," Carroll said.

The snap was bad. The wet ball slipped on release, a wormburner that dribbled back toward Stabler way low. Carroll could feel it as soon as it left his hand, and his heart sank.

Fortunately, Stabler had been handling a wet football all day long—which came in handy, just as Bryant thought—and he used no small amount of his significant athletic skill to pull the ball down and shovel it onto the tee, slightly crooked, just as Davis's leg reached the target. The 17-yard kick was not pretty, but it was good. Alabama led, 11–10, with 3:23 remaining in the game.

"Thank goodness for Stabler," Carroll said. "I'm glad I didn't have to live with that for the rest of my life . . . costing us a game with one bad snap."

Prominently mentioned in Alabama's detailed scouting report for Tennessee was a warning about tight end Austin Denney: "Do not let him off the line of scrimmage. He does not have great speed but he can catch the ball."

The Crimson Tide defense knew about all Denney. The 6'2", 234-pound senior from Nashville entered the game with three touchdown passes in Tennessee's first three games, and he burned 'Bama for number four in the first half. "Every time I tackled him, my head would be ringing for two or three plays," said defensive back Mike Sasser. The Tide managed to contain him and the other Vols receivers for most of the rest of the game. For the first twenty-seven minutes of the second half, Alabama allowed Tennessee quarterback Dewey Warren to complete just 2 passes for a total of 4 yards. Even considering the inclement weather, this was a significant feat against a player who would finish the season as one of the country's most efficient passers. Johnny Sullivan, Richard Cole, and Louis Thompson clawed at his face all day.

But it was the fourth quarter. The game was on the line. Tennessee, like Alabama, wanted it bad. As far as the guys from Knoxville were concerned, the fourth quarter belonged to Tennessee, not Alabama.

After Warren connected with tailback Bill Baker for a 22-yard reception on first down, pushing the Vols to their own 49 as the clock dipped below three minutes, the Alabama defense expected another pass. When Denney handed off to halfback Charles Fulton, it looked for a moment like a sweep, and Alabama linebacker Stan Moss misread a check off and went for the halfback, noticing after it was too late that he had left the tight end uncovered.

"All of a sudden, the ball's snapped and I'm in no-man's land," Moss said.

Before Moss reached him, Fulton lofted a perfect strike to Denney, who raced into the open field. He was bound for glory, and despite what the scouting report said, he could pick it up and put it down pretty swiftly. Dicky Thompson lunged for him but missed. Finally, Johnny Mosley, not one of the fastest players on the team, somehow ran Denney down and slammed him to the ground at the 'Bama 13 yard line, saving the game.

"Coach Bryant always used to say: Do your job and then go help somebody else," Moss said. "That play was a perfect example of what he was talking about. Mosley saved my butt . . . saved the whole season."

Tennessee went back to the ground game and inched toward the goal line, but the clock was running out. With less than half a minute remaining, and the Vols facing a third and goal from the 3 yard line, Tennessee called a time-out and sent Heflin, Alabama, native Gary Wright on for a chip-shot field goal.

Ends coach Dude Hennessey walked toward the bench and turned his back. He could not bear to watch.

Inside his bedroom in Arab, Alabama, a small town southeast of Huntsville, eleven-year-old Terry Robinson was on his knees, praying with all his might. He loved Alabama football, and he was not above asking for a little divine intervention.

"We got to block this! We got to block this!" he mumbled to himself as he listened to 'Bama radio announcer John Forney describe the scene.

Robinson never knew his daddy. He left one day when his son was very young and never came back.

He and his mother were "just poor people trying to get by the best we could," Robinson said. "We didn't have much but each other."

Needing something to believe in, Robinson gravitated to the Alabama Crimson Tide when he was about eight years old. He read all he could find about Bryant and the players, and on Saturdays in the fall, when his mother was working, he would lie on his bed all alone and listen to the games on the radio. Sometimes, he closed his eyes and tried to imagine he was in the stadium, watching from up close, holding one of those red and white shakers he had seen on television. Sometimes, his thoughts drifted to the father he had never known, wishing he could share the experience.

"Alabama football gave me something to hold on to," Robinson said. "It was just everything in the world to me. A way of life. Back then, if we lost a game, it was like the end of the world."

In an era when only a small number of games were telecast—and in a year when Alabama would not be seen on live TV until the seventh Saturday of the season, against LSU—John Forney was more than just a play-by-play announcer. He was the primary connection between the team and its fans, the essential conduit between the Crimson Tide and all those supporters, young and old, male and female, black and white, who invested it with their hopes and dreams. The radio network, organized by Tuscaloosa broadcasting executive Bert Bank in the years after World War II, stretched to every city and town in Alabama and various other parts of the South.

For most fans in 1966, football existed much more in the mind than in the eye, and Forney was the central figure who informed and empowered their imaginations. Concentrating and conjuring mental images was part of the joy of being a football fan in those days, and in 1966, Alabama supporters closed their eyes and tried to envision what Ray Perkins looked like catching a pass over his shoulder, or how close Austin Denney came to breaking free and scoring the game-winning touchdown. In a time before bold yellow lines emblazoned across television screens removed most of the guesswork from first down markers, fans from Dothan to Florence waited breathlessly to hear whether their man ran far enough to move the chains. They could not see it, but they could imagine it, which made the experience part of them in a way that would be lost on future generations spoiled by the ubiquity of televised games.

All across the state, an audience approaching one million people crowded around radios in homes, cars, and offices, waiting anxiously for Forney to call the kick no good, despite their gathering fear. It was the beginning of hunting season, and many fans carried transistor radios into the woods, including injured defensive end Jimmy Israel and several of his friends from Haleyville. Like his teammates on the field in Knoxville, Israel worried about the rough practices sure to follow a loss to the Volunteers.

Like both the Alabama and Tennessee teams, Forney was exhausted by the time Gary Wright stepped on the field. "That game took more out of me as a broadcaster than any I can recall," said Forney, the co-owner of a Birmingham advertising agency.

At least once per week, Alabama took time out of practice to simulate blocking kicks. The special area of the field reserved for this purpose was a sawdust pit, to cushion the players' falls as they repeatedly leapt toward the ball. The sawdust tended to get stuck down inside their practice jerseys, leaving many itching and scratching and trying to jiggle the sawdust out for the rest of practice.

Donnie Johnston's speed and the sound technique he developed in the sawdust pit made him the obvious choice to go after the Tennessee field goal. A sophomore from Birmingham who played at Banks High School—where he was a teammate of Bobby Johns—Johnston was the son of a Baptist minister who was studying to be an architect.

When Bryant yelled his name on the sideline, he came running. "You know what to do," he said.

On his way into the game, Perkins grabbed him from behind. "You can have my tickets to the next game if you block this," he said, an incentive worth more than $100 in 1966 dollars.

Before taking his stance second from the outside, next to Johns, Johnston walked up to the line of scrimmage, drug his cleats on the Alabama edge of the neutral zone, and made his mark. He wanted to give himself a clear view of his boundary, so he could get as close as possible without risking an offsides penalty.

When the ball was snapped, Johnston juked past a lineman and lunged toward the ball, hands extended, just as Wright was stepping into it. A photograph printed on the cover of an ABC Sports college football promotional booklet clearly showed him in position to get a piece of the ball. However, Wright, forced to negotiate a difficult angle, watched in agony as his twenty-yard kick sailed wide right—just barely.

"I was looking right down at the ball as I came in," Johnston said. "If it had been straight, I probably would have caught it in my gut."

Buried by the surging Tennessee line, Alabama's Louis Thompson could not see the kick take flight, so when he finally was able to look up from under the pile, he saw head manager Sang Lyda jumping up and down. "I couldn't see the scoreboard from that angle, but I didn't need to," he said. The image of Sang celebrating told him all he needed to know about Alabama's dramatic 11–10 victory over Tennessee.

When Forney, with his eyes trained on the telling expression of a Tennessee manager standing just beyond the end zone, announced to his huge audience that the kick had failed, Terry Robinson started dancing around his bedroom. "I couldn't believe," he said. "I just couldn't believe it. That kicker was so good, and it was such a short kick. I couldn't believe he missed it."

Coming off the field, as the stadium erupted, defensive linemen Randy Barron and Mike Reilly were stunned to see some frustrated Tennessee fan's pocket knife land at their feet, the blade plunging into the dirt. Reilly picked it up and kept it as a souvenir, and they resumed their jog into the darkness.

Moments later, the jubilant visitors locker room was quickly filling up with cigar smoke. Whenever Alabama beat the Volunteers, head trainer Jim Goostree passed out victory cigars. For the Alabama players, nothing tasted so sweet as a ceremonial stogie on the third Saturday in October, especially under the circumstances, especially behind enemy lines in Knoxville.

Just about the time Bryant was assuring the assembled newsmen, "If the kick had been straight, we would've blocked it," the would-be hero was bent over a trunk in the middle of the locker room, receiving a shot in his hip. In the crash to the ground that followed his rush toward the kick, Donnie Johnston had fallen hard enough to sustain a nasty hip-pointer, which hurt like hell. Instead of becoming a household name in the state of Alabama, Johnston was relegated to a footnote in the annals of one of the most storied rivalries in college football.

"I've never been prouder of a team," a grinning Bryant told reporters. "They certainly proved to me they have class. It takes a lot to come back, come back, come back, and then keep coming back."

Indeed, the Crimson Tide had seized the opportunity to prove something— to Tennessee and to itself. The Bear's wily halftime speech would be cited many times in the years ahead as an example of his motivational mastery, and deservedly so, but Alabama did not win the game at the half or even in the fourth quarter. The intangibles required to cause a bunch of individuals to unite as a team and battle back from adversity are instilled over time. The game against Tennessee was very nearly lost in the fourth quarter, but it was won long before, in the intensity of gym class, the heat of two-a-days, the pressure of spring practice, the discipline of dorm life, and the desperation of hundreds of gut checks, when the players learned to push beyond their own mental and physical boundaries.

The road between Knoxville and the threepeat was long and treacherous, but at least one thing regarding the 4-0 Crimson Tide appeared unimpeachable. Those boys knew how to fight.

8. THE KEY

The way the Crimson Tide rallied in Knoxville to stay unbeaten filled every member of the team with a whole new level of confidence. "After that, we knew nobody could touch us," said linebacker Bob Childs. No one else would get so close. Everyone involved with the Alabama program was beginning to realize the 1966 edition of the Crimson Tide was a special bunch, even by Tuscaloosa's elevated standards.

At the beginning of the week, football fans across two states were still talking about the game, sure to go down as one of the all-time classics in the series. Meeting with reporters on Sunday, with the sting of heartbreaking defeat still surging, Tennessee head coach Doug Dickey praised the poise Alabama demonstrated in the final minutes. "They put on one of the greatest drives I've ever seen there in the fourth quarter," he said. "I doubt there will be a better drive than that on any football field in the country this year."

Champions are made in such moments, but unfortunately, the national championship seemed increasingly out of 'Bama's control. In a day of limited television coverage, the writers and coaches who voted in the wire service polls relied mostly on newspaper coverage to rank teams, and in the one-dimensional realm of newsprint, Alabama's 11–10 victory looked like nothing more than a narrow escape. The line of scores in the paper could not adequately reflect how the Crimson Tide proved incredibly resilient in overcoming significant adversity.

As a result, 'Bama dropped from third to fourth in both the AP and UPI polls on the Monday following the Tennessee victory. After four weeks atop the rankings, Michigan State was supplanted as the No. 1 team by longtime media darling Notre Dame, which moved up from second after crushing Oklahoma, 38–0.

All football seasons invariably are seen through the lens of narrative arcs, and as Notre Dame jumped and jumped and kept jumping, until it leap-frogged right over Michigan State, the plot of the 1966 season was building toward a dramatic conclusion.

It was becoming increasingly clear that Alabama would have to pursue the threepeat while contending with the powerful emerging narrative, being promoted by the national news media, of the November 19 Michigan State-Notre Dame game in East Lansing, still a month away but already being billed as the definitive and climactic showdown for the national championship. Practically no one mentioned the inherent problem of justifying the awarding of the national championship without the participation of undefeated, two-time defending title holder Alabama—at least no one outside the South. In the eyes of the sportswriters hyping the upcoming clash of the titans, Alabama was just a needless distraction.

So how did the Crimson Tide respond to this mounting frustration?

It crushed Vanderbilt, 42–6.

The outcome could have been much worse. Five plays into the game, Bobby Johns intercepted a Commodores' pass and returned it 33 yards for a touchdown, lighting the match that would build into an inferno. Bryant started substituting before halftime, eventually using fifty-eight players, including eleven ballcarriers and all three quarterbacks. The Crimson Tide, which improved to 5–0, out-gained the Commodores 353 yards to 114 and punted just once, methodically dominating every phase of the contest.

The Alabama defense, which had allowed just two touchdowns and a total of seventeen points in its first four games—including victories over two bowl teams, Ole Miss and Tennessee—was even stronger, due to one key personnel change. After breaking down the Tennessee film and watching diminutive Tom Somerville struggle at noseguard against Tennessee's larger offensive line, Bryant reassigned him to offense, where he would spend the rest of the season backing up guard Johnny Calvert. This allowed the Tide to anchor Johnny Sullivan at nose and Louis Thompson and Richard Cole at the tackles, an upfront combination that would prove practically impenetrable in the weeks ahead.

"We were never actually in the game," lamented Vandy head coach Jack Green, whose team was headed to a 1–9 finish. "You have to play the perfect game if you have any hopes of staying with Alabama. We were far from perfect."

Five and a half minutes after Bobby Johns's heroics, the ball zipped through the air like a bullet.

Les Kelley knew how to zoom it when he had a man wide open.

Ray Perkins extended his hands, caught the ball, tucked it away, and kept running, never breaking stride. Kelley's halfback option—his first and only pass attempt in college—was right on the money, and so was Perkins's route, as usual. The swift, sure-handed senior turned on the gas and motored into the end zone for a twenty-nine-yard touchdown, his third of the season.

Perkins grunted when he ran. From a certain distance, it sounded like he was humming, which is why, in later years, teammates nicknamed him "the Hummingbird." The grunting was the physical manifestation of his straining to go faster, ever faster—the sound of his untrammeled ambition, pulsating like a second heartbeat, a constant reminder that the poor boy from Mississippi was determined to go places, far beyond the nearest end zone, far beyond his daddy's toolbox.

Nothing could silence his grunting. Not even his frightening brush with death.

Riding in the backseat of his daddy's car on the way home from a trip to the Mississippi Gulf Coast beaches when he was no more than eight or nine years old, Ray Perkins was mesmerized by the expanse of unspoiled woods surrounding the two-lane highway. The tall pine trees loomed in the distance for as far as he could see.

"I remember wishing that someday I could have a piece of property where I could own everything for as far as I could see," he said.

While many boys of his age dreamed of playing centerfield for the New York Yankees or riding off into the sunset alongside Gene Autry, Ray Perkins was focused instead on becoming a landowner, which said a mouthful about his powerful need to transcend his modest upbringing.

Thomas Perkins, his father, worked hard as a carpenter, but he barely earned enough to support Ray, his younger sister, and their mother, who suffered from a chronic illness that left her bedridden for significant periods. Perkins learned to work hard from watching his daddy hammer and saw, and from an early age, he was good with his hands. The desire to get out on his own and start earning his own money motivated Perkins when he was still very young, filling him with the ambition to be a man, to stand on his own two feet, long before most boys ever started to think in such a way. "I always wanted more than my father could provide," he said.

Bored with school, Perkins dropped out in the middle of the eighth grade and eventually landed a job painting houses for his uncle. He also worked for a time as a carhop at a popular local drive-in, where he once saw Elvis Presley pull up in a brand-new Cadillac.

Soon after he started making his own money, Ray approached his father, who drank too much too often, and offered to pay him $20 per month if he promised to stop hitting the bottle. The teenage son could see how the alcohol abuse was affecting the whole family, and was willing to tempt his father into sobriety with a significant incentive, the equivalent of more than a day's pay on the construction trail.

Thomas dismissed the thought with a sneer. "Keep your money," the father told his son.

Earning his own money liberated Perkins from his father to a certain degree, and while he continued to live at home and maintain a good relationship with his old man, Ray essentially supported himself from the time he was fourteen. He never took another nickel from his father, except a $20 bill Thomas gave him after watching the 1965 Alabama-Mississippi State game in Jackson, the first and last time he saw his son play football. With his beloved, devout mother—who insisted he attend church every Sunday—sick so much of the time, Ray handled many of the chores around the house, including washing his clothes and cooking some meals.

While his father and mother seemed powerless to prevent him from throwing away his education, others could see he was making a big mistake. Several months after he dropped out, Perkins was mowing the lawn when Ed Palmer stopped by to see him. Palmer, a math teacher and assistant football coach at his old school, told him to go inside and pack a change of clothes. He was taking a bunch of junior high school kids to football camp, and he wanted Ray to come along. "You're gonna play football and we're getting your butt back in school," Palmer said. Perkins didn't argue. He just gathered his things and jumped in the back of Palmer's car, not quite understanding that he was riding off into a future profoundly shaped by one act of kindness.

More than four decades later, Perkins looked back on the moment as a life-altering event. "Ed Palmer just happened to come by my house at the right time, and it changed everything," he said. "I owe everything I've done since then to that one guy."

The need to stay eligible to play football and three other sports motivated Perkins to take his schoolwork more seriously, and he never again thought about dropping out of school. The serious, driven teenager, mature beyond his years, landed a job at a service station across the street from his high school when he started the ninth grade. A couple of months later, Marcus James, the owner of the station, called the wiry freshman into his office.

"Hold your hand out," James said, and then he placed a set of keys in Perkins's right palm. "I want you to start opening up in the morning and closing up at night."

Stunned, Perkins struggled for words.

Him?

Marcus James was handing him a set of keys?

The fifteen-year-old grease monkey, who pumped gas and handled a variety of minor automotive repairs around the full-service station, could hardly believe his ears. Burdened with low self-esteem, still unsure of where all his hard work might someday lead, the carpenter's son could hardly believe that James was willing to entrust him with the keys to his business, and the feeling of those keys in his hand validated him in a way he was still too young to fully appreciate. It made him feel special, perhaps for the first time in his life. More than the money he earned, the responsibility symbolized by those keys, the faith, made him feel like a man.

"Marcus believed in me, when I needed somebody to believe in me," Perkins said.

For the next four years, Perkins opened the station at dawn and worked until he went off to school, then returned after football practice to handle the night shift. He worked from daylight to dusk on Saturdays and Sundays. James, who became a father figure to his young employee, eventually cosigned the $500 bank note that enabled Perkins to purchase his first car—a 1955 Ford Farlaine. By the time he was old enough to get his driver's license, Perkins was already an accomplished mechanic, and he tinkered with the Ford until it ran like a scalded dog. Once, when Perkins ventured to the nearby city of Hattiesburg, the cops arrested him for disturbing the peace with his loud muffler, and instead of calling his father, he phoned Marcus, who bailed him out of jail.

His mother never wanted him to play football. Afraid her little boy would get hurt playing the rough game, she tried to stop him, but he assured her he knew what he was doing. Always one of the most tenacious players of his age group, Ray slowly matured into a tough-to-topple fullback on an outstanding Petal team that captured a conference championship in his senior season of 1961. He was blessed with good moves and a nice little burst of speed, but he much preferred lowering his head and running over defenders.

"I'm not quite sure when I realized football was my ticket, but if it hadn't been for football, I'm not sure what would have happened to me," Perkins said at his Mississippi home on a fall day in 2004. "In fact, if it hadn't been for the combination of Ed Palmer, Marcus James, and Coach Bryant . . ."

His voice trailed off and he stared into the distance.

"You're talking about three people who had a deep impact on my life, probably deeper than I'll ever know."

Not much interested in the larger sports world growing up, Perkins nevertheless heard all the stories about Paul "Bear" Bryant, who seemed like his sort of guy. From the time a local Alabama alumnus gave him a 'Bama media guide during his sophomore year, he wanted to play for the Crimson Tide, and although the cocky kid made Dude Hennessey work for his signature, he would have walked to Tuscaloosa to play for the greatest coach in the business. For months, he carried a letter from Bryant folded up in his wallet, pulling it out from time to time just to read it once more.

"I figured if I could play for him, I could play for anybody," Perkins said. "I was just another guy who felt like he had something to prove."

When the Alabama coaches started talking to him seriously during the 1961 season, when the Crimson Tide was hot on the trail of Bryant's first national championship, a friend who thought he knew the score told Perkins he might be able to get a little something extra if they really wanted him. "They might get you a wardrobe," the friend said, meaning a set of clothes.

Several days later, after watching Mike Fracchia, the greatest runner he had ever seen, lead the Crimson Tide to a 26–7 victory over North Carolina State—quarterbacked by future Los Angeles Rams great Roman Gabriel—Perkins was sitting in the passenger seat of assistant coach Pat James's car. Behind the wheel, James, a former Kentucky player, who would leave Tuscaloosa after the 1964 season to join Charley Bradshaw's staff at his alma mater, was leading the recruit on a tour of the campus, pointing out the various buildings and offering his best sales pitch.

Not quite knowing how to broach the subject, Perkins slowly gathered his courage. Finally, he just blurted it out.

"Coach," he said, "I'm not a rich man by any means, and I don't have any good clothes to come to school in. I sure would like to get some clothes as part of this deal."

The silence was icy.

James pulled up to the curb and stared at Perkins.

"Son," he said, suddenly looking hurt, "we want you to come to the University of Alabama to play football and get your education, but we don't do that sort of thing. We're offering you a scholarship and that's it."

Perkins was crushed, not because he apparently was not getting a new wardrobe as part of his deal, but because he had obviously offended someone who was offering him a wonderful opportunity.

"I never felt so small in my life," he said.

Ever since Marcus James made him feel big for the first time, he understood the full measure of feeling small. The two moments loomed like psychological bookends for the young man straddling the fence between adolescence and adulthood, and just as he would forever carry the pride of holding those keys in his hand for the first time, he would also carry the shame of asking Pat James for something under the table.

Soon after signing with Alabama—as one of sixty-five incoming freshmen, including sixteen fullbacks—twenty-year-old Perkins graduated from high school at the end of the term in early January 1962 and then married his girl-friend Carolyn, a pretty blonde several years older, who taught at his school. Ready to settle down and have a family, Perkins had already worked out the details with the Alabama coaching staff, allowing the couple to live off-campus in married student housing. Wanting to earn some good money before reporting to Tuscaloosa during the summer, Perkins and his new bride moved to Texas, where the Alabama staff helped him land a job as a lighting maintenance man at an office building owned by Houston Oilers founder Bud Adams. He borrowed some cleats from a local high school coach, which allowed him to spend much of his spare time working out, preparing for the enormous test awaiting him in Tuscaloosa—as if anything could.

In high school, Perkins thought he was tough. Everyone around Petal thought he was tough. Many folks had watched him lay his body on the line time and time again, which was the definition of toughness in their little corner of the world. "I wasn't nearly as tough then as I thought I was," he said.

Like all of his new teammates, he was unprepared for the rigorous demands of playing big-time football at Alabama. Feeling unappreciated by the coaches, he even considered transferring during his freshman season, especially after his poor study habits led him into academic trouble. He reconsidered, however, and worked hard to pull up his grades. In time, he started to learn that the kind of mental toughness required to survive in Tuscaloosa was much more complicated than having the ability to withstand physical pain.

"When I got to Alabama, like all players, I got to a certain point where I thought I was wasted, and my inclination was to stop," Perkins said. "Well, I still had some more to give, but I didn't know it yet. I could go farther, because the coaches pushed me . . . showed me how to break beyond that barrier in my head. I learned that I could take a lot more than I thought I could."

During spring practice heading into his sophomore year in 1963, Perkins took a pitch from the quarterback and darted across the line. When defensive back Billy Piper moved in to tackle him, both athletes lowered their heads, each one preparing to punish the other. The collision of helmets, a thunderous lick, knocked both players to the ground. Piper quickly pulled himself off the grass, but Perkins was out cold.

Rushed to Birmingham's University Hospital, Perkins was diagnosed with a blood clot on his brain. The prognosis was dire. With his life hanging in the balance, doctors performed risky brain surgery to deal with the clot, which was exerting tremendous pressure on his brain and could have exploded in a fatal burst at any time. In 1963, operating on the brain was still shrouded in mystery and dread, and the procedure doctors performed was nearly as perilous as the condition itself. The surgeons drilled two holes in his head and drained the clot, but contrary to some reports, no steel plate was installed.

His wife Carolyn, scared to death, was comforted by the constant presence of Bryant, who maintained a vigil at the hospital for the next nine days. He assured her that her husband's scholarship would be honored, regardless of whether he could ever return to the football field. At least he could get his education. Bryant had seen many of his players sustain devastating, career-ending injuries, but he had never watched so helplessly while one of his boys fought for his life.

When he woke up in intensive care with a pounding headache, which would linger for several days, Perkins asked his doctors how soon he could suit up. "We'll see," one of them said, trying not to shatter his spirits. The man in the next bed, who had also sustained a head injury, lay in a coma, and Perkins soon would come to understand how lucky he was just to be conscious.

Nearly everyone believed his football career was over.

"We truthfully never thought Ray would play another down," Bryant confided three years later.

The close call made Perkins realize the importance of finishing his education, especially with a wife to support. They were starting to think about children—Tony, the first of his two sons, would be born in 1964—and he felt the tug of increasing responsibilities. Redshirted during the 1963 season, he spent the next several months running and working out, without taking contact.

"There was no way I was going to put it in my mind that I wasn't going to play again," he said. "I just wouldn't allow myself to even consider the possibility. They [the doctors and coaches] were going to have to tell me no."

After Perkins briefly toyed with the idea of kicking, assistant coach Gene Stallings suggested to Bryant that they try him at receiver, where he would face fewer potentially dangerous head-on collisions. During practice, while the rest of the team scrimmaged and drilled in pads, he stood on the sidelines in sweats, catching passes from trainer Jim Goostree and anyone else he could find to throw to him. "Ray just wouldn't be denied," Goostree later said. "He was determined to make himself into a receiver and to get back on that football field, no matter what it took." While teaching himself to catch, to run routes, to think like a receiver—while periodically returning to see his doctor for checkups—he also experienced a transformation in the way he approached the game.

"You never know how much something means to you until it's taken away," Perkins said. "Having the game taken away made me want it so much more."

Like many others, Perkins was predisposed to put up with the rigors of Alabama football because the game meant so much to him. Playing football was not just something he did. It was a large part of his identity—the ultimate expression of his toughness, his ambition, his self-esteem, his commitment to excellence, his need to prove his worth to others and to himself. Without the game, a big part of him felt empty and unfulfilled. The accident made him even hungrier, even more dedicated, and his drive to return to action was in reality a desperation to reclaim part of himself.

The mental part of recovering from any significant injury is usually the toughest aspect, because even after the doctors and therapists have solved the physical problem, the brain naturally wants to react by telling the body to be tentative, even fearful. In Perkins's case, the severity of the injury, the knowledge that he was lucky just to be alive, lingered in his head at all times. Far beyond the ability to sustain physical pain, even past the imaginary threshold that all Alabama players were challenged to ignore, Perkins demonstrated his mental toughness by learning a new position while suppressing the urge to wonder if his next tackle might be his last.

After observing him for more than a year and putting him through various tests, Dr. Griff Harsh finally cleared him to play toward the end of the summer in 1964. No one could say whether the condition might reoccur, or whether playing the game placed him at a greater risk than anyone else walking down the street, but the signs were all positive. He returned to live action in a world full of unknowns.

"The day they told me I could play again was one of the happiest of my life," Perkins said.

The same injury that threatened Perkins's career eventually enhanced it. Without it, he might never have been moved to receiver. Without it, he probably would have finished his playing career in 1965. Without it, odd as it may seem, the faith of Ed Palmer, Marcus James, and Paul Bryant might never have been fully realized.

Some tackles are bigger than others, and for all the pain it caused at the time, Billy Piper's collision turned out to be one of the most important licks of all in shaping the 1966 Crimson Tide. Imagining the 1966 Alabama team without Ray Perkins is like trying to contemplate the Super Bowl–winning

Pittsburgh Steelers of the 1970s without Lynn Swann. Or the Beatles without Paul McCartney. In many ways, Perkins was the face of the 1966 Crimson Tide—the personification of drive, perseverance, and mental toughness.

Partially because he was so much older than most of his teammates and because, as one of a handful of married players, he lived away from Bryant Hall, Perkins struck most as distant, even cold. "Ray was something of a loner," said receiver Dennis Homan. Forever serious, forever focused, he never joined in the festivities at The Tide—in fact, he never drank a beer until he was 27—and he was not known to go hunting or fishing with the boys. He cultivated an image as a tough guy not to be messed with, and while he was widely admired and respected for his leadership on the field and off, few players on the team felt especially close to him.

Like the other married couples, the Perkinses lived in a tiny apartment at Northington Campus, a converted World War II–era Navy hospital located on the site of Tuscaloosa's present day University Mall. Haphazardly carved out of the old medical complex, each apartment was slightly different. One place had once been an operating room, and the university officials who had rushed to reconfigure the building in the years after the war, to meet the housing demand caused by the sudden surge of ex-servicemen, neglected to remove more than half a dozen sinks randomly positioned around the apartment. Needing a little more space for his home, Perkins bought several pieces of plywood, appropriated a hallway adjoining his flat, and used the carpentry skills he had learned from his daddy to build another room. No one cared. In fact, everyone marveled at his ingenuity, squeezing a little more value out of his $41 monthly rent.

Always anxious to make an extra buck to supplement his scholarship, Perkins enlisted in the Alabama National Guard, which kept him occupied one weekend a month; offered his services as an auto mechanic to his teammates and coaches; bought and sold appliances discarded by graduating students; and brokered tickets he had procured from underclassmen. He repaired backfield coach Ken Meyer's washing machine, even painted ends coach Dude Hennessey's house. After selling the old Ford Marcus James had helped him buy, Perkins gave line coach Howard Schnellenberger $50 for his old junker, primarily because it contained a still-valid faculty parking decal, which allowed him to drive right up to his classes without having to walk for blocks to find one of the few on-campus student spaces. A green sticker was like gold.

On the field and off, Perkins was a hustler in every sense of the word.

"Ray could not catch the ball very well when he started," said receivers coach Richard Williamson, a graduate assistant at the time of Perkins's injury. "He was so determined, and he taught himself how to catch before he ever got to me. It was sheer will. When he set his mind to do something, he was bound and determined to find a way to do it."

After a solid sophomore year catching passes from Joe Namath and an even better junior year teaming with Steve Sloan, Perkins attracted the whole country's attention in the 1966 Orange Bowl. Perkins entered his senior season widely regarded as one of the nation's outstanding receivers. At the end of the year, he joined offensive tackle Cecil Dowdy, defensive back Bobby Johns, and defensive tackle Richard Cole on various All-America teams.

For all his acrobatic skills, which often amazed defenders and his own teammates, Perkins was not especially graceful, like some receivers. His 4.4 speed in the 40-yard dash set him apart, and he could run forever without tiring. "It seemed like he hardly ever drew a breath," said Richard Williamson. The secret to his success was not so much finesse, but toughness. Even as he taught himself to be a receiver mechanically, he thought more like a linebacker or a fullback, attacking every play determined to beat and punish the guy in front of him—with the ball or without it.

"Ray was one of the most intense guys I've ever known," said backup receiver Richard Brewer, who caught a touchdown pass against Vanderbilt. "He could not stand to make a mistake."

In addition to his demonstrated pass-catching skills, he also became a dedicated blocker. When 6', 183-pound Perkins slammed into someone, he knew he had been blocked. Despite his brush with death—or perhaps because of it—no one could ever accuse Perkins of avoiding the rough and tumble aspects of the game. He might have heard the nagging little voice ringing in his head, but if so, he chose to ignore it, which was a lesson to all.

Instead, he paid attention to other voices, from within and without, exhorting him to strain, push, reach, perform.

"Catch it! Catch it! Catch it!"

Even in his sleep, Perkins sometimes could hear the sound of Williamson encouraging him, challenging him as he ran a route and chased down a pass during practice.

After watching Perkins set a regular season school record by catching nine passes against Ole Miss, Tennessee assistant coach—and one-time All America back—George Cafego marveled at his skill. "That Perkins is the smoothest thing around, isn't he?"

The 1966 Alabama offense was heavily influenced by Perkins's presence at split end, even more than his stats might suggest. In addition to his 33 regular season catches for 490 yards—a 14.8 yard average—and 7 touchdowns, the threat he represented opened things up for Dennis Homan. Having two game-breakers with 4.4 speed, sure hands, and great moves caused opposing defenses fits. In fact, no team in the country could boast two such outstanding receivers. Opponents who tried to shut down Perkins by double-teaming him usually were left vulnerable to Homan, and vice versa. The friendly rivalry with Homan, who caught 23 passes for 377 yards—a 16.4 average—and 5 touchdowns from the flanker position, also motivated Perkins to keep challenging himself.

The greatest impact of the Perkins-Homan tandem was how it kept the defense honest while strengthening the running game. The Crimson Tide's option-oriented offense used the pass primarily to set up the run, and as long as defenses were forced to cover two great receivers and try to stop the ground game, quarterback Kenny Stabler could use his skill in running, passing, and faking to maximum effect.

Beyond strategy and tactics, Perkins's quiet leadership was a powerful force across the entire team. Elected one of the team's permanent co-captains—along with defensive lineman Richard Cole—he rarely said much, but his remarkable comeback was like a monument to the whole concept of perseverance and paying the price. He inspired his teammates one grunt at a time.

With the exception of Kenny Stabler, none of the players on the 1966 Alabama football team showed up in Tuscaloosa thinking seriously about the possibility of playing pro ball, despite the program's history of producing athletes who advanced to the next level.

One of the first 'Bama players to make the leap, in fact, had been Bryant's former teammate, All-America end Don Hutson, who revolutionized the passing game as a receiver for the Green Bay Packers before World War II. When the National Football League launched its annual draft in 1936, No. 1 pick—and initial Heisman Trophy winner—Jay Berwanger declined to turn pro, leaving the second selection, Alabama back Riley Smith, with a historic distinction: He became the first drafted player to sign and play, spending three seasons with the Boston franchise.

In 1966, teams in the NFL and the rival American Football League featured more than a dozen former 'Bama players, including Packers quarterback Bart Starr, Jets quarterback Joe Namath, Cowboys linebacker Lee Roy Jordan, and Cardinals tight end Ray Ogden.

Except for the occasional studs like Namath and Jordan, most of the players on the 'Bama teams of the era were considered too small and ungifted for the NFL. Besides, salaries for all but the stars remained relatively modest, not much more than could be earned in professions with much longer life spans, where the other folks around the office were not capable of breaking your legs in the course of the daily routine.

Developing yourself into a bone-crushing defender or a runner with break-away speed was not yet the equivalent of holding a winning lottery ticket. For those who entertained the idea of sweating for pay, love of the game and the chance to avoid a regular job for a few more years represented much bigger fac-tors than the opportunity to get rich quick. When 'Bama kicker Tim Davis was offered a free agent contract after graduation in 1964, it was not attractive enough to distract him from medical school. For the vast majority of players at Alabama and elsewhere, college football remained an end in itself, not a launch-ing pad to multimillion-dollar contracts.

Ray Perkins arrived in Tuscaloosa planning to become a high school coach. "I never gave pro football the first thought when I signed with Alabama," he said.

The explosion in salaries and the symbiotic relationship between college and pro football evolved over time, but more than any other player, Alabama's Joe Namath started the fire. At a time when $10,000 was a good salary—and many pro football players earned less—Namath's record-setting haul seemed like a fortune. The competition between the NFL and AFL drove up the prices for the stars and eventually for marginal players as well.

Toward the end of the 1965 season, to Perkins's surprise, Baltimore of the NFL and Boston of the AFL drafted the future rights to him. His stock rose dramatically after the 1966 Orange Bowl, when the whole country watched his dazzling performance. Eligible to be drafted a year before he could actually sign, because he had been redshirted, Perkins started thinking for the first time about postponing his coaching plans.

The week heading into the 5-0 Crimson Tide's game against Mississippi State at Denny Stadium, Perkins stopped by to see Bryant at his office. He wanted to ask a favor.

Because of his role as president of the A Club and as a cocaptain of the squad, Perkins was closer to Bryant than anyone on the 1966 team. They shared a special relationship—which probably had more than a little to do with his head injury—and while most of the players avoided the boss's office at all costs, circumstances had conspired to make Perkins feel more comfortable around a man whom he saw as a father figure.

The whole process of negotiating a sports contract was foreign to Perkins, and the concept of the sports agent was still in its infancy. Former teammate Joe Namath told him he should get someone he trusted to represent him, and he trusted Bryant implicitly, so he walked right into his coach's office and asked if he would mind serving as his agent.

Forty years later, in the shadow of a much more complex system, the thought boggles the mind on several different levels. But at the time, under the circumstances, it was a perfectly logical request, so Bryant, who thought very highly of Perkins, said he didn't know much about the process, either, but that he would be happy to entertain offers on the player's behalf.

"It took me a while to get up the nerve to go in and ask him, and I was really relieved when he didn't turn me down," Perkins said.

He walked out of the office and tried to put the uncertain future out of his mind, because he still had a championship to win.

9. ONE FINE DAY

The journey always began with such hope. Every athlete who arrived on the Alabama campus believed he was going to run out onto the field wearing the red jersey and take his place in a long line of hard-hitting warriors exalted by the grateful Crimson Tide nation. This possibility was the source of much of the program's inherent strength, motivating young men from various backgrounds to reach and endure. But like all college football teams, the Crimson Tide was filled with players who never quite measured up to their expectations or the coaches', their dreams shattered by injuries or simply the vagaries of the competitive process.

If you want to truly understand a football team, or any group of competitive individuals, follow the heartbreak. Follow the disappointment. Follow the tears.

In this sense, it is impossible to comprehend the full measure of Alabama's success in 1966 without considering what the sometimes excruciating journey of Wayne Trimble said about the Crimson Tide.

Entering the fourth quarter on a warm late October Saturday at Denny Stadium, undefeated, fourth-ranked Alabama led stubborn Mississippi State, 13–0. The defense was dominating, having allowed the Bulldogs to cross midfield just once. But the offense kept sputtering, twice turning the ball over inside the MSU 20 yard line, including an errant Kenny Stabler pass intercepted in the end zone.

Underdog State—in the middle of a twenty-two-year losing streak against Alabama, stretching from the early days of rock 'n' roll to the last days of disco—came to play against the two-time defending national champions, leaving a bone-jarring impression on the Crimson Tide. On the fifth play of the quarter, the usually precise Stabler threw another interception deep in Alabama territory, only his third of the season, in sixty-two attempts. This one hurt. The turnover set up a three-yard touchdown run by State's Prentice Calhoun, which closed the gap to 13–7 with 11:40 remaining.

When Bryant, fed up with Snake's uncharacteristic inability to stick the ball in the end zone, sent backup Wayne Trimble into the game to ice it, he said simply, "See what you can do." The directive belied the personal drama rumbling under the surface. Trimble, one of the most gifted athletes ever to suit up in an Alabama uniform, a player with marvelous talent and horrible luck, was nearing the end of a disappointing four-year ride. It was difficult to see him as anything less than a tragic figure.

But redemption can be a mighty force. Redemption can happen right in the middle of someone else's nightmare.

Trimble never understood how anyone could even consider leaving the Alabama football team voluntarily. "Sure, we worked hard, real hard," he said, "but we got to live in a nice place with air-conditioning and eat steak all the time, and they paid for our education. Sounded like a great deal to me, and they weren't about to run me off. It sure beat shoveling coal."

He hated shoveling coal.

Before Wayne was born, his father, R. O. Trimble, bought the mineral rights to a small coal mine near Arkadelphia, south of their Cullman County home, in the north central part of Alabama. The family business consisted of mining the coal, transporting it to a storage location in Cullman, and then selling it by the $1 sack load to individuals to heat their homes. They spent most of the hot summer months building inventory, piling it up into a mountain of black, in order to meet the demand of all their steady customers come winter. The coal business was dirty, exhausting, backbreaking work, and Wayne learned the value of his own sweat at an early age.

Danger forever lurked in the shadows. When Wayne's older brother Murray was about five, he accidentally tripped a dynamite blasting cap used in the mining operation. Lucky not to have lost his life, he lost most of his right arm in the explosion. One morning in 1959, their forty-six-year-old father was heading down the road toward the mine driving a front-end loader. Somehow, he lost control of the vehicle on the steep, narrow grade, and it flipped over. The impact crushed him, leaving Wayne fatherless as he transitioned from junior high school in the rural community of Hanceville to high school in the county seat of Cullman.

Determined to keep the small business alive, his strong-willed mother continued to support the family with the demand for coal dust. On Saturday mornings, the office telephone started ringing shortly after dawn, and Wayne and his mother typically spent the whole day delivering the orders to families throughout the area, from the back of a dusty pick-up truck.

"It was a living, but I knew pretty early on that I didn't want to do that for the rest of my life," Trimble said.

Fortunately, the 6'3", 203-pound Trimble was one of the most talented football players ever to come out of northern Alabama, and football would save him from shoveling coal for the rest of his life.

"Wayne was the best damn athlete I had ever seen," said high school and college teammate Johnny Calvert. "Absolutely amazing."

As the quarterback for Oliver Woodard's powerhouse Cullman Bearcats, who finished undefeated and claimed a mythical state championship in his senior year of 1962—four years before the Alabama High School Athletic Association launched its playoff system—Trimble could run, pass, and turn busted plays into moments of awe-inspiring, head-shaking magic.

Football was in his blood, and so was his connection to the Bear.

Soon after Bryant arrived at Texas A&M in 1954, he received a discouraging telephone call from Elmer Smith, one of his assistant coaches, who was having very little luck scrounging for available high school talent at an all-star game in Alabama.

"Are there any that aren't signed, and who can play?" Bryant related in *Bear*, the 1974 autobiography he wrote with John Underwood.

"Yeah, there's one."

"Then sign him."

"Well, coach, there is one thing. He's only got one arm."

Impressed by the way Murray Trimble attacked, despite his disability, Smith signed him to play for the Aggies. Two years later, Stubby, as he was affectionately known to friends, became an All-Southwest Conference guard, helping A&M win its first league title in more than a decade. He loved Bryant like a father, and the feeling was passed down to his little brother.

When Wayne became a prep All-American and started attracting attention from college recruiters, he declined to accept any official visits, not wanting to lead anyone on. Auburn's Shug Jordan called the house one night and told him he had a scholarship with his name on it, but Trimble left no room for interpretation. "Coach, I really appreciate the offer, but my mind's already made up," he said. He was heading to Alabama to play for the Bear, a decision enthusiastically supported by his mother, who had been charmed by the coach during his A&M days. "There was never any discussion about it, and there was never any doubt," he said.

On the day Bryant drove up the driveway in his big black Cadillac to make it official, Wayne was standing outside in the yard with some of the neighborhood kids. He watched the coach climb out of the car and thought to himself, "That's the biggest man I've ever seen in my life." The next hour was a blur. He could not wait to pull on one of those red jerseys.

All the folks around Cullman expected him to be the next Joe Namath.

The torment started even before Trimble reported for his freshman year at Alabama. During practice leading up to the state high school all-star game at Denny Stadium, he snagged a punt, started heading upfield, and broke a bone in his foot, which left him hobbling into the 1963 season.

After surgery, the pride of Cullman made a complete recovery and moved up the depth chart during his first spring with the varsity, winning the job as backup quarterback behind Namath. No doubt about it, the kid with the rifle arm looked like the heir apparent to the man destined to be known as Broadway Joe. However, the first time he carried the ball in a varsity game, in relief of Namath during a season-opening drubbing of Georgia in 1964, a Bulldogs tackler crushed him with his helmet, breaking three ribs. The concessive crash collapsed a lung.

By the time he returned to action several weeks later, junior Steve Sloan—the starter in the 1964 Sugar Bowl, in Namath's absence—had already reasserted himself as the backup, which made him the heir apparent the next year.

Because he was too good of an athlete to stand and watch, the coaches moved Trimble to fill a need—for the first of several times. He finished the year at tailback, eventually overcoming a separated shoulder to catch a touchdown pass from Namath in the Orange Bowl. In 1965, with Kenny Stabler firmly established as Sloan's backup, Trimble found a home at defensive rover, before moving back to tailback, then to quarterback heading into his senior season.

None of Trimble's various injuries represented a knockout punch, but the time they cost prevented him from competing at full strength against Sloan and Stabler. His tremendous athleticism actually worked against him, blocking him from settling in at any one position, unwittingly undermining his bid to become the next great Alabama quarterback.

"Wayne could have been an all-star quarterback at a lot of schools," said backfield coach Ken Meyer. "He just had the misfortune of having to compete against three tremendously gifted quarterbacks [Namath, Sloan, and Stabler]."

The archetype of unfulfilled promise is as old as the game itself. The sport is filled with Wayne Trimbles, young men who appear to have all the ability in the world and somehow stumble on the road to greatness. Amid all the overachievers who somehow found a way to start on Alabama's championship teams, the immensely talented Trimble worked diligently and yet could not overcome his combination of poor injury luck and lousy timing, two things completely beyond his control.

"I guess you could say I had a disappointing college career," Trimble said four decades after the fact. "But I wouldn't trade going to Alabama for anything in the world. I'm proud to have a couple of national championship rings, and all I ever wanted was to help Alabama win the best I could."

If he had signed with Auburn, Tennessee, Georgia, or any of the other schools that came calling, Trimble's name might very well be splattered all over the record books. Of course, he could have transferred at any time, to a place without a Namath, without a Sloan, without a Stabler. In later years, when the rising tide of individualism swept over the game, when athletes started arriving on campus more concerned with protecting their NFL draft status than contributing to a winning team, it would become commonplace for gifted players like Trimble to migrate elsewhere rather than sit on the bench.

Trimble's continued dedication in the face of repeated frustration reflected something important about the 1966 Alabama team as it chased a third straight national championship. Like most of the athletes he played alongside, Wayne loved Alabama so much, loved winning so much, that he would rather be a small part of a winning team in Tuscaloosa than go somewhere else and be a star. The roster was full of players who felt this way, but none paid quite as high a price for the feeling as Trimble. The team was full of players who sacrificed at the altar of building a championship team, but no one sacrificed quite like Trimble. He threw more than just his body into the crucible. He unwittingly gave up his dreams.

Instead of taking his place in the line of venerated All-America quarterbacks who led the Crimson Tide to championships, becoming the next man in the parade of Trammell, Namath, and Sloan, he wound up spending his senior year as the backup to Stabler. Naturally, he was crushed.

Despite all his talent, despite his hard work and dedication, despite his intense love of Alabama, he was reduced to a marginal figure in the history of Crimson Tide football. Trimble saw plenty of playing time and contributed to 'Bama's success throughout the season, but still, he came close enough to his dream to touch it, then watched it dangle just out of his reach. His heartbreak could not be seen from a distance, but up close, among the brotherhood, it was deeply felt, yet rarely discussed.

As Bryant took great pains to teach his players, learning to deal with adversity and disappointment is a big part of football and life, and instead of quitting in disgust or pouting about the situation, Trimble accepted his role with a smile and kept working his butt off to help his team win. Every day. Every snap. He knew it was his job to be ready, just in case, but he also knew it was his job, as a senior and as a quarterback, to demonstrate leadership by going full speed all the time, forever pushing himself to get better, setting a good example for the younger guys on the team. Any athlete on the squad who watched Trimble suck it up and give it everything he had, in spite of his career of disappointment, was motivated by the experience to follow his lead, and in ways that could not be seen from a distance, this was one of a thousand minidramas which contributed to the ultimate strength of the 1966 team.

Like every man on the squad, his desire for team achievements far surpassed any need for individual glory, because wearing the red jersey meant everything to him. Trimble yearned to be part of something larger than himself, and while this desire could not be clocked or weighed or converted into some easily digestible statistic, it was powerful, and it was pervasive throughout the carpeted corridors of Bryant Hall.

While it is impossible to deny that Trimble left Tuscaloosa in a haze of personal disappointment, wondering what might have been, the true measure of a college football player is not how many yards he piles up, how many games he starts, or how much ink he generates. Rather, it is how he responds in the moment of truth when his team needs him.

Sometimes, the opportunity arrives without warning.

Heading into the fourth Saturday in October, eight major college teams remained unbeaten, but the ranks were thinned to six when fifth-ranked Southern Cal was upset by Miami, 10–7, and tenth-ranked Wyoming lost to Colorado State, 12–10. The three teams ahead of the Crimson Tide in the wire service polls stayed unblemished. On an afternoon when Terry Hanratty tossed two touchdown passes to lead No. 1-ranked Notre Dame past Navy, 31–7, No. 2 Michigan State's defense dominated Northwestern to key a 22–0 victory, and No. 3 UCLA knocked off Air Force, 38–13, Alabama's defense was smothering Mississippi State. But Kenny Stabler was having an off day.

After throwing a touchdown pass in relief of Stabler during the first half— a 26-yarder to Ray Perkins—Wayne Trimble took over at his own 29 yard line early in the fourth quarter, knowing the Crimson Tide needed another touchdown to put the game out of reach. After Kenny Martin ran for 2 yards, Trimble kept it on the option around right end, picking up another 4. A pass interference call gave the Tide a first down, then Martin and Trimble gained 2 and 3 yards, respectively, leaving a critical third and 5 call from the State 48 yard line.

Sensing the time was right for a little trickery, Trimble called the play and looked across the huddle at Jerry Duncan, who grinned big. It was time for the offensive tackle to have a little fun.

Never known as a great offensive innovator, Bryant nevertheless spent a significant amount of time tinkering with Xs and Os as well as studying the rulebook. No coach in the history of the sport invested more energy in trying to exploit obscure loopholes in the rules to give his team an edge, and nothing personified his eternal search for a way to catch the defense offguard more than the tackle-eligible pass play.

Usually, the quarterback may pass only to other backs and the ends, who must be positioned at the far edges of either side of the line of scrimmage. The rules require seven men on the line of scrimmage. However, in those days, a tackle became an eligible receiver when the flanker, instead of lining up in the backfield, positioned himself on the line. The toughest part of the play was finding a tackle who could catch and run, since most linemen tended to be relegated to the line because they could neither catch nor run.

Executed well, the pass almost always caught defenses by surprise—because it was such a little-known rule, because it was so rarely seen, and because it was difficult to realize in the heat of battle when the tackle had become a legal target. Typically, the tackle plowed through his block and moved several yards upfield without inviting the defense's suspicion, and by the time he turned around, allowing the quarterback to dump the ball off short, most defenses were completely fooled.

Bryant first used the gimmick at Kentucky. In fact, until his dying day, he remained bitter about the Wildcats' 1950 regular season finale, when his undefeated, third-ranked Kentucky team lost in a snowstorm, 7–0, to once-beaten, ninth-ranked Tennessee in Knoxville. Three times, he called the tackle eligible. Three times, All-America quarterback Babe Parilli caught the defense napping and churned up big yardage with the pass. But the officials, apparently unfamiliar with the rule, brought all three plays back, and the SEC champion Wildcats—who went on to halt Oklahoma's thirty-one-game winning streak in the Sugar Bowl—saw their undefeated season spoiled.

At Alabama, Bryant's teams made the play famous. In fact, the Crimson Tide exploited the gadget to such remarkable effect that in the late 1960s, after being victimized several times by it, Ole Miss head coach Johnny Vaught went on a personal campaign to outlaw the tackle eligible. Longtime Arkansas head coach Frank Broyles remembers Vaught's insistence during a meeting of the NCAA football rules committee, to which they both had been appointed. "Johnny wasn't going to let us adjourn the meeting until we got rid of that play," Broyles said.

Among some members of the 1966 Alabama football team, the outlawing of the tackle eligible is known, somewhat facetiously, as the Jerry Duncan Rule. No one was more associated with the play than the tenacious former high school fullback from North Carolina, who stuck . . . and stuck . . . and stuck, even as the coaches desperately tried to run him off.

Instead, he ran straight into the hearts of Alabama fans everywhere.

During both his junior and senior seasons, Duncan, blessed with good hands, led the nation in pass receptions and yards from the tackle position, which sounded like a made-up stat. It was not. Hard as it was to believe, the same guy who swapped licks with opposing defensive linemen, laying down the 'Bama block with precision and force, became known throughout the nation as one of the Crimson Tide's most potent, if infrequently used, weapons. In the Orange Bowl victory against Nebraska, he caught three for a total of thirty-two yards.

"We could have run it all night on Nebraska," Duncan said. "They were totally confused every time we ran it."

The play gave Duncan a taste of unexpected notoriety. While most offensive linemen toil in the shadows, their names brought to the forefront only when something goes wrong, Duncan emerged as one of the most popular and well-known players on the team. All across Alabama, young people wore replicas of his No. 77 jersey with pride and aspiring offensive linemen walked a little taller. Snake Stabler and Ray Perkins may have been the big guns on offense, and Cecil Dowdy may have been the most devastating blocker, but Jerry Duncan, one of the least gifted players on the whole team, became a folk hero. The tackle eligible was an example of Bryant's determination to find a way to win, however unconventionally, and Duncan's consistent execution of the gimmick secured for him a place of honor in the lore of Alabama football.

During picture day heading into the 1966 season, Duncan tried to talk Bryant into letting him have his photo taken with the receivers. The idea didn't go over very well, and he dropped it, but his buddies on the line never let him live it down. "Ole Duncan got to where he thought he was more of a receiver than a lineman," center Jimmy Carroll said with a laugh, adding, "We all heard about that tackle eligible a time or two."

All of the quarterbacks worked on the play from time to time in practice, knowing they would use it when the situation was warranted.

"In certain situations, it was just about unstoppable," said backfield coach Ken Meyer. "Defenses were very vulnerable to that play."

When the Crimson Tide lined up and Jimmy Carroll snapped the ball,

Trimble lunged to his right, like he was going to run the option, and just as the linebacker bit on his fake, Duncan, who was about five yards downfield, turned around. The pass was a perfect zip. Duncan caught it cleanly and turned toward the end zone to discover he was wide open, nothing between him and the goal line but a seam of green grass bigger than his daddy's milking barn.

"I've never been so wide open in my whole life," he said.

Although not the fastest player on the team, the old fullback lumbered toward the end zone, kicking it into overdrive, and no one came close to catching him. Steve Davis's extra point gave Alabama a commanding 20–7 lead with 9:15 remaining.

Two series later, after the swarming 'Bama defense held State on three and out twice, allowing a total of 3 yards, Trimble led the Tide on another scoring march. His 37-yard toss to Perkins made it 27–7 with 3:29 left, giving the backup quarterback, the heartbreak kid, 3 touchdown passes on the day in a total of 9 pass attempts. He finished with 5 of 9 for 136 yards, and also ran 6 times for 49 yards.

Suddenly, Wayne Trimble's name was rolling off the tongue of every 'Bama fan among the crowd of 56,500, as well as the huge radio audience.

He may not have been the starter, but on that memorable day, he was a hero, nonetheless. In fact, Trimble's three touchdown passes tied the school record, shared by several different players, placing his name alongside Joe Namath and Steve Sloan, among others.

"I understood my role, was comfortable with my role, which was to be ready to step in," Trimble said. "When Snake was having a tough time, I stepped in and had some success. It wasn't any more complicated than that."

When Alabama needed him, Trimble responded like a champion. He stepped up, proving he could lead under the gun, achieving a moment of splendid redemption few people beyond his teammates completely appreciated. Watching him drill the ball and lead the team with authority, many of his friends could not help wondering what might have been.

Trimble would lead other scoring marches the rest of the year, but none would matter so much—to his team or to himself.

Alabama's 27–14 victory—which included a meaningless touchdown by State as time expired, against the Tide's second-team defense—proved to be the highlight of Trimble's career.

Praising the senior's clutch performance, Bryant told reporters, "I don't know what we would have done without him."

One sentence, from the man in the big black Cadillac, made every disappointing aspect of Trimble's college career melt away.

Whatever happened, the old coal shoveler would always have that one glorious afternoon against Mississippi State, when his heroics kept the Crimson Tide on the road to the history books.

10. SUNDAY MORNING

A steady trail of cigarette smoke curled toward the ceiling.

The Chesterfield fog could not obscure the look of disappointment plastered all over Paul Bryant's chiseled face.

Les Kelley would never forget that look.

The look would haunt him for years.

The night before, after Alabama knocked off Mississippi State to go 6–0 on the season, Kelley, the Crimson Tide's starting fullback, a senior leader for the two-time defending national champions, had peeled off into the darkness with a good mad on. Nothing in particular brought the feeling bubbling to the surface. Instead, it was the accumulation of so many things: the way the coach kept singling him out, kept pushing him, kept expecting so much of him, kept demanding more, always more.

The 6'3", 203-pound native of Cullman, one of the most imposing physical specimens on the whole team, jumped in his car and headed off to Birmingham with some buddies to have a good time. The more he drank, the less Kelley worried about his curfew, which came and went as he continued to party and blow off steam.

Kelley was starting to sober up by the time he parked behind Bryant Hall a few minutes before five o'clock on Sunday morning, his buzz giving way to fear and dread. The sun would be piercing the darkness soon, and the young man who had worked so hard for so long, enduring every one of Bryant's numerous gut checks, charging toward the line time and again on the unforgettable winning drive against Tennessee, was starting to think about the consequences of his actions.

Creeping toward the back of the brick building, hoping to sneak in without detection, Kelley was startled to see dorm director Gary White standing near the back door—like a sentry—smoking a cigarette. White, a small man with a big job, looked him over carefully and said not a word. As Kelley stopped in his tracks, somewhere between the edge of the parking lot and the back door, White raised his arm and pointed toward the athletic offices in the distance, like a bird dog on the hunt, and even in his diminished state of lucidity, Kelley needed no interpretation.

"I knew what he meant," Kelley said. "I knew I was in the dog house, and he was telling me to take my case to Coach Bryant."

Sunday morning, coming down.

Bryant was already at his desk by the time Kelley walked in and took a seat on the couch with no springs, which swallowed him like quicksand, forcing him to gaze up at the boss, who peered down at him with that look, the one he could never shake.

After quickly debriefing the player, making him feel small and insignificant in his smoke-filled office, Bryant told him he would need to talk to his coaches and pray on the matter.

"Come back at five o'clock this afternoon," he said.

Great, Kelley thought to himself as he got up to leave. He had all day to worry.

When Kelley started playing organized football as a fourth grader in Cullman—the year some local civic leaders launched the town's first pee-wee league, and he played for a squad sponsored by Ponders department store—the game was all about having fun. The excitement of strapping on the pads was a new experience for everybody, and the thrill of running, passing, catching, tackling, and blocking required no higher purpose. It was a kick just to play. Even as the pressure to win increased when he started running for the Cullman High School Bearcats—the whole town living vicariously through their exploits—Kelley attacked the game with a smile on his face and a spring in his step. The night he joined four of his teammates in signing with Alabama at the house of Dr. Frank Stitt, a prominent local 'Bama alumnus—just about the time the All-Steak restaurant in downtown Cullman, a northern Alabama landmark, went up in flames—was one of the happiest of his life.

Kelley loved pulling on that red jersey, which filled him with tremendous pride. However, the harder the 'Bama coaches pushed him, he gradually felt much of the joy being drained out of the football experience. "Somewhere along the way at Alabama, it stopped being fun and became work, and that bothered me," he said.

"Football was always a game to me," Kelley said, "but it was much more than a game to Coach Bryant. He was always real clear about that."

The tone was set early during Kelley's rookie year, when the 'Bama freshmen walked into the locker room at the half trailing Ole Miss by two touchdowns. Assistant head coach Sam Bailey, a usually subdued figure, rattled their cages with a speech no one would forget. "You've heard all this talk about the pride of wearing that red jersey. Well, you can forget about all that!" Bailey roared. "When you go back out there in the second half, you're gonna be fighting for your goddamned lives!"

While he was able to look back on the moment with a totally different perspective after four decades of adult experiences, Kelley never forgot the terror he felt at the time. "It wasn't a matter of life or death, of course, but it sure seemed like it to us then," he said. "You have this dread, this fear. If you quit and go back home, you have to face all those people, so you can't afford to quit. You're caught. You're trapped. You wonder, what in the world are they going to do to us if we lose? Man, that was an awful feeling."

Kelley's experience demonstrated the inevitable tension between loving the game as an experience and needing it as a form of validation. All Alabama players faced some variation of this psychological tug-of-war, but everyone was wired a little differently. Some players actually enjoyed proving their ability to withstand pain and mental strain. Some players took great pride in showing the coaches, their teammates, and themselves how they could keep striving to be better. The bond developed over time, the sense of brotherhood, enhanced this feeling among many.

The concept of the breaking point existed for all. Every person on the team could be driven past the line, wherever it was, but the catalyst was not always some specific action. In Kelley's case, the unplanned, spur-of-the-moment decision to blow his curfew resulted from a feeling which had been building up in him since he first arrived in Tuscaloosa.

One of the hallmarks of the Alabama program in those days was Bryant's tendency to equate good size with ability, and as hard as he worked the little guys who dominated the ranks, he was known to push the physically gifted even more relentlessly. Often, the tall, strapping Kelley found himself struggling to meet his coach's elevated standards, like the time headed into the 1966 season when he spent what seemed like an eternity on the practice field blocking the end on play after play, being berated by the boss, until he mastered the maneuver to Bryant's satisfaction.

"He stayed on me all the time," Kelley said. "I think he thought I had more ability than the average player but that I wasn't living up to that potential. I thought I was doing about as good as I could do."

The gap between what Bryant perceived as Kelley's potential and his performance on the field left the player forever chasing a distant horizon.

Backfield coach Ken Meyer, who was responsible for Kelley, said, "I think Coach Bryant expected more out of Les, because he was, for the time, a pretty big guy. Coach Bryant never thought he was as good as he should have been."

Like every other player on the team, Kelley reached deep and kept trying to please the boss, but the effect of the constant pressure on him slowly undermined the feelings that drew him to the game in the first place, which left him vulnerable to his own internal triggers. Instead of on the practice field, his breaking point occurred while trying to relax in the aftermath of a hard-hitting game, when something in him snapped and he momentarily lost sight of the consequences of his actions.

The Alabama team was filled with incredibly self-motivated individuals, and yet, all of the players needed help in bursting through the ceiling of their potential. Some needed more help than others, and Bryant's ability to recognize which athletes required what kind of motivation played a large part in his success. Even Bryant would admit in later years that he sometimes played the part of the demanding coach too well, often becoming a prisoner of his zeal to turn even the most talented players on his team into overachievers. Whether Kelley would have performed at a higher level if Bryant had spent more time encouraging him and complimenting him, rather than challenging him and humiliating him, is impossible to know, but in the years after his college career ended, Kelley found himself wondering what might have been.

"I think I could have been a better football player if Coach Bryant had handled me differently," Kelley said. "He made me better, no doubt about it, but I think I would have responded better if he hadn't pushed me so hard all the time."

Of course, if Bryant had not leaned on him so relentlessly, he might never have become as good a player as he wound up in 1966.

In contrast to the 1965 season, when bullish Steve Bowman rushed for 770 yards, the 1966 Crimson Tide chased history without one dominant ballcarrier. The runner by committee system played into 'Bama's depth at the position, but also placed more emphasis—and pressure—on Stabler's ability to run the option. Snake became the first quarterback since Pat Trammell to lead the team in rushing (397 yards on 93 carries, a 4.3 yard average, with 3 touchdowns), followed by Les Kelley (309 yards on 94 carries, a 3.3 yard average, with 4 touchdowns), David Chatwood (271 yards on 74 carries, a 3.7 yard average, with 3 touchdowns), Gene Raburn (176 yards on 45 carries, a 3.9 yard average), Wayne Trimble (142 yards on 46 carries, a 3.1 average), Ed Morgan (132 yards on 38 carries, a 3.5 yard average), and Frank Canterbury (104 yards on 34 carries, a 3.1 yard average, with 1 touchdown).

Widely considered the best of Alabama's running backs, Kelley was not very fast, but he could be terribly effective fighting for the tough yards up the middle. In the Tennessee game, he showed everyone something. The Volunteers kept pounding on him in those terrible conditions and he continued to churn, moving his feet, using his body to punish anyone who got in his way.

But in Bryant's world, playing time was something that could only be earned with winning behavior—on and off the field.

Four years of tension hung heavy in the air on the Sunday after the Mississippi State game, as Kelley spent the whole day sweating his coach's response to his violation of the curfew rule. When he returned to the office at the appointed time, Bryant told him he had given the matter significant thought, and had also spoken with some of the other players. When the coach suspended him indefinitely, and told him to move out of Bryant Hall, and not to associate in any way with the players or coaches, he was not surprised. He was devastated, but not the least bit surprised, because, as much as he hoped the coach would overlook the matter and give him a second chance, he knew he deserved to be punished.

"I was real mad at Les when I heard," said fellow fullback David Chatwood, one of his closest friends on the team. "I couldn't understand why he would do something so stupid, so late in his college career."

When the news hit the papers the next day, as the Crimson Tide was starting preparations for LSU, Bryant told reporters, "It will be up to Les to prove to me that he is worthy of another chance."

Exiled from his teammates in dilapidated, vacant Friedman Hall—the former athletic dorm, on the verge of being condemned—Kelley spent the next several days beating himself up and contemplating his next move.

"I was miserable," said Kelley, who watched helplessly while time started to run out on his senior year. "Like something inside me had died."

The big game against tradition-rich Louisiana State University always represented a major test for Alabama.

One of the SEC's most consistent winners for decades, LSU reached a high water mark in 1958, when Paul Dietzel led the Bengal Tigers, featuring eventual Heisman Trophy–winning halfback Billy Cannon and the famed Chinese Bandits defense, to the national championship. After a 10-1 season in 1961, Dietzel left Baton Rouge to take over the once dominant program at Army, where he became the man who followed the man who followed the legendary Earl "Red" Blaik. As Dietzel and Army slowly faded toward irrelevance, LSU continued to win under the guidance of Charley McClendon, who played for Bryant at Kentucky. After being contested only sporadically for many years, the

Alabama-LSU game became a fixture of both program schedules starting in 1964. The Crimson Tide entered the 1966 game at Legion Field with a two-game winning streak in the series, including the 31–7 blowout in 1965, over a team that finished the year 8-3, capped by a 14–7 victory over Frank Broyles's unbeaten Arkansas Razorbacks in the Cotton Bowl.

Despite the mounting rivalry, Bryant and his one-time pupil—who coached the Tigers to a 135-61-7 record and thirteen bowl bids over eighteen years—shared a close relationship. "I thought a lot of Coach Bryant and owed him so much, but when we kicked it off, there was nobody I wanted to beat more," said McClendon, who went 2-14 against the Bear, including a run of nine straight losses. The 2-14 figure was cited often in later years, when LSU made a big mistake by running off its most successful coach of all time, but Bryant was a stout 43-6 against his former coaches and players, and the man universally known as Cholly Mac was the only one who ever managed to beat him twice.

In the middle of a rebuilding year, after significant losses from the previous season's Cotton Bowl team, LSU entered the game 3-3-1 and a decided under-dog to the undefeated Crimson Tide, which was looking increasingly unbeat-able, even without Les Kelley.

Still working his way through the various stages of suspension—the process started with denial, and acceptance was nowhere in sight—Kelley took off for Cullman to try to get away from his problem. But he could not escape it, espe-cially in his hometown, especially around his parents' house, where his older brother Max, an assistant football coach at Huntsville's Butler High School who had played fullback for the Crimson Tide during the mid-1950s, tracked him down and started making him feel like an embarrassment to the whole family.

One of the primary reasons Kelley and his teammates endured the enor-mous stress of Alabama football was the knowledge that their families, friends, and neighbors were counting on them, that quitting was ultimately more painful than staying, so the trip he made home represented every player's sweaty nightmare. In the world of broken plates, there was no hell quite like staring into your big brother's disappointed face. The guilt was enormous, and every player on the team secretly dreaded such a gut-wrenching experience, a thought which motivated a significant amount of the hard work that trans-formed the 1966 Crimson Tide into a powerful football team.

Rambling around his parents' house, feeling sorry for himself, not quite sure what to do, Kelley kept a close watch on the time. He didn't want to watch the Alabama-LSU showdown, the Crimson Tide's first televised game of the sea-son. In fact, he wanted to be out of the house when the game kicked off on ABC, and as he started out into the yard, he happened to pass by the television set—just as the Crimson Tide was running onto the field in Birmingham. Without him.

"That about killed me," he said. "I knew right then I had made a big mistake, that I had to do something to get back on the team."

Unable to pull himself away from the set, he sat down and watched, burdened with an overriding feeling of helplessness and anxiety.

Some thirty-five miles to the southeast, in the vibrant blue-collar town of Tarrant—a close-knit community where most folks worked at a local rock quarry, a coke foundry, or one of the steel mills in nearby Birmingham—humiliation and frustration were nowhere in sight. The family and friends of local hero Mike Hall crowded around television sets trying to catch a glimpse of the sophomore linebacker, playing for the first time on live TV.

The pipeline from Tarrant to Tuscaloosa was already firmly established by linebacker Tim Bates and halfback Hudson Harris, who helped the Crimson Tide win national championships in 1964 and '65. Hall, a 5'11", 210-pound specimen with tremendous upper body strength, grew up idolizing Alabama All-America Lee Roy Jordan, the prototype for an entire generation of linebackers, who graduated to an All-Pro career with the Dallas Cowboys.

"I wanted to be Lee Roy Jordan," Hall said.

By the first Saturday in November, Hall was on his way to making his name respected and admired by Crimson Tide fans everywhere, too.

On the fourth play of the game, after Louis Thompson sacked LSU quarterback Freddie Haynes, the Tigers lined up to punt inside their own 10-yard line. Hall slid past his block an instant after the ball was snapped, and as the punt left the foot of Mitch Worley, Hall got a great big piece of it. The ball dribbled out of the back of the end zone for a safety, giving 'Bama an early 2–0 lead.

The cheering erupted all across Tarrant, and in Alabama homes all across the South. In fact, it rarely stopped over the next three hours.

From the first snap until the last, the Crimson Tide dominated LSU. The 21–0 victory was never in doubt.

Johnny Mosley, Bobby Johns, and Stan Moss picked off the LSU quarterback. Moss's big play set up a touchdown by Frank Canterbury. Nine other LSU possessions ended on three and out as Wayne Owen, Richard Cole, and Bob Childs had big days.

Few defenders in Alabama history ever played the pass as ferociously as All-America Bobby Johns.

The one-time quarterback sometimes appeared to have a sixth sense about where and when a ball was going to be passed. The way he covered receivers and broke to the ball set a standard for the whole team, helping him record a team-high seven interceptions in 1966.

Sometimes, he was too into the moment, like on the fifth play of the Vanderbilt game, when he picked off the Commodores quarterback and raced 33 yards for a touchdown.

"I was feeling pretty proud of myself," he said.

Momentarily lost in his accomplishment, Johns trotted off the field—forgetting his duty of holding for the extra point. As quick-thinking Kenny Stabler filled in for him, Bryant's voice could be heard thundering along the sideline, "Where the hell is Johns?"

Determined to never make such a mistake again, Johns's mind momentarily flashed back to the incident as he stepped in front of an errant LSU pass in the third quarter and raced 40 yards for a touchdown.

He was still feeling pretty good about putting six points on the board, but this time, he was the first man to line up for the extra point.

"Some lessons, you have to learn the hard way," he said.

Held to just 90 total yards, the Tigers failed to penetrate the 'Bama 40 yard line until the closing moments, when a desperate fourth and one stab from the 21 was halted at the line of scrimmage by . . . Mike Hall.

Somewhere, perhaps an ambitious young athlete was dreaming about becoming the next Mike Hall, but all Les Kelley could think about was getting his jersey back.

Soon after the game ended, he climbed in his car and headed for Tuscaloosa. When he knocked on Bryant's office door before dawn on Sunday morning, Kelley told his coach he had learned his lesson and asked for another chance. Bryant looked him over, told him he would have to think about it, and instructed him to return later in the day for his answer. In the meantime, several of Kelley's teammates—including Johnny Mosley and Ray Perkins—stopped by the office and asked the coach to consider reinstating him. "I think he's learned his lesson, coach," Mosley said.

After sweating out another day of waiting and wondering, Kelley returned to the office and caught a break.

"Coach, you won't be sorry," he said with a big smile, exiting the room as Bryant returned to his work, the smoke from his cigarette flowing into the distance.

Two days later, the invisible obstacle in Alabama's quest for a third straight national championship was bathing in the thunderous applause of his constituents. His role was obscured only for those who refused to see.

Forbidden by state law from succeeding himself in the governor's mansion, Democrat George C. Wallace was not the sort of man to allow a little technicality to separate him from power, so he convinced his wife Lurleen, a fine Southern lady admired by all, to stand for election in November 1966. Assuring voters with a wink and a nod that ole George would be the power behind the nation's only female governor was child's play for a man of his significant political acumen, so when Lurleen trounced Republican Jim Martin in the general election in the wake of Alabama's victory over LSU on the football field, no one was the least bit surprised. Staying in the governor's mansion was the critical first step in his grand plan to run for the White House in 1968.

Once considered a liberal on matters of race, Wallace lost his first gubernatorial bid in 1958 to John Patterson, who struck a much harder line on the still-building civil rights movement. In the aftermath of the bitter defeat, he remarked, "I'll never be out-niggered again." And he was not. Like some tragic Shakespearean figure, Wallace abandoned his principles and became a prisoner of his ambition, which led him down a dark path. Sweeping into office in 1962, he vowed to defend segregation at all costs, which led directly to the stand in the schoolhouse door. Painting himself as a defender of the Southern way of life against the intrusion of the federal government, "outside agitators," and the elites he liked to call "pointy-headed intellectuals," the onetime boxer, onetime circuit court judge became a hero to a great many people in Alabama and throughout the South. In fact, Wallace was well on his way to striking a chord with disaffected voters all across the country.

Appealing to the fear of many white voters who saw forced integration, African-American suffrage, and other aspects of the civil rights movement as a threat, Wallace proved to be little more than an irritant against the historic struggle led by Dr. Martin Luther King Jr. During his four-year term, virtually every remaining aspect of segregation was destroyed or mortally wounded and King emerged as the international embodiment of nonviolent resistance to an unjust system, winning the Nobel Peace Price in 1964. Two years later, it was only a matter of time before the last vestiges of state-sponsored racism were swept away for good.

Instead of offering Alabama the statesman-like leadership it desperately needed, uniting the people and leading them into an inevitable new era, he shamelessly pandered, legitimizing defiance in face of the civil rights movement, further stratifying the racial divide. His intolerant rhetoric set a poisonous tone, and in this sense, his fingerprints could be seen all over the various acts of resistance and violence.

His fingerprints could also been seen all over the state of Alabama's negative image across the rest of the country, which represented a significant problem for the 1966 Crimson Tide. In addition to contributing mightily to the fact that 'Bama still fielded a segregated team and faced difficulty in attracting integrated opponents, Wallace gave people across the country an easily recognizable symbol of the state, an infamous figure to compete with, and in some cases, helped define Bear Bryant's powerful football program. During the 1966 campaign, the overt segregationist rhetoric was diminished, but the decision by Alabama voters to keep a man with such a history in the governor's mansion—one way or another—reinforced the mental linkage all across the country, just as the Crimson Tide needed all the help it could get in competing against the Notre Dame mystique.

After UCLA stumbled against Washington, Alabama moved back up to third heading into the eighth game of the season against South Carolina, but Notre Dame and Michigan State remained entrenched at No. 1 and No. 2, respectively, one week prior to their widely anticipated clash of the titans.

With the national championship decided by what amounted to a popularity contest from writers and coaches all across the country, the Alabama football team could not separate itself from the state of Alabama's image problem. By midseason, anyone with a knowledge of college football history who considered the situation logically could only conclude that some number of voters were, perhaps subconsciously, punishing the Crimson Tide for the sins of others, as well as its own continued segregation.

At the very least, Alabama was receiving none of the benefit of the doubt usually accorded undefeated defending champions.

If the situation had been reversed, and Notre Dame was undefeated and bidding for a third consecutive title, the Fighting Irish most certainly would have been ranked No. 1.

Given the chance, Alabama could have beaten Notre Dame, Michigan State, or any of the other contenders for the title.

But the Crimson Tide was no match for George Wallace and all he represented.

Many of the same people who voted for the enormously popular Wallaces lived and breathed Alabama football. As fans all across the Heart of Dixie gradually began to see the poll slight as yet another shot at the state by the national media, few probably considered the irony that their decision to twice elect the Wallaces effectively empowered their critics. The voters' continued validation of the politician who stood in the schoolhouse door did not excuse the behavior of any panelist who equated George Wallace with Bear Bryant, but it certainly enabled it.

————————

When he returned to practice on the Monday heading into the 7-0 Crimson Tide's homecoming game against South Carolina, Kelley looked at the depth chart on the wall of the locker room to find his name was not listed. The backs with a place on the personnel roster included Gene Raburn, David Chatwood, Junior Davis, and Harold Moore, but the leading rusher was nowhere to be found, which was an unmistakable signal. He did not need anyone to draw him a picture.

"I knew I would have to prove myself all over again in Coach Bryant's eyes," he said.

In addition to demonstrating Bryant's determination to maintain a strict sense of discipline—when many other coaches would have swept the minor in-fraction under the rug—the Kelley suspension highlighted one of the Alabama program's most powerful hidden assets: jersey lust.

Even though Kelley sometimes resented how the Alabama system turned the once fun experience of playing football into something closer to work, it also unwittingly infused the game with greater meaning in his life. The frivol-ity may have been mostly gone, but in its place was something more substan-tial. Football gave him purpose. Although he often chafed at the way Bryant leaned on him, Kelley's self-esteem was every bit as intertwined with playing for the Crimson Tide as Ray Perkins's or Jerry Duncan's, and when the boss cut him off from his support system and left his pride to have a long talk with his brain, his bid to return to the team and toe the Bear's line was practically in-evitable.

In his own eyes and in the eyes of everyone he knew, Kelley was defined by what wearing the red jersey demonstrated about him. It said he was tough enough to play for the Bear. It said he was something special. The pride he felt inside and attracted from people back home was something he believed he had earned, and losing the right to wear the red jersey was, in the minds of Alabama people everywhere, worse than never having donned it in the first place. With-out the possibility of shame, pride can have precious little currency, and so it was with Kelley as he wrestled with his dilemma.

"I knew I could never come back to Cullman, if I didn't somehow make the situation right," Kelley said. "I knew I'd have to move somewhere else, 'cause I never could have shown my face around here again. The shame would have been too much to live with."

The psychological dance between pride and shame played a large role throughout the shaping of the 1966 Crimson Tide, and during the second week in November, it brought the team's best runner back to Bryant Hall, back to the practice field with a renewed sense of purpose, as 'Bama thundered into the homestretch of the season.

The way Kelley responded to the situation demonstrated something important about the 1966 Alabama football team. The Crimson Tide was a better team with him, no doubt about it, but 'Bama could have survived without him just fine. However, he would have had a very difficult time dealing with permanently losing his identification with the team, especially so late in his career. The loss of his jersey would have left him struggling to deal not only with the shame of facing his family and friends, but also with the fundamental question of who he was without it. In this sense, his return to the fold suggested that he needed Alabama football a lot more than Alabama football needed him, which could have applied to virtually every player on the team. The knowledge of this was a powerful tool in shaping the Crimson Tide, and it was also a source of enormous strength in preserving the team as the various players bumped up against their breaking points while caught between loving the game and needing it.

With Kelley back in uniform, the homecoming festivities began with the annual parade down University Boulevard, featuring grand marshal Jim Nabors. Nabors, like most of the dignitaries who visited campus in those days—including Senator Bobby Kennedy and Reverend Billy Graham—stayed overnight at Bryant Hall. The gleaming expansion of Denny Stadium to 59,000 seats was finally complete, transforming the once modest, two-sided, 12,000-seat shell, originally opened in 1929, into a complete bowl for the first time. All the old grads went home happy. Playing one of its most complete games of the season, Alabama crushed South Carolina, 24–0, to go 8-0 on the season.

Gamecocks coach Paul Dietzel, leading his third program of the decade, was asked by a reporter how Alabama compared to the top two teams in the rankings. "No one can match Notre Dame or Michigan State in terms of personnel, but if either one of them played Alabama, I'd have to pick Alabama," he said.

Even the usually cautious Bryant was impressed by the way his Tide played. "It'll take a real good football team to beat us," he said, which was the verbal equivalent of the old poor-mouther breaking out into song.

Decimated by injuries, South Carolina never threatened against the punishing Alabama defense. Unable to penetrate the Tide 45 yard line until the closing moments, the Gamecocks managed just five first downs, clearly outmatched even after Alabama started clearing the bench.

Quarterback Kenny Stabler led 'Bama on two long drives in the first quarter. During the first, junior David Chatwood bulled his way for one short gain after another, finally breaking a fifteen-yarder to give the Tide a first and goal at the one. Stabler then called his old Baldwin County buddy's number, and Chatwood plowed through the crowd to give 'Bama a lead it would never relinquish.

When backup quarterback Wayne Trimble trotted on the field to lead 'Bama's third drive of the game, with time winding down in the first quarter, Bryant called for Les Kelley.

On 5 of the next 12 snaps, Trimble handed off to Kelley, who churned straight ahead, for gains of 3, 4, 6, and 2 yards. Finally, in the early moments of the second quarter, he rambled in from the 3, giving Alabama a 14–0 lead, on the way to an impressive 16-carry, 64-yard day.

The play of the day for Kelley may have been the thunderous block he landed in the third quarter to spring Frank Canterbury for a first-down run. Not everyone saw it. Most eyes were focused on Canterbury, who made a terrific play and was having one of the best days of his senior year as well. Kelley's block was not a moment of personal glory, and it was not as much fun as running with the football, but the impressive knockdown—the kind Bryant had envisioned during all those pressure-cooker moments in practice—was instrumental in making the play successful, and such unselfish acts, invisible in the statistics, proved critical in helping the Crimson Tide win football games.

Playing football at Alabama was like work, and even as the boyish fun of the game faded, Kelley and his teammates were all gradually learning one of the lessons that would frame the rest of their lives: Sometimes the most joyful experience of all is the sweet satisfaction of a job well done.

11. TWO WORLDS

The road to the most infamous moment of the 1966 football season can be traced to a daring display of offensive trickery.

The University of Notre Dame began playing football in 1887, five years before the game spread to the University of Alabama, and by the first decade of the twentieth century, the tiny Catholic school located in South Bend, Indiana, was learning how to kick a little butt. In fact, the independent Fighting Irish regularly scheduled the larger, more prestigious institutions of the Western Conference, including Michigan, Wisconsin, and Purdue, sometimes pulling off upsets. Twice rejected for admission to the league, later known as the Big Ten, because the haughty presidents of the elite universities looked down on the little school, which they considered insignificant and academically inferior, Notre Dame eventually was snubbed altogether by the members of the powerful conference.

When the Big Ten schools dropped Notre Dame from their schedules, leaving the Fighting Irish with a slate consisting entirely of nearby small colleges—lightweights including Butler, Wabash, Olivet, and Morris Harvey—the administration and most others were perfectly satisfied to play a less ambitious schedule. Since the conventional wisdom of the day held that Notre Dame could not hope to compete with the giants in educational stature, pressing the point athletically seemed pointless.

Jesse Harper refused to buy such timid logic. Harper, an Amos Alonzo Stagg disciple who became Notre Dame's head coach in 1913, wanted to aim higher, aspiring to make his football program more than the master of St. Viator, Loyola, and Ohio Northern.

With nothing to lose, Harper wrote letters to the coaches of various bigger schools across the country, pitching unknown Notre Dame as a worthy opponent for the next football season. Intersectional matchups remained rare in those days, given the high cost of travel and the meager budgets of the teams, so when the Fighting Irish accepted a game against the University of Texas in Austin to finish the 1913 season, it was billed as one of the longest road trips in the sport's history. He also signed up a visit to Penn State, a home game against

South Dakota, and a journey to the banks of the Hudson River in West Point, New York, to face Army, one of the strongest teams in the football-rich East.

Nineteen Notre Dame players rode the train overnight to reach the storied U.S. Military Academy—according to reports, they shared fourteen pairs of shoes—where a crowd of some five thousand spectators wandered into Cullum Hall Field on November 1, 1913, without paying a nickel, most of them expecting to see an Army rout.

No one outside the official travel party from South Bend knew what quarterback Gus Dorais and end Knute Rockne were planning.

Most football historians credit St. Louis University as the first college team to utilize the forward pass, as early as 1907, but the weapon languished in obscurity in an era when brute strength dominated every aspect of the sport, still contested without pads or the slightest hint of finesse. The ball, fatter, rounder, tougher to grip than modern pigskins, was an obstacle in itself, limiting most aerial adventures. Passing was considered an act of desperation, and even the teams who tried to toss the ball on occasion usually wound up flicking it for no more than a few yards.

But the pass was about to be drenched in cool.

After Dorais and Rockne spent the off-season perfecting a revolutionary passing and receiving technique, and convinced even the skeptical Harper that they were onto something, the Fighting Irish threw the ball with great success in their first two games. However, since news coverage of the unheralded Midwestern team was extremely limited, and the Irish cleverly shelved their innovation during the one game Army coaches scouted, the boys from West Point were unaware of the team's newfound passing potency.

Catching the unprepared Cadets completely by surprise, Dorais threw the ball with abandon against Army. The military descendents of U.S. Grant, Robert E. Lee, and Stonewall Jackson struggled to figure out how to defend the aerial bombardment by the Irish, who stunned Army, 35–13. "Hopelessly confused and chagrined," was the post-mortem assessment of the writer dispatched from *The New York Times*. Employing the pass as a strategic weapon, Dorais completed 13 of 17 attempts for an astonishing 243 yards, including a breathtaking 40-yard touchdown connection with Rockne, hailed as the longest and most spectacular pass play in college history.

More than an isolated victory, more than a demonstration of how the pass could be harnessed to fundamentally alter the sport, the game transformed Notre Dame into a college football power.

In the years after the charismatic Rockne was named head coach in 1918, launching one of the greatest stretches in college football history as the country entered what journalists would one day refer to as the golden age of American sports, Notre Dame emerged as the game's most celebrated program. Fawning coverage by big-city sportswriters, especially Grantland Rice of New York's *Herald Tribune*, mythologized Rockne and his team, including the fabled Four Horseman and runner George Gipp, soon to become synonymous with the term "tragic hero." Before long, Notre Dame's anointed status was accepted as a matter of fact all across the country, which became a self-fulfilling prophecy.

"The media treated Notre Dame differently," said Jeff Coleman, Alabama's longtime athletic business manager. "They were a national team, like Army. The rest of us, regardless of what we did on the field, seemed to be forever caught in the shadow of Notre Dame."

Guiding the Fighting Irish to five perfect seasons and an overall .881 winning percentage before his untimely death at the age of forty-three in 1931, Rockne set a new standard of excellence, preeminence, and innovation, on the field and off. Frank Leahy, who led Notre Dame for eleven seasons starting in 1941, eventually earned a place alongside the immortal Rockne, posting a .855 winning percentage and capturing four national championships in seven years, when star players including Heisman Trophy winners Johnny Lujack, Angelo Bertelli, and Leon Hart assumed iconic status with fans from coast to coast.

Despite the vast distance between them, geographically and culturally, Alabama and Notre Dame shared a common thread. In addition to their power on the football field—and the marriage of the two bloodlines accomplished when former Irish quarterback Frank Thomas, the Gipper's college roommate, began a highly successful tenure in Tuscaloosa in 1931, creating a direct link between Knute Rockne and Bear Bryant—the two universities exploited the game to enhance their respective institutions.

When the Crimson Tide won the first of its Rose Bowl appearances in 1926, Dr. George Denny, the University of Alabama's forward-thinking president, saw an opportunity to raise the onetime military academy's profile. Even as the success of the football team helped cement the so-called Capstone as the state of Alabama's most important center of higher learning, Denny used the national publicity to recruit students from across the country, particularly the northeast. At a time when many esteemed institutions—especially those in the WASP-dominated Ivy League—discriminated openly against Jews and other ethnic minorities, maintaining strict admission quotas, Alabama placed newspaper advertisements trumpeting the school's famous football team, solid academics, and warm climate, welcoming any and all to come South. By 1930, despite its important place in a Bible Belt culture dominated by Protestant Christianity, a large percentage of the University of Alabama's student body was Jewish, including hundreds of young people attracted from the northeast by the gathering fame of the Crimson Tide.

At the same time, Notre Dame used the celebrity garnered by its football program to escape obscurity and become the most important Catholic institution in the whole country. The success of the Fighting Irish transformed all-male Notre Dame into a hallowed destination, a magical place of distant dreams for young men all across America. Catholic mothers from coast to coast longed to someday send their sons to study under the golden dome, seeing it as an extension of the church itself. Millions of so-called subway alumni, seduced by radio, newspaper, and, eventually, television coverage—not to mention the sentimental splendor of the 1940 Hollywood classic, *Knute Rockne All American,* which starred a young Ronald Reagan as the Gipper—adopted the Fighting Irish as their favorite team, empowering the university in ways no one could possibly have imagined on that fateful day in 1913. Never again would the schools of the Big Ten be able to look down their noses on the sons of South Bend. Notre Dame slowly gained the stature of an elite, academically rigorous institution capable of choosing from among the nation's best and brightest.

Just as the Crimson Tide gave beleaguered Southerners a source of enormous pride when the rest of the country looked down on the region, the Fighting Irish became a potent symbol of self-esteem for Catholics, who faced widespread discrimination and marginalization all across America, including the South, where the Ku Klux Klan espoused hatred toward Catholics and Jews as well as blacks. Each in their own way, Alabama and Notre Dame rose to prominence defiantly resisting condescension and outright hostility toward the groups who gravitated to them and bathed in the reflected glow of their glory.

Despite the common thread, however, the two institutions occupied starkly different positions in American society in 1966, symbolizing the cavernous divide between North and South, between integration and segregation, between the scorn of the dominant media culture and the embrace of the dominant media culture. The two powerful football programs could not even agree on one of the sport's most sacred principles. Football united the two giants, and football also divided them.

As undefeated, two-time defending national champion Alabama enjoyed an off week heading into the ninth game of the season against Southern Mississippi in Mobile, the impending clash between No. 1 Notre Dame and No. 2 Michigan State in East Lansing on November 19 sucked all of the air out of the entire sport. As far as the national media was concerned, No. 3 Alabama's pursuit of a historic threepeat was irrelevant to the coronation.

The first Super Bowl was still two months away, but from the vantage point of history, the game was hyped like one of those Roman numeral affairs. "The buildup was so overwhelming. It's all anyone wanted to talk about that week, and for several weeks before," recalled ABC play-by-play announcer Chris Schenkel, who compared the surrounding buzz to the landmark 1958 National Football League championship game, won in sudden-death overtime by the Baltimore Colts over the New York Giants, which he also called. Some 745 media credentials were granted to the game, easily exceeding the demand for any of the early Super Bowls. Even *The Wall Street Journal,* which rarely covered sports, ran a page-one article examining the frenzy.

So unbelievable was the clamor for tickets, one desperate fan purchased a newspaper ad offering to trade his liquor store for a pair on the 50 yard line. However, like millions of other fans, he was forced to watch the action from the comfort of his living room.

Like the 1958 NFL title game, widely credited with launching the modern era of pro football, Notre Dame-Michigan State cast an even larger shadow because of the enormous power of television. It also reflected how the sport was still struggling to deal with the rapid changes in culture and technology.

The National Collegiate Athletic Association controlled the rights to all live college games in those days, and in an attempt to promote broadcasting equity among its various members, the NCAA's all-powerful television committee strictly limited individual teams to no more than one national appearance per season. Because Notre Dame had already appeared coast-to-coast against Purdue—and Michigan State had played the Bob Griese-led Boilermakers before a regional audience—ABC was contractually prohibited from televising the biggest game since the invention of the shoulder pad to the entire country. Instead, ABC planned to broadcast Notre Dame-Michigan State as a regional game to more than half of the country, while parts of the Southeast and Northwest were to be shown a relatively meaningless Tennessee-Kentucky game, which satisfied the NCAA's rigid sense of justice.

When news of the partial blackout hit the media, the network and the college governing body were bombarded with cards, letters, and telegrams of protests. One southern fan filed suit against ABC, the NCAA, and the Federal Communications Commission, claiming his rights were being violated because he was being deprived of his constitutionally guaranteed ability to watch the event being breathlessly described as the Game of the Century. The negative publicity generated by the NCAA's dilemma served only to throw gasoline onto an already raging fire—it was pure Adam Smith, demand far exceeding supply, combined with the hype of P. T. Barnum—as evidenced by the fan from Miami

who told a newspaper reporter he planned to fly to New York and rent a hotel
room so he could watch the game on the tube.

Carved out during a period of antitelevision hysteria in the early 1950s—
when college officials believed fans would stop buying tickets if they could stay
home and watch games for free—the NCAA's strict television policy was primarily intended to muzzle Notre Dame. In 1950, both Notre Dame and the
University of Pennsylvania broadcast their entire home slates on network television, such as it was, and various other schools telecast their games locally. Fear
of competing against Notre Dame every week prompted the vast majority of
the NCAA's membership to act in what they saw as a self-defensive posture,
and the tightly controlled television system that remained in force in 1966 was
a testament to Notre Dame's anointed status with the football public. Yet, the
system intended to mitigate Notre Dame's dominance left the NCAA and ABC
with a peculiar dilemma.

Finally, after several days of heated debate, the NCAA announced a com-
promise, allowing ABC to show Notre Dame-Michigan State to the blacked-
out regions, but only on tape delay, three hours later than the rest of the
country. Two years before the infamous *Heidi* game—when NBC executives
learned an unforgettable lesson by breaking away from the climactic ending of
an Oakland Raiders victory over the New York Jets to show that children's
movie, which forever changed network tactics on late-running games—the suits
still believed in the infallibility of their judgment, which valued entertainment
over sports, precise schedules over unpredictable drama. Within a few years, de-
laying the biggest game of the year to satisfy some arbitrary standard would be
unthinkable—as unimaginable as broadcasting in black and white.

Even as the brass at the NCAA headquarters in Kansas City endeavored to
mitigate the promotional dominance of the Fighting Irish while simultaneously
trying to sell the videotape solution as an experiment, the message was clear:
Notre Dame was special, and required special treatment.

"Notre Dame was the biggest thing in college football, and while that might
not have mattered on the field, the mystique of Notre Dame was a big force off
the field," said ABC's Schenkel.

For all the hype surrounding the big game, other things were happening in
the world during the third week in November. Sports fans all across the country were saddened to hear of the premature retirement of Los Angeles Dodgers
pitching ace Sandy Koufax, forced to walk away from the mound at the peak of
his brilliant career because of severe arthritis. In Red China, former leader Mao
Tse-Tung was making noise about regaining power. More than one hundred
prominent Americans, including former President Dwight D. Eisenhower,

joined to issue a warning that "extremist" criticism of U.S. policy in Vietnam could endanger a future peace settlement. "Let us hope that the distinction between responsible dissent and unfounded attacks upon our society and its leaders will be recognized by the dissenters themselves," the statement said, reacting to the still relatively small but growing antiwar movement.

According to an analysis by *The New York Times,* for the first time since Reconstruction after the Civil War, the black vote—spurred by the 1965 Voting Rights Act—played a pivotal role in several major Southern elections, helping elect South Carolina's Ernest Hollings, a Democrat, to the Senate and Winthrop Rockefeller, a Republican, to the governor's mansion in Arkansas. In Birmingham, state officials announced construction of a massive interchange connecting interstate highways 59 and 65 on the edge of downtown would begin in December. The first legs of the interstate system across Alabama were open, but most sections remained under construction.

For the last time ever, the Notre Dame football team left South Bend on a train.

Notre Dame, undefeated and untied after eight games, arrived in East Lansing with a team already being compared to the greatest of all time. The Fighting Irish played a smothering brand of defense, led by All-America end Alan Page, the future Minnesota Vikings star. In eight games, the unit had allowed just 28 points, including five shutouts. The potent offense, averaging a national best 37 points per game, featured the pinpoint passing of sophomore quarterback Terry Hanratty and the tough running of All-America halfback Nick Eddy, although he would miss the Michigan State game with an injury.

The game marked the season finale for 9-0 Michigan State. Since being upset the previous January by UCLA in Pasadena—one part of the three-piece miracle required for Alabama's second consecutive trophy—the Big Ten champion Spartans had proven nearly as untouchable as the Fighting Irish. Michigan State had knocked off eventual No. 6 Purdue, 41–20, as well as escaping a challenge against Woody Hayes's Ohio State Buckeyes, 11–8. Led by 6'7", 283-pound All-America end Bubba Smith, the bruising Michigan State defense also featured All-Big Ten linebacker Charlie "Mad Dog" Thornhill, the pride of Roanoke who had been steered away from South Bend and to a happy landing in East Lansing by none other than Paul Bryant. The Spartans offense, which averaged 31 points per game, included their own All-America running back, Clint Jones, and a quarterback in Jimmy Raye with a quick release and a good eye for open receivers, especially the elusive Gene Washington.

In many ways, the collision lived up to all the hype. Early in the first quarter, Bubba Smith—with an assist from Charlie Thornhill, who recorded sixteen tackles on the day—knocked Terry Hanratty out of the game with a separated shoulder. Backup quarterback Coley O'Brien, who suffered from diabetes, came off the bench and gave a gutty performance for the Irish, but the game became a war of defense and field position. With Michigan State leading 10–7 as the fourth quarter began, Parseghian sent kicker Joe Azzaro on to boot a 28-yard field goal, which tied the game, leaving ABC announcer Chris Schenkel and color man Bud Wilkinson scrambling to describe the tension and excitement filling the air.

Both coaching staffs started mentally sifting through their playbooks, looking for ways to exploit the other's defense and win the game. Notre Dame came closest. After driving inside the State 20 and being repelled, Parseghian turned once more to Azzaro, who missed a 41-yard field goal attempt, wide right, ever so slightly, with 4:39 left.

When Michigan State stalled at its own 36, with less than two minutes remaining, Daugherty faced a difficult decision. He had gone to the air four times on the drive, and clearly was trying to win, but fourth and four from his own 36 was a big gamble. Believing a failed stab would hand the game to Notre Dame, he punted and counted on his defense to force a turnover.

The clock showed 1:24 left when Notre Dame took over at its own 30 yard line—plenty of time to try to win the football game. Time to go deep for the big one. Time to dink it off short several times and run out of bounds to stop the clock. Time to push down close enough to attempt a field goal.

But Ara was not thinking about trying to win the game.

Instead, he was determined not to lose it.

Fearing a turnover, Parseghian instructed Coley O'Brien to keep the ball on the ground and avoid a turnover. In other words, the coach of America's Team instructed his quarterback to run out the clock.

Two plays into the drive, when the clock dwindled to under a minute and a chorus of boos started rising from among the capacity Spartan Stadium crowd, the Michigan State defense lined up and started taunting the Notre Dame players. Bubba Smith and Charlie Thornhill began yelling across the neutral zone, "You don't want it! C'mon. Throw the ball! Try to win!"

"I couldn't believe it," Thornhill said nearly four decades later. "I couldn't believe they would just sit on the ball and not even try to win the game."

On a fourth-and-one call from his own 39, O'Brien sneaked up the middle, picking up the first down and allowing Notre Dame to keep possession. Two plays later, it was over. The stunning 10–10 tie glowed from the end zone scoreboard as the crowd fell eerily silent. One of the many fans with access to the field approached the Notre Dame players and started hurling insults. "They went for a tie," he shouted. "They didn't want to win."

The result hit the players on both sides hard.

"I felt like somebody had ripped my heart out," Thornhill said.

All across America, even as Parseghian stood in the visitors' dressing room and tried to explain his reasoning to the players, Notre Dame fans questioned his decision to run out the clock. In Tuscaloosa, many Alabama players watched the game—or listened to it live on radio—with a combination of disbelief and relief.

"None of us could understand why they didn't try to win the game," recalled center Jimmy Carroll. "It was the opposite of everything we believed, everything we had been taught. The flip side of it was, we thought for sure that would make us No. 1."

Ara knew better.

Because Notre Dame occupied a special place in college football, Parseghian believed his team could still win the national championship as long as it walked off the field without losing, and so his decision to sit on the ball and avoid a turnover at all costs was not just a carefully calculated tactical gambit. It was the most cynical act in college football history.

On an electric night seventeen years later, millions of NBC television viewers watched Tom Osborne standing on the sideline at the Orange Bowl, facing a choice that would define him for the ages.

After quarterback Turner Gill led a furious comeback and a late touchdown, undefeated, No. 1-ranked Nebraska still trailed upstart, No. 4-ranked Miami, 31–30, in the final moments. The Big Eight champion Cornhuskers, who featured Heisman Trophy winner Mike Rozier at tailback and a pair of All-Americans in Gill and flanker Irving Fryar, entered the matchup averaging fifty-two points per game. Long before the Orange Bowl, the 1983 Nebraska team was being hailed as one of the greatest of all time, and as he wrestled with the decision of whether to go for one or two, Osborne understood that because no other teams remained undefeated and untied, he could probably secure at least a piece of his first national championship by kicking the extra point.

With an easy out in his back pocket, Osborne still called for a two-point pass to win the ball game, and as soon as Gill's toss was batted down in the end zone, handing the victory and the national championship to Howard Schnellenberger's underdog Miami Hurricanes, the debate began swirling across the country. Should Osborne have played for the tie?

In some quarters, the classy, erudite Nebraska coach—who would eventually cap his 255-victory career by leading the Cornhuskers to three national championships in four years during a remarkable run in the 1990s—was ridiculed for placing principle above practicality.

But he did the right thing.

Kicking the ball would have been more than the wrong decision. It would have been a disgraceful act.

In the eyes of many football fans all across the country, fans who saw the fundamental meaning behind his choice, Osborne became a symbol of something wonderfully profound and yet painfully simple. Like any coach worth the price of his whistle, Osborne understood that champions always play to win in such a situation, regardless of the possible consequences. Winning may not be everything, but trying to win certainly is, and Osborne's bold act on that memorable night in the Orange Bowl reinforced a core value just as it was being assaulted by the forces trying to elevate the acquisition of a trophy as an end worthy of any means. Even shameful cowardice.

In the days before college football adopted the overtime rule in the late 1990s, coaches grappled with the choice all the time. In most cases, ties resulted as a matter of course from two teams slugging it out and trying desperately to go for the kill, such as the 1965 Alabama-Tennessee game. Even though Bryant was fond of saying "A tie is like kissing your sister," an admonition that hung over his program like a rotten tomato, some underdog teams understandably took great pride in managing to strike even. Case in point: In 1981, Southern Miss kicked a late field goal to tie Alabama, 13–13, which felt like a mighty victory to the folks from Hattiesburg.

After No. 1-ranked Alabama's two-point try failed against Georgia Tech in 1962, Bryant explained: "When you're the champ, you don't go for a tie. You're out there to win."

The players and their fans respected it as a call consistent with the values of Alabama football. The highly publicized failure communicated quite loudly what they were all about.

By contrast, the closing moments of Notre Dame's hard-fought 10–10 tie with Michigan State represented a departure from the program's proud and distinguished heritage. More than just an isolated decision, it left an indelible stain on the house of Rockne.

Watching Notre Dame run out the clock shattered the image of the program, which in so many ways personified old-fashioned American ambition and bravado. It was like seeing John Wayne parade around the room in high heels and a strapless gown.

In his postgame press conference—and for years afterward, until he stopped answering questions on the matter altogether—Parseghian tried to justify his decision by saying his primary goal was to capture the national championship, and that going for the win represented too great of a risk that Notre Dame could lose. Protecting the tie was his very calculated attempt to play the percentages, because he believed that, if he could escape without a loss, the Irish could still win the trophy by finishing unbeaten the next week against Southern Cal. He was right, of course, but that was hardly the point.

Ara took a beating from many in the media. Perhaps *Sports Illustrated*'s Dan Jenkins summed it up best: "No one really expected a verdict in that last desperate moment . . . But they wanted someone to try."

Several days later, Cecil Dowdy, Alabama's All-America offensive tackle, told a reporter: "One thing is certain. If we had been faced with an identical situation as Notre Dame and we were the top team in the nation, we would have lost before settling for a tie. Coach Bryant would have scoffed at the idea of running out the clock when there was a chance at victory."

Somewhere, Knute Rockne and the Four Horsemen and George Gipp and Gus Dorais—and Frank Thomas—must have been fuming. Love them or hate them, the Fighting Irish had always stood for something, something admirable, something sacred, and Parseghian's decision to run out the clock demeaned every single man who had ever laid his body on the line for the little Catholic school that dared to dream big.

How in the world can you call yourself a champion if you are too gutless to try to win the biggest game of the year?

Ara could rattle on about the risk of turning the ball over as some abstract concept, like an accountant hovering over a spreadsheet, but despite the story he tried to sell to the country, becoming a champion is not about avoiding conflict and risk. Rather, becoming a champion has always been and will forever be the act of persevering and triumphing in the face of a season-long minefield of conflict and risk. Becoming a champion is about taking the field and proving something. At the core, it is the very American act of earning something that cannot be bestowed. Becoming a champion is not and will never be about cowering in fear and taking the path of least resistance.

Without the possibility of losing, what good is winning?

Often, the risk of losing leads to the defining moment of a champion—as it did for Alabama against Tennessee—but unfortunately for a talented Notre Dame team that played its guts out and deserved better, Ara was too concerned with winning a championship to allow his players to act like champions. He was too preoccupied with protecting them from the possibility of failure to al-

low them the chance to earn their success, to prove they were a team for the
ages.

And this was America's Team?

Asking to be rewarded for avoiding risk?

In John Wayne's America?

Could this possibly be the program aspiring to stand as a shining example
of excellence in a country reaching at that very moment for the moon? The in-
spiring words of the late John F. Kennedy—the nation's first Irish Catholic
President—still rang in ears from sea to shining sea: "Why does Rice play
Texas? We go to the moon! We go to the moon! We go to the moon in this decade and do the other things. Not because they are easy, but because they are
hard!"

Lowly Rice played powerful Texas because the Owls aspired to reach, to
dream, which was the American way. In a world in which Rice annually played
Texas, knowing the odds, it was inconceivable that Notre Dame, the biggest
name in college football, could actually be proud of sitting on the ball in the
most hyped game in the history of the sport.

In Bear Bryant's America, where football meant something, Parseghian's
caution was widely ridiculed.

"Everything at Alabama is based on winning," a frustrated but tactful
Bryant told reporters in the game's aftermath. "I couldn't go for a tie late in the
game. . . . In our region, our football players have a far-reaching effect on
young people. Some of them are going off to Vietnam everyday, and I hope
they aren't going over there for a tie."

In 1966, Bryant's off-the-cuff connection between the game being snidely
referred to as "Tie One for the Gipper" and the escalating conflict in Vietnam
probably sailed right over most heads—especially since the thought of losing or
tying the war still seemed unthinkable—but four decades later, the comment
jumped off the yellowed, crinkled page, eerily prescient, at least in a vague
sense, of the storm brewing on the horizon.

Because football dominated the culture in various ways, because the game's
lessons were invested with such meaning by so many, the thought of not trying
to win in such a situation touched an exposed nerve. In the context of the day, it
was a rebellious and utterly antiestablishment act. Subtler than bra burning, less
provocative than protesting the war, less dangerous than dropping acid, Ara's decision nevertheless represented a challenge to the most sacrosanct beliefs of the
American establishment, at least those who viewed football through a larger lens.
Ara's decision mocked everything the Alabama program stood for—and everyone who saw the Crimson Tide as a reflection of their little corner of the world.

Instead of leaning on his administration to abandon its long-standing policy of declining bowl invitations, which would have allowed Notre Dame to honorably challenge two-time defending national champion Alabama in New Orleans or Miami to decide the issue on the field, Parseghian deftly exploited the media's love affair with the Irish and the widespread anti-Southern bias working against the Crimson Tide.

This is how his cautious maneuver catapulted out of the stunned stillness of Spartan Stadium to become the most cynical act in college football history.

Because he understood that Notre Dame played by a different set of rules, and would not be punished by most poll voters for sitting on the ball—even those who criticized it—Parseghian's move effectively said to Alabama: "I know you're the only undefeated, untied team in the country. I know you're the two-time defending national champion. But I don't care, because I have the votes in my back pocket, and I can shut you out of the title even without beating Michigan State, even without playing in a bowl game. The fix is in. Try doing something about it!"

Several factors handicapped Alabama as the national championship race came down to the wire in late November and early December. The Crimson Tide's relatively weak schedule gave some voters an excuse, especially the glaring presence of Louisiana Tech, necessitated by Tulane's withdrawal from the SEC and the vagaries of the racial situation.

"Louisiana Tech has to be the chink in the Tide's case for No. 1," wrote *The Birmingham News*' Alf Van Hoose, the only Alabama journalist with a vote on the fifty-eight-man AP panel. "It cannot be easily explained to voters."

From the standpoint of combined opponent records, Notre Dame faced the toughest schedule of the three contenders (54-46-2, .530), significantly stronger than both Michigan State (48-49-2, .490) and Alabama (51-61-1, .460). Both Notre Dame and Alabama played three teams with eight or more wins. Michigan State played two. The Tide played six teams with winning records, compared to five for the Irish and three for the Spartans.

The way the Crimson Tide won the 1964 and 1965 titles likely gave some voters pause and drained support away from the 1966 edition, especially considering the historic ramification of a third straight championship. "There was no way they were going to let a southern team win three in a row, if they could help it," theorized offensive tackle Jerry Duncan, a view shared by many of his teammates. Unlike 1964 and 1965, voters had the chance to crown a nonsouthern team at the end of the year.

In the end, the title would rest not on the powerful argument represented by Alabama's perfect season, but on a popularity contest between Notre Dame and

Alabama, between dynamic and easily clichéd symbols of North and South, which was no contest at all. Not in 1966.

In this respect, the real villain was not Ara Parseghian, but George Wallace. Wallace and all of the negativity he symbolized gave the voters all the ammunition they needed. He loaded the gun.

Boston Globe sports columnist Bud Collins, conceding the poll bias raging against the Crimson Tide, wrote: "Alabama . . . it's a great place to march, but you wouldn't want to stay. . . . Obviously, the United States would be better off trading the state to Europe for Spain or Switzerland, but until the deal can be made we may as well recognize that our best team is located in Tuscaloosa."

Amazing. Even a rare member of the national media taking up for the Crimson Tide could not do so without dabbling in condescension.

Around the same time, *Los Angeles Times* columnist Jim Murray—who once famously lampooned the Sugar Bowl as "the White Supremacy Bowl"—suggested the folks in Alabama change the lyrics to "Dixie," ever so slightly: ". . . do the folks keep segregatin' . . . till I cain't win no polls."

It is possible to look back on the continued segregation of the Alabama team in disapproval, even shame, and still see the unfairness of a system that bastardized a sport supposedly based on merit by allowing some unknown number of voters to punish the Crimson Tide because it was all-white. If the reverse had been true, and Alabama had fielded an all-black team, such behavior would have been every bit as bigoted. Segregation was just plain wrong, and yet so was allowing any consideration of skin color to affect the awarding of college football's national championship. In this respect, anyone who sought to rank a truly deserving Alabama team lower simply because it was segregated was no better than George Wallace or Bull Connor.

In addition to its treasured status as one of the biggest brand names in American sports, Notre Dame was riding an additional sentimental wave because the Fighting Irish, reeling from all those years of mediocrity, had not captured the big prize since 1949. When voters in other parts of the country thought of Notre Dame, their first image probably was of Knute Rockne or some great player. Alabama was not so fortunate. The impact of George Wallace, Bull Connor, and all the other forces of hate and division could not be quantified, but it was significant, and when it came down to a contest between a media darling with a national constituency and a team emblematic of a state seen by many Americans as a national pariah, the Crimson Tide never had a chance. Not even with a better record. Not even if 'Bama had crushed the Green Bay Packers.

The fact that Bryant's team was still segregated played into the hands of those who wanted to punish Alabama—and the South—and made blurring the lines between Wallace and the Bear easy and convenient. However, even the black and white issue was filled with shades of gray. The battle between Alabama and Notre Dame was a struggle between segregation and integration, but only in the narrowest terms. In 1966, Notre Dame featured just one African American on its roster: All-America defensive end Alan Page. Meanwhile, five of the teams ranked among the AP's final top ten in 1966 remained segregated, so by that standard at least, Notre Dame was far ahead of the curve.

The contrast between Michigan State, the most integrated of all major teams, and nearly all-white Notre Dame was impossible to deny. The racial angle was rarely mentioned in the media, though it was a prism through which the Michigan State players could not help viewing the still largely segregated and tokenized world.

According to Mike Celizic's book on the showdown, *The Biggest Game of Them All,* in the huddle during the final series, Bubba Smith told his teammates: "If this game ends in a tie, Notre Dame is going to win [the championship]. All the sportswriters are Catholic. We got too many niggers on this team to win the national championship [that way]."

Initially, the tie filled Alabama players and fans with a glimmer of hope, especially with the knowledge that no team in college history had ever won back-to-back championships, finished undefeated and untied in the third year and been denied the title. Theirs was the only perfect team, and perfection was the recognized standard. Now, they thought. Now the pollsters will come to their senses. Now the voters will do the right thing. Now.

When the wire service polls were announced the following Monday, hopes all across Alabama were dashed. The AP still ranked Notre Dame first, Michigan State second, and Alabama third. The UPI survey gave a narrow lead to Michigan State, followed by Notre Dame and Alabama.

How could this be?

The Alabama players were dumbfounded. It was one thing for the Crimson Tide to be outvoted if all three teams finished with perfect records, which was bad enough considering the issue of defending the title, but how the writers and coaches could in good conscience vote against 'Bama under the circumstances left every man on the team in a state of shock and disbelief.

With Southern Cal on the horizon, the Fighting Irish still had time to change a few minds and capture both titles. So did Alabama.

Around the Alabama program, the 1961 national championship team was universally revered. While the members of the 1925 team, who first staked the program's claim as a major college power by knocking off Washington in the Rose Bowl, were looked up to as the founding fathers of the Crimson Tide's football dynasty, the sons of 1961 rescued 'Bama from the nightmarish Ears Whitworth years and reestablished the tradition. Hard-nosed young men including Pat Trammell, Billy Neighbors, Lee Roy Jordan, Tommy Brooker, Darwin Holt, and Billy Richardson would always hold a special place in Bryant's heart, because their hard work and sacrifice set the tone for all that was to come. They made Alabama Alabama again, and in this sense, their story is inexorably linked to the boys of 1966.

More than anything else, the 1961 team was exemplified by the ferocious way it played defense. "They acted like it was a sin to give up a point," Bryant often said.

In 10 regular season games, the undefeated, untied Crimson Tide surrendered a total of 22 points—2.2 points per game—and recorded 6 shutouts. The field goal 'Bama allowed in the 10–3 Sugar Bowl victory over Arkansas prevented the bunch from ending the year with 6 consecutive shutouts, which ticked them all off.

"We took a lot of pride in those goose eggs," recalled Lee Roy Jordan.

Toward the end of the 1966 season, the buzz around the program grew steadily louder and louder. The 1966 Crimson Tide was increasingly being compared to the 1961 bunch, which was as provocative and complimentary around Tuscaloosa as speaking of a baseball team in the same breath as the 1927 Yankees. The 1961 Tide was the gold standard, and the 1966 Tide was bidding up its value with every dominating performance.

The environmental differences between the one-platoon 1961 team and the two-platoon 1966 team render any sort of head-to-head comparison little more than a fool's errand, even though Kenny Stabler's gifts at the quarterback position clearly exceeded Pat Trammell's, making the 1966 offense significantly more dangerous. However, one thing was abundantly clear: The 1966 Crimson Tide defense was well on its way to setting a new standard for the new age. In 10 regular season games, while matching the 1961 team's 6 shutouts and allowing just 5 touchdowns, Alabama surrendered a total of 37 points—3.7 points per game—making it not only the toughest defense in the country for the year—by a single point over Notre Dame—but also the stingiest defense of the entire two-platoon era, from 1964 to 2005. No major college football team since the British Invasion has guarded the end zone like the 1966 Alabama Crimson Tide, which held every single opponent scoreless in both the second and third quarters.

Equally tough against both the run and the pass, Alabama held its opponents to 174.1 yards per game and forced a nation's-best 35 turnovers, for a sterling giveaway/takeaway ratio of plus 19. The numbers might have been even more impressive, but Bryant emptied the benches every week.

Playing defense for the Crimson Tide was not just a matter of execution and pursuit. It was an attitude—a defiant, resolute, punishing attitude—and no one personified the mental line drawn arrogantly in the dirt like defensive line coach Ken Donahue. A terrific teacher of technique who also exuded significant influence over Alabama's defensive scheme, the intense former Tennessee player provided a critical link between the General and the Bear.

"Our philosophy was that the defense should always attack the offense and make them earn whatever they get the hard way," said Donahue, eventually promoted to defensive coordinator. "We also had the philosophy that football's kinda like war. You fight till you drop with everything you've got."

Football was Donahue's life. His fierceness surged across the practice field like a kinetic force, forever pushing his players to move faster, hit harder, reach deeper.

"Coach Donahue was one of the toughest men I've ever known, and he was especially hard on me, probably because I needed it," recalled defensive tackle Louis Thompson. "Some days, I just hated him, he leaned on me so hard. But I grew to love him to death, because he helped make me a better football player."

The key to Alabama's success was the dominance of the all-senior three-man front. After some shuffling of personnel early in the season, the lineup of 6', 191-pound noseguard Johnny Sullivan, 6'2", 213-pound tackle Louis Thompson, and 6'2", 204-pound tackle Richard Cole stifled offenses like few units in school history. What they lacked in size they more than compensated for with an abundance of quickness and tenacity, routinely stopping the run and putting pressure on the quarterback.

The sense of oneness that lifted the bunch of no-names and overachievers to a championship performance level had been tested by fire in various ways. Off the field, tackle Richard Cole was an incredibly mild-mannered, devout young man, an officer in the campus chapter of the Fellowship of Christian Athletes. Between the white lines, however, he was one of the Crimson Tide's most competitive athletes, and his teammates learned to respect—and trust—his fierceness.

During his junior year in 1965, Cole became increasingly frustrated by senior linebacker Jackie Sherrill's tendency to push off of his butt to get a head start, especially when he was required to back up into a zone to cover the pass. Cole kept warning him to stop pushing off, because the shove sometimes left him scrambling.

Finally, after Sherrill pushed off during the first half of the LSU game in Baton Rouge, Cole turned to him in the huddle with a nasty expression. "I done told you! Don't you ever do that again! If you do, I'll slug you!"

Several plays later, Sherrill broke his promise never to push off again, sticking his hand once more where it did not belong, as Cole struggled to retain his footing. After the play, Cole walked up to Sherrill in the huddle, looked for the exposed, V-shaped area underneath his shoulder pads, and punched his teammate in the gut as hard as he could. The force knocked Sherrill to the ground, right in the middle of the game for all to see. He never again touched Cole's rear end. The linebackers in 1966 knew better than to challenge him, and all of his teammates appreciated and knew they could count on his toughness, which was usually applied against the opposition.

While the 'Bama lineup included no giant physical specimens like Bubba Smith, the guys in red shirts swarmed to the ball, leveled thunderous, bone-rattling licks, and played with a chemistry that defied description. No team hit harder. No team chased its potential more relentlessly.

In addition to being supremely conditioned, thanks to gym class and all the other moments of formative hell, the Alabama defense was always extremely well prepared. Donahue and the other members of the defensive staff—linebackers coach Pat Dye, secondary coach Mal Moore, and ends coach Dude Hennessey—excelled in teaching and reinforcing solid technique as well as getting their players ready to defend against opponents' strengths and exploit their weaknesses. The coaches made sure they were ready for every possible contingency, and when one of them made a big stop or forced a turnover in front of a huge throng, it was merely the climactic moment following years of repetition and preparation in a sweaty, desperate world far from the maddening crowds.

"Our players always went into games believing that nobody they faced could have worked harder or be better prepared than them," said Mal Moore. "Because of that, they played with an enormous amount of confidence."

The Crimson Tide played a tough brand of football and also a smart brand of football. No one exemplified this potent combination better than linebacker Bob Childs.

After being recruited out of Montgomery's Sidney Lanier High School as an offensive guard, Childs caught a break when one of the starting linebackers in the state high school all-star game suffered an injury on the first play of the game. He had tried to sell himself as a linebacker to the Alabama staff—without success—and when the all-star coach inserted him into the defensive lineup to replace his fallen teammate, Childs seized the unexpected opportunity. After watching him intercept two passes and make a bunch of tackles, Bryant decided to give him a shot at linebacker.

Blessed with photographic recall, the cerebral Childs, who was thinking about a career in medicine, memorized the Alabama playbook during his freshman year, which helped him read and anticipate well enough to make several big plays in the 1966 A-Day game. Though not the most physically gifted linebacker on the roster, Childs earned a starting role—and the important job of calling the defensive coverages up front—by learning how to apply his knowledge while exploiting his athleticism. Not only was he was a vicious tackler, his demonstrated ability to memorize opponents' tendencies became a tremendous asset for the Crimson Tide.

"Childs was probably the most underrated linebacker in the whole conference," said Mike Hall, a dominating presence at the other linebacker slot, especially when he routinely neutralized the tight end.

By owning the line of scrimmage and constantly putting pressure on the quarterback, Alabama played to the strengths of its mobile and athletic secondary, which covered the pass as well as any unit in the country. The Crimson Tide allowed a stingy 94.4 passing yards per game, held opposing quarterbacks to a 41.3 completion percentage, and recorded 24 interceptions, by far the best in big-time college football.

"The thing that made that bunch so good was that it was a team in every sense of the word," said noseguard Johnny Sullivan, a native of Nashville. "We didn't think like a bunch of individuals. We truly thought like a team, and that can be a pretty powerful thing."

A stiff breeze whipped across Mobile's jam-packed Ladd Stadium as the captains approached midfield for the coin toss.

Several minutes before, in the home dressing room underneath the ancient arena—site of the annual Senior Bowl all-star game—Bryant had instructed Cecil Dowdy and Johnny Mosley to "kick to the clock" if they won the toss against Southern Mississippi. At one end of the stadium, the old-fashioned dial clock—the style prevalent before the advent of modern electronic scoreboards—loomed as a recognizable landmark and a reminder of a vanishing era.

In addition to playing about four games per year at Birmingham's Legion Field, the largest stadium in the state, the Crimson Tide always played one game at Ladd Stadium in the state's second-largest city. In 1958, eleven-year-old David Chatwood sat in the Ladd Stadium stands with his father watching

Billy Cannon and eventual national champion LSU rally to knock off Alabama, 13–3, in the historic first game of the Bryant era. As he looked out at the players darting around the field and soaked up the electric atmosphere of his first college football game, Chatwood decided right then and there that he wanted to wear the red jersey when he grew up. A big portion of the stands collapsed during the game, and wide-eyed Chatwood heard the crash over the roar of the crowd, turned to check on the commotion, and then returned his eyes to the hard-hitting action on the field. He could not wait to grow up.

Taking the state's favorite team to the city by the bay was a good way to connect with the fans at a time when Denny Stadium was still relatively small and the world was less mobile, and besides, it was tradition. In the years before Bryant returned to the Capstone, Alabama also reserved one game each season for Montgomery's Cramton Bowl, but eventually, the Crimson Tide outgrew the facility located just a few blocks from the state capital, site of the annual Blue-Gray Game. The expansion of Denny Stadium to 59,000 seats in 1966, and the surging demand for tickets, would eventually cause Alabama to curtail the annual pilgrimages to 40,000-seat Ladd Stadium, too. After 1968, Alabama played all of its home games in Tuscaloosa and Birmingham, where the stadiums would grow bigger still, unable to keep up with the ever-growing demand.

As the officials prepared to flip the coin, Cecil Dowdy and Johnny Mosley could be seen throwing blades of grass into the air, testing the wind. Clearly, the direction of the breeze had changed since Bryant instructed them to "kick to the clock," and in the tense moment after Alabama won the toss, Dowdy and Mosley could not agree on a course of action. Should they follow the boss's orders, even though the conditions had changed? Or should they adapt to the new wind?

"I wanted to go the other way, because I thought that's what Coach Bryant would want to do, under the circumstances," recalled Mosley. "But ole Cecil wanted to do what Coach Bryant told us to do, period."

Finally, Dowdy blurted out, "Kick to the clock."

In many ways, playing football for Paul Bryant was like being in the military. The coach expected his orders to be followed, and ordinarily, this was not the least bit problematic. To every last man on the team, his word was law. However, Bryant also expected his leaders on the field to act like leaders, which sometimes required them to know how and when to improvise. The line was fine and fraught with peril, and the pregame debate between the two captains was a perfect example of how two driven, disciplined, well-coached athletes could reach completely opposite conclusions when forced to make a decision in the heat of the moment.

With Alabama's Dudley Kerr forced to kick into the wind, Southern Miss wound up with good field position to start the game. Then the Crimson Tide's defense lowered the boom. On first down, Charley Harris charged through the line and tackled a runner for a two-yard loss. On second down, Richard Cole slammed the door shut on an off-tackle run, giving up a single yard. On third down, Mike Ford sacked the quarterback for a four-yard loss.

Three plays. Minus five yards. The tone was set for another dominating day by the Crimson Tide.

Early in the second quarter, after Kenny Stabler threw a 25-yard touchdown pass to Ray Perkins, staking the Crimson Tide to a 6–0 lead—set up by a fumble caused by Louis Thompson and recovered by Mike Hall—Southern Miss was still looking for its initial first down of the afternoon. In their first 13 offensive snaps, the Golden Eagles gained 6 net yards. Still, Southern Miss, headed for a 6-4 season, had taken Bluebonnet Bowl-bound Ole Miss to the wire before losing, 14–7, and the Alabama players knew better than to relax against the underdogs from Hattiesburg.

After studying his scouting report all week, defensive signal caller Bob Childs probably knew more about Southern's tendencies than anyone else on the field. "Bob had some genius in him," said starting monster Wayne Owen. "He had a real gift for being able to take a playbook and absorb it better than anyone I ever saw. He could always tell you what a team was statistically likely to do in a certain down and distance."

His knowledge was power. Sometimes, however, it led him toward that fine line where Cecil Dowdy and Johnny Mosley danced in the breeze.

After Childs called a blitz, Southern quarterback Mike McClellan read it, avoided it, and completed a pass for a first down. Moments later, reserve lineman Mike Reilly trotted onto the field with a message. "Coach Bryant says you need to run the blitz," he said.

"Nah. It won't work. I called it a minute ago and he read it," Childs said to Reilly, who ran off the field.

When Southern gained seven yards on the next play, a fuming Bryant sent Reilly back into the game, determined to stop the drive cold. "Bob, Coach Bryant said to tell you that he's the head coach and you're going to run that blitz or you won't be able to stand up in practice next week," Reilly said.

Needing no further elaboration on the subject, Childs followed orders and called the blitz. Then Mike Ford sacked the quarterback for an eleven-yard loss, forcing the Golden Eagles to punt and proving Bryant right.

Childs managed to avoid the boss until the half, but when the time expired and the teams headed off the field with Alabama leading 12–0—thanks to another Stabler touchdown pass, a one-yarder to Wayne Cook—Bryant collared him and stayed in his face until they reached the lockerroom. He was not whispering sweet nothings.

"I was not even thinking about not doing what Coach Bryant told me to do," Childs said. "It's just that I was so into the moment. After he got through fussing at me, I thought to myself: How dumb am I? The bottom line is, he was right. Obviously, he saw something that I didn't, and we sacked the quarterback. I was reading too much into the fact that he had read the blitz the first time."

The Crimson Tide's 34–0 victory was never in doubt. In running its record to 9–0, Alabama churned up 348 yards on the nation's No. 1-ranked defense, more than twice the Golden Eagles' average for the year. The Crimson Tide's defense, destined to finish the season ranked second nationally in yards allowed—Notre Dame was fourth, Michigan State eighth—held Southern to 103. The Eagles never crossed the 'Bama 40.

Alabama's combination of superior conditioning and enviable depth always loomed large, especially late in the game, so when one of Southern's 230-pound defensive linemen, who had played every snap, lined up in the fourth quarter against another diminutive but fresh Tide offensive guard with a clean uniform, the exasperated look on his face told a familiar tale.

"How many damn little ole farts have y'all got?" he said to the latest reserve entering the fray, while settling into his stance.

The Golden Eagle was spent, with no reinforcements on the way, even as the little farts from Tuscaloosa kept coming, rested and ready to rock.

While Alabama moved within one step of an undefeated, untied regular season, Notre Dame crushed Southern Cal, 51–0, to finish 9-0-1. On Sunday, as 'Bama started preparations for Auburn, the hope still lingered in every mind at Bryant Hall. Now that the UPI poll was prepared to make its final selections, surely the coaches would take a step back and consider Alabama's strong case for No. 1.

The news hit the wires on Monday afternoon, and even after a whole season of playing catch-up, the Alabama players could not believe their ears.

Notre Dame?

Was this some sort of joke?

Could the UPI coaches poll actually have voted to reward not only an inferior record but also gutless behavior in the face of their perfection?

The UPI vote was an insult—an unmistakable slap at the 'Bama program. At the SEC. At the South. At the most sacred principles of college football.

In the final UPI poll, Michigan State finished second, followed by Alabama, Georgia, UCLA, Purdue, Nebraska, Georgia Tech, SMU, and Miami.

Adding salt to 'Bama's fresh wound, the National Football Foundation, which had joined in the selection process starting in 1959, announced that its eight-man panel had chosen to award the MacArthur Bowl trophy to Michigan State and Notre Dame as cochampions. Like the title presented by the Football Writers Association of America—still to come—the MacArthur Bowl was much less prestigious than the ubiquitous AP and UPI polls, especially considering the small number of participating voters centered around the Northeast, who included former head coaches of Army and Columbia and a former Yale athletic director.

"The reasons are rather obvious why we divided the award," explained MacArthur Bowl chairman Vincent dePaul Draddy. "It seemed the only fair thing to do with a couple of excellent teams like Notre Dame and Michigan State."

Hello?

Was Alabama invisible?

The UPI and MacArthur Bowl boards appeared to be in such a hurry to prove the irrelevance of the nation's only undefeated, untied team, they could not even wait until Alabama completed its regular season the next week against archrival Auburn. This struck the 'Bama players as a particularly galling slight. The decision by the AP, announced the previous summer, to revert to the traditional process of closing the polls at the end of the regular season left Alabama with one last chance to move the needle and convince the writers to award the Crimson Tide a third straight AP title. With one week to go, the AP top ten was nearly identical to the UPI: Notre Dame, Michigan State, Alabama, Georgia, UCLA, Nebraska, Purdue, Georgia Tech, Miami, and SMU.

Even before the writers filled in their final ballots, the coaches vindicated Ara Parseghian's cynical calculation. He was shameless in his pursuit of a championship, but he sure knew how to count the votes in his back pocket.

12. FAMILY TIES

Suddenly, the whole world seemed not to make sense. Suddenly, all those harrowing moments in gym class . . . all those excruciating days on the practice field . . . all those rigid rules around the dorm . . . all those hard-hitting games . . . seemed like a gigantic waste of time. The whole Alabama football experience suddenly felt like one big tease, one big con, one big lie.

After the UPI vote, it was hard for the 'Bama players not to view their rejection through such a prism, because every aspect of the demanding system was geared around competing for the national championship.

More than some abstract concept, the national championship was the North Star of the Alabama football universe, pointing the Crimson Tide forever home, to the promised land, and to watch it vanish under such conditions, despite their various sacrifices, despite their perfection, the players felt absolutely lost.

It was as if somebody had moved the North Star.

As the Crimson Tide prepared for the season finale against Auburn, with one final chance to convince the AP voters, the game loomed as more than an opportunity to clinch an undefeated, united regular season and capture a share of the national championship. It was one last chance to return some sense of order to their universe.

The Alabama players were accustomed to dealing with distractions, as evidenced by the mounting threat of the war in Vietnam.

One afternoon late in the season, dorm director Gary White called upstairs and said he needed to see Nathan Rustin and Richard Cole.

After checking on the matter, which was nothing important, Cole, who roomed with Don Shankles, and Rustin, who roomed with Bruce Stephens, returned upstairs and decided to have a little innocent fun.

"What's it all about?" asked Stephens, the Tide's starting right guard.

About that time, Shankles, a reserve defensive end from Fort Payne, walked up.

Cole flashed a worried expression. "There was an army recruiter down there and he had draft notices for a bunch of guys," said the Crimson Tide's All-America defensive tackle, milking the moment for all it was worth. "I saw the list, and both your names are on it!"

"No!"

"You're lying!"

Rustin, a reserve lineman from Phoenix City, played along, and they kept the gag going for several minutes.

"We were just carrying on like a bunch of kids, not thinking they would believe us," Cole recalled. "But we had 'em going. Had 'em convinced that they were on the list and that they were headed to Vietnam."

The war, which had once seemed like a distant abstraction, prayed on the mind of every draft-age young man across America in 1966. The rules regarding college deferments would change several times in the coming years, and the number of Alabama players signed up for ROTC was a testament to how seriously they all took the threat of being compelled to fight in a jungle war whose wisdom was just starting to be questioned. Several were destined to eventually serve their country honorably, and the team was filled with patriotic young men who were taught to believe in the rightness of American ideals. Most of the coaches had served in the military at one time or another, including linebackers coach Pat Dye, who finished his army hitch in 1965, just missing the major buildup in Vietnam. While most of the Alabama players wanted to avoid the draft at all costs, the sense of duty, honor, and country pervading their lives dictated that they all be prepared to do the right thing if called to serve.

The change looming on the horizon, with regard to Vietnam and many other things, would be evident in a conversation less than a year later, early in the 1967 season, between kicker Steve Davis and his father, the hard-nosed high school football coach. "My father was a real right-winger . . . [who believed] anything the United States government did was right," recalled Davis. "He hated hippies and all that antiestablishment stuff. But one day we were talking and he looked at me and said, 'Son, if they drafted you, I wouldn't blame you at all if you went to Canada.' You talk about a change. I never thought I would hear him say something like that. Never. But by that time, [having seen] several of his players get killed and badly wounded in Vietnam . . . affected the way he thought."

The 1966 Alabama team was straddling a cultural fault line, and nothing symbolized the revolution in thought quite as well as Pig Davis's slowly awakening conscience on the subject of the Vietnam war.

When David Chatwood's draft notice arrived after graduation in 1968, when the war was tearing the country apart, when young men from all sorts of backgrounds were fleeing to Canada, when many others were burning draft cards in the streets, the fullback from Baldwin County paid all of his bills and made arrangements to report to infantry school at Georgia's Fort Benning. Lord knows, he didn't want to go, but he was prepared to do his duty, because that's how the men who played for Paul Bryant were trained to think.

As he walked out the door, his mother cried, because she knew. Her little boy was headed for Vietnam, which, by that time, Walter Cronkite had pronounced unwinnable, leading a stunned President Lyndon Johnson to tell an aide, "If I've lost Cronkite, I've lost middle America." He was right, and by then, Chatwood's mother had every reason in the world to believe her son might never come back. At his last physical, however, an army doctor found something wrong with Chatwood's ear. "Get out of here," the doctor finally said, which was not so much a command as a reprieve. Having a bad ear might very well have saved his life, a fact that would cross his mind often in the years ahead.

The country was heading toward uncharted territory, yet, as the Crimson Tide chased history in the fall of 1966, it remained on the front side of the fault line, unable to imagine the world just over the horizon.

Like several of his teammates, Richard Cole had taken the bus to Montgomery for his army physical, where he was led to believe he would eventually receive a deferment. Several days before the regular season finale against archrival Auburn, he stopped by his mailbox in the lobby of Bryant Hall and retrieved a letter. As soon as he ripped open the envelope and started reading, the little joke he had pulled on Don Shankles and Bruce Stephens several weeks before took on a whole new meaning.

His heart raced as he read every word of the three-page draft notice, which included a "report to duty" demand.

"It scared the devil out of me," he recalled. "I read through the first two pages, and all I could think about was that I was about to line up to go to Vietnam."

Finally, the devout young man from Crossville breathlessly turned to the third and final page, all the while trying to suppress panic, wondering if he could somehow delay his induction until after the Crimson Tide's two remaining football games. Then he saw it. The word "deferment" jumped off the page.

"I've never been so relieved in my life," he said.

When he calmed down, Cole walked back to his room and prepared to head off to practice. He tried to put the scare out of his mind, because the serious business of the state of Alabama's upcoming football civil war required every ounce of his attention.

The greatest rivalry in college football began on a brisk winter day at Lakeview Park in Birmingham, where a grandstand ticket could be purchased from a man in an open-air booth for twenty-five cents. "Tuskaloosa vs. Auburn," proclaimed the little yellow stub, the Indian spelling of Alabama's hometown still holding sway. The date was February 22, 1893, which just happened to be George Washington's birthday. According to the local newspapers, a crowd estimated between four thousand and five thousand gathered to see the epic first meeting on the gridiron between the University of Alabama and the Agricultural and Mechanical College—later to become Alabama Polytechnic University, and eventually, Auburn University. Both campuses chartered special trains to bring students to Birmingham, and the railroad also brought spectators from as far as Montgomery, Anniston, and Eufaula. "The whole state has its eyes turned to Birmingham and is eagerly awaiting to learn who will be the vanquishers," a writer for *The Birmingham News* declared. "Never before was there such enthusiasm over an athletic contest in the state."

The previous February, Auburn had played its first football game, knocking off the University of Georgia, 10–0, to launch the South's long-running rivalry, nearly seven months before Alabama joined the revolution sweeping across the country's college campuses. After losing to Duke and North Carolina and beating Georgia Tech, Auburn challenged the boys from Tuskaloosa and procured F. M. Balliet, a former Pennsylvania player, to coach the team for the big game.

Auburn's 32–22 victory was hailed by *The Birmingham News* as "the greatest football game ever played in the State of Alabama." Since it was roughly the eighth college football game ever played in the state, this was probably true. Within a few months, the captains of the teams—it would still be a long time before either school featured anything resembling an athletic department—started discussing another match. The second game occurred on November 30, 1893, as most teams across the South fell into a pattern of playing the sport only in the autumn months. Auburn won the second renewal in the series, 40–16, and Alabama beat Auburn for the first time the next year, 18–0. The 1894 game was bathed in controversy because Auburn complained that Eli Abbot, Alabama's new coach, was being paid a salary.

Quickly, the rivalry took on great importance at both campuses and among fans across the state who began to identify with one school or the other. Tensions sometimes spilled beyond the field of play.

Led for five formative years by John Heisman, whose name would one day be immortalized by the most coveted individual honor in college football, presented annually by New York's Downtown Athletic Club, Auburn held the upper hand in the series before Alabama pulled off consecutive victories in 1905 and '06. Some months after the 1907 game ended in a 6–6 tie, the representatives from the two teams started making plans to play again in 1908, but a dispute over money proved to be a mighty stumbling block. When Auburn demanded a per diem of $3.50 for twenty-two men, since Alabama was to be the host team for the game at the Birmingham Fairgrounds, Alabama resisted, proposing a compromise of $3 for twenty players. The teams also disagreed on officiating. Alabama wanted a referee from the South. Auburn, believing no official from the region was qualified, held out for a northern football man to officiate the proceedings.

Thus began the most unusual cold war in college football history.

Over a relatively small amount of expense money ($34) and the issue of refereeing—Alabama insisted that obtaining an official from the North, where football was more developed, would cost too much—the state's two biggest schools stopped playing each other. Despite several attempts to revive the rivalry, the bitter feud would last for forty-one years—from the trust-busting days of Teddy Roosevelt to the buck-stopping days of Harry Truman.

Slowly, as the sport began to take on a structure—the formalization of conference play, the earliest forms of recruiting, the first thrust of stadium construction—Alabama emerged as a national power, and Auburn wallowed in mediocrity. Between 1922—the year of Alabama's seminal victory over Pennsylvania—and the end of World War II, as the Crimson Tide posted a widely envied 175-40-11 record, and captured five national championships and eight league titles, Auburn struggled to a 107-99-19 mark.

Although they toiled in the same league—first the Southern Intercollegiate Athletic Association, then the Southern Conference, and finally, the Southeastern Conference—and for a time were both coached by disciples of Knute Rockne who ran the Notre Dame box offense, Alabama and Auburn shared precious little else in common. While Alabama was playing in Rose Bowls and carrying the banner of Southern pride, Auburn lacked the clout even to attract some SEC teams to play at the small facility in the so-called loveliest village on the plain. Even after 7,500-seat Cliff Hare Stadium was completed in 1939— at a time when Alabama's Denny Stadium could accommodate 22,000—the Tigers were forced to play an inordinate number of games on the road.

"We felt like second-class citizens in those days," said Babe McGehee, who scored the first touchdown at Cliff Hare Stadium.

Under pressure from the state legislature, Alabama and Auburn agreed to meet for the first time in a generation, on December 4, 1948, the last game of the season for both teams. "They'll take the bandages off a forty-one-year-old football wound tomorrow to see if the scar is healed," wrote *The Montgomery Advertiser*'s Sterling Slappey, reflecting the tremendous anticipation for the event.

Prior to the game, leaders from the two campuses met at Birmingham's Woodrow Wilson Park to bury a ceremonial hatchet. So great was the demand for tickets at 44,000-seat Legion Field in Birmingham, a local television station made a deal to beam the game via closed-circuit technology to the armory across the street. A packed house paid the $1 admission price to see a fuzzy black-and-white picture of the action.

As expected, Alabama crushed Auburn, 55–0. The score roughly indicated the distance between the two programs at the time.

The next year, even though the Crimson Tide was moving into a mediocre era under the leadership of Harold "Red" Drew, 6-2-1 Alabama entered the season finale as a prohibitive nineteen-point favorite over the 1-4-3 Tigers. Then Auburn stunned the football world, pulling off a 14–13 victory, ranking among the biggest upsets in the storied history of the SEC.

Alabama people considered the 1949 game a fluke, but even though the Crimson Tide won the next four in the series by a combined score of 90–14, the direction of both programs pivoted on the arrival of Ralph "Shug" Jordan in 1951. Jordan, a former Auburn player and assistant coach, took over the Tigers' program on the heels of a winless 1950 season. With Alabama up and down under Drew, and then hitting the skids under the inept J. B. "Ears" Whitworth, Jordan turned long-suffering Auburn into a power, capturing the AP national championship in 1957. Even as the Tigers won four straight in the series—by a combined 128–7—Auburn was hit with NCAA sanctions for recruiting violations three times, probably costing the school at least three major bowl bids. Many Auburn supporters blamed Alabama for providing the information leading to the penalties, serving only to heighten the rivalry's already fevered tensions.

Just when Alabama fans feared Auburn might permanently control football in the state, Paul "Bear" Bryant returned from Texas A&M and changed everything. After a narrow 14–8 loss to the Tigers in 1958, Bryant quickly reestablished Alabama's dominance. Shug Jordan would produce several more good teams before retiring with a 176-83-6 mark—especially those featuring the record-setting tandem of Heisman Trophy–winning quarterback Pat Sullivan and All-America receiver Terry Beasley from 1969 to 1971—but he would spend the rest of his career in Bryant's enormous shadow.

Entering the 1966 game, Alabama had won six of the last seven in the series.

Sometimes the game was competitive, sometimes not. The Crimson Tide shut out the Tigers four straight times between 1959 and 1962: 10–0, 3–0, 34–0, and 38–0. After Auburn pulled off a 10–8 upset in 1963, the game was nationally televised for the first time in 1964. Viewers were treated to one of the best games in the history of the rivalry, as Alabama clinched the national championship by holding off stubborn Auburn, led by All-America halfback Tucker Fredrickson, 21–14. 'Bama sophomore Johnny Mosley stepped in front of an Auburn pass near the goal line in the fourth quarter, helping preserve the victory. The Tide's 30–3 win in 1965, which placed Bryant's program within reach of another national title, was never in doubt.

Instead of quelling the rivalry, Alabama's stranglehold on the series during the 1960s intensified the level of animosity.

Especially in the years after the schools started playing again, the meaning of the game extended way beyond the football field, becoming the most important point of identification for the vast majority of the state's citizens. From an early age, children in the Heart of Dixie made a choice—Alabama or Auburn—and the decision tended to brand them for life. Like other agricultural schools—including Texas A&M, Mississippi State, and Oklahoma State—Auburn was looked down upon by the supporters of the state university as a "cow college." While Alabama produced most of the state's doctors, lawyers, bankers, and such, Auburn was known primarily for turning out pharmacists, engineers, and county extension agents. Whom you pulled for said much about your lot in life. Alabama fans enjoyed stereotyping Auburn fans as hicks with inferiority complexes—and chips firmly attached to their shoulders. Auburn fans derided Alabama fans as elitist, arrogant snobs. Alabama graduates dominated the legislature, and whenever anyone across the state ran for mayor or a seat on a city council or school board, his university affiliation was always an asset or a liability, depending upon the demographic makeup of his constituency.

Most people who pulled for the Crimson Tide could trace no formal connection to the university, and many identified not only with Bryant's unparalleled record but also the classy image he created, as a symbol of aspiration. The Bear sold an image of Alabama as first class all the way, and the implication that Auburn was not permeated the rivalry and reverberated throughout the culture. With the publicity savvy Bryant often throwing out an occasional reference to the "cow college," the class warfare represented by the rivalry needled Auburn people who were already predisposed to think of themselves as outsiders.

"Coach Bryant . . . was able to portray Alabama as better than Auburn in every way," remarked former Auburn athletic director David Housel, who attended the university during the period, "and an awful lot of Auburn people took that to heart, got wrapped up in it."

Around his team, Bryant often referred to the Auburn people as "those country bastards," making sure his players understood that he expected to dominate the Tigers as a matter of course. His choice of words was terribly ironic, because, despite his national reputation, despite his friendship with prominent figures in a variety of fields, despite his wealth and status, no one was more country than Bryant himself.

During Bryant's playing days, in the midst of the forty-one-year feud, the big enemy in Tuscaloosa was Tennessee, and while he retained a special hatred for the Volunteers, he learned to reserve a unique kind of venom for Auburn. Because the Crimson Tide and Tigers competed head-to-head for players as well—not to mention the hearts and minds of the state—the rivalry existed on a slightly different plane than Tennessee. The game itself was the annual culmination of a conflict forever raging on a variety of levels—a 365-day battle for bragging rights. The entire foundation of the Alabama program required that the Crimson Tide keep Auburn subservient and submissive, so it was hard to overstate the importance of the season-ending grudge match. Over the course of his quarter-century in Tuscaloosa, Bryant's 19–6 record against the Tigers simultaneously lifted Alabama to one championship after another and kept Auburn forever struggling to keep up.

Even in the 1960s, many Auburn people resented Alabama's insistence to play the annual game in Birmingham, which was touted as neutral ground but struck the folks in orange and blue as Crimson Tide territory. Like 'Bama, Auburn played several other games each year at Legion Field, the state's largest facility, but soon, the Tigers would start moving some of those to campus, out of Alabama's enormous shadow.

Bryant, who usually arrived at his office long before the sun rose and probably worked longer hours than anyone in the game, liked to tell the story about the call he placed to the Auburn athletic department at about seven o'clock one morning. When he asked to speak with Shug, whoever answered the phone told him that the coach was not in yet. "What's the matter," he snorted. "Don't you folks down there take football seriously?"

The point of the story was lost on no one on either side of the rivalry: Alabama deserved its anointed status because the game meant more to the Crimson Tide, because Alabama people worked harder.

Despite the heated rivalry, the two coaches maintained a cordial and friendly relationship, sometimes even spending time together at their nearby vacation homes on Lake Martin in the southeastern part of the state. The amiable Jordan, a decorated veteran of the D-day invasion, was a gentleman in every sense of the word, but he was also a competitive individual who must have resented that he allowed Bryant to steamroll right over him, rendering Auburn to the role of a periodic spoiler, rather than a consistent threat.

As he watched Bryant's legend grow, Jordan liked to tell the apocryphal story about a day when they went fishing together and the Bear decided to see whether he could truly walk on water, as so many Alabama fans seemed to believe. According to the tall tale, Bryant climbed out of the little rowboat, took one step into the water and sank like a stone. When Jordan fished him out of the drink, Bryant made him promise not to tell anyone that the mighty Bear could not walk on water.

"OK, Paul," Shug said, "as long as you'll promise not to tell anybody I saved you!"

At some point during his childhood, Stan Moss chose the orange and blue of the Auburn Tigers.

Growing up the son of a printing equipment salesman in Ensley, on the western edge of Birmingham, Moss became a big Auburn fan. He was also a good athlete, gifted and tough, and eventually, his talent carried him from the backyards near his home to the local high school, where he became an All-America back, drawing the attention of college recruiters, especially those representing Alabama and Auburn. Three of his high school teammates accepted scholarships to Auburn, and everyone expected Moss to sign on the dotted line with Shug Jordan's Tigers.

However, like many other youngsters across the state, Moss was in awe of Bryant, even though he was the enemy to Auburn fans, and the chance to play for the best in the business—and win championships—overshadowed his history as an Auburn fan.

His father, who never attended college and wanted better for his son, never tried to influence his decision. "To him, it was irrelevant whether I played football or not," Moss said. "He was going to make sure I went to college."

However, his uncle Woody, a huge Auburn fan who never attended the school but recruited the area for the Tigers, was devastated by his choice. Several hours after Stan announced he was signing with Alabama, Woody, his father's only brother, showed up at their house about one o'clock in the morning, holding an early copy of the next morning's *Birmingham Post-Herald,* which contained the news. The feeling of betrayal was written all over his face.

"My uncle could not believe it," Moss said. "He was just furious. It was a pretty tough family deal. He pretty much disowned us."

The decision shattered their close-knit family. For a period of about five years, Woody refused to have anything to do with his only brother's family, including the difficult period when his father died suddenly, and his brother truly needed him. Finally, Woody died unexpectedly himself at the age of forty-six, without reconciling with his brother or nephew.

The experience taught Stan a critical lesson at a young age. "Football is important, and there's nothing wrong with making it important," he said. "And, yes, I wanted to beat Auburn more than anything in the world. But football's not more important than your family. Some people just take it way too far, and unfortunately, my uncle was one of those people. It really hurt my father. He never said it, but I know it hit him hard, to have his brother turn on him like that over a football deal."

The Moss story illustrates the power the sport held over the culture of the state of Alabama. So many aspects of the society valued the lessons of football, especially in cultivating strength, toughness, and discipline, yet, it was difficult for some fans to know where to draw the line. Some things, football could not teach. Some things could only be learned off the field of play, and a small number of fans like Woody Moss spent so much time investing the game—and their allegiances—with so much meaning, they failed to see how an otherwise wonderful sport could turn ugly when they allowed it to consume them to the point of losing all perspective.

Because the fans took their allegiances so seriously, the Alabama-Auburn rivalry routinely divided family and friends all across the state. The intense passion usually produced less extreme behavior, but as the undefeated Crimson Tide walked onto the playing surface at Legion Field to warm-up for the nationally televised game against the 4–5 Tigers, the electricity in the air surged with more than a little good old-fashioned hate.

In the distance, smoke from nearby steel mills drifted toward the clouds, a constant reminder of the Magic City's steel-making prowess. Often referred to as "the Pittsburgh of the South," Birmingham reflected the flower of American industrial might at a time when the whole world lived in the wake of the country's manufacturing preeminence. Founded in 1871, Birmingham exploded as a steel mecca at the end of the nineteenth century after the discovery nearby of the three ingredients required to produce the metal: iron ore, coal, and limestone. In 1966, the various steel companies employed a huge chunk of the city's population.

In the days leading up to the Alabama-Auburn game, Leslie B. Worthing-

ton, the president of giant U.S. Steel Corporation, the largest of the city's em-
ployers, told local business leaders, "The rapid industrialization of the South
will continue . . . and consequently, the steel market will continue to grow,
causing a need for more and more steel production facilities."

It was inconceivable that, slightly more than a decade later, the American
steel industry would be on its knees, forcing the Magic City to reinvent itself.

Like every other facet of Birmingham society, the steel mills were still trying
to deal with a legacy of segregation. The racial strife of the decade left all Alabamians feeling beleaguered, but the burden of calling Birmingham home in
those days was especially severe. All across the nation, Birmingham was a symbol of hate, and it would take the city a long time to overcome the haunting image of Bull Connor's fire hoses and the thought of those four little girls.

Most people tried to put such lingering negativity out of their minds, of
course, and at Legion Field on the first Saturday in December, men wearing
suit coats and skinny ties sat alongside women adorned in fancy dresses and
high heels, attesting to the formality of the era and the importance of the day.
Isolated shouts of "Roll Tide!" and "War Eagle" echoed across the 67,000-seat
municipal facility, where the tickets were split down the middle, where a sign
painted onto the upper deck proclaimed, BIRMINGHAM FOOTBALL CAPITAL OF
THE SOUTH. South, hell. As far as Alabama and Auburn people were concerned,
Legion Field at that moment was the center of the universe. The Alabama
cheerleaders busied themselves handing out red and white shakers, which could
easily be seen on TV. Some fans held hand-made posters and prepared to flash
them for the cameras.

Somewhere in the stadium, a colorful character named Shorty Price was
running his mouth and attracting a crowd. Price, who wore a funny-looking hat
and a button proclaiming himself "Alabama's No. 1 fan," was considered by
some the Crimson Tide's unofficial mascot. A folk hero who ran for governor
several times—like Alabama's answer to Pat Paulsen—Price was often ejected
from the stadium for openly violating the school's prohibition against alcohol
in the stadium. He was not the only one taking a nip. The place was a sea of
carefully concealed hip flasks and bottles, especially the Alabama student section, where some enterprising fraternity boys and sorority girls arranged their
seating assignments based on their choice of poison. All the guys had short hair,
all the girls wore girdles, and the coming age of rebellion still seemed unimaginable as they all cheered for the ultimate expression of their neatly ordered
world.

Before the teams returned to their dressing rooms, Auburn assistant coach
Gene Lorendo, who had unsuccessfully recruited Stan Moss, approached the

Alabama linebacker with a serious expression. "You'd better buckle up your chin strap," Lorendo said, and walked away.

Many of the players on both sides had been offered scholarships by both Alabama and Auburn, including Kenny Stabler, Dennis Homan, Les Kelley, and Johnny Mosley. When Mosley called Shug Jordan to break the news, the coach responded with a terse stock answer: "You'll never play down there." Mosley remembered the tense phone call when he picked off the ball near the goal line in the fourth quarter of the 1964 game, and the memory rattled around in his head as he took the field to face the Tigers for the final time in 1966.

Auburn's team included much larger players, especially on the line, and several members of the Crimson Tide had been rejected as too small or untalented by Jordan's program, including All-America defensive tackle Richard Cole, starting linebacker Bob Childs, and reserve lineman Billy Johnson. Cole grew up liking Auburn, and as he matured into one of the best defensive linemen in the country, he never forgot who was willing to give him a chance and who could not see beyond his rather unimposing frame.

After a patriotic pregame ceremony involving an army sergeant who marched the length of the field to salute the American flag—and the introduction of another army sergeant wounded in Vietnam, who was bathed in thunderous applause—Auburn took the opening kickoff and drove to midfield before Alabama stiffened and forced a punt, setting the tone for a defensive first quarter.

Special teams play was always a priority at Alabama, and the members of the Crimson Tide's punt return unit took tremendous pride in the way they stifled opponents. Entering the Auburn game, 'Bama had allowed a net average return of about *one foot*—an amazing stat. When Steve Davis punted from his own 20 in the first quarter, with Alabama closing in on an NCAA record, Auburn speedster Bobby Beaird fielded the ball and headed upfield. Jerry Duncan lunged for him and missed, leaving the runner to scamper into the open field for a 28-yard gain, before Davis, the kicker, tackled Beaird and saved the touchdown.

"Duncan and the rest of the guys were just sick over that missed tackle," Davis recalled. "That's a record nobody ever would have touched."

The game was still scoreless with ten minutes left in the half, when Kenny Stabler methodically drove the Tide down Auburn's throat, from his own 28 to the Tigers' 15, only to watch as Davis missed a 31-yard field goal.

When the defense held Auburn to three and out, Stabler returned to the field and went right for the jugular, hitting a streaking Ray Perkins for a 63-yard touchdown strike. The Alabama fans went wild, hoisting those shakers in the air, creating a sea of red and white exuberance visible throughout the country as the ABC cameras panned across the crowd.

Moments later, after the dominant 'Bama defense forced another Auburn punt, Stabler went back to work, leading the Tide on a 9-play, 48-yard march, culminating with Les Kelley's 1-yard touchdown run.

After the defense stuffed the Tigers once again, Stabler drove 'Bama within field goal range and Davis booted a 23-yarder with one second remaining, giving the Crimson Tide a commanding 17–0 lead at the half.

Firing on all cylinders, both offensively and defensively, Alabama was making a strong case for No. 1, well aware that millions of fans across the country were watching the Tide for the first time, especially the voters in the AP poll, who were due to hand in their final ballots over the weekend.

Win, lose, or tie against Auburn, Alabama was headed for a rematch against Big Eight champion Nebraska, this time in the Sugar Bowl in New Orleans on January 2. In the press box at the half, Nebraska assistant coach Tom Osborne, scouting the Tide, told a reporter, "There's no doubt in our minds that we will be playing the best team in the country."

Alabama was happy to play Nebraska, the highest ranked available opponent, which gave the players a chance to prove that the previous year's Orange Bowl was not a fluke, but the Crimson Tide and its enraged fans wanted Notre Dame. Hand-lettered signs of protest could be seen all over the stadium, including one asking the rhetorical question: IS NOTRE DAME AFRAID OF THE TINY GIANTS? Another demanded: WE WANT THE IRISH (STEWED!)

Several of the banners caught the eye of the ABC crew and eventually flashed across the nation's television screens, including one carried around the concrete walkway encircling the field, which captured the frustration of many:

> **BAMA PLAYS FOOTBALL**
> **N.DAME PLAYS POLITICS**
> **IN YOUR HEART YOU KNOW WE'RE NO. I**

In the second half, the domination continued. Alabama hammered Auburn on both sides of the ball.

Moments after Bobby Johns intercepted Auburn quarterback Loran Carter, Stabler led the Tide downfield with a combination of runs and short passes, culminating with Les Kelley's 12-yard touchdown ramble, which gave 'Bama a 24–0 lead with 5:20 remaining in the third quarter.

The potent Stabler, who finished with one of the best days of his career, hitting 11 of 16 through the air for 169 yards and running 9 times for another 51 yards, never played another snap the rest of the day. Bryant knew the game was won and, despite the fact that he was playing for the national championship, he did not believe in running up the score, as evidenced by the fifty-six players who saw action for the Crimson Tide, including all three quarterbacks and nine ballcarriers.

"Kenny Stabler probably played his greatest game," Bryant would say later.

Three plays later, Alabama end Wayne Owen, a 5'10", 185-pound sophomore from Gadsden, lined up and waited for the ball to be snapped. Mature beyond his years, Owen started school at the age of five, and arrived in Tuscaloosa as a cerebral seventeen-year-old freshman. While he would insist years later that he was only the third-best running back on his high school team, Owen somehow wound up with a scholarship to Alabama, and somehow became a significant player on the varsity in 1966 despite not starting on the previous year's freshman team. Like so many others on the unit who toiled in relative anonymity—a long list that included Mike Sasser, Bunk Harpole, Frank Whaley, Wayne Stevens, and Brownie Sides—his was not a name that would roll easily off the tongue for 'Bama fans in the years ahead, as they remembered the butt-kicking dominance of the 1966 defense, but Owen's significant contributions to the cause could not be overlooked.

One of several sophomores to play major roles on the unit, Owen fired off the ball, made a terrific play on a deep route, and intercepted the Auburn quarterback, putting the Tide offense in business once again at the Tigers' 41 yard line. Two plays later, Wayne Trimble hit Donnie Sutton for a 41-yard touchdown, giving the Crimson Tide a 31–0 lead with 3:19 still to play in the third quarter.

As Bryant emptied his bench, Trimble and third-string quarterback Joe Kelley took turns running the offense and eating the clock. Despite all the substitutions, Auburn could not penetrate the Alabama 45 yard line as the smothering 'Bama defense—led by Richard Cole, who recorded eight tackles and a fumble recovery, and Louis Thompson, who played one of his best games—held the Tigers to 70 net rushing yards, a stingy 1.6 yards per snap.

On his way off the field, Stan Moss, who made several stops against the Tigers, pulled his chin strap off his helmet and walked up to Auburn assistant coach Gene Lorendo, who glared at him, arms folded. "Thought you might want this," Moss said with a sly grin, pushing the chin strap to Lorendo's chest. He then just walked away, grinning from ear to ear.

Lorendo was having an especially bad day. About the same time, Bob Childs introduced himself to the Auburn coach, who had once turned the Montgomery native down for a scholarship, although he said he might have something for him later, if he was willing to wait and gamble. "I just wanted to thank you for not offering me a scholarship," said Childs, who intercepted a pass in the fourth quarter and made six tackles on the day.

The 34–0 rout, which clinched the ninth undefeated, untied regular season in Alabama history and a share of the school's ninth Southeastern Conference championship, extended the Crimson Tide's winning streak to a nation-leading sixteen games, making a powerful statement about the two-time defending national champion's historic quest.

Praising the Alabama defense, Jordan said simply, "They don't intend for you to score on them."

Asked about the impending final AP vote, Bryant refused to politick, but pointed out, "They said our boys were No. 1 before the season and we haven't lost."

On his Sunday replay show, Bryant said he believed the poll voters would "vote their convictions" and urged everyone to "keep [their] mouths shut about the way they vote [because] nothing we can say will make any difference."

He was right.

The vote was anticipated, but it still hit the Crimson Tide like a punch in the stomach.

On Monday, the AP's survey of sports journalists crowned 9-0-1 Notre Dame the national champion, with 506 points and 41 first-place votes. Michigan State (9-0-1) was a distant second, with 471 points and 8 first-place votes. Alabama (10-0-0, with one game to play) was an even more distant third, with 428 points and 7 first-place votes.

"The voters have spoken," said a clearly disappointed Bryant. "I don't agree but that's that. I congratulate two great teams with two great coaches."

Despite Bryant's graciousness and class, the coach and every member of his organization were crushed.

When the news hit the streets, some players sat in their rooms in stunned silence, trying to deal with the devastating shock of it all.

The AP poll results hit the seniors hardest of all. After spending four years of their lives reaching, enduring, and believing, every moment of it invested as a down payment toward the national championship . . . after winning two previous titles . . . after finishing a perfect regular season . . . after seeing the other two contenders stumble . . . the seniors felt betrayed by the whole process.

"We really didn't know how to take it," said offensive tackle Jerry Duncan. "Losing the national championship was like the end of the world to us, 'cause [the pursuit of it] was what drove everything. You take that away and what were we chasing? What were we working so hard for if they were just going to take it away from us after we'd earned it?"

The 1966 Alabama Crimson Tide was not just outvoted. It was robbed, the victim of the greatest injustice in the history of the national championship selection process.

The sport has seen many controversial finishes and close calls through the years, but the 1966 Alabama Crimson Tide occupies a dubious distinction.

In the history of college football, no other team has ever won back-to-back national championships, finished undefeated and untied in the third year, and been denied the title.

In the history of college football, no other team has ever been ranked No. 1 in the preseason AP poll, finished perfect, and then been denied the title.

In 1966, the pollsters appeared to be saying that winning was irrelevant, or at least not the decisive factor, in the national championship process, effectively moving the goalposts even as Alabama chased history. Not only was this an insult to an Alabama team that took on all comers, it undermined faith in the process, and no one in 1966 could predict how the inequities in the polling system would be challenged in the years ahead.

Believing the racial situation cost him the title, Bryant took the offensive and announced that the Crimson Tide was trying to schedule regular season games against integrated, non-Southern programs—a small step, but one loaded with symbolism and significance.

"A few years ago, we had segregation problems," he told reporters after the votes were totaled. "But now we'd like to ask the help of you fellows up North who've been our critics. Help us get games with the Big 10, the Big 8, and the Pacific Coast."

Saying nothing about integrating his roster just yet, he had no way of knowing that the long, drawn-out process of placing black faces in red jerseys was already in the works, without his knowledge. Even though the Crimson Tide was preparing to play an integrated team in a bowl game for a second consecutive year—and several integrated teams from the North, including Boston College, had turned down the chance to play Alabama in 1966, because of the racial climate—the public gesture was interpreted by some in the national media as a capitulation. At the very least, it was a signal, to the Alabama fans and to the nation, that the world was changing and that the Crimson Tide wanted to keep up.

Frequent critic Jim Murray of the *Los Angeles Times* remarked that Bryant was "tired of winning the Magnolia championship" and said the decision by the Alabama coach could be summed up by one phrase: "The South asks for terms."

The first team Alabama wanted to play was Notre Dame, but Bryant joked, "Ara won't return my calls." In fact, Alabama was willing to challenge both Notre Dame and Michigan State to prove where the national championship trophy belonged, even though Bryant knew he had no prayer of convincing the Irish and the Spartans to give him a game, at least right away. "That [Sugar Bowl] game isn't until January 2, and if one of those other teams wanted to square off before then, I think we've got some boys who believe they could out-quick 'em and would like to try," he said.

A couple of weeks later, just before Christmas, Parseghian stood before a packed house at Notre Dame's annual banquet and presided over a raffle for a football autographed by the entire Irish team. "Would you believe the winner is from Alabama?" he announced from the dais with a laugh, and then he threw the ball to Bloomington, Indiana, resident Jack Saks, a native of Gadsden, who had been given the ticket by a friend.

Saks, a huge Crimson Tide fan, told Jimmy Smothers of *The Gadsden Times* that he subsequently approached Parseghian and asked him to sign the ball. "But I've already signed it," Ara said.

"Yes, I know," Saks responded, "but I want you to write underneath that in your heart you know Alabama is No. 1."

This was like asking Willie Sutton to return his loot. Fat chance.

Parseghian chuckled and politely declined.

13. SOMETHING TO PROVE

When Bryant broke the news, an unusual and unexpected feeling shot through every fiber of Jimmy Sharpe's body.

Terror.

"Thought I was going to have a heart attack, right there in the staff meeting," said Sharpe, the Crimson Tide's twenty-six-year-old offensive line coach.

His mind immediately flashed back to a summer trip to Tallahassee.

Before the season, the boss had sent Sharpe to represent him at the annual coaching clinic hosted by his friend Jake Gaither, the highly successful head coach at Florida A&M. Bryant often attended the clinic himself; in fact, he and his wife Mary Harmon enjoyed playing bridge with the Gaithers. The coming integration of southern football was bound to dramatically impact all of the historically black schools, but in 1966, Florida A&M still attracted many of the best African-American players across the region, making the Rattlers one of the most consistent winners in black college football.

The big name on the program was Nebraska head coach Bob Devaney. Naturally, Devaney was interested in learning all he could about the Alabama team, especially considering the Crimson Tide had upset his Cornhuskers, 39–28, in the most recent Orange Bowl. After the lengthy teaching sessions on the field, the guest lecturers convened at Coach Jake's house for dinner three nights in a row, where shop talk was inevitable. The curious Devaney made sure he sat next to the young assistant coach from Tuscaloosa, who was more than happy to answer his questions.

"I told him how our off-season program worked, how we ran specific plays, our blocking philosophy, all kinds of stuff," Sharpe said. "I didn't think a thing in the world about it, 'cause I was a young assistant coach dealing with a big-time celebrity coach . . . and really never thought I would see him again."

When Bryant informed his coaches, during a staff meeting toward the end of the regular season, that he had arranged a rematch with the Cornhuskers in the 1967 Sugar Bowl, Sharpe started replaying the various conversations in his mind.

"I'm thinking to myself: Oh, my goodness! What in the world did I tell them?" Sharpe said. "Did I share any secrets?"

As Alabama prepared for its NCAA-record twentieth postseason trip, the sport's major teams approached bowl games in strikingly different ways.

Three decades after the Orange Bowl in Miami, the Sugar Bowl in New Orleans, and the Cotton Bowl in Dallas joined the pioneering Rose Bowl in Pasadena to form what came to be known as the Big Four, the system included a total of only eight major college games. Bowling remained a coveted reward for a successful season. In addition to the most prestigious New Year's Day events, the holiday season also offered four lesser major college affairs: the Gator Bowl in Jacksonville, the Liberty Bowl in Memphis, the Bluebonnet Bowl in Houston, and the Sun Bowl in El Paso.

The Rose Bowl was annually hosted by teams from the Big Ten and AAWU, but the selection process sometimes left college football fans scratching their heads. The Big Ten maintained a rule forbidding a school from playing in the Grandaddy of Them All in consecutive years. Meanwhile, the AAWU chose its representative through a vote of the members. In 1966, these two rules combined to shaft two deserving top ten teams: Despite going undefeated in conference play and fielding a team being hailed as one of the strongest in college history, second-ranked Michigan State was forced to stay home with a 9-0-1 record while 8-2 Purdue—which had lost to both Michigan State and Notre Dame—headed west for the holidays. Equally bizarre was the vote by the AAWU athletic directors to send 7-3 Southern Cal to the Rose Bowl, instead of fifth-ranked UCLA, which finished 9-1, including a 14–7 victory over the archrival Trojans.

The two conferences prohibited their teams from playing in other games, so it was California or bust.

The Southwest Conference champion hosted the Cotton Bowl against the best available team, usually selected from among the Southeastern Conference, the Big Eight, or the major independents. Darrell Royal's Texas Longhorns or Frank Broyles's Arkansas Razorbacks routinely headlined the party at the state fairgrounds in Dallas, but SMU won the right to carry the flag after a 9-1 season, including the Mustangs' first victory over Texas in nearly a decade. Vince Dooley's Georgia Bulldogs, who finished 9-1 and ranked fourth—losing only to ninth-ranked Miami (Florida)—earned the trip to Dallas after sharing the SEC championship with Alabama. Due to the vagaries of schedule luck, 1966 marked the sixth time in SEC history that two teams were declared cochampions because they finished unbeaten in league play without facing each other, but most Alabama folks didn't give Georgia's cochampionship a second thought.

For many years, the Orange Bowl gained security and prestige by providing a home for the Big Eight champion, but in the mid-1960s, the Miami game was playing the field while going after blockbuster matchups, placing it in direct competition with the Sugar Bowl. The New Orleans game usually featured an SEC team—sometimes two, especially during the worst days of the civil rights movement—but the arrangement was strictly informal.

Because the SEC exerted no authority over its members' postseason activities, and because his championship team represented a marquee name sure to generate sizeable ticket sales and television ratings, Bryant wielded tremendous clout in the bowl process. His teams played in a then-NCAA record twenty-four straight bowl games, including seventeen combined trips to New Orleans, Miami, and Dallas. In any given year during the period, the Bear could typically chose between the Sugar, Orange, and Cotton bowls, and once he pulled the lead string, other selections fell into place. Unable to line up a shot at either Notre Dame or Michigan State, Bryant figured Nebraska was the best available opponent, and besides, he knew Devaney was itching for a rematch, so, after playing in consecutive Orange Bowls, he brokered a deal to face the Cornhuskers in New Orleans. Consequently, the Orange Bowl matched 9-1, eighth-ranked independent Georgia Tech against 9-1 Florida, the SEC's third-place team, led by Heisman Trophy–winning quarterback Steve Spurrier.

The absence of Notre Dame probably enhanced Bryant's postseason leverage throughout the era, but it devalued the whole system. The boycott was defended by university officials for more than four decades as a necessary step to prevent the football program from trampling on academics, which had been a problem during Notre Dame's first and only postseason adventure, a 27–10 victory over Pop Warner's Stanford powerhouse in 1925. The word came down from on high soon after Rockne's team returned from Pasadena, and Irish coaches knew better than to question the reasoning behind the policy, even as it made the program look like an increasingly elitist, out-of-touch institution, anxious to enjoy the spoils of the modern game but unwilling to pay the price of admission. Besides, Notre Dame saw little need to play in bowl games, especially when it could win the national championship without the risk, as it did in 1966, playing keep away with the trophy. Dismissing Alabama's all-southern regular season schedule was a popular activity in some circles, and yet, it was the Irish who were dodging a bowl showdown with the Crimson Tide, enabled by the complicit media, who never questioned the fairness or the logic of awarding the national championship to a team unwilling to lay its ranking on the line in the postseason.

The tension between the forces who wanted to look upon the bowls as meaningless exhibitions and those who preferred to see them as culminating events in the national championship process was nearing a fever pitch. Despite the decision by the AP, UPI, and MacArthur Bowl officials to hold their final votes before the bowls, the less well-known Football Writers Association of America planned to wait until after the Big Four to award its championship, which gave Alabama one final chance to win a trophy.

After ten days of practice in Tuscaloosa, the Crimson Tide headed off for New Orleans on Christmas Day. By the time the team's two chartered airplanes lifted off from the Birmingham Municipal Airport, bound for New Orleans, defensive back Johnny Mosley was starting to sweat.

Like several of his teammates, Mosley had received permission to take his own car and meet the rest of the Crimson Tide in the Crescent City—as long as they all arrived at the Fountainbleau Motor Hotel in time for the squad meeting prior to dinner. After celebrating Christmas with his family in Montgomery, Mosley sped off in his Chevy Malibu, picked up Bruce Stephens, and headed south by southwest. The plan was to stop in Mobile to add two other players to the party, which was about all the sporty coupe could comfortably hold.

For some reason, a total of four players showed up at the appointed place looking for a ride, so when Mosley pulled up in his little car and started counting bodies and luggage, he knew he had a big problem.

"We were all getting worried, because there was no way I could get all those guys in my car, and we could not be late," Mosley said. "If we were late we might as well not go at all."

Thinking fast, the players plotted a course for the nearest state patrol headquarters. Walking through the door to the place in their official Alabama red blazers, they all looked sharp, and as they explained the predicament to the lieutenant in charge—who, naturally, was a Tide fan—the guy was sympathetic to their plight. But it was a holiday, he was incredibly shorthanded, and under the circumstances, he said there was really nothing he could do to help.

Looking at his watch, Mosley politely asked to borrow the phone.

A few minutes later, he was on the line with Chief Smelley, Bryant's personal bodyguard and one of the highest-ranking officials on the state police force. Smelley was already in his hotel room in New Orleans.

"What jail you in?" Smelley said.

"I ain't in no jail," Mosley said, "but I need your help . . ."

When Mosley turned the phone over to the low-ranking officer manning the desk in Mobile County, the players watched an expression of urgency suddenly consume his face.

"Yes, sir! Yes, sir! Yes, sir!" was about all he said, before hanging up and ordering a patrol car back to base.

The Crimson Tide was one of the state of Alabama's biggest assets, and Smelley made clear to the young officer that the state needed to help the distressed players in their time of need.

Soon the heroes from Tuscaloosa were speeding toward New Orleans, sirens blaring, lights flashing. Big Tide fans, the troopers relished the chance to talk football with some of Bear's boys. With the officers leaning on the gas across lower Mississippi and into Louisiana, the players made it to their meeting on time, which may have prevented several key players from being punished heading into the Sugar Bowl.

"Those guys saved our butts," Mosley said.

Sometimes it really paid to wear a red blazer.

The Nebraska players knew the feeling. With no big-time professional sports and no other major college teams to compete with, the Cornhuskers owned Nebraska, a sparsely populated, largely rural state still getting used to the idea of having a winning football program.

Although the Cornhuskers produced occasional good teams through the years, the program spent most of the 1940s and 1950s under the thumb of Big Eight powerhouse Oklahoma. While Bud Wilkinson's Sooners were busy compiling winning streaks of 31 and 47 games, Nebraska produced 17 losing seasons over a twenty-one-year period. When Bob Devaney arrived in Lincoln in 1962, after a short tenure at Wyoming, and immediately produced an 8-2 season to secure only the third bowl bid in school history, he was hailed as a savior. Wilkinson, whose program was already in decline, retired after the 1963 season to make an unsuccessful bid for the U.S. Senate, leaving a void that Devaney's Cornhuskers quickly filled, capturing Big Eight championships in 1963, 1964, 1965, and 1966. The heated Oklahoma-Nebraska rivalry went back and forth, and as Jim Mackenzie stumbled to a 6-4 finish in Norman in 1966, his first and only season at the helm, he guided the Sooners to a 10–9 upset of Nebraska in the season finale, spoiling the Cornhuskers' bid for a second straight undefeated regular season.

Like Notre Dame and Michigan State, Nebraska under Devaney cast an increasingly wide recruiting net. More than half of the players on the Cornhuskers' Sugar Bowl roster hailed from out of state—29 of 56, or 51 percent—compared to just 16 of 62 for Alabama, or 25 percent.

After the shellacking Nebraska took in the previous Orange Bowl, the Cornhuskers were anxious to prove it a fluke by cutting Alabama down to size. In the days leading up to the game, as the two teams practiced and saw the sights of New Orleans, the papers, radio, and TV were full of comments from Nebraska players talking the 1960s version of trash. All those trick plays in Miami caught them by surprise, the Cornhuskers kept saying, and this time, they would be ready and eager for revenge.

Although the possibility of capturing the last of the four national championship trophies dangled in the humid New Orleans air, most folks around the country considered the AP and UPI polls the definitive word on the race for No. 1. The best Alabama could hope for was to muddy the waters a bit, to deprive Notre Dame of a unanimous title. The Crimson Tide entered the Sugar Bowl determined to prove something to the whole country, especially the AP and UPI voters, not to mention the members of the MacArthur Bowl board, who appeared to be unaware of any football being played south of Fourteenth Street in Manhattan.

"We went to New Orleans on a mission," said receiver Dennis Homan. "We wanted to prove that we were the best football team in the country . . . to remove any doubt."

The mimeographed Alabama playbook for the Sugar Bowl contained a hand-scribbled challenge: "Be prepared to do whatever it takes! We have come too far to lose it now! You can do it if it means enough! You can and you will because you are the No. 1 team in America! Act like champions and you will be champions!"

Two or three days before the game, Bryant called his offensive coaches to his hotel suite for an urgent meeting.

The previous season, the Bear had scrapped his usually conservative offensive philosophy against heavily favored Nebraska, relying much more than usual on the pass and attacking the Cornhuskers in a variety of unorthodox ways. This proved to be one of the boldest strokes of his entire coaching career, demonstrating how he was willing and able to radically alter his thinking, to be pragmatic, in order to find a way to beat a team that looked much better than his on paper.

The original game plan for the Sugar Bowl was typical conservative 'Bama football, but he experienced a change of heart after a few days in New Orleans.

"We go in there to meet with Coach Bryant and he has almost completely rearranged the approach to the game," said backfield coach Ken Meyer. "He knew we had a better defense than the year before, and so instead of a game where we were going to play it close to the vest, he decided to attack more and to use more options with Stabler. It was a much more aggressive offensive game plan, including the first play, which he had already decided on."

Unbeknown to the 'Bama coaches, Nebraska was still tinkering, too. Determined to find an edge against the Tide's small but quick offensive line, Devaney switched his defense from an odd-man front to an even-man front. Compared to Alabama, Nebraska was huge, especially on the offensive and defensive lines. In fact, the Cornhuskers brought twenty-two men to New Orleans heavier than 6'2", 213-pound Louis Thompson, the largest player on the Tide roster. "Bear Bryant," New Orleans sportswriter Peter Finney pointed out, "is winning with athletes who, because of their size, aren't even considered by the pros."

Several days before the game, Bryant called his team together and apologized for scheduling the game against such a superior opponent. "We knew what he was doing," remarked linebacker Bob Childs, "but it was still an incredibly effective thing to do."

By the time Alabama reached New Orleans, the players could cite various chapters and verses on how the boss had manipulated their minds through the years. In the isolation of the moment, some had struck them as odd or unnecessary, but the seniors who arrived in New Orleans riding a powerful wave of confidence could see how all of the various motivational techniques had conspired to push them toward greatness. With the grand sweep of their college careers drawing quickly to a close, their combined affection for Bryant was a powerful force. During the days of formative torture, it had been easy, even for those who believed with all their might in the rightness of his overall plan, to wonder why, on a variety of levels. Many days, they hated his guts for pushing them so hard. But somewhere along the line, most learned to love him, like a demanding father. Of course, they never said it out loud, because hard-ass athletes in the world shaped by folks like Bear Bryant and John Wayne didn't talk in such ways, especially in 1966. But they felt it just the same. They saw Bryant as a man who gave them all a special gift, teaching them how to see the enormous possibilities in life, how to overcome their own feelings of weakness and tap into their inner strengths, how to see the world as a place where anything was possible if they were willing to work hard enough. They loved him for giving them a gift that would define the rest of their lives.

While revamping the game plan and deftly managing the psychology of his team, Bryant also finalized negotiations between Ray Perkins and the Baltimore Colts. On the day before the game, the coach collared Perkins in the hallway at the hotel and told him what the Colts were willing to pay for his services, although he could not consummate the deal until after the Sugar Bowl. "I couldn't believe Coach Bryant would take time out of preparations for a big bowl game to help me like that," Perkins said. "It really made me feel good. It was a real honor. That's just the kind of guy he was."

As Perkins and his fellow seniors neared the end of the line, Ronald Reagan was starting a new career. The former actor was due to be sworn in as California's governor the next day, around kickoff time in New Orleans, promising to cut the bureaucratic fat out of state government. Even as the war in Vietnam appeared to be widening, the North Vietnamese rejected a proposal by British intermediaries to consider a cease-fire. According to military officials, Air Force Col. Robin Olds led a mission into the north that resulted in the downing of seven Soviet-made MIG fighters, a one-day record. Despite recently being sentenced to an eight-year prison sentence for pension-fund fraud, Jimmy Hoffa remained president of the Teamsters. In Houston, Gus Grissom, Ed White, and Roger Chaffe were busy preparing for the first flight of the Apollo program, scheduled for the end of the month, unaware that they were destined to become the first martyrs of America's space program. In New York, former Alabama star Joe Namath was recovering from knee surgery, anxious to get out of his $79-a-day hospital room and start working his way back onto the field for the New York Jets. Television's *The Fugitive* was building toward a dramatic conclusion, and much of the country was caught up in the hype surrounding *The Monkees,* NBC's made-for-TV pop band, who topped the charts with "I'm a Believer."

When reserve halfback Ed Morgan found out his wife was pregnant and was due around the first of the year in 1967, he never mentioned it to the coaches, fearing that Bryant would leave him at home. On the day before the Sugar Bowl, the news arrived by phone: His wife had given birth to a beautiful baby girl. Both mother and daughter were fine, and the proud papa was bouncing off the walls. Supressing the urge to catch the next bus for Alabama, he tried to concentrate on the business at hand, but slept very little on the night before the big game.

"I was a little distracted," Morgan said.

Not for long.

The young men who entered the dressing room underneath ancient Tulane Stadium before noon on the second day of January in 1967 seemed incredibly ordinary. At first glance, Dicky Thompson, Jerry Duncan, Bruce Stephens, Tom Somerville, and so many others looked like spectators who had gotten lost on the way to the concession stand. Each man in the room had endured various hardships to arrive at this place in time, learning how to fight against obstacles unseen, how to appreciate the connection between hard work and achievement, how to invest in the pride and significance of wearing the red jersey. In the process, they had altered the trajectory of their own lives and given an entire state a reason to believe.

Something mysterious happened when they all pulled on those jerseys, pads, and helmets and walked through the tunnel. The uniform was not just a protective shield, it was a cloak of transformation. The boys from Tuscaloosa became fierce competitors who saw every snap as a referendum on their lives. In their minds, they were no longer ordinary. Wearing those jerseys, they felt like champions. Wearing those jerseys, they felt invincible.

The sky loomed dark and gloomy a few minutes before kickoff, and the field was soaked from several days of precipitation. Conventional wisdom held that a wet field favored Nebraska. Just as Bryant walked onto the field prior to the coin toss at Tulane Stadium, where a capacity crowd of 82,000 gathered, most in rain gear, the sun pierced through the clouds and the drizzling rain stopped. The Alabama players took it as a good sign. "We all thought Coach Bryant had some kind of higher power anyway, but that was pretty spooky," Kenny Stabler said.

"We were so fired up, I guarantee you, we could have beaten the Green Bay Packers," said linebacker Bob Childs.

Moments before, between the locker room and the tunnel, Bryant walked up to his quarterback. "Stabler, I want you to throw the son of a bitch as far as you can on the first play of the game."

Throwing a bomb to start the game was completely out of character for Alabama, and Bryant was counting on the element of surprise to work in the Tide's favor. He wanted a knockdown punch, to make Nebraska desperate, which he figured would play to the strengths of the Alabama defense.

Stabler, who entered the season unproven as a passer, arrived in New Orleans four months later as a star being compared to the likes of Joe Namath. A left-handed Namath—that's what they called him. In addition to his cool-headed leadership and his slithery moves on the option, Snake had matured into one of the nation's finest passers. While Florida's Steve Spurrier completed 179 of 291 attempts for 2,012 yards to lead the SEC in all three categories, Stabler's aerial talents were often obscured by Alabama's ball-control offense, which used the pass sparingly. However, within the constraints of Alabama's conservative philosophy, Snake's potency and efficiency were impossible to deny. During the regular season, he completed 74 of 114 for 956 yards, 9 touchdowns, and 5 interceptions. His 64.9 completion percentage set a new SEC record. He could throw it underneath all day and could burn opponents long with a perfect touch, when the boss took the handcuffs off.

"Any way you slice it, Kenny had a terrific year," said backfield coach Ken Meyer. "He just kept getting better and better . . . and tougher for teams to defend against."

The Nebraska defense, which allowed 8.4 points per game, tenth best in the nation, was led by 6', 239"-pound All-America noseguard Wayne Meylan, and also featured 6'2", 251-pound tackle Jim McCord and 6'5", 261-pound tackle Carel Stith. The Alabama offensive line, which averaged 192 pounds, looked like a bunch of boys next to all those men.

After 'Bama won the coin toss and Mike Sasser returned the kickoff to the 28 yard line, Stabler gathered his offense and called the first play: 55 sprint out, with Perkins running a go route. The plan was to test the Nebraska defense. If Perkins was double-covered, Stabler had other options, but when Perkins outran his coverage, Snake let it rip. The pass was right on the money. Stabler drilled it, Perkins caught it at about the Nebraska 40, and ran it down to the 28, putting Alabama within striking distance seconds into the football game. On the next play, as the offensive line created a perfect seam, Les Kelley, the prodigal son, ran right up the gut of the Nebraska defense for a 10-yard gain and another first down.

Five plays later, with 'Bama facing a second and goal from the one, Stabler accidentally lined up behind one of the guards. Center Jimmy Carroll whispered something, and he moved down, shoving his hands up underneath Carroll's rear end, as his teammates, on the field and off, tried to conceal their laughter. After the snap, Stabler handed off to Kelley, who ran it in for the touchdown—his fifth since returning from his late-season disciplinary problem. He was right. Bryant was not the least bit sorry about having given him another chance.

Coming off the field, Stabler was collared by head manager Sang Lyda, who tried to hide his amusement. "God dang, Kenny! You lined up under the guard!"

Stabler smiled big. "I wasn't nervous, was I?"

Beyond all the intense training and the enormous pressure of a big bowl game with championship implications, the Alabama players were just a bunch of kids living in a still mostly innocent time. Tough as he was, shaped by such hardship, even Stabler could be forgiven for momentarily losing his way in all the excitement. The joy of playing the game permeated every fiber of his being, and the young man from lower Alabama who was destined for a lifetime of fame was at the peak of his college playing experience. By the time Snake arrived in New Orleans with his teammates on Christmas Day, his twenty-first birthday—which he celebrated with a cake and a photo op with his smiling coach—he stood on the verge of taking his place alongside Pat Trammell, Joe Namath, and Steve Sloan in the pantheon of the Crimson Tide's championship quarterbacks of the memorable and incredibly successful 1960s. In the years ahead, the four men would be forever linked in the minds of grateful 'Bama fans, venerated from Huntsville to Mobile like the original Mercury astronauts of the modern era of Crimson Tide football.

Long before Alabama arrived in New Orleans, the boss decided he might be able to trust a left-handed quarterback after all.

After the first drive, the rout was on, but not without a key casualty.

The touchdown run, 66 drive, was simple power football, with the end doubling down and the fullback kicking out. Heading into the end zone, Kelley braced himself to be clobbered. "In that situation, you expect to get hit from about every direction," Kelley explained. "You get your body leaning." But the line did such a good job, no one touched him. "Instead of getting hit, I just fell in there, sort of clumsily."

The impact with the ground separated Kelley's shoulder, although he did not realize it at the time. His shoulder was throbbing with pain but he struggled to hide it, because he wanted to play.

On the Cornhuskers' first play from scrimmage, Nebraska quarterback Bob Churchich—who had burned the Tide for 232 yards in the Orange Bowl—hit split end Tom Penney for a 17-yard gain. Then the Alabama defense stiffened and forced a punt.

Starting from his own 29, Stabler went back to the air. On a second and one call, he found Perkins at the Nebraska 48, and the speedster from Petal turned on the juice once again, showing his All-America moves, demonstrating why the pros were hot on his trail. The 42-yard pass play gave Alabama a first down at the Nebraska 20.

Nebraska called a safety blitz on the play, and Les Kelley stayed home to block for Stabler. When he hit the defender with his shoulder, slamming into the guy with the kind of lick that made the boss proud, echoing back to all those harrowing days on the practice field, Kelley felt the most excruciating pain of his life.

"I just died when I threw my shoulder into the guy," Kelley said. "I knew I was hurt bad."

Prematurely, Kelley's Alabama career was over.

Two plays later, Stabler called his own number, running the option to perfection. Too quick and too good, he faked it just so, and was gone in the blink of an eye, dancing toward the end zone, beyond anyone's reach. The 14-yard touchdown and Steve Davis's second extra point gave Alabama a 14–0 lead with 7:28 remaining in the first quarter.

Putting tremendous pressure on Churchich on virtually every snap, the Alabama defense came up with one big play after another, including a fumble recovery by Charley Harris to set up another 'Bama score. Six plays later, after another great run by Stabler, Steve Davis kicked a 30-yard field goal to extend the Tide's lead to 17–0 with 28 seconds remaining in the first quarter.

When Alabama got the ball back, Bryant inserted backup quarterback Wayne Trimble, who led the Tide on a ten-play, 71-yard march. New father Ed Morgan, who entered the game with only 38 carries all season, was forced into action by Kelley's injury and gained 13 yards on an off-tackle run. "It's amazing what you can do when you're scared to death," joked Morgan, who finished with 37 yards on 10 carries, by far his best day of the season. "With a new baby and us dominating such a good team like that . . . I was having one of the best days of my life."

The key play of the drive was a 31-yard pass from Trimble to seldom-used receiver John David Reitz, who broke two tackles to achieve the most memorable moment of his junior year. Trimble's 6-yard run gave 'Bama a staggering 24–0 lead with 7:02 remaining, which is how it stayed at the half.

By switching to a 4-3 defense and focusing on the Tide's guards, instead of putting the noseguard directly on center Jimmy Carroll, Nebraska's defense was trying to mitigate Alabama's quickness. As the game progressed, however, it became increasingly clear that Nebraska's strategic maneuver instead enhanced the Tide's ability to overcome the Cornhuskers' tremendous size advantage.

"The change actually played to our strengths," said offensive line coach Jimmy Sharpe. "It allowed us to use our full toolbox . . . [to do] things that we could not do when the center was covered."

Concerning the amazing sight of diminutive Alabama routinely clobbering gigantic Nebraska all afternoon, *Sports Illustrated* remarked: "It was embarrassing, like getting mugged by a kindergarten class."

The romp on the sloppy field continued in the second half, as Stabler tossed a 45-yard touchdown pass to Perkins and Davis kicked a 40-yard field goal. Except for one solid drive at the end of the third quarter, culminated by a 15-yard touchdown pass from Churchich to Dick Davis, the Alabama defense owned Nebraska. The Tide recorded five interceptions in the second half, including three by All-America cornerback Bobby Johns and one each by linebackers Stan Moss and Bob Childs. Forced to play catch-up from the early moments of the game, Nebraska's powerful running attack was completely neutralized, an effort led by tackle Louis Thompson, who recorded a team-leading seven tackles.

Playing a nearly flawless game, the Tide turned the ball over just once—third-string quarterback Joe Kelley threw one into a crowd in the fourth quarter—and, for the twenty-second straight game, the offense finished without a holding penalty.

Considering the way Jerry Duncan repeatedly burned the Cornhuskers on the tackle eligible in the Orange Bowl, Nebraska must have spent an inordinate amount of time in practice learning to recognize and defend against the trick play. Naturally, the Tide failed to run it once in the first half. Sometimes a bluff can be every bit as useful as a full house.

By the time Stabler called the play midway in the third quarter, Alabama led 24–0 and the game was essentially over. The pass caught Nebraska completely by surprise, landing right in Duncan's hands, but he lost his footing, fumbled the ball, and then fell on it, preserving the ball and the first down, one of the key plays in a drive culminated by Davis's second field goal, which extended the lead to 27–0 with 3:31 remaining in the third quarter.

The guys in the huddle gave Duncan plenty of brotherly grief for dropping the ball, but in his defense, he insisted, "Man, that was a helluva route!"

Alabama football was going to miss Jerry Duncan.

The Crimson Tide's 34–7 victory was one of the most dominating performances ever seen in a big bowl game. The rout represented a powerful statement, demonstrating to millions of fans watching on television all across the country—and the stubborn wire service voters—how ridiculous it was to overlook the nation's only undefeated, untied team.

In the jubilant Alabama locker room, after Bryant told the players how proud he was of each and every one of them, the athletes started throwing their coaches in the showers—even the Bear himself, who smiled broadly as the water dripped from his towering frame.

Dude Hennessey, the defensive ends coach, had already changed into his street clothes by the time the players came for him, and he begged them to spare him. Dude was wearing a brand-new suit, which was a big deal to a guy who came to Alabama making $6,500 a year.

Standing nearby, Bryant pulled a wad of cash from his pocket. "Dude, you may not be able to afford another new suit, but I sure can," he said with a grin, dropping several bills at Hennessey's feet, which the players took as a sign of approval from the boss. In a matter of moments, Dude and his brand-new suit were all wet, too.

When he went off to meet with reporters, Bryant's usually reserved tone was gone. Forever playing down his team's performance, forever poor-mouthing, he rarely spoke in superlatives, so when he told the assembled crowd of newsmen, "This is the greatest college football team I've ever been associated with," it meant something. It meant everything. It meant the world.

After all those moments of formative hell, all those days of physical pain and mental anguish, the members of the 1966 Alabama football team had achieved a reward none of them ever imagined was possible.

"It is the greatest college team I've ever seen, too, and they proved it today," Bryant added. "Needless to say, my limited vocabulary doesn't permit me to say how proud I am of these boys. We had stars and superstars out there today. Every man, every down played as if their own performance meant everything."

Someone asked him the question, and he left no room for interpretation. "They deserve to be No. 1 and if I had a vote, they would be," he said.

Kenny Stabler, awarded the Miller Digby Trophy as the game's Most Valuable Player, finished the greatest game of his career by completing 12 of 18 passes for 218 yards, with no interceptions and 1 touchdown—including 7 receptions by Perkins for 148 yards. Stabler, who also ran for 38 yards and another touchdown, kept the Nebraska defense lunging for him in vain all day long.

"Stabler was just too quick for the people we had chasing him," Nebraska head coach Bob Devaney said.

"Alabama is several touchdowns better than the team that beat us last year," lamented Devaney, who added, "They are better than the score indicates. Alabama is the best football team I have ever seen."

He didn't stutter, either.

On the subject of polls, Art Burke wrote in the next day's editions of *The States-Item,* a New Orleans newspaper, "If Bear Bryant's 'Bama team must be ranked No. 3, I would have to say the No. 1 and No. 2 teams must be the Green Bay Packers and the Kansas City Chiefs," referring to the champions of the NFL and AFL, heading for the upcoming clash not yet known as the Super Bowl.

Writing in *The Tuscaloosa News,* Charles Land opined, "Maybe it isn't the Alabama quickness that makes the Crimson Tide so great. Maybe it isn't pride, either, or the intense preparation. Maybe Alabama is just stubborn. The Crimson Tide of Paul William Bryant just keeps refusing to believe any claims that it isn't the best college football team in the nation."

More than a decade before portable computers entered the scene, sportswriters transmitted their stories back to their papers via Western Union, and several hours after the game ended, just as he was heading out the door of the press box to attend the post-game banquet, Bill Lumpkin, sports editor of the *Birmingham Post-Herald,* received a frantic call from his office. Where were his stories?

"About scared me half to death," Lumpkin said. "We had been finished for a long time . . . and had no copy of what we'd sent."

Forced to start re-creating all of the stories from memory as the paper's deadline approached, Lumpkin eventually found out that the telegraph lines leading to Tulane Stadium were completely soaked by the intense rain. The telegrapher hired by the paper had been forced to take all of the copy downtown, to be sent from the central office, which caused an enormous backlog. The desk in Birmingham eventually called to say the dispatches were finally coming in from New Orleans, preventing the unthinkable: No coverage of one of Alabama's greatest wins of all time in the next morning's paper.

"It's funny to think how all that rain had no impact on how Alabama played, and yet, nearly caused a catastrophy at my paper so far away," Lumpkin said.

The scene offered a powerful reminder of how technologically primitive the world remained as 1967 arrived. More than a century after the invention of the telegraph, sportswriters on assignment still relied on Samuel Morse's nineteenth-century invention to communicate with readers.

By the time Lumpkin solved his problem, Alabama's celebration was in high gear.

Mingling with their Nebraska counterparts during the postgame banquet, a posh event held in a ballroom at the Jung Hotel, the Alabama players and coaches relaxed over adult beverages and a delicious meal. Sang Lyda, the head manager, was bellied up to the bar alongside several of the 'Bama players when one of the Nebraska players walked up. "He said, 'Last year, you beat us with all those trick plays, and this year we thought we were going to crush you. But you just whipped our ass.' I thought that was a pretty classy thing for him to say," Lyda recalled.

Some time later, Bryant walked to the microphone and started handing out the commemorative Sugar Bowl watches to his team. He said something nice about every member of his organization, sometimes making a good-natured joke. When skinny Sang Lyda stepped forward, Bryant dead-panned, "For two or three years, I thought he was Chinese!" And the whole place erupted in laughter.

When Bryant called Les Kelley's name, the injured back walked to the front of the room, his shoulder throbbing. For four years, Bryant had challenged him to reach. For four years, Kelley could never seem to do anything to satisfy his demanding coach. Bryant pushed him to the edge and beyond, before pulling him back, rescuing him from his own immaturity, and as Kelley stood at the end of the road, he was still struggling to come to grips with why, on so many different levels.

Bryant started telling the audience a little about the pride of Cullman County, finally saying, "This young man is truly a great football player."

The complimentary words tumbled over and over in Kelley's head, as he stood before the huge crowd in disbelief, never having heard anything remotely resembling the phrase come out of his coach's mouth.

"I'll never forget how it felt to hear him say that, after all I'd been through," Kelley said. "That meant more to me than anything he could have said."

In later years, Kelley and his teammates would come to understand the full measure of why Bryant pushed them all so hard and handed out compliments so sparingly. He wanted to keep them all reaching beyond their grasp, regardless of how well they performed, because he knew they could always attack harder, play better, give more. In the sophisticated system of motivation conceived and manipulated with such skill by Bryant across their careers, some rewards took four years to achieve. A few words of praise carried enormous weight, which is the way he intended it. By withholding approval while pushing his players to the edge, where they teetered precariously between his enormous expectations and their true potential, he lifted them to greatness.

Sometimes, his most effective tool of all was silence.

When the news hit the wires two days later, the Alabama football team was back in Tuscaloosa, preparing for the start of the spring semester. Some of the guys heard it on the radio, which treated it like an obituary.

The five-man panel of the Football Writers Association of America had awarded the national championship to Notre Dame, joining the AP and UPI. The Fighting Irish received 18 points and 3 first-place votes, followed by No. 2 Michigan State, with 14 points and 1 first-place vote, and No. 3 Alabama, with 13 points and 2 first-place votes.

Even though the FWAA vote carried much less weight than the wire service rankings, it was their last hope, and besides, the Alabama players believed the organization's decision to wait until after the bowls represented a desire to consider the bowl results in determining the national champion. Apparently not.

Instead, from the vantage point of the Alabama players, the football writers' vote turned out to be nothing more than an elaborate tease.

"We beat everybody on our schedule. What else did they want? Did they want us to beat the Green Bay Packers?" wondered defensive back Bobby Johns.

Relaxing with some of the guys at The Tide when the news hit, Sang Lyda was so distraught, he forgot to pick his wife up from her job at a Tuscaloosa doctor's office. They were still newlyweds, and Lanny was not happy when she waited around for more than an hour and was eventually forced to find another way home. "I was pretty mad," she recalled. "At the time, not winning the national championship was not exactly No. 1 on my list."

In time, of course, she came to understand what a body blow the final vote represented. "After that, it was pretty clear to us that there was nothing in the world we could have done," recalled linebacker Mike Hall. "There was no way they were going to give it to us. What an awful feeling. We were just devastated, absolutely devastated."

The pursuit of a third straight national championship motivated and propelled the Alabama football team, from the challenging note tacked onto the door of the cafeteria after the 1966 Orange Bowl through the final seconds of the 1967 Sugar Bowl. The national championship was not just an abstract concept—it was the reason for their existence. No one talked about winning the Southeastern Conference championship or any other secondary goal. Every player on the team made a commitment to do whatever it took—to work hard, to sacrifice, to reach, to persevere—in order to place the Crimson Tide's name in the history books, and from their standpoint, arguing against the weight of their perfection defied logic and justice.

If 'Bama had stumbled somewhere along the way, at least the players would know whom to blame. But who were they to see about finishing with a perfect record and then being robbed of an accomplishment they had clearly earned?

The finality of winning all the battles but losing the war landed with full force after the FWAA verdict, leaving every member of the team enormously demoralized. "To do everything Coach Bryant asked of us, and then not to win the national championship . . . for reasons that had nothing to do with what we did on the field . . . was an awfully hollow feeling," remarked center Jimmy Carroll. "We really didn't know how to deal with it, because that was the first time Coach Bryant had ever told us something that didn't turn out to come true."

Undefeated. Untied. Uncrowned.

In the glow of an electrifying Sugar Bowl victory, capping a season for the ages, the Crimson Tide was forced to wrestle with a most dubious distinction.

The ring the players chased with all their might was not just a high-priced trinket. It was the proof they all sought, the tangible symbol not only that they had achieved something historic, but also that their incredibly consuming and demanding world ultimately made sense.

"I couldn't wait to get mine," recalled fullback David Chatwood. "I planned to give it to my daddy. I wanted to give him that ring for everything he had done for me."

Several players stopped by to see the boss to petition him to award rings commemorating the Crimson Tide's SEC championship, but he explained what the players already knew: Alabama stood for the pursuit of the big prize. Rewarding anything less—even considering the unfairness of the situation—would have undermined the whole program. Telling them no was not the act of a gruff father figure denying his players a reward as some sort of punishment. Instead, it was a symbol of his respect for all the sacrifices they had made to produce a perfect season, and he was not about to water down the accomplishment by trying to diminish their feelings of disappointment, which he saw as a critical part of the whole process, for those players and the athletes yet to come.

Late in the season, when Alabama continued to trail Notre Dame and Michigan State and the players wondered what they could do to change the voters' minds before it was too late, Bryant said something to a reporter about his players' attitude that still rang true, even as they discussed the ring that slipped away. "I hope they're bothered by it," he said. "I hope they're bothered a great deal by it."

Instead of lowering Alabama's standards by recognizing the SEC title in such a way—or simply declaring themselves the national champion, as some Tide fans no doubt wanted—Bryant was communicating to his players and the entire Alabama nation a respect for the goal and the process, which, under the circumstances, was as incredibly mature act. "The fact that he thought we were the best team in the country was beside the point," said defensive end Wayne Owen. "Losing the national championship in that way, as frustrating as it was, taught us all a lesson: The world is not always just."

Indeed, the classy way Bryant dealt with the situation struck a powerful chord with his team and Alabama fans everywhere. He was deeply hurt by the whole affair, which he took as a personal assault on everything he stood for, but he did not rant or rave or wage a public relations battle through the media. He took it like a man. Even though he said he disagreed with the decision, Bryant congratulated both Notre Dame and Michigan State, and then moved on to the business of competing once more for the national championship in 1967, no doubt wondering how he would be able to motivate his next team to chase the big prize under the circumstances, when the national championship suddenly seemed more theoretical than tangible.

With the frustration still surging, football fans all across the country devoured the next week's issue of *Sports Illustrated,* which provided comprehensive coverage of the major bowl games, including Purdue's 14–13 squeaker over

Southern Cal in the Rose Bowl, Florida's 27–12 victory over Georgia Tech in the Orange Bowl, and Georgia's 24–9 thrashing of SMU in the Cotton Bowl. Alabama dominated *Sports Illustrated*'s all-bowl team, which featured Ray Perkins, Cecil Dowdy, Kenny Stabler, Jimmy Carroll, Bobby Johns, Dicky Thompson, Charley Harris, and Bob Childs. In a feature called "Best and Worst of the Bowls," the magazine's appreciation for the Crimson Tide was impossible to miss:

Best Team: Alabama.

Best Offense: Alabama.

Best Strategy: Alabama.

Best Player: Stabler of Alabama.

Best Receiver: Perkins of Alabama.

Best Defender: Johns of Alabama.

Best Blocker: Dowdy of Alabama.

Best Kicker: Davis of Alabama.

"Be truthful now, Notre Dame and Michigan State," wrote *SI*'s Dan Jenkins. "Would you really want to play Alabama? Would you honestly care to spend an afternoon trying to swat those gnats who call themselves linemen and swirl around your ankles all day? Why, Heavens to Bear Bryant, nobody ought to want to play Alabama unless it just enjoys going to football clinics. Which is exactly what last week's Sugar Bowl was—a clinic, with Bear Bryant instructing the nation on what a top-ranked team is supposed to look like . . ."

There was no trophy to go along with Jenkins's remarks, but they sure endeared him and *SI* to Alabama fans desperately looking for a validation for their rage.

The rising tide of resentment sweeping across the state of Alabama, and indeed, the South, led two enterprising Crimson Tide fans—lyricist Billy Overstreet and vocalist Jake Antonio—to record a protest song, "In Our Hearts We're No. 1," to the tune of the chart-topping 1966 hit, "The Ballad of the Green Berets."

More than a century after the end of the Civil War, the divide between North and South still defined the country in a variety of ways, and many Southerners were still inclined to hear echoes of the lost cause in any conflict between the regions. The wound still ran deep, and in many ways, football was a kind of proxy for a hundred years of frustration. Viewed through the prism of the historic rivalry between North and South, the battle for the 1966 national championship took on even greater meaning to many Southerners, as demonstrated by a popular cartoon that began circulating after the final votes were counted. The drawing showed an outraged man wearing a Confederate cap and belt buckle, holding a copy of the AP poll in one hand and a 'Bama pennant in the other. In the years after the Civil War and Reconstruction, "Forget, Hell!" became a rallying cry for demoralized southerners, so the caption on the cartoon, "Number 3—Hell!" cleverly tapped into a history of shared angst.

At a time when it remained acceptable in the North to look down on Southerners, to stereotype anyone living south of the Mason-Dixon Line as an ignorant, racist, inferior hick, when southerners invested football with even greater meaning because it gave the region an opportunity to compete against the North on supposedly equal footing, the 1966 vote struck many Southerners as yet another indignity foisted upon the region by the North's superiority complex. How else were Southerners to interpret the fact that two northern teams with inferior records were ranked ahead of a southern team with a perfect record bidding for a third straight title? Obviously, victories up North counted more than victories down South, highly publicized ties up North might as well be wins, and southern teams need apply only when a suitable northern team was not available for the coronation. How else were southerners to react when the national media bestowed superiority on Notre Dame, without forcing the Fighting Irish to prove it by challenging two-time defending national champion Alabama on the field? The competition served only to intensify the widespread feeling among Southerners that people and institutions up North were judged by a whole different set of standards, that they played by different rules, and it was difficult to argue with such logic.

Beyond the hollow feeling of the greatest misjustice in college football history, the Alabama players achieved something no group of self-appointed experts could bestow. Nor could anyone ever take it away. Their perfection was an enormous accomplishment in and of itself, as was the overall 30-2-1 record produced by the senior class of 1966, one of the finest three-year runs in the storied annals of Alabama football.

Some victories could not be seen so easily.

While professional football ignored most of the players on the 1966 Alabama team, the NFL's Baltimore Colts moved quickly to sign All-America receiver Ray Perkins after the Sugar Bowl. His $250,000 contract was a significant sum for the day, including a $41,000 signing bonus, which immediately gave him the kind of financial security his carpenter father had never known.

More than one of the greatest receivers ever to wear an Alabama uniform, Perkins represented something profound about the entire team. Born into a modest family, burdened with low self-esteem, he had gravitated to football as a way out of a dead-end life, benefiting along the way from the kindness of

Ed Palmer and Marcus James as well as the life force of Paul Bryant, and while paying a high price during his Alabama career, he very nearly died. Yet, he fought his way back, literally teaching himself how to be a receiver, and battled through all the difficult days of the Alabama football experience by learning to believe in himself, but also, in the power of something bigger than himself.

His unlikely journey from oblivion to first-round draft pick was living proof of what could be accomplished with faith, perseverance, and old-fashioned hard work, the foundations of the whole program.

Soon after the deal with the Colts was finalized, with his pockets full for the first time in his life, the one-time dropout found himself standing on the back porch of a little house on a large spread of land near Tuscaloosa, looking out into the surrounding piney woods.

"How far does the property go back?" he asked the owner.

"As far as you can see."

His mind flashed back to a long ago moment, on the road to Petal, when he felt small, insignificant, trapped, and yet made the conscious decision to dream of a better life, not imagining how far his ambition would someday lead.

"I'll take it," he said.

Sometimes even a championship ring is no substitute for a lump in your throat.

14. FINGERPRINTS

The integration of the Alabama football program began on an ordinary February day in 1967, as the chilled morning air blanketed Dock Rone's face. During the walk from his dorm to the athletic offices, Rone tried to fight off his nerves, but the freshman engineering student from Montgomery knew he was headed for a world of unknowns. The thought of walking onto the most dominant football team in the land represented an enormous challenge for any athlete, but as an African American seeking a place on a segregated squad so often seen as another fist shaken defiantly at the civil rights movement, Rone was heading into uncharted territory.

"I really didn't know what Coach Bryant would say," Rone recalled.

Several minutes after he politely asked the lady in the lobby if he could see the man in charge, Bryant greeted him warmly and escorted him into his office. The conversation lasted only a few moments, but sometimes, history can flash by in the blink of an eye. When Rone told the coach what he had on his mind, Bryant listened intently, explained how tough it would be, both in terms of football and race, and then told the former high school athlete that he would be glad to have him, providing he could pass a physical.

"I admire your courage, young man," Bryant said, as he looked out from behind his desk.

The warm reception Bryant gave the aspiring player was understandable. While the coach believed it was still too soon to start recruiting black athletes, he probably thought having African-American nonscholarship players trying to earn a spot on the roster alongside many whites would help ease the team and the fans into the integrated era while mitigating his program's image problem. The fact that the turbulent racial climate helped cost Alabama the national championship played no role in Rone's decision to chase his dream, but the events of 1966 certainly invested his pioneering step with even greater significance. His journey represented the first tentative step toward making sure 1966 never happened again, the first halting step toward healing the state's racial wounds.

A few weeks after meeting with Bryant, when Alabama convened spring practice, Rone started drills with the Crimson Tide, where he was joined by four other African-American players—Arthur Denning, Andrew Purnell, Jerome Tucker, and Melvin Leverette—apparently following his lead. Before spring practice began, the coaches informed the returning varsity players about the history-making change.

"We were told there were going to be some black players out there with us . . . that we shouldn't make a big deal about it . . . just to treat 'em like everybody else, which we did," recalled Tom Somerville, heading toward his senior season.

Somerville, who frequently faced off against Rone, remembered him as "a tough little guy" who "battled you on every play."

Like the forty-two white players who walked on at the same time, the black athletes faced an enormous uphill climb to make the team, but Rone and Purnell both played in the A-Day intrasquad game, the culminating event of spring practice. For the first time in Alabama history, black faces appeared in Crimson Tide uniforms at Denny Stadium, without incident. It was a small step, but it was a step in the right direction.

"I got a fair shot," said Rone, who received a few letters of hate mail when his name was printed in the paper. "The coaches treated me fine . . . [they] really went out of their way to make me feel welcome. I expected to get a chance to play the next season."

Unfortunately, family problems forced Rone to quit school during the summer of 1967, which may have prevented him from becoming the first African American to play in a varsity intercollegiate game for the Crimson Tide. No one can say whether he could have survived and worked his way up the depth chart, or whether the state of Alabama was truly ready for such a leap in 1967. By the time he returned to the university to earn his degree three years later, the thought of playing football no longer held the same allure, so he left the banner of progress to be carried by others.

Addressing Rone's bid several years later, Bryant said, "I don't think he would ever [have been] a starter, but I think he would have played someday . . . helped us someday."

Through the years, the story of the integration of the Alabama program has largely obscured the pioneering efforts of Dock Rone, a historic but mostly forgotten figure in the annals of Crimson Tide football. Nevertheless, he took a courageous step into the darkness, helping pave the way for the full-scale integration of the program in the years ahead.

After the 1966 season, Bryant told his players that the racial climate was the decisive factor in their loss of the national championship. A different sort of coach, in a different sort of place, might have exploited the situation to sell integration to his fan base, overtly framing the choice so emblematic of so many aspects of the evolving social order. But for reasons about which historians can only speculate, Bryant chose not to make a big issue of the change he knew was coming. It would provide a tidy ending to the whole story of the 1966 Crimson Tide if the frustrating product of their tragic flaw had produced an immediate new age of enlightenment in Tuscaloosa, but the reality was much more complex. Dock Rone came along at just the right time, and Bryant was glad to have him, but his journey was just the first step in an evolution toward the integration of the Alabama football program. Just as the 1966 season marked the beginning of the end of some things that were very right about Alabama culture, it also represented the beginning of the end of something that was very wrong.

In addition to the steady growth of integrated high school teams across the state in the late 1960s, which conditioned even the most resistant fans to the inevitability of the new era, the minor league Birmingham Barons broke important ground. After disbanding in 1961, rather than comply with the segregation laws, the Double-A Southern League baseball team returned as an integrated franchise in 1964. Throughout the late 1960s, the Barons featured many outstanding black athletes, including future major leaguers Reggie Jackson and Vida Blue, and local baseball fans—black and white—embraced the team enthusiastically. Legion Field also hosted several integrated NFL exhibition games during the late 1960s.

In the first two years after Rone, several more African Americans walked on to the Alabama team, but for various reasons, none permanently stuck. The climate remained volatile, especially considering the experience of basketball player Perry Wallace, who broke the color barrier at Vanderbilt and endured various incidents of intimidation. "The first time I played at Ole Miss I got spat on at halftime by four generations of one family," Wallace once said. Many fans openly called him "nigger" and threatened his life—simply because he dared to play sports in the Southeastern Conference.

The civil rights movement destroyed institutionalized racism, but changing the hearts and minds of many people accustomed to a separation of the races would not happen overnight. Some things existed outside the reach of the law. No one understood this better than Bryant, who remained wary of placing any of his athletes in a climate where they would be taunted—or worse—by a bunch of thugs.

Even as powerful forces among the university's supporters opposed the integration of the athletic program and wanted to delay it for as long as possible,

Bryant felt increasing pressure to break the barrier. In 1967, just as Rone and the other walk-ons were suiting up, the American Civil Liberties Union filed a complaint that spurred an investigation by federal education authorities, but it eventually fizzled. Two years later, the university's Afro-American Association filed a suit in federal court, contending 'Bama's apparent unwillingness to provide scholarships to blacks violated the Civil Rights Act of 1964. The suit was dropped when the school finally inked its first African-American athletes.

Early in 1969, Bryant gave C. M. Newton, his new head basketball coach, the go-ahead to sign Wendell Hudson, who became the school's first African-American scholarship athlete in any sport. A few weeks after Hudson arrived on campus in the fall of 1969, Tennessee crushed the Alabama football team, 41–14, at Legion Field. One of the men inflicting the damage was sophomore linebacker Jackie Walker, an African American who intercepted a Scott Hunter pass and returned it twenty-seven yards for a touchdown.

Even before the landmark first integrated major college game in the state of Alabama, the coaching staff was hot on the trail of the right young man to shatter the Crimson Tide's color barrier. Bryant believed the first man needed to be especially tough in order to withstand the mental strain, and especially good in order to avoid giving those opposed to black players any further ammunition.

The search for such a figure led the Alabama coaching staff to Wilbur Jackson, a gifted receiver destined to become the Jackie Robinson of Alabama football.

Growing up in the small southeastern Alabama town of Ozark in the days of Wallace's stand, Jackson never experienced any racist violence up close, but nobody needed to tell him about the indignities of segregation. The separate water fountains always bugged him. "When you're a young kid, you wonder: What's the difference in the water?" he said.

Buster Jackson, his father, worked forty-five years as a laborer for the railroad, repairing ties, driving spikes, using his strong back, and supplemented his income by cutting the hair of neighborhood folks in his home. Late one night, when he was supposed to be in bed, Wilbur overheard him talking to a customer. "You know," he said, "some nights, everybody in this house is asleep but me, and I'm lying there in bed wondering: 'How am I going to make it?' "

The moment marked Wilbur deeply. "I'll never forget how it felt to hear him say that," he said. "We didn't know."

In time, Wilbur would learn how his father, who had dropped out of school in the third grade to help support his mother and his brothers and sisters, repeatedly found ways to borrow against his house in order to send his other three children to college. In time, Wilbur would learn so many of the hardships his father had endured without complaint, while dutifully endeavoring to always take care of his family and live up to his obligations. The world saw Buster Jackson as an uneducated black man with a menial job, but to Wilbur, he was a heroic figure who taught him what it meant to be a man. Not a black man. A man.

Like many of the athletes who provided countless thrilling moments on the gridiron while helping the Crimson Tide win championships in the 1960s, Jackson grew up shaped by strong values and a desire to earn an education and make something of himself, and in this sense, his connection to young men like Jimmy Carroll, Dicky Thompson, Ray Perkins, and Louis Thompson transcended race. His skin color should have been irrelevant, but in Alabama in the 1960s, skin color was never irrelevant.

Even as Wilbur matured into one of the most talented athletes in Ozark, Jimmie Mae Jackson refused to sign the papers to allow him to play football. Like many mothers, Jimmie Mae, a gentle woman who worked for many years as a domestic, feared for her son's safety. Then came the luckiest break of his life, the break that would affect the racial evolution of an entire state. During his sophomore year at all-black D. A. Smith High School, Wilbur broke his foot playing basketball.

After watching her boy hobble around the house for six weeks in a cast, Jimmie Mae gradually softened on the football idea. Wilbur worked on her hard, finally convincing her that football was no more dangerous than basketball, which was a whopper, of course, but she finally relented.

"Once she realized I could get hurt playing basketball, the same as football, she wasn't so adamant about it," Wilbur recalled. "She still wouldn't sign the papers—she didn't want to have that on her conscience—but at least she didn't object when I got my daddy to sign."

The rest is history. In his junior year, Wilbur used his speed and hands to become a dangerous receiver. When integration arrived in 1969, leading him to traditionally white Carroll High School, Jackson attracted enough attention to be recruited by Alabama assistant coach Pat Dye and graduate assistant Joe Kelley, the third-string quarterback on the 1966 team, who had grown up nearby and whose father ran a clothing store in Ozark where the Jackson family sometimes shopped.

When Dye arrived at the Jackson house to talk about making their son a pioneer, Jimmie Mae fretted over the decision. It was still hard for black people of their generation to separate George Wallace and Paul Bryant, instruments of the same white power structure that had conspired to keep blacks down for a century. She remembered all too well the day the governor stood in the school-house door, but just as he had once convinced his mother to let him play foot-ball, Wilbur won her over.

"I didn't have a real understanding of the significance of the whole thing," Jackson said. "At the time, I was just looking for a way to take the load off my dad, who was determined to send me to college. I didn't want to be Jackie Robinson."

The courting of Wilbur Jackson was a turning point in the history of the state of Alabama.

Fourteen years and twelve days after Rosa Parks refused to move to the back of a Montgomery bus, igniting the civil rights movement, Wilbur Jackson's signing with Alabama on December 13, 1969, represented the final nail in the coffin of segregation. In the culture of the state, Parks and Jackson are forever linked, generational bookends in the struggle for civil rights. The decision by an instrument of the white establishment to recruit a black man for one of the most exalted positions in Alabama society slammed the door on the turbulent era of violence and resistance.

As the only black on the roster in his freshman year of 1970, Jackson under-standably felt somewhat isolated, but he insists he never encountered any racial problems at Alabama. Bit by bit, the moments of shared sacrifice mitigated the racial differences, as the athletes slowly began to see beyond their stereotypes. Gradually, Wilbur, quiet and something of a loner, started to make friends on the team, and if some of the white boys who had been raised during the poison-ous time of segregation had a problem with his presence, they never expressed such feelings to him. Bryant made clear he would not tolerate any problems, as evidenced by a conversation with Jackson during the courting process.

"Coach Bryant pulled me aside [during a recruiting trip] and told me two things," Jackson said. "He said, 'Wilbur, if you come here, I'll make you the best receiver in the nation. And if you ever have a problem, you bring it to me and we'll handle it.'"

No one wanted to give the boss anything to handle.

Some connections can be seen only from the long view of history, so when Bryant switched Jackson to halfback and asked halfback Rod Steakley, who was white, to room with him, he probably had no idea that the Huntsville native had been on the leading wave of integration since playing against Leonard "Rabbit" Thomas during the landmark Butler-Huntsville game in 1966. The system in those days called for Alabama players to be grouped according to po-sition, and yet, a black man and a white man sharing a room represented an-other barrier that needed to be surmounted.

"Coach Bryant was making a very important statement," said Steakley, who later became an attorney for Alabama A&M, the historically black university in Huntsville. "He wasn't going to tolerate segregation of any kind, and he wasn't going to treat Wilbur differently. That sent a signal to the rest of the team."

On the way out of a hotel on a road trip to Mississippi, some redneck walked up to Steakley and Jackson with an angry expression. "Nigger lover!" he shouted.

"That guy didn't have a clue what we were about," Steakley said. "We just sort of laughed it off."

During another road trip, the teammates were trying to relax in their hotel room, when a program about the Underground Railroad filled the television screen, providing a stark reminder of the legacy of racial trouble the roommates were still struggling to surmount. Not wanting to change the channel, not knowing quite what to say, Steakley was relieved when Jackson eventually told him, "It's OK, Rod. I know where your heart is."

By the time of the season opener in 1970, the Alabama football program was successfully integrated. Some people apparently do not realize this. Wilbur Jackson was sitting in the stands with some of his teammates on the night Alabama hosted Southern Cal at Legion Field, because he was a freshman. Freshmen would remain ineligible for varsity competition for another two years, so the only reason Alabama's only African-American football player was not on the field was simply a result of an NCAA rule soon to be abolished. The suggestion that Bryant was looking for a way to convince Alabama people that it was time to integrate heading into the USC game, which has been floated for years, is pure fiction, and an insult to the pioneering leap Wilbur Jackson was already negotiating. Nor—as even Tennessee fans know—was the 1970 Alabama-Southern Cal showdown the first integrated game in the state of Alabama, as has been cited time and again in the national media. Furthermore, during the period, Alabama continued to play integrated teams in bowl games. In the losses to Missouri in the 1968 Gator Bowl (35–10) and Colorado in the 1969 Liberty Bowl (47–33), many of those delivering the blows to two struggling Alabama teams had black skin. The implication that the Crimson Tide was sheltering itself in a purely segregated world until the 1970 Southern Cal game is a distortion of the facts.

However, the importance of Southern Cal's visit to Legion Field on September 12, 1970, cannot and should not be diminished. The game did not cause Alabama to integrate, but it certainly strengthened Bryant's hand.

Watching John McKay's fully integrated Trojans crush Bryant's all-white team, 42–21, made a powerful statement. It was impossible to see the game as anything less than a clash between the future and the past, and even the most bigoted 'Bama fans wanted their Crimson Tide to be riding the jet to the future. In this sense, USC was a powerful weapon against the forces of bigotry.

Through the years, most of the attention has gravitated to the dominating performance of tailback Sam "Bam" Cunningham, who proved virtually unstoppable while rushing for 135 yards and 2 touchdowns. But the case of Clarence Davis was dripping with irony. Davis, who ran for 76 yards, grew up in Birmingham, a short drive from Legion Field, was unwanted by the still-segregated Crimson Tide.

The suggestion by some that Bryant orchestrated the Southern Cal game with his friend McKay knowing his team would be blown out is a compelling idea, but is without foundation and frankly, implausible given the coach's incredibly competitive nature. From the vantage point of history, Alabama's weak 1970 team undoubtedly aided the forces of integration, but Bryant was doing everything within his power to reverse a three-year slide—which produced seasons of 8-3, 6-5, and 6-5-1 in 1968, 1969, and 1970—and anyone who believes the Bear brought USC to Birmingham knowing he would get creamed does not have a clue about what made him tick.

Several weeks after ending the disappointing 1970 season with a 24–24 tie against Oklahoma in Houston's Astro-Bluebonnet Bowl—the last time Alabama fielded an all-white varsity team—Bryant made a trip to the West Coast, where he played in a golf tournament with McKay. While having a cocktail the USC coach started talking about a fine junior college player they were pursuing who just happened to be a native of Alabama. Some time later, Bryant excused himself and made a telephone call to one of his assistants back in Tuscaloosa, the first step toward stealing a talented defensive end named John Mitchell right out of McKay's pocket.

Years later, McKay could laugh about how it happened. "Paul was so competitive," he said. "I learned to keep my mouth shut about unsigned players after that."

When Alabama walked onto the field to face fifth-ranked Southern Cal at Los Angeles Memorial Coliseum on September 10, 1971, the shadows were filled with whispers. The once-dominant Crimson Tide was expected to wallow around the middle of the pack in the SEC for a third straight year, and many inside and outside the state of Alabama were starting to believe the Bear was over the hill. What no one outside the program knew was that during the summer, Bryant had secretly converted from a drop-back passing game to the option-oriented wishbone, developed by his good buddy Darrell Royal and top assistant Emory Bellard at Texas. With the program and Bryant's future on the line, Alabama entered the game as a two-touchdown underdog. Especially after the drubbing of 1970, not even Alabama people gave the Crimson Tide much of a chance.

Unveiling the wishbone, the Crimson Tide stunned Southern Cal, 17–10. The pivotal upset launched not only a perfect regular season but also the winningest decade in college football history, as Alabama headed for a record 103 victories, three national championships, and eight SEC titles in the 1970s.

Lost amid much of the excitement over the debut of the wishbone was one of the changes destined to make Alabama dominant again: black faces.

John Mitchell, the first African American to start for the Crimson Tide, offered a powerful statement about the future of Alabama football by making the tackle on the opening kickoff. As a senior in 1972, Mitchell was recognized as Alabama's first All-American with a black face. By 1973, about one-third of the team's starters were African Americans, including Wilbur Jackson, an All-SEC selection who led the team's powerful wishbone offense in rushing. Not that the boss ever spent any time thinking about arbitrarily influencing the number. He believed in merit, period, and once the door opened, the Alabama football team became a model of racial integration and harmony.

During the period, a reporter from out of state asked Bryant how many black players he had on his team. "I don't have any black players," he said.

The man asked Bryant how many white players he had. "I don't have any white players, either," he said. "I only have football players."

The African-American athletes who played for Bryant in those days invariably say he treated them just the same as the whites, and their respect and affection for him is undeniable.

When he was selected in the first round of the NFL draft and signed his first professional football contract, Wilbur Jackson went home to Ozark to visit his parents. There was something he needed to do.

When Wilbur told his daddy that he had paid off his home mortgage—the one he had borrowed against repeatedly to send his children to college—a look of disbelief was written all over Buster's face. The moment was one of the proudest and most fulfilling of both their lives. After all those years of hard work and struggle, Buster had accomplished something even more powerful than being a man who lived up to his word and endeavored to do the right thing. He had produced a man who followed proudly in his footsteps.

After a decade in the NFL, playing for the San Francisco 49ers and the Washington Redskins, Jackson and his wife Martha moved back to Ozark, not too far from where he grew up, so they could raise their daughter Emily in a nice small-town environment, where people, black and white, look out for one another. He started a commercial cleaning business, employing eleven people. Martha was elected to the school board.

During the 1998 season, Wilbur packed up the family and headed off for Tuscaloosa to watch an Alabama game, where the Crimson Tide's 1973 national championship team was being honored on the occasion of its twenty-fifth anniversary. The old guys mobbed Jackson, not because of his pioneering status, but because everybody always loved Wilbur. At a separate reception for the 1970 freshman team, his teenaged daughter looked around the room and, in a private moment, whispered, "Where are the other black players, dad?"

The question itself was a comment on how far Alabama, the team and the state, had come. Emily really didn't understand what a giant figure her father was.

Later in the day, after laughing and telling stories with the old guys, Wilbur felt the need to teach a little history, so he led his daughter over to Foster Auditorium to show her where Wallace stood in the schoolhouse door on that awful day in 1963. Then they strolled over to Denny Chimes, where Alabama's football captains have smashed their handprints into the concrete since the days of Wallace Wade.

"See right there," he said, pointing to his very own prints, circa 1973, "that's from being elected cocaptain by my teammates ten years after Wallace stood in the doorway."

At that moment, perhaps for the first time in her young life, Emily understood.

In a larger sense, the fingerprints of Wilbur Jackson, John Mitchell, and so many other African-American players of the era can be seen all across the new Alabama they helped to create.

During his pro football days, Jackson often encountered athletes who could not believe he played for Bear Bryant, whom many considered a symbol of segregation, or that he continued to maintain a home in Alabama, which they saw as a bastion of hate. "It was always, 'Man, how can you live down there?'" Jackson recalled. "They just didn't get it. This is home. I love my state. This is where I feel most comfortable."

The integration of the Alabama football program profoundly affected the state's culture. Martin Luther King Jr. and others broke down the legal barriers, but the effort led by Paul Bryant reached into the hearts and minds of people across the Heart of Dixie. Because so many Alabamians invested so much of themselves in the Crimson Tide, watching great athletes like Wilbur Jackson, Johnny Davis, Sylvester Croom, and Ozzie Newsome sweat, bleed, and achieve for the glory of Alabama challenged the way many people thought and dealt a devastating blow to the forces of hate and division, uniting Alabamians in a common cause. Having black faces in red jerseys did not create a color-blind society in Alabama, but it certainly helped forge a much more tolerant and integrated culture than anyone would have imagined possible during the turbulent 1960s. A once unfathomable level of racial harmony transformed the state in many ways, and the role of the Crimson Tide in this process cannot be denied. At a time when public schools were still being desegregated amid a climate of fear and mistrust and people of both races remained vulnerable to the learned behavior of seeing the world through a prism of black and white, the state's most treasured cultural institution set a powerful tone, becoming a catalyst in the healing of the devastating wounds of the 1960s. The next generation grew up with no direct knowledge of segregation, while at least some aspects of the society were conditioning them to see the world differently than their parents, especially the integrated example of all those beloved Alabama players.

In his eloquent "I Have a Dream" speech on the steps of the Lincoln Memorial in 1963, just as the state of Alabama was resisting the civil rights movement in a variety of ways, King looked metaphorically into the future and imagined a day in Alabama when ". . . little black boys and black girls will be able to join hands with little white boys and white girls and walk together as sisters and brothers . . ." He probably could not have imagined a day when the sons of white people who voted for George Wallace would fight for the right to "be" African-American Alabama football players like Wilbur Jackson and Calvin Culliver in backyard pickup games. He could not have imagined the day white Alabamians who once believed in segregation as a just institution would cheer the descendents of slaves and take them to their hearts, because being an Alabama football hero ultimately was a stronger force than the legacy of hate and division.

Far from the glare of the national media, hearts and minds were changed on the subject of integration, and slowly, a whole new Alabama emerged—an Alabama that owed every bit as much to young men like Leonard "Rabbit" Thomas, Wilbur Jackson, and John Mitchell as to Martin Luther King Jr. and Rosa Parks.

While Bryant was quietly practicing integration and setting a powerful example for all Alabamians, George Wallace was still preaching division. The rhetoric was somewhat muted, compared to the "segregation forever" days, but as he ran for the White House in the tumultuous year of 1968—while his wife, Lurleen, the governor, succumbed to cancer—Wallace garnered a surprisingly strong 13.5 percent of the vote and helped tilt the close election to Richard

Nixon by appealing largely to white fear all over the country. Two years later, his successful campaign to regain the governor's mansion against incumbent Albert Brewer was filled with racial innuendo, including a photo, which proported to show Brewer making nice with Nation of Islam leader Elijah Muhammad and boxer Muhammad Ali. As a candidate for the Democratic presidential nomination in 1972, he scared the hell out of Nixon. His support was surging with disaffected voters all over the country, far beyond the issue of race, and when lunatic Arthur Bremer shot Wallace during a campaign stop in Maryland, leaving him permanently paralyzed and confined to a wheelchair, the shape of the Democratic Party was fundamentally altered.

Perhaps the greatest testament of all to the healing of Alabama on the issue of race was Wallace's own conversion. In later years, he apologized for his racist stand and actually won a majority of the African-American vote in his final bid for the governor's mansion in 1982. In the end, he was just another sinner who eventually found his way, and Alabama people of both races understood and forgave.

Still, in some ways, the past remains a burden the state may never be able to shake.

When former Tide quarterback Mike Shula, who is white, was selected as Alabama's new head coach in 2003, some believed the job should have gone to former Tide center Sylvester Croom, who is black, and charges of racism filled the air. This gave some elements in the national media another reason to fall back on the stereotype of Alabama as a place defined by bigotry, as Reverend Jesse Jackson and others played the race card with glee. No evidence was presented to substantiate the notion, and while some Alabama fans will never be prepared to accept a black man in what will always be Bear Bryant's job, many others could care less about the skin color of their coach. They want to win, period. At the very least, the controversy demonstrated that, despite all the progress, the Crimson Tide remains deeply affected by the lingering residue of 1966.

The tension between the past and the present may never be completely extinguished, at least as long as those awful images of Bull Connor's dogs and fire hoses can be seen on television, haunting Alabamians like a recurring nightmare, but if you want to understand how far Alabama has come since 1966, how gloriously far, take a step back to October 22, 2005.

As a young child in segregated Birmingham, Condoleezza Rice was forever shaped by the infamous church bombing of September 1963, which murdered one of her friends. However, her father refused to let her get caught up in the poisonous climate. Among other things, Condi's old man taught her to be an

Alabama football fan, even at a time when people of her color were not welcome in Tuscaloosa. Instead of a symbol of division, she saw the Crimson Tide
as an example of excellence.

Four decades later, after pulling for the Crimson Tide from afar for all those
years, Rice returned to her home state and walked out onto the field at Bryant-
Denny Stadium to administer the coin toss prior to a big game against Tennessee. The capacity crowd cheered the Secretary of State like a rock star. For
anyone with a sense of history, the chill-bump factor was high. All across the
stadium, the sons and daughters of those who had once opposed the integration
of the University of Alabama bathed Rice in thunderous applause, many of
them hoping to have the chance to vote for her for president someday.

Forty years after the lost threepeat, even as the state of Alabama has grown
more prosperous and sophisticated, it continues to rank near the bottom of
most national statistics, particularly in terms of education and economics, making many folks hold tighter than ever to the Crimson Tide, which still gives
them a rare chance at national superiority in something. Many people insist Alabamians invest too much meaning in football. This viewpoint is simplistic at
best, ignorant at worst, especially in terms of race, because the meaning Alabama people attach to the game has been harnessed for a profound purpose. It
cannot be charted or graphed, but it could be seen on that day when Condi
Rice's world came full circle.

Just as the various statistics fail to capture the high-tech glow of
Huntsville . . . the transformation of Birmingham into one of the region's leading medical and financial centers . . . cultural institutions like Montgomery's
Alabama Shakespeare Festival and Huntsville's U.S. Space and Rocket Center . . . and the unrivaled quality of life in dozens of charming, peaceful towns
from the Tennessee Valley to the Wiregrass, the rankings will never be able to
adequately reflect Alabama's long journey out of the darkness. The stats will
never demonstrate how Alabama's obsession with football actually helped the
state surmount the most formidable obstacle of all.

Some people believe Alabama has little to be proud of, only because they re-
fuse to see.

After Bryant's sudden death in 1983, the massive crowds who lined the
route from Tuscaloosa to Birmingham's Elmwood Cemetery cut across all
racial, social, and economic boundaries. The shock was enormous, the hurt universal.

At the graveside service, Joe Kelley, one of the boys of 1966, stood between
Joe Namath and Mel Allen, two giant figures in the history of American sports.
Out of the corner of his eye, he saw an elderly, rail-thin, African-American

woman, shabbily dressed, leaning against the door of the hearse that had brought the Bear to his final resting place, silently paying her respects. Tears streamed down her cheeks. Like many other Alabamians, she had lost someone special in her life.

"I was truly touched by that moment . . . how real it was," recalled Kelley. "To know where we had come from, and to see something like that . . ."

Some images dance right past the eyes and pierce the heart.

When former Alabama offensive guard Bruce Stephens returned from a tour in Vietnam in 1971, the first lieutenant in the U.S. Army's Signal Corps flew into an installation in Washington State, where he was amazed to have to walk through a tunnel designed to protect the servicemen from a large and persistent crowd of antiwar protesters. "They were out there spitting on us and calling us baby killers," Stephens recalled. "I never thought I would see something like that in my own country."

It was not 1966 anymore.

In the years after the denied threepeat, as the country descended into a cauldron of cynicism and civil unrest . . . as establishment institutions were challenged at every turn . . . as traditional values were mocked . . . as illicit drug use mounted . . . as Vietnam exploded into the defining issue of a generation, even the University of Alabama was rocked by the changes roiling American society. Some aspects of the revolution arrived later in Tuscaloosa than elsewhere, but they arrived, all the same.

Bryant continued to try to insulate his football program from the temptations of the outside world, with varying degrees of success. Bothered by the rule demanding short hair, when long hair, more than anything else, symbolized youth, a group of players petitioned the coach in 1970 to change his policy. When he gave a little on the hair issue, the decision was a measure of his pragmatism in changing with the times, not an abdication of his sense of discipline. The positive impact on morale was unmistakable. However, about the same time, Bryant discovered his team had been infected with a fairly widespread drug problem, and he reacted decisively. Several players were banished. Even in an age of longer hair, he continued to run a very tight ship.

In the years after 1966, as the two-platoon system slowly altered the sport, Alabama's ability to win with small, quick players gradually diminished, contributing to the late-1960s slide. About the same time black faces started showing up in red jerseys, the Crimson Tide began recruiting much larger athletes. When the rules changed to allow linemen to use their hands at the point of attack, quickness was no longer able to compete with size and strength. Adjusting to the demands of the new era, Bryant altered some aspects of his regimen, abandoning gym class and replacing it with a comprehensive weight training program.

Once able to factor a significant amount of attrition into the process, Alabama was forced to adjust with the advent of NCAA-mandated scholarship reductions, which took full effect in 1976. The days of recruiting an unlimited number of players and running off those who proved unworthy were over for good.

As salaries in the NFL escalated dramatically, more players started showing up in Tuscaloosa with an eye on the pros, many of them taking the academic process much less seriously.

Slowly, the world that produced the boys of 1966 was erased like a blackboard.

Despite all the changes, the Crimson Tide remains a source of pride and inspiration for many people who see it as much more than a football team. In this sense it may always be 1966 in Alabama.

The controversial finish in 1966 was like a struck match. Over the next three decades, the flicker of discontent over the inequities in the national championship process slowly built into a mighty inferno, leading eventually to the formation of the Bowl Championship Series (BCS).

In 1968, the Associated Press responded to the growing importance of the postseason and the controversy of 1966 by permanently moving its annual final vote after the bowl games. The United Press International held firm by awarding its trophy before the bowls, which merely added to the controversy some years, but finally joined the AP in waiting until January, starting in 1974.

The 1969 season once again demonstrated the inherent flaws with the problematic bowl structure, the popularity contest represented by the polls, and the difficulty in contending with a powerful narrative storyline being promoted by the national media. In the summer before the season, ABC Sports convinced Southwest Conference rivals Texas and Arkansas to reschedule their big game until the end of the year, to maximize the effect of a blockbuster TV showdown. Roone Arledge's brainstorm was a masterstroke, because, just as the network hoped, both Darrell Royal's Longhorns and Frank Broyles's Razorbacks entered the early December clash undefeated and occupying the top two places in both wire service polls. With the whole country anticipating the game for weeks, the electric atmosphere resembled the 1966 Notre Dame-Michigan State game. Much like 1966, the media hype led by ABC validated the perception of the game as the definitive showdown for the national championship. After millions of fans watched as No. 1-ranked Texas pulled off a thrilling 15–14 victory, President Richard Nixon presented the Longhorns with his own special trophy signifying the national championship.

As he watched the scene unfold in the Texas locker room, a steaming Joe Paterno beat the rush. He started loathing Richard Nixon long before Watergate.

On the verge of finishing their second consecutive undefeated, untied season, Paterno's Penn State Nittany Lions were completely shut out of the process once again. In both 1968 and 1969, Penn State became one of only two teams with perfect records, but wound up ranked second both years, without being allowed a shot at either eventual national champion in a bowl game. In addition to representing a terribly tone-deaf political maneuver, Nixon's grandstanding act magnified the weakness of a system that for some reason could not place the only two teams with perfect records on the same field.

The same year, Notre Dame finally bowed to the mounting pressure—and increasing financial incentive—by accepting its first bowl invitation in more than four decades. The ninth-ranked Fighting Irish lost to the national champion Longhorns, 21–17, in the 1970 Cotton Bowl. More than any other single event, Notre Dame's return to the bowl scene invigorated the postseason and strengthened its link to the national championship process.

The 1966 season turned Notre Dame into a curse word across Alabama. A whole generation of Crimson Tide fans grew up seeing Notre Dame as the enemy, a feeling intensified when Bryant's program lost four close games to the Fighting Irish over an eight-year period—by a total of thirteen points—including a 24–23 thriller in the enormously hyped 1973 Sugar Bowl, considered one of the greatest games of all time.

Losing to the house of Rockne on the field, fair and square, was tough enough, but in 1977, Alabama once again saw a national championship slip away thanks to the power of the Notre Dame mystique. After upsetting top-ranked Texas, 38–10, in the Cotton Bowl, the 11–1 Irish leapt from fifth to first, catapulting right over third-ranked, 11–1 Alabama, which crushed Ohio State, 35–6, in the Sugar Bowl. In the frustrating aftermath, many enraged Tide fans sported bumper stickers posing the rhetorical question: "Ask Ole Miss Who's Number 1." While 'Bama had rebounded from an early season loss to tenth-ranked Nebraska, Notre Dame's lone blemish had come at the hands of an Ole Miss team with a losing record, which the Tide had crushed, 34–13. Being outvoted once again by the most celebrated name in college football intensified the feelings of Alabama fans who were already conditioned to believe the two programs were judged by a whole different set of rules.

When Alabama captured back-to-back national championships in 1978 and

1979, the 1977 vote assumed even greater meaning. For a second time, Notre Dame's ability to muster what amounted to political strength in the poling process prevented the Crimson Tide from accomplishing a history-making threepeat. Long after the racial issue had been solved, Alabama could not seem to escape the lingering dilemma of 1966.

Undermined for years by the various deals tying conference champions to specific bowls, the road to a more just system began in 1986, when the once lowly Fiesta Bowl lured independent powerhouses Miami and Penn State to Tempe to determine the national title—the Nittany Lions' 14–10 upset clinched Joe Paterno's second national title—but overturning the flawed structure would take more than another decade. Several additional controversial finishes helped lead to the eventual formation of the BCS, including yet another undefeated Penn State team being outvoted in 1994.

The BCS, which abolished the problematic conference tie-ins and diminished the importance of the subjective polls while arranging a unified national championship game, nevertheless repeatedly became a victim of its own inherent flaws. In 2004, Auburn understandably felt dissed by the process when Tommy Tuberville's Tigers finished as one of three unbeaten teams but were shut out of the big game, which could accommodate only two.

When Pete Carroll's Southern Cal powerhouse entered the 2006 Rose Bowl against Texas with a chance to become the first team in college history to capture a third consecutive national championship, the boys of 1966 watched with a certain ambivalence. The possibility brought back all those old feelings of frustration among many, especially considering that all USC needed to do was win the big game. When Texas, led by the incredible performance of quarterback Vince Young, drove the length of the field in the closing moments to capture the big prize with an electrifying 41–38 victory, the boys of 1966 could identify with how the Southern Cal players must have felt. Whether on the field or at the ballot box, seeing a history-making achievement disappear right before your eyes can be an excruciating experience.

Forty years later, the wound remains fresh.

"It still hurts," said defensive lineman Johnny Sullivan. "It probably always will . . . till they put every last one of us in the grave."

Many times, Bryant—who won 6 National Championships, 15 conference titles, and 323 games—would refer to the 1966 bunch as his greatest team, and while the notion invariably leads to a heated debate wherever two or more Alabama fans gather, the victims of the denied threepeat cherish the compliment like an invisible diamond, nonetheless. It shines in every one of their hearts.

Through the years, the story of the Missing Ring has been passed down in the great oral history of Alabama football between parents and children, along-side the suspension of Joe Namath, the landmark 1971 victory over Southern Cal, and so many other important milestones. In the culture of Alabama foot-ball, 1966 lives as a monument to injustice, which explains why, forty years later, Bryant-Denny Stadium always erupts in cheers when the public address announcer tells the crowd Notre Dame is losing.

Forget, hell.

EPILOGUE

None of the boys of 1966 walked on the moon or cured cancer in the years after pulling off the red jersey for the final time. Sometimes they succeeded, beyond even their own enormous expectations, cultivated by an experience that was all about learning to dream big. Sometimes they failed. But when the men who learned much about life in the crucible of Alabama football got knocked down, they always climbed off the deck and went back to work, forever strengthened by the memory of all those formative moments, never quite forgetting how it felt to have a broken plate.

In various ways, those years in Tuscaloosa set the tone for the rest of their lives.

"You're talking about a guy who wouldn't let you be ordinary," remarked Jerry Duncan, speaking about his former coach. "That spilled over into everything . . . that way of thinking. It affected all of us in so many ways."

Duncan became a highly successful stockbroker in Birmingham. For twenty-four years, he also served as the colorful sideline reporter on the Alabama radio broadcasts. Since 1971, the Alabama football program has presented the Jerry Duncan "I Like to Practice" Award to an especially hungry player. His old teammates laugh every time they hear the phrase, because they still insist Duncan didn't like to practice any more than they did.

Suburban Atlanta teacher Bruce Stephens, a former coach, likes to tell his ninth-grade students how he played on a championship team at Alabama as a 5'11", 181-pound lineman. They think he's kidding.

"I sometimes make a point of telling my students that if you want something bad enough and you're willing to do whatever it takes to achieve your goal, you can find a way to do it, regardless of the obstacles," he said. "That's something I learned under Coach Bryant at Alabama."

Byrd Williams, Alabama Regional President of BancorpSouth, spent his entire career climbing the ladder in the extremely competitive financial industry, achieving a level of success that amazes even some of his old teammates. "I learned more about management from Coach Bryant than from all my college professors and superiors combined," he says. "He was a tremendous influence on my life."

Invariably, the players talk about how playing for Bryant infused them with a desire to have class in everything they do and to live within a certain ethical framework. "The program was all about character and integrity, and that shaped every one of us who came through there," said Joe Kelley, who became the CEO of a Nashville-based insurance company and also served as the chairman of the Music City Bowl.

Nearly every athlete on the squad eventually earned an undergraduate degree from the University of Alabama, which represented a significant, life-altering achievement. Several were awarded advanced degrees. The bunch includes doctors, lawyers, and professionals in various fields. In the four decades since the memorable season of 1966, all have married—some more than once—and raised families. Many have become grandparents. As the fortieth anniversary of their historic quest approached, the eldest members of the team inched toward retirement, most in professions far removed from the football field.

Several of the boys of 1966 served their country honorably in Vietnam, including Wayne Cook, Bruce Stephens, Richard Brewer, Harold Moore, and Mike Reilly. They all came back, although Moore died in recent years, along with Cecil Dowdy and Nathan Rustin.

Moore, a fullback from Lupton City, Tennessee, a tiny community near Chattanooga, spent most of his Alabama playing career in a supporting role. His was not a name easily remembered even by the most ardent Crimson Tide fans. However, he was tough and tenacious and fought for every yard, which served the one-time ROTC cadet well when he was shipped out to Vietnam. Far from the electric crowds of Denny Stadium, Moore became a genuine American hero.

His helicopter crashed somewhere near the border.

Moore rarely spoke of the incident, because he was not the kind of guy to brag. Nor was he the kind of man to spend much time looking back.

On a harrowing day in 1969, Captain Moore, a U.S. Army helicopter pilot, was hauling a platoon of soldiers toward the border separating South Vietnam from Laos. The chopper took a direct hit and fell violently out of the sky.

The details after the crash remain fuzzy, but Moore and his small band wound up fending off several North Vietnamese soldiers in hand-to-hand combat, saving the lives of two injured Americans in the process. The patriotic country boy was awarded the Silver Star for valor, one of the highest of all military honors. During his tour in Vietnam, he also received two Bronze Stars. Making a career in the military, he became one of the earliest pilots of the Blackhawk helicopters toward the end of the Cold War.

Several athletes continued their playing careers in the NFL.

After starting the year 1967 as the MVP of the Sugar Bowl, Kenny "Snake" Stabler's carefree ways finally landed him in Bryant's doghouse. He was suspended indefinitely during the spring heading into his senior season, and conceded, "I was capable of throwing it all away." Then the most unlikely man of all came to Snake's rescue: his father.

For all the darkness bubbling up out of Slim Stabler when he drank, he loved his boy, and was willing to do anything in his power to prevent him from making a disastrous mistake. With Snake seemingly unconcerned about his predicament, his daddy conspired with a lawyer friend to concoct a phony draft letter, which convinced Kenny he was headed to Vietnam unless he found some way to get back in school—and back on the team. With further help from some of the assistant coaches—especially Jimmy Sharpe—Stabler gathered his courage and made the lonely pilgrimage to the boss's office.

"Stabler," Bryant told him through a fog of smoke and disappointment, "you don't deserve to be on this team."

Scared to death of losing everything, Stabler persevered and eventually convinced Bryant to give him another chance.

"He saved my ass," Stabler said. "I was going to throw it all away, but he saw something in me worth saving. He disciplined me and challenged me at exactly the moment I needed it."

After working his way out of Bryant's doghouse, Stabler led the Crimson Tide to a 8-2-1 season in 1967, highlighted by his dazzling forty-seven-yard touchdown run in the mud to beat Auburn, the moment which, more than any other, cemented his Alabama legend. Drafted in the second round by the Oakland Raiders, Stabler signed a four-year contract worth $126,000, including a $50,000 signing bonus, which made him feel rich. Stabler was not quite ready for pro ball, at least mentally. After a difficult year on the taxi squad, he abruptly quit the Raiders and caught a plane back to Alabama, thinking his football career was over. However, the story has a happy ending. In fact, the story has a glorious ending.

After begging the Oakland management to give him another chance, Stabler spent three years as a third-string quarterback before winning the starting job and becoming one of the NFL's signature QBs of the disco era. Stabler led the league's renegade franchise to five straight AFC Championship Games and a 32–14 victory over the Minnesota Vikings in Super Bow XI. Snake, who also played for the Houston Oilers and the New Orleans Saints, throwing for 27,938 yards and 194 touchdowns over the course of his fifteen-year pro career, remains one of the most beloved figures in Alabama football history. He has been the distinctive and informative color analyst for the Alabama radio network since 1998 and lives in the Mobile area.

Several others wound up signing NFL contracts as well.

Ray Perkins played for the Baltimore Colts for five years, where the man who had caught passes during his college career from three different All-America quarterbacks wound up teaming with Hall of Famer Johnny Unitas. About the time Stabler was finally finding his way in Oakland, Perkins traded his shoulder pads for a whistle. After several years as an assistant, the carpenter's son from Petal was named head coach of the New York Giants in 1979.

Four years later, after leading the franchise to its first playoff bid in sixteen years, Perkins returned to his alma mater to accept the enormous challenge of following his mentor, Paul "Bear" Bryant. His tenure was turbulent. The same tenacity and abrasiveness that made him an outstanding player sometimes worked against him as the successor to the greatest coach in the history of the game. In 1987, after leading the Crimson Tide to a 32-15-1 mark—including a team that finished 10-3 and ranked ninth in 1986—he was lured back to the NFL by a record wad of cash to coach the Tampa Bay Buccaneers. Since then, he has worked as an offensive coordinator in the NFL and as a college head coach, and pursued various business deals. In 1990, he was inducted into the Alabama Sports Hall of Fame. Perkins, who now lives in Hattiesburg, Mississippi, still owns the patch of land in Tuscaloosa County, where the woods still extend for as far as his aging eyes can see.

Dennis Homan, who earned All-America acclaim as a senior in 1967, was drafted in the first round by the Dallas Cowboys. After three seasons with the Cowboys and three with the Kansas City Chiefs, he also played with the Birmingham franchise of the World Football League. Homan, who still owns the Alabama record for career touchdown receptions (eighteen), was inducted into the Alabama Sports Hall of Fame in 1999. "Of course, the best catch of my life was my lovely wife," he says often, and means it. Homan has spent nearly three decades in medical sales.

Drafted by the New Orleans Saints, Les Kelley wound up playing five years in the NFL, although his career was significantly hampered by injuries. He eventually moved back to Cullman County and spent most of his adult life as an educator. Sometimes he thinks about what his coach said after the Sugar Bowl. It still makes him smile.

Wayne Trimble, who now lives in Arab, Alabama, played briefly for the San Francisco 49ers and eventually moved into high school coaching and college teaching. A few days after his Alabama career ended, Wayne finally asked Barbara to marry him. No longer afraid of how his coach might react, he took her out for a bite at a local deli and, on the way home, told her to look in the glove compartment of his car. "Might be something you like in there," he said, like he was offering her a piece of gum. Ah, romance. They carved out a wonderful life, and Wayne never had to go back to shoveling coal.

In addition to Perkins, the 1966 team produced several other men inspired to walk in Bryant's footsteps.

Louis Thompson, who nearly threw it all away on that demanding day prior to the 1966 season, became one of the most successful high school coaches in his home state of Tennessee, compiling a record of 221-125-1 over 31 years. His Lincoln County High School team won state championships in 1990 and 1993.

Chris Vagotis started his career as a student coach at Alabama, later coached in high school—where he also worked as a special education teacher—and has spent most of his career on the sidelines alongside former 'Bama offensive line coach Howard Schnellenberger. Vagotis, currently the defensive line coach at Florida Atlantic University, worked under Schnellenberger at Miami, Louisville, and Oklahoma. In the 1984 Orange Bowl, he won a national championship ring because the opposing coach—Nebraska's Tom Osborne—had the guts to try to win the game and the title. How's that for irony?

Stan Moss was a high school coach for twenty-five years, including stops at Pleasant Grove, Ensley, Ider, Arab, and Bibb County, before moving into administration.

Jimmy Fuller built a powerful small college football program at Jacksonville State University before he returning to his alma mater, where he spent thirteen seasons as offensive line coach during the regimes of Ray Perkins, Bull Curry, and Gene Stallings, capped by the Crimson Tide's most recent national championship in 1992. He is currently the athletic director at Jacksonville State.

Bobby Johns, who still shares the Alabama record for interceptions in a bowl game (three), spent more than three decades as a coach on both the college and high school level, including assistant coaching stints at the University of North Alabama, Valdosta State, South Carolina, and Florida State, and a tenure as the head coach at West Alabama.

Jimmy Carroll, who served as an assistant athletic director at his alma mater during the Perkins era, works as a rehabilitation consultant for athletes and lives in the Mobile area.

Eddie Bo Rogers coached high school ball for several years and then moved into real estate development. He and a partner now own two shopping centers.

Steve Davis, who became an Academic All-American and a Phi Beta Kappa, turned down the chance to play professionally so he could attend medical school. He became a primary care physician in internal medicine and lives in Mobile.

Mike Hall, who earned All-America honors as a senior in 1968, lives near Moundville and owns and operates All-American Signs.

Mike Sasser sells real estate in his hometown of Brewton.

Richard Brewer manages the pest control department at Alabama Professional Services in Birmingham.

Frank Canterbury moved back to Birmingham to take over the family business, Canterbury Electric.

Sang Lyda served for many years as the assistant trainer at Alabama, working with both the football and basketball teams. He's now retired and living near the Gulf Coast in Baldwin County.

Soon after graduation, Ed Morgan was offered a job selling limited partnerships in the gas and oil business. Like a great many of the players through the years, Morgan sought his coach's council on important decisions, and after Bryant made a few phone calls to check out the people Morgan was going to work for, just to make sure they were solid folks, he handed him a list of sixty-three prominent and well-heeled individuals.

"I want you to call these people," the coach told him, "and say this and exactly this: 'Coach Bryant suggested I give you a call. He feels like I have something that you might be interested in.' "

This was the Alabama version of "abracadabra."

"That list," Morgan said, nearly four decades later, "became the basis of my business. Got me started in a big way. People just don't understand how much Coach Bryant did for people after they quit playing for him. You didn't have to be a star. All you had to do was work hard and keep your nose clean, and he was always there for you."

Morgan later was elected mayor of Hattiesburg, Mississippi, and to a seat in the Mississippi state senate.

When David Chatwood dodged the Vietnam bullet, Bryant called him into the office and said he had a good job for him, a sales position with a mobile home manufacturer. No interview was required. He was one of the Bear's boys, which told the owner of the company all he needed to know. Chatwood, who now lives in the Mobile area, works in sales with a large concrete and asphalt company.

Richard Cole became a public school principal and administrator in Albertville.

Johnny Mosley works as an administrator for the Alabama Development Office.

Tom Somerville, who lives in Montgomery, spent many years in management with BellSouth.

Wayne Owen is a district court judge in Gadsden.

Bob Childs, an Academic All-American in 1967, became a lawyer. He eventually formed a firm specializing in workplace discrimination law, with offices in Birmingham and Washington, D.C.

Frank Whaley pursued a career in industrial management. He worked for many years as a plant superintendent in the trucking business, before being forced to retire early with a medical problem. He lives in Anniston.

Conrad Fowler became a lawyer in suburban Birmingham.

David Bedwell has spent nearly four decades as a high school teacher. He lives in Cedar Bluff.

Donnie Johnston, who earned a master's degree in architecture, spent several years in the construction business and now works as an owners' representative in the hotel industry.

Billy Johnson, who lives in Camden, was in the sawmill business for many years and now runs a land management operation.

Randy Barron has worked in the mortgage business for more than twenty years. He lives in Guntersville.

Johnny Calvert, who lives in Haleyville, is the general manager of a manufactured housing plant.

Dudley Kerr, who spent many years working for an engineering firm in Birmingham, owns his own home-building and remolding business and lives in Northport.

Billy Scroggins is a nondenominational pastor who lives in Tuscaloosa.

John David Reitz owned a retail sporting goods business for many years before retiring early.

Dicky Thompson, who still shares the Alabama single-game record for interceptions in a regular-season game (three), has spent many years in the manufactured housing business, both in sales and production. He lives in Haleyville.

The 1966 Alabama coaching staff was one of the best in the game, and through the years, this became abundantly clear.

Pat Dye left Alabama in 1974 to become the head coach at East Carolina, followed by a stint at Wyoming. In 1981, he took over the moribund Auburn program and built it into a power. Under his guidance, the Tigers won four Southeastern Conference championships. In 2004, Dye was inducted into the College Football Hall of Fame, joining his old boss and eventual rival, whose plaque was enshrined in 1986.

Ken Meyer left Alabama in 1968 to take the first of several positions in the NFL. He eventually became head coach of the San Francisco 49ers. He is retired and lives in Gadsden.

Jimmy Sharpe left the staff in 1974 to become the head coach at Virginia

Tech. He later moved into real estate development and now lives in Destin, Florida.

Richard Williamson left the Alabama staff in 1971 and eventually became the head coach at Memphis State. He has spent most of his career as an assistant in the NFL. Currently, he is the receivers coach for the Carolina Panthers and lives in Charlotte.

Jim Goostree, Ken Donahue, Mal Moore, Jack Rutledge, Clem Gryska, Sam Bailey, Gary White, and Dude Hennessey all remained on the Alabama staff for the rest of the Bryant era. Their hard work and skill helped the Crimson Tide capture three more national championships and nine more SEC titles between 1971 and 1981. After many years as 'Bama's offensive coordinator during the ultrasuccessful wishbone days, Mal Moore now serves as the school's athletics director. Most of the rest have long since retired from the university or moved on to other things, but Gryska (a consultant at the Bryant museum) and Hennessey (an associate in the Tide Pride office) remain on the job, providing a vital link to Alabama's glorious past.

As the boys of 1966 approach the fourth quarter of their respective lives, their reverence for Bryant is forever evident.

Because of the coach's foresight and generosity, any child of a former Crimson Tide player during the period from 1958 to 1982 may attend the University of Alabama for free. The Paul Bryant Scholarship is one of the most remarkable aspects of his legacy and the result of a gesture unprecedented in the history of college athletics. It has helped hundreds of young people pursue their education over the last quarter-century. This was his way of trying to give something back to all the young men who fought so hard for him.

Every time Jimmy Fuller walks into the home of his daughter and sees her University of Alabama diploma hanging on the wall, he cannot help thinking of his old coach, who paid for his little girl's college education.

"I tell people about [the Bryant Scholarship] and they don't believe me," said David Chatwood, whose son attended Alabama on the program.

The sense of brotherhood cultivated all those years ago remains powerful, even among those who rarely see each other. Most every year, a group of athletes from the 1964, 1965, and 1966 teams gathers for a reunion weekend of hunting, fishing, and socializing, usually at a home owned by fullback Steve Bowman or lineman Billy Johnson.

Johnson's teenage son Forrest often joined in the festivities during the reunions, and one morning, after he headed down the road in in a pickup truck with Richard Cole, Ray Perkins, and Cecil Dowdy, Billy took a measure of pride in pointing out, "Son, did you realize you had three first-team All-Americans with you?"

He and Dowdy really hit it off, which was hardly unusual. Everybody loved Cecil, a charming, fun-loving guy who carved out a successful career as an advertising salesman. When Forrest got sick, Dowdy came by to see him in the hospital several times. He always had a way of making Forrest perk up.

On the way out of the hospital room on November 23, 2002, Dowdy told him, "I'm leaving in the morning to go duck hunting. I'll come see you when I get back."

But he never came back.

No one knows exactly what happened. He was out in the woods, in a duck blind by himself. When his hunting buddies, scattered across the field, got ready to call it a day, they started trying to contact Dowdy on his walkie-talkie. He didn't respond.

Somehow, he must have accidentally tripped the trigger, perhaps as he was climbing out of the blind.

"It broke my heart when Cecil didn't come back," said his old friend Billy Johnson.

The funeral at the big church in Tuscaloosa was incredibly sad, especially for his beloved wife Carol and their two daughters. His family and friends tried to make it a celebration of Dowdy's life, and a group including Wayne Owen and Terry Kilgore took turns telling stories about his zest for so many things, especially his family and friends, but it was impossible for the aging boys of 1966 to see the event as anything less than a significant passage.

Mortality has a way of creeping up on us all, and on that tragic day when they buried the best offensive lineman on a team for the ages, a fifty-seven-year-old man in the prime of his life, a loving father and husband, a helluva guy who pursued everything at full speed with a big smile on his face, at least two dozen of his former teammates came from far and wide to pay their respects.

"I hadn't seen Cecil in about thirty years," said Tom Somerville, who drove in from Montgomery. "But I felt an obligation, because of that oneness. We had this incredible bond, all of us, and losing Cecil so unexpectedly hit us all pretty hard."

After the service, one of Dennis Franchione's assistant coaches, taking note of the huge turnout of former players, walked up to Wayne Owen, one of Dowdy's closest friends. "Now I know what they mean when they talk about the Alabama family," he said.

All those years ago, the man with the chiseled face tried to prepare his young men for tough times. He taught them all to strive and win, but he also taught them all not to panic or lose heart in the face of adversity, and most of those athletes never fully appreciated the full measure of his message until they grew older and faced hardships unimaginable in the splendor of youth. "Tough times don't last," he would often say in those afternoon meetings. "Tough people do."

Less than a month after Dowdy's death, Forrest Johnson died from an infection that followed an auto accident. "We all learned a lot about how to be tough from playing football," Billy Johnson remarked, "but there's nothing that can prepare you for the pain of losing a child." Several of Billy's old teammates showed up at the funeral to pay their respects and support their old comrade. It was a family thing, and on that day like so many others, he knew he was part of something special.

The news of Dowdy's death reached Frank Whaley too late, and he missed the funeral. The best man in Cecil and Carol's wedding was crushed. Two years later, a lifetime after the embarrassing day when he left his Orange Bowl watch to cover a $5 gas bill, Whaley's wife gave him a special Christmas present: A framed photograph of the two buddies back during their Alabama days, when they were young and cocky and still had their whole lives ahead of them.

"I got really choked up by that," Whaley said.

In time, Dowdy's old teammates dealt with the shock of seeing one of their own fall when he was still so full of life. They scheduled other reunions, perhaps cherishing the events even more, and while it was not quite the same without him, they hunted, fished, played cards, laughed, and regaled each other with stories about times old and new, looking ahead with hope instead of back in regret.

After all, the fourth quarter belongs to the mighty Crimson Tide.

ACKNOWLEDGMENTS

The idea for The Missing Ring *began to take shape in my head in 2001. From the beginning, two people bought into my vision for what this book could and should be: David Black and Pete Wolverton.*

David, my literary agent, encouraged and nurtured this work at a critical stage in my career, while motivating me to keep moving my own personal goal posts. I'm truly fortunate to work with such a wise and tenacious professional.

Pete, my editor, brought to the task of editing this book the powerful combination of literary sensibility and football knowledge. One of the most zealous Alabama fans in New York City—along with his lovely wife, Lindy—Pete understood from the start what kind of chords I was trying to strike with this project, and, while providing me with the critical elements of time and a discerning eye, he deftly helped me negotiate the fine line between music and noise.

Like Coach Bryant, Pete pushed me, time and again, to reach beyond my grasp, and I am grateful for his significant contributions to this work.

Thanks also to assistant editor Katie Gilligan, who handled a variety of important duties with skill and poise. Her help was instrumental in many ways in making this project come to life.

While my dad, who taught me to love sports, especially Alabama football, unwittingly planted the seed many years ago by telling me about the frustrating result of the 1966 season—which happened as I was turning two—the love of history I inherited from my mother is alive in these pages. No single person has been more supportive of this project, in a variety of ways.

The research for *The Missing Ring* included hundreds of hours of interviews, stretched over more than two years. I am indebted to many people whose names appear in the narrative, and many others who helped me chase down a lead, flesh out a storyline, or find a telephone number.

To place the story in the proper context, I often strayed beyond the 1966 Alabama team, so I would also like to acknowledge the important participation of Leonard Thomas, John Meadows, Charlie Thornhill, Jo Ann Boozer, Ginger Turner, Roberta Allison, Dock Rone, Bruce Graham, Terry Robinson, and Wilbur Jackson.

The Alabama athletic department provided much-needed assistance throughout the process. Thanks especially to Larry White, Barry Allen, Becky Hopf, Brenda Burnette, Roots Woodruff, Kevin Almond, Jeff Dunnavant, and Melanie Gray.

The staff of the Paul Bryant Museum, headed by Ken Gaddy, was indispensable throughout this process. I cannot thank them all enough, especially Taylor Watson, who was my go-to guy in many ways. Taylor was always eager and able to help, and I am forever grateful.

A long list of colleagues and friends helped me in important ways during this project. I am especially grateful to my old friends John Pruett and Mike Marshall of *The Huntsville Times* for their generous help with the Rabbit Thomas story. I would also like to thank Paul Finebaum, Bill Lumpkin, Gilbert Nicholson, Fred Estanich, Alex McRae, Joe Chandler, Natalie Bishop, and Laine Filasky, as well as a long list of family and friends who are too numerous to list here.

In addition to the sportswriters from the 1960s who provided a rich foundation of journalism, several fine books proved to be invaluable resources. These include *The Crimson Tide,* by Clyde Bolton; *Bowl, Bama, Bowl* and *Third Saturday in October,* both by Al Browning; *Alabama's Family Tides,* by Tommy Ford; *The Biggest Game of Them All,* by Mike Celizic; *Bear,* by Paul Bryant and John Underwood; *The Crimson Tide,* by Winston Groom; *The Legend of Bear Bryant,* by Micky Herskowitz; *Snake,* by Ken Stabler and Berry Stainback; *Southern Fried Football,* by Tony Barnhardt; *And the Walls Came Tumbling Down,* by Frank Fitzpatrick; *Braggin' Rights,* by Bill Cromartie; and the *ESPN College Football Encyclopedia,* edited by Michael MacCambridge.

The essential element in bringing the story to life, of course, was obtaining the cooperation and participation of the available players and coaches from the 1966 Alabama team. I was enormously gratified by the participation of nearly all of the players on the roster. Some indulged several different interviews. They all have my sincere thanks—for their time, their candor, and their trust to get the story right. The texture of the book owes a huge debt to the players who were willing to reach deep into their memories to help me reconstruct the dialogue that brought important scenes to life.

The 1966 Alabama players who granted me interviews included: Randy Barron, David Bedwell, Richard Brewer, John Calvert, Frank Canterbury, Jimmy Carroll, David Chatwood, Bob Childs, Richard Cole, Wayne Cook, Steve Davis, Jerry Duncan, Conrad Fowler, Jimmy Fuller, Mike Hall, Dennis Homan, Jimmy Israel, Bobby Johns, Billy Johnson, Donnie Johnston, Joe Kelley, Les Kelley, Dudley Kerr, Ed Morgan, Johnny Mosley, Stan Moss, Wayne

Owen, Ray Perkins, Eddie Propst, John David Reitz, Eddie Bo Rogers, Mike Sasser, Billy Scroggins, Tom Somerville, Kenny Stabler, Bruce Stephens, Johnny Sullivan, Dicky Thompson, Louis Thompson, Wayne Trimble, Chris Vagotis, Frank Whaley, and Byrd Williams.

Thanks also to assistant coaches Clem Gryska, Richard Williamson, Pat Dye, Mal Moore, Ken Meyer, Jack Rutledge, Jimmy Sharpe, and Dude Hennessey; dorm director Gary White; and head manager Sang Lyda.

Their individual stories have been living inside my head for some time now, and the opportunity to connect the dots between their lives and the life of my home state has enriched me beyond words.

SOURCE NOTES

Unless otherwise indicated, all direct quotes were taken from interviews conducted by the author.

p. 7   "It was as remarkable to some": Winston Groom, *The Crimson Tide* (Tuscaloosa: University of Alabama Press, 2000).

p. 21   "In the meantime, we'd checked": *The Birmingham News,* Dec. 30, 1965.

p. 51   "If he comes down to Tuscaloosa": *The Tuscaloosa News,* July 12, 1966.

p. 56   "We didn't deserve to win": Al Browning, *Bowl, Bama, Bowl* (Huntsville: Strode Publishers, 1977).

p. 64   "You don't win games in the movies": *The Birmingham News,* Sept. 21, 1965.

p. 66   "Dear Coach Bryant": Correspondence archive, Bryant Museum.

p. 67   "Pat, how long have you": *The Atlanta Journal-Constitution,* May 19, 2005.

p. 72   "If the No. 4-ranked Tide isn't voted": *The Birmingham News,* January 2, 1966.

p. 81   "The South stands at Armageddon": *USA TODAY,* Dec. 30, 2005.

p. 87   "Danny Treadwell's heart was pounding": *The Huntsville Times,* March 10, 2006.

p. 88   "If he was my kid": Deposition of Paul Bryant, lawsuit brought by Afro-American Association of University of Alabama, July 8, 1970, Archives, Bryant Museum.

p. 88   "It was kind of ridiculous for us to think": Deposition of Paul Bryant, lawsuit
           brought by Afro-American Association of University of Alabama, July 8,
           1970, Archives, Bryant Museum.

p. 94   "I thought I was dying": *The Tuscaloosa News,* June 12, 1966.

p. 94   "I always heard": *The Tuscalooa News,* June 12, 1966.

p. 94   "Just another exercise in hoopla": Associated Press story, Jan. 3, 2004.

p. 95   "Bryant, himself, scoffs": 1966 Alabama football media guide.

p. 96   "We have an opportunity": *The Birmingham News,* Aug. 14, 1966.

p. 96   "It's awful easy for people to read": *Birmingham Post-Herald,* Aug. 18, 1966.

p. 96   "I'm stall-walking": *The Birmingham News,* Aug. 14, 1966.

p. 96   "Biggest thing we've got": *The Decatur Daily,* July 13, 1966.

p. 96   "Meet me in New York": *Sports Illustrated,* Aug. 11, 1966.

p. 98   "Why, yes, we've got a weakness": *The State,* Aug. 24, 1966.

p. 104   "I'm sorry I opened my mouth": *The Birmingham News,* Aug. 13, 1966.

p. 112   "I didn't recognize anybody": *The Huntsville Times,* Sept. 14, 1966.

p. 113   "Anybody could look at the statistics": *The Birmingham News,* Sept. 25, 1966.

p. 129   "Stabler surprised us": *The Clarion-Ledger,* Oct. 2, 1966.

p. 130   "Kenny Stabler answered once and for all": *The Birmingham News,* Oct. 3,
           1966.

p. 130   "They're a better football team": *The Clarion-Ledger,* Oct. 2, 1966.

p. 131   "Hell, Bear": Paul Bryant and John Underwood, *Bear* (New York: Little,
           Brown, 1974).

p. 131   "I notice that Bear's got": *The State*, Oct. 3, 1966.

p. 132   "By God, Bear": Paul Bryant and John Underwood, *Bear* (New York: Little, Brown, 1974).

p. 133   "There must be times": *Birmingham Post-Herald*, Sept. 22, 1966.

p. 143   "The only trouble": *The Tuscalusa News*, July 31, 1966.

p. 147   "... in the unlikely event": Al Browning, *Third Saturday in October*, (Nashville: Rutledge Hill Press, 1987).

p. 148   "You never know": Al Browning, *Third Saturday in October*, (Nashville: Rutledge Hill Press, 1987).

p. 155   "This is the vehicle": James Schefter, *The Race* (New York, Doubleday, 1999).

p. 166   "Do not let him off the line": Tennessee scouting report, Bryant Museum.

p. 169   "That game took more out of me": Al Browning, *Third Saturday in October*, (Nashville: Rutledge Hill Press, 1987).

p. 170   "If the kick had been straight": *The Tuscaloosa News*, Oct. 16, 1966.

p. 170   "I've never been prouder of a team": *The Tuscaloosa News*, Oct. 16, 1966.

p. 173   "They put on one of the greatest drives": *Nashville Banner*, Oct. 17, 1966.

p. 174   "We were never actually": *The Tuscaloosa News*, Oct. 23, 1966.

p. 180   "We truthfully never thought": *The Tuscaloosa News*, Nov. 12, 1966.

p. 189   "Are there any that aren't signed": Paul Bryant and John Underwood, *Bear* (New York: Little, Brown, 1974)

p. 195   "I don't know what:" *The Birmingham News*, Oct. 30, 1966.

p. 208   "No one can match Notre Dame or Michigan State": *The Tuscaloosa News*, Nov. 14, 1966.

p. 208   "It'll take a real good football team": *Birmingham Post-Herald*, Nov. 15, 1966.

p. 212   "Hopelessly confused": Mike Celizic, *The Biggest Game of Them All*, (New York: Simon & Schuster, 1992).

p. 217   "Let us hope that the distinction": *Birmingham Post-Herald*, Nov. 15, 1966.

p. 218   "You don't want it": Mike Celizic, *The Biggest Game of Them All*, (New York: Simon & Schuster, 1992).

p. 219   "They went for a tie": Mike Celizic, *The Biggest Game of Them All*, (New York: Simon & Schuster, 1992).

p. 220   "When you're the champ": *Nashville Banner*, Nov. 19, 1962.

p. 221   "No one really expected": *Sports Illustrated*, Nov. 28, 1966.

p. 221   "One thing is certain": *Florence Times-Daily*, Dec. 2, 1966.

p. 222   "Everything at Alabama": *The Tuscaloosa News*, Dec. 4, 1966.

p. 223   "Louisiana Tech has to be the chink": *The Birmingham News*, Dec. 5, 1966.

p. 224   "Alabama . . . it's a great place to march": *Boston Globe*, Nov. 24, 1966.

p. 224   ". . . do the folks keep segregatin'": *Los Angeles Times*, Dec. 8, 1966.

p. 225   "If this game ends in a tie": Mike Celizic, *The Biggest Game of Them All*, (New York: Simon & Schuster, 1992).

p. 233   "The reasons are rather obvious": *The New York Times*, Nov. 29, 1966.

p. 238   "The whole state has its eyes": *The Birmingham News*, Feb. 21, 1893.

p. 238   ". . . the greatest football game": *The Birmingham News*, Feb. 23, 1893.

p. 240   "They'll take the bandages off": *The Montgomery Advertiser*, Dec. 3, 1948.

p. 245   "The rapid industrialization": *Birmingham Post-Herald*, Dec. 2, 1966.

p. 247   "There's no doubt in our minds": *The Tuscaloosa News*, Dec. 4, 1966.

p. 248   "Kenny Stabler probably played": *The Tuscaloosa News*, Dec. 4, 1966.

p. 249   "They don't intend for you to score": *The Birmingham News*, Dec. 4, 1966.

p. 249   "They said our boys were No. 1": *The Birmingham News*, Dec. 4, 1966.

p. 249   ". . . vote their convictions": *Birmingham Post-Herald*, Dec. 5, 1966.

p. 249   "The voters have spoken" *The Birmingham News*, Dec. 6, 1966.

p. 250   "A few years ago": *Birmingham Post-Herald*, Dec, 6, 1966.

p. 250   ". . . tired of winning the Magnola": *Los Angeles Times*, Dec. 8, 1966.

p. 251   "Ara won't return my calls": *Birmingham Post-Herald*, Dec. 6, 1966.

p. 251   "That game isn't until January 2": *The Tuscaloosa News*, Dec. 4, 1966.

p. 251   "Would you believe": *The Gadsden Times*, Dec. 20, 1966.

p. 258   "Be prepared to do whatever": Nebraska scouting report, Bryant Museum.

p. 259   "Bear Bryant is winning": *The Times-Picayune*, Jan, 3, 1967.

p. 264   "It was embarrassing": *Sports Illustrated*, Jan. 10, 1967.

p. 265   "This is the greatest college football team": *Birmingham Post-Herald*, Jan. 3, 1967.

p. 266   "They deserve to be No. 1": *The New York Times*, Jan. 3, 1967.

p. 266   "Stabler was just too quick": *The Birmingham News*, Jan. 3, 1967.

p. 266   "If Bear Bryant's Bama team": *The States-Item*, Jan. 3, 1967

p. 266   "Maybe it isn't the Alabama quickness": *The Tuscaloosa News*, Jan. 3, 1967.

p. 270   "I hope they're bothered by it": *The Birmingham News,* Nov. 12, 1966.

p. 271   "Be truthful now": *Sports Illustrated,* January 10, 1967.

p. 277   "The first time I played at Ole Miss": *The Tennessean,* Jan. 12, 2003.

p. 283   "I don't have any black players": Paul Bryant and John Underwood, *Bear* (New York: Little, Brown, 1974).

INDEX